Dugard of Rouen

Dugard of Rouen

French Trade to Canada and the West Indies, 1729–1770

by Dale Miquelon

McGill–Queen's University Press · Montreal and London

© Copyright McGill–Queen's University Press 1978
ISBN 0 7735 0299 8
Legal deposit second quarter 1978
Bibliothèque nationale du Québec

Design by Richard Hendel
Printed in Canada by
T. H. Best Printing Company Ltd.

This book has been published with the help of a grant from the Canada Council

Contents

LIST OF TABLES AND FIGURES   vii

PREFACE   ix

I. Introduction: The Context of Prosperity, 1715–1770   1

II. The Founders and Their City   13

III. The New Company, 1729–1742   27

IV. Questions of Finance, 1729–1742   39

V. Cargoes Outward   49

VI. Quebec: A Colonial Trading Factory   69

VII. Trade in the West Indies   91

VIII. Destructions and Diversions   119

IX. The Lord Taketh Away   139

X. Conclusion: From Business History to the History of Society   155

Appendix A. Profiles of the Dugard Fleet   167

Appendix B. The Ships and Their Voyages   171

Appendix C. Voyages: Chronological List   191

Appendix D. Investment, Outlay, and Profit   197

ABBREVIATIONS USED IN THE NOTES   215

NOTES   217

PRIMARY SOURCES   259

BIBLIOGRAPHY   263

INDEX   271

Tables and Figures

TABLE

1 The *Alçion* to Léoganne, St. Domingue, 1742–43; Breakdown of Cargo   56

2 The *Imprévû* to Cul de Sac Marin, Martinique, 1743; Breakdown of Cargo   56

3 The *St. Mathieu* to Cul de Sac Marin and Fort Royal, Martinique, 1743; Breakdown of Cargo   57

4 The *Union* to St. Pierre, Martinique, 1744; Breakdown of Cargo   57

5 Breakdown of the Fourteenth Cargo, 1743   61

6 Gathering the Fourteenth Cargo; Percentages of Various Goods Obtained in Rouen and Elsewhere   65

7 Inflation of Invoice Prices in Canada, 1743   74

8 Level of Profit in Excess of Invoice Inflation (*Bénéfice*), Quebec, 1740–47   75

9 The Accumulation of Debts Owing (Promissory Notes and Obligations), 1730–38   79

10 The Declining Importance of Bills of Exchange in Returns from Quebec, 1730–44   81

11 Receipts and Returns of the Quebec Factory, 1732–45   85

12 Sale of Outward Cargo, *Alçion* to Léoganne and Region, 1742–43   107

13 Sale of Outward Cargo, *Imprévû* to Cul de Sac Marin, 1743   108

14 Profits on Selected Commodities: Beef, Flour, Red Wine, Kettles, *Toiles*, 1742–46 110

15 Profits on Return Cargoes, 1742–55 114

16 Cargo vs. Costs; the *Union* to Martinique, 1744 116

17 Possible Combinations of Profits on Outward and Return Cargoes Yielding Net Profits of 15 Per Cent 116

18 The Impact of Wartime Insurance Premiums, the *Union* to Martinique, 1744 117

19 Robert Dugard's Financial Position, 23 March 1762 149

20 Voyages of the *Louis Dauphin* 172

21 Voyages of the *St. Mathieu* 174

22 Voyages of the *Ville de Québec/Union* 176

23 Voyages of the *Alçion* 178

24 Voyages of the *Fleury* 180

25 Voyages of the *St. Louis* 182

26 Voyages of the *Centaure* 184

27 Voyages of the *Imprévû* 186

28 Voyages of the *Astrée* 186

29 Voyages of the *Trois Maries* 188

30 Profits in Colonial Trade, 1729–55 202

31 Value of Ships with Amount of Annual Depreciation 204

32 Depreciated Value of Ships at Each Year's End 206

33 Financial History of Dugard and Company, 1729–48; Hypothetical Reconstruction 212

34 Reconstructed Balance Sheet of Dugard and Company, 31 December 1748 214

FIGURE

1 The Fourteenth Cargo, 1743; Flow of Goods 67

2 The "Curve of Returns," 1730–43 86

3 Graph of the Investments and Outlays of Dugard and Company, 1729–55 209

Preface

In 1953 the proprietor of the château of Bonneval at La Haye-Aubrée par Routot in the Norman department of Eure presented the French National Archives with a collection of eighteenth-century papers. They had been brought to the château by previous owners at the time of the French Revolution. The proprietor was unrelated to these shadowy figures, and the papers concerned neither his family nor the estate.[1] Now deposited at the Archives Nationales in Paris, the 45 cartons of letters and business papers tell the story of the business activities of the Dugard family of Rouen.[2] The earliest item in the collection is a bill of exchange dated 3 January 1658/59, and the last letter is from 1794. Most of the papers concern Robert Dugard, 1704–70, and a number of companies formed by him and several other Rouen merchants, among them the Société du Canada.

Dugard and Company, as the Société may be called with less formality, was founded in 1729 to exploit the trade of Canada with France and the West Indies. Soon it directed its attention to the development of a Franco-Caribbean trade independent of its North-Atlantic commerce. After 1743 maritime warfare seriously injured the company and made a continuation of operations seem unattractive. The members were in any case responding to other economic opportunities that demanded the full dedication of their talents and fortunes. When officially dissolved in 1759, the company had long since become a caretaker operation.

When I arrived in Paris in 1967 with the intention of undertaking research on the Canadian bourgeoisie before 1760, the Dugard Papers were brought to my attention as being of possible interest. They were not about the Canadian bourgeoisie, but they explained much about trade relations between France and Canada in the eighteenth century that was essential for an understanding of this key social and economic group. Canada's story seemed so often to have been written in the margin of history, although beside some very important paragraphs. Here was an opportunity to link the colonial glosses with the main text. I therefore surrendered to the imperialism of the metropolis and accepted, at least in part, Richard Pares's dictum, "The most important thing in the history of an empire is the history of its mother country. Colonial history is made at home." [3]

The present history is a case study of a business partnership. The size and structure of eighteenth-century French business enterprises, the nature of French business finance, methods and maritime insurance, French commodities of trade and markets, and the relation of French business to government are all examined. So too is the manner and extent of the penetration of French business into Canada and the West Indies. This examination of business and businessmen, both metropolitan and colonial, will also be relevant to the history of society.

Phillippe Wolff has written, with regard to economic and social history, that its chief preoccupation is with the average man: "A l'opposé de l'individu plus ou moins exceptionnel, du grand homme à l'étude duquel s'est longtemps complus l'histoire politique, nous entendons par là le représentant d'un groupe social plus ou moins vaste, de son régime économique, de son statut juridique, de ses habitudes mentales." [4] As members of a class and children of an age, and more particularly from an institutional point of view, Dugard and his partners have that representative character that is always the *raison d'être* of the case study. It is also true, however, that they demand our attention as unique individuals. The company was of uncommon importance in Canada in the 1730s and 1740s. It was represented by agents that figure prominently in the documentation of the time. Certain members of the company were associated with industrial experiments and undertakings at Rouen that were of a singular importance. Thus Robert Dugard and his circle cannot be denied that interest in their individuality that has always been the special mark of historical studies.

Archivists and librarians in France and Canada have been extremely helpful to me in the pursuit and elucidation of documents; to them is owed a large debt of gratitude. I also wish to acknowledge the role of Professor James Pritchard of Queen's University, who drew my attention to the Dugard Papers. Special thanks are owed to Professor W. J. Eccles of the University of Toronto, astute in criticism and unfailing in support. Professors J. M. Hayden and J. R. Miller, colleagues at the University of Saskatchewan, have read the typescript which benefited from their comments. From archives to final draft, my wife Patricia has been the constant companion of my ups and downs; but my debt to her extends also to her knowledge of business law and her fine sense of style. Without the financial assistance of the Canada Council during my first three years of research and writing, the present work could not have been written; an earlier version was awarded a Canada Council doctoral thesis prize. The President's Publications Fund of the University of Saskatchewan aided materially in the final preparation of the manuscript.

The Context of Prosperity, 1715–1770

Gathering prosperity, a novel air of optimism: these are the context in which the history of Dugard and Company unfolds. To reconstruct the world of its founders, seeing the horizon of possibilities as they saw it, is the aim of the present chapter, which reviews the lineaments of the period and recalls the basic structures within which the company was conceived and operated.

At the time of the company's foundation, Rouen and the other French Atlantic ports were being transformed by the building of new townhouses and neo-classical public buildings paid for by the colonial trades—Canadian furs, North-Atlantic cod, and the rich Caribbean cargoes of tropical produce. The New World colonies provided food for the imagination as well as material exports, the unspoiled country and primitive inhabitants that made their appearance in travel books and copper-plate engravings teasing the still provincial, somewhat credulous minds of eighteenth-century Frenchmen. Similarly, increasing commercial contacts with the Far East confronted them with highly sophisticated manufactures and ancient civilizations, transforming French taste with *chinoiserie* concepts of art and decoration. The accepted notions of a once-isolated Europe were being challenged by the relativism implicit in this wider world of diverse societies and cultures. For some at least, the horizons of the intellect rolled back as readily as the horizons of the globe.

At home, life was becoming more secure. France was spared invasion by foreign soldiery, and the danger from brigands had lessened considerably. Many roads had become true highways and could be travelled in safety. The transport of foodstuffs to the towns or to areas where crops had failed was less difficult than it had been. Industrial wages, meagre though they were, added to the purchasing power of the proletariat, both urban and rural. Still less important than this extension of cottage industry, but marvelled at by contemporaries, were the cumbersome new machines that betokened the future revolution in industrial technique. It was an age of rising expectations, very real, although grafted precariously into a powerful tradition of fatalism.

When Louis XIV died on 1 September 1715, the future had not seemed so promising. Twenty years of war had made considerable demands on French blood and treasure. The depredations of the tax collector had been augmented by monetary devaluation that added greatly to the risks of trade. Famines had occurred twice, in 1709–10 and 1713–14. The treaties of Utrecht (1713) and Rastatt (1714) that ended the War of the Spanish Succession blasted French hopes of European hegemony and sealed British supremacy in the maritime colonial world. Early in the war, Great Britain had already gained access to the Brazilian market by the Methuen treaty of 1703. Now the *asiento*, or monopoly of the slave trade to the Spanish-American colonies, passed from the French to the British, who also were granted limited access to the Spanish colonial market for manufactures. In North America, all French rights to Newfoundland, peninsular Acadia, and Hudson Bay were surrendered to Great Britain; and the British foothold in the Mediterranean gained by the acquisition of Gibraltar and Minorca threatened French naval supremacy and hence the Levant trade. The triad of British competition in trade, naval supremacy, and political stability was henceforth one of the principal limiting conditions of French commercial growth.

Despite all these tribulations, the peace was not vindictive, perhaps because in the last analysis the "Grande Alliance" of France's enemies did not have the power to make it so. France suffered only minimal territorial loss in Flanders; the real basis of French power remained unimpaired. The wartime crop failures proved to be the result of a meteorological interlude, and good yields and moderate prices had returned by 1715. The French presence remained intact in Canada, Louisiana, India, and Senegal. Most important of all, France retained her significant West-Indian possessions whose exploitation had really only begun. It is true that British control of the Atlantic had become almost complete, and the vigorous French maritime expansion discernible in the later seventeenth century had received a temporary check. But it had not been so fundamentally damaged as to prevent its postwar resuscitation.

The necessary condition of future economic development was peace, a condition that might not have been achieved had it not also been required by dynastic interests.[1] With a five-year-old king and a succession disputed by the Duc d'Orléans and Philip V of Spain, who had disavowed his renunciation of all rights to the French throne, France needed security and an alliance to ensure it. The new Hanoverian dynasty in England, lacking either historical sanction or the love of the people, was equally in need of friends abroad. The first British diplomatic moves after Utrecht had been directed towards the reconstruction of the Grand Alliance. But the old allies were unfriendly and of doubtful utility. Holland had been obliged to give up its role as a great sea power to devote its straitened resources to continental defence and was inclined to opt for a policy of neutrality. Neither Spain, shorn of its power base in Belgium and Italy and ostensibly friendly, nor Austria, which had gathered up the shearings but was greedy for more, were happy with or likely to support the Utrecht settlement. Only in France did Great Britain find a willing partner in the defence of the *status quo* that, although founded on French humiliation, was also the firmest support of French security.

The Anglo-French alliance was held together by internal weakness, the fear that a War of the English Succession or a War of the French Succession was not inconceivable, and by an external pressure brought to bear upon that weakness—the continual machinations of Austria and more particularly of Spain that threatened to undo Utrecht to promote dynastic interests. Great Britain and France together acted as international policemen, maintaining the European equilibrium by diplomacy, congresses, even preventive war. The gift of peace was internal security and a great prosperity based upon open sea-lanes and near-balanced budgets. Even though the birth of a *dauphin* in 1729 did away with any French dynastic necessity for a continuation of the alliance, the Cardinal Minister Fleury persisted in it because of the benefits of peace. The peace was still maintained when the alliance finally dissolved in 1733 under the stress of conflicting diplomatic aims, France returning to a Spanish alliance to break up the Austro-Spanish connection and Great Britain allying with Austria in direct reaction. It withstood the War of Jenkins' Ear and the early phases of the War of the Austrian Succession, succumbing only when British diplomatic initiatives among the smaller states of Germany threatened the French "Westphalia system" of clientage east of the Rhine. March 1744 thus saw the end of three decades in which France and Great Britain, each in its own interest, co-operated to maintain the peace, competed with each other within its shelter, and finally refrained from war in spite of hostility. Dugard and Company was only one of hundreds of maritime commercial enterprises that owed their birth and uninterrupted growth to this Thirty Years Peace and that were badly mauled or destroyed by the return to war, undertaken with inadequate preparation on the Atlantic front.

Not that France had no conception of an Atlantic and maritime destiny: regarding the Spanish succession, Louis XIV himself had written, "The principal object of the present war is the trade of the Indies and the wealth that they produce."[2] But it is also true that the Crown viewed this extension of commerce primarily from the standpoint of an anxious tax collector. Social and political structures had not that welcoming elasticity to accommodate trade and traders that characterised the financial administration. If eighteenth-century monarchs became enthusiastic about commerce, it was because the British victory consecrated by Utrecht seemed to be a clear demonstration of the increase of national power resulting from a far-flung maritime trade. For this reason the elaboration of commercial policy became an item of high priority. The support given John Law's schemes by the Regent was a fresh expression of faith in the usefulness of trade. It should not be dismissed as an example of Palais Royal irresponsibility because the bursting of the Mississippi Bubble in 1720 confirmed French doubts about financial reform and vast commercial undertakings. But Law's failure to keep a tighter rein on ambition and imagination was unfortunate, for conservatism was thus given sanction by events. This can only have reinforced the unsavoury associations that attached to finance in the French mind, given popular expression at the time by a woodcut of a squatting man in the Rue Quincampoix being fed coin through a funnel while shares in the Compagnie des Indes were drawn from his nether end.[3] Commercial and financial policy was thereafter more modest in its aims and less spectacular in its means.

This policy was fashioned and executed by an institutional infrastructure that dated from the beginning of the century.[4] On 29 June 1700, the Conseil de Commerce was founded to co-ordinate the policy of the two departments concerned, the Marine and the Contrôle-générale. Because its role was solely advisory, executive decisions coming from the Controller General or the Conseil d'Etat, it was more appropriately designated a *bureau* in 1722. The business community was accorded a consultative voice in the Bureau; and to facilitate the election of deputies from within it, chambers of commerce were established in major centres, that of Rouen, for example, being founded in 1703. The deputies were joined by another set of advisers who were in addition responsible for administering policy, the intendants of commerce, first created in 1708, and their immediate inferiors, the inspectors general. A third group within the membership was composed of councillors of state, including the Secretary of the Marine (or Navy) and the Controller General, although the latter two rarely attended. The Bureau was thus an excellent institution that brought together the views of business, administration, and executive, disseminating policy decisions by the same channels that facilitated the collection of information. It framed laws, regulations, and proposed exemptions with regard to commercial institutions, commerce, and industry. From time to time the minutes of the Bureau record Robert Dugard's requests for exemptions. The same is true of the correspondence files of the Department of the Marine, the seat of executive power regarding maritime commerce. Government can there be seen intervening directly in the history of Dugard and Company, although even for the company its most important role lay in general economic policy. The Bureau, for example, was partly responsible for the decree of 26 May 1726, that stabilized the French currency at a level that remained nearly constant until after the First World War, providing a sound basis for commercial transactions. Fleury's parsimonious collaborator, the Controller General Philibert Orry (1730–45), consistently reduced royal deficits and in 1738 balanced the budget for the only time in the century. It was Orry who also supervised the improvement of the roads by means of the *corvée des grands chemins*, with obvious benefits for trade.

After 1744 new ideas on the administration of commerce came to the fore. The Bureau was allowed to decline in importance because of a new distaste for its excessive regulation.[5] The supervision of trade and industry was taken over from the President of the Bureau, hitherto a powerful administrator, and given to a Director of Commerce. These directors (Rouillé, Trudaine, and Trudaine de Montigny) cut down the number of inspectors upon which the system reposed and instituted a program of liberalization—one that depended for its efficacy on royal decree rather than the vagaries of laissez faire. The new policies, like the old, would be of significance in the careers of Dugard and his business associates.

Of course, the importance of government policy should not be overstated. It was not primarily responsible for that trend of economic improvement that is reflected in the healthy price rise traced by Ernest Labrousse, starting around 1733, increasing in speed and angle of ascent after 1759, finally sinking into stagnation in the years beyond 1770.[6] This was part of a phenomenon of international proportions.

The addition of Brazilian gold and Mexican silver to the European monetary stock doubled and perhaps tripled the volume of French currency between 1715 and 1789. Plentiful bullion enhanced by a proliferation of commercial paper resulted in a steady and healthy inflation. At the same time, the agricultural sector increased its output, managing this primarily by an extension of the area under cultivation and the planting of crops of high market value, such as wheat, vines, and flax. After 1715, even the climate co-operated.

While the identification of causes may be a perilous business, the essentially responsive character of agricultural improvement directs the searcher to the marketplace, where the lubricant effect of abundant money escalated the interplay of supply and demand. As France had no mines of its own, it was trade that was responsible for the influx of bullion by which trade in turn was stimulated. It was the increasing ability to satisfy wants that improved the agricultural market, spreading the effects of the new prosperity throughout the country, resulting in the disappearance of plague and famine and the increase of baptisms over burials.

French foreign trade experienced at least a fivefold increase between Utrecht and the Revolution.[7] In this, the tenfold increase of colonial trade, which gave rise to re-exports to diverse parts of Europe, was of considerable importance. After 1730 there was a parallel increase in industrial output. Colonial production of raw cotton made possible a cotton textile industry. The markets of Portugal and the Levant stimulated increase and improvement in the production of French woollens, which soon drove the British product out of both. Industry was everywhere falling into the hands of merchant capitalists who became putters-out, having raw materials manufactured for them by a rural proletariat beyond the reach of the urban guild structure. New industries such as cotton, without any tradition of manufacture, were particularly open to the introduction of technology. Dugard and some of his associates were typical of these trends, both putting-out and experimenting with factories. Commerce and industry, for them so closely connected that they might be regarded as a single sector of the economy, thus experienced change and expansion far more spectacular than the extension of agriculture or the demographic rise.

The strengthening of the agricultural foundation, not only of France but of Europe as a whole, was nevertheless a major stimulus to mercantile expansion. As Hubert Luthy has persuasively argued, there were two economic kingdoms of France: the agricultural and the mercantile-industrial.[8] The first, the French economy perceived by the physiocrats, provided basic necessities for the producers and yielded up to a *rentier* class Quesnay's "produit net," which the second absorbed in return for the provision of the means and the marks of luxury. The second economic configuration was marginal and dependant, and its social expression, the middle class, was similarly denied a position of primacy. "The profession of trader is vilified and despised by officers and gentlemen," the Conseil de Commerce complained in 1701.[9] There were changes in attitude, at least in some localities, but business still remained a mark of inferiority on the eve of the Revolution.[10]

The business with which the present study is primarily concerned is the trade with colonies. The richest colonies were those of the West Indies, where both the French and the English had become established in the 1640s.[11] By 1661, when Jean-Baptiste Colbert took in charge the Department of the Marine, the Dutch had been for 20 years the masters of the trade with the French islands. Colbert put muscle into French mercantile regulations by building up the French navy; and although his West India Company was a failure, it was a useful instrument for breaking into the trade and arousing the interest of the French trading community. The numbers of French ships trading to the Caribbean each year rose from three or four in 1662, to 89 in 1672, and 205 in 1683, the year of Colbert's death.

The French traders held their own in war as in peace until the disastrous defeat of the French navy at La Hougue in 1692. The wars of the League of Augsburg and the Spanish Succession ruined French Atlantic trade; its reconstruction was a major preoccupation of French business after Utrecht. The colonial basis for prosperity was unimpaired. Martinique seems even to have prospered under the aegis of Danes and Dutch; the number of plantations rose from 207 in 1694 to 264 in 1710. In the three decades of peace after 1713 the number increased to 456. French exports to the island for 1743 have been estimated at 30,000,000 livres, their highest level. Martinique had become "a second Peru."[12] The French half of the island of Saint Domingue, the haunt of pirates and the buccaneers, who hunted wild cattle descended from Spanish herds, only became an important plantation colony after 1714, the year in which it was given its own government separate from that of the French Windward Islands. Because of its great size, it quickly became the wealthiest French colony, a *nouveau riche* among the ordered ranks of older sugar islands, its name a byword for opulence and extravagance.

The French reclamation of maritime empire was superintended from 1723 to 1749 by Jean-Frédéric Phélypeaux, Count Maurepas, a vigorous Minister of Marine who well understood the importance and the interdependence of colonies, trade, and a powerful navy. He was never able to restore the navy to the pre-eminence it enjoyed in the days of Colbert, yet with the support of Fleury and the Admiral of France, the able Count of Toulouse, he built up a small navy of well-designed and solidly-built ships, supported by improved arsenals, adequate stockpiles of naval stores, and budget provision for repairs.[13] The French consoled themselves for the inferior size of their navy by persisting in the belief that superiority in naval architecture was more important than having a large number of ships and that a small navy was really more efficient than a large one, especially when manoeuvred with Gallic dash and flair. In any case, maritime warfare was held to be the job of privateers who preyed on enemy commerce, while between escort assignments it was the duty of the navy to lie in port and draw the attention of, and hence immobilize, the enemy navy. The experience of Dugard and Company among others in the 1744–48 war would woefully reveal the inadequacy of the strategy of the fleet-in-being.

In the welter of legislation generated by the Department of Marine and the Bureau of Commerce with the intention of re-establishing French Atlantic trade, the letters patent of 1717 and 1727 are of primary importance.[14] They provided elaborate procedures for policing the trade, consolidating numerous edicts and regulations. They were policy statements as well as legislation, announcing the State's intention to enforce the *pacte coloniale*. The system constituted by these and other items of legislation was not inflexible. Foreign goods permitted entry to France were also admitted to the colonies with an identical burden of taxation. The re-export from France of colonial produce in an unimproved state was also provided for, laying the foundation for the French conquest of the European sugar market. The colonies themselves were allowed to send refined sugar direct to Spain. After 1717, French traders were given the privilege of taking Irish salt beef to the islands duty free, indeed after 1728 even the necessity of entrepôt in a metropolitan French port was waived. If French external trade quintupled between 1715 and 1789, as official statistics suggest, the Caribbean trade and the re-export of colonial produce were to a considerable extent responsible.

In their attempt to contain the trade of the sugar islands within their empire, the French were largely successful. The colonists had less incentive to deal with smugglers after 1730, when keen competition within the growing body of French traders rectified the problems of shoddy merchandise and extortionate prices.[15] To the great frustration of the Department of Marine, the system at its most efficient still left unsatisfied a growing colonial demand for wood, foodstuffs, and live horses and cattle to drive the crushing mills. It also failed to provide a market for two important by-products of sugar production, molasses and rum. These problems were of secondary importance at St. Domingue, where a considerable hinterland provided wood, neighbouring Spaniards provided cattle, and sugar was exported in an unrefined state. But the situation in the Lesser Antilles was quite different. There a brisk trade had developed with New England traders who were happy to provide the necessary provisions in exchange for the by-products of clayed (semi-refined) sugar. The molasses and scum produced in sugar boiling, two "excrements of sugar," as Governor De Caylus of Martinique described them, produced only rum, "a species of brandy of very disagreeable taste" used by the inscrutable English to make "*La punch*, their usual drink." [16] Successive administrators at Martinique were won over to the belief that the New England trade was essential. Their apologetic dispatches explaining its necessity contrast sharply with Marine outward correspondence in which their statistics are questioned, their arguments dismissed, and their integrity sometimes doubted. [17] Even the import of cattle from Spanish Santo Domingo was regarded as unsatisfactory because the Spaniards bought little French merchandise and preferred to be paid in gold. "Whether it is indifference or hatred for luxury, or uncleanliness, which seems to be more believable," a French administrator puzzled, the Spanish colonial was content with four shirts in his closet, to the great detriment of French industry. [18]

The experience of De Fayet, administrator at St. Domingue, was typical of that of all colonial administrators who resisted smuggling. In 1733, De Fayet determinedly arrested the most notorious smugglers, later to find that they were also the agents of the biggest merchant houses in Nantes. The resulting harm to legitimate *Nantais* trade was so great that De Fayet was forced to release them. He was neither the first nor the last servant of the Marine to complain, "I am alone against all the colony." [19]

Maurepas's response to New England trade was consistent and categoric. It could not be countenanced except in the most straitened circumstances. That it might be inconvenient for a French colonial to do his duty to the Crown was immaterial. Maurepas recommended that ranches be established in St. Domingue and that the mule trade with Spanish Central America be encouraged. In particular, it was the possibility of a considerable trade between the Antilles and Canada that captured the ministerial imagination. [20]

It was the fate of Canada, the oldest of the Atlantic colonies, that it could not fulfill the promise that it appeared to hold.[21] Its population was as small as its geographical extent was vast. Although centred on one of the principal water entries to the North American continent, the river's mouth was lamentably far to the north, distant from Caribbean markets and barred with ice in winter. The area of settlement was inland, drawn there by the fur trade and driven there by the inhospitality of the pre-Cambrian highlands that dominated the coastal areas. The Canadian economy was based upon the wheat of the riparian farms of the St. Lawrence valley and the staple export of fur, especially beaver fur. It was the fur trade that raised the standard of living above subsistence, although in the decades after Utrecht agriculture and trade in agricultural products became of some significance.

The Wars of the Iroquois that had endangered the very existence of the colony had been brought to an end in 1701, and by 1714 the glut of beaver that had brought the fur trade to a point of stagnation had vanished as stocks were disposed of by obliging rats and vermin. The marketing of a wider variety of furs and the development of new markets by metropolitan importers brought a return of prosperity to the trade. In spite of this, the imperial economy did not absorb the full output of the Canadian fur trade, and the colony was not free of those eighteenth-century stock characters, the smugglers. Considerable but untallied quantities of furs disappeared down the wilderness waterways to New York receivers.

The Department of Marine was primarily interested in encouraging the production of raw materials to supply French manufacturers and traders or to answer the needs of the Caribbean colonies. However, most ministers of the Marine, who could never forget that colonials were themselves Frenchmen with a right to the King's paternal regard, applied their mercantile policies with some flexibility. The Canadian ship-building industry was subsidized by the Crown, and the forge at Trois Rivières, which produced simple iron manufactures, was first subsidized and then taken in hand by government. From 1729 to 1748 the colony found in Gilles Hocquart a dedicated and competent intendant.[22] The impact of the Crown upon the economy, finally, cannot be fully appreciated without reference to the manna of military expenditures made in the colony for the maintenance of troops and Indian alliances and the building of fortifications.

The developing Canadian economy was materially affected by the founding of the colony of Ile Royale in 1713.[23] The new colony was intended to take the place of Plaisance, a major French fishing base in Newfoundland lost at the Treaty of Utrecht. It was the fishery and the trade based upon it, wrote the minister, "which ought to be regarded as the principal object of the establishment of Ile Royale."[24] Only a year after this sentence was written was the idea conceived of building the fortress town of Louisbourg "capable of annihilating all ships that will arrive from across the ocean" and thus to protect the maritime approach to New France.[25]

The Cape Breton fishery and the Louisbourg garrison were a new market for Canadian wood and provisions, and Louisbourg facilitated Canadian trade with the West Indies. It also became the resort of smugglers. Contraband trade between France, the French West Indies, and the Anglo-American colonies became the foundation of the entrepôt business, thrusting the fishery into the background and over-shadowing Canada's role in the West Indies trade. But Canada's modest success in the Caribbean trade, either direct or via Louisbourg, and the appearance of even greater success given it by the identification of New England merchandise leaving Louisbourg as Canadian, helped to nourish the tenacious idea that Canada would one day re-place New England as a supplier to the French sugar islands.

The gamut of Canadian possibilities that fascinated Maurepas was also responsible for drawing together Robert Dugard and the other Rouen merchants who founded the Société du Canada. The company's experience in exploiting the Canadian trade, the extent to which it also became involved in the West Indian trade, and the result of its attempts to link the two together are an accurate reflection of the problems and possibilities of French colonial trade as a whole.

The chronological boundaries imposed upon the present study by the formation and dissolution of the company and by the lifespans of its members are of wider significance. They correspond closely with the contours of French history that have been sketched here. The company's rise parallels the moderate and steady improvement of the French economy beginning in the 1730s, and its dissolution in 1759 occurs just prior to the spectacular acceleration of French economic activity in the 1760s. The wartime attrition suffered by the company, while not a reflection of national economic calamity, is an example of the tribulations that beset the maritime sector. The partners' loss of interest in the company and their absorption in other economic pur-suits correspond with the major trend in the economic history of Rouen. The death in 1770 of the head of the company, Robert Dugard, coincides with the end of the era of prosperity and the begin-ning of economic stagnation that marked the penultimate years of the Ancien Régime.

CHAPTER TWO

The Founders and Their City

Even today the centre of Rouen is a maze of narrow streets lined by half-timbered houses with jutting midriffs and leaded windows. In spite of the extensive damage of the Second World War, the visitor can still make contact with the trading city of centuries past through this architectural legacy. Many of these streets were not very different in 1729, when Robert Dugard and five other Rouen merchants founded the Société du Canada. They would recognize the famous clock of the town hall on the Rue de la Grosse Horloge, the Parlement de Normandie, with its high-pitched roofs and forest of pinnacles a block north on the Rue aux Juifs, and countless unnamed buildings holding memories for them of which we can know nothing.

Their city was an important administrative centre, being the seat of a governor and of admiralty and having an intendancy, a Grand Maître des Eau et Forêts, the Vicomté d'Eau, Monnaies, Lieutenant-général de Police and Bureau des Finances, charged with collecting the *taille*.[1] But it was even more important as a commercial centre. A city of more than 50,000 persons standing on the right bank of the Seine at the apex of a great bow,[2] Rouen owed its existence to the river that carried the flat-bottomed *chalans* loaded with merchandise up and down the 188 kilometres of meanders between Rouen and Paris, and the one-masted hoys the 118 kilometres between Rouen and Le Havre. It was an old saying even in 1729 that the first citizen of Rouen was a ferryman and the second a merchant.

The part of the city that was most particularly the merchants' domain, the quays and the nearby streets, is now completely changed. Only its name links the long Rue des Charettes where Dugard lived with its eighteenth-century past. The Palais des Consuls, the legal

centre of the merchants' world, housing the Juridiction consulaire de
Rouen and the Chambre de Commerce de Normandie, has disappeared.[3] There, on the ground floor, had been the bourse, a large hall
where Rouen's merchants transacted their business in bad weather.
Their preference on fine days was for an outdoor bourse on the quay
beside the custom house, bounded by the city wall in rear and on its
opposite side by a row of trees, in 1729 still newly planted.[4] In later
years the bourse was provided with a fence and gate to exclude traffic.
Much of the history of Dugard and Company must have happened
there among the strolling or seated knots of outfitters and commission
agents, wholesalers and putters-out, brokers and hangers-on. Only a
short distance away the tangle of horses and carts, sailors, stevedores,
merchants, soldiers, and taxmen, the rolling of barrels, and the lifting
of crates, were visible and audible all along the busy quay.

Rouen's merchants had their own court in the Consular Jurisdiction, which had been founded by royal edict in 1556 to try causes
arising out of trade.[5] It had soon been restricted to cases between merchants, and its unique jurisdiction over maritime commerce and insurance had been transferred to the admiralty.[6] The Chamber of Commerce had been established by an *arrêt* of 19 January 1703 for the
purpose of sending a deputy to the Bureau of Commerce, the merchants' link with the central government.[7] The Chamber was empowered to levy a tax, the *octroi des marchands*, for expenses related to
the public good. These expenses, however, were decided for it by the
central government, although it might raise additional money for its
own purposes.[8]

The consular institutions also fulfilled a social function for the merchants among whose opulent houses the Palais des Consuls was built.
Those who had held office in either the Chamber or the Jurisdiction
retained a certain status thereafter; they were collectively "la Compagnie."[9] A kind of consular nobility had come into existence and
exercised its authority whenever the Chamber felt the need for support
in its decisions. These might include questions concerning the conditions, laws, and usages of commerce, the composing of *parères*, the
establishing of contributions and, as it was euphemistically described,
the guiding of elections.[10]

The three judges of the Jurisdiction and the five syndics, who together constituted the Chamber, were elected by the business community. But election did not imply democracy. Election to the Jurisdiction
had been hedged about from an early date by the provision that junior
officials would succeed to higher positions as a matter of right so that
only the two lowest positions were open to election.[11] The system was

tightened even more in 1707, when authority to nominate candidates was restricted to a committee of the Company, which from 1715 also drew up the list of 250 eligible voters.[12] This electoral group, flagrantly over-representing the merchants as opposed to the craftsmen of the city,[13] also chose the syndics of the Chamber.[14] The middle class shared the elitist values of their age.

Le Havre and Rouen acted together as a kind of funnel through which all manner of raw materials entered France. Most of these were transformed into manufactures in the region and were then distributed throughout France. Because these goods were sold on the national market, imports at Le Havre-Rouen always exceeded exports.[15] The most important industries bequeathed by the seventeenth century were the making of fine draperies, or woollens, and coarse linen for the trade to Cadiz.[16] But the eighteenth century saw the rise of a new manufacture—cotton. Gradually, workers were leaving woolworking for the cleaner and more agreeable work in cotton. The Rouen manufacturers had already resigned themselves to producing the inferior kinds of woollen cloth, and the making of fine draperies had moved to the neighbouring towns of Louviers, Elbeuf, and Darnétal. But through the agency of the putting-out system, the spinning and weaving of cotton was spreading through the countryside. By mid-century, the region's woollen industry was everywhere either extinct or in decline.

Cotton had begun its spectacular climb to prominence in 1694.[17] In that year, according to the most common version of the story, a Rouen merchant named Etienne De la Rue, having found himself overstocked with raw cotton hitherto used only for ribbons, had persuaded two weavers, Bigault and Thierry, to weave it with a warp of silk. The result had been named *siamoise* because of its superficial resemblance to the clothing of the Siamese ambassadors who had visited Louis XIV in 1684 and 1686. The use of silk had made the cloth too weak for general use, however; and linen had been substituted. The new, improved *siamoise* had been an immediate success and was to hold its own in the market even after the legalization of printed textiles in 1759.[18] According to the *Manuel du Fabricant*, 1727, there had been in that year some 25,000 artisans making *siamoises*, plain cotton cloth, *futaines*, and handkerchiefs, this last manufacture having employed some 4,000.[19] In contrast to woolworking, the linen manufacture was not supplanted by cotton; and there was little variation in its production until after the American Revolution.[20]

Rouen was also famous for its faience, glazed in blue and white or blue, white, yellow, and red. Along the three little rivers that ran through the town, the Robec, the Aubette, and the Renelle, were the many mills of tanners and dyers. There were a soap factory, a starch factory, and five sugar refineries, although the latter industry was in decline. Playing cards and pipes, ribbons and hats, stockings, brushes and books, candies and jams, were all among the city's manufactures.

Because of Holland's free trade principles and its role as an entrepôt, Dutch trade with Rouen was extensive. Of the great variety of commodities Rouen imported, the most significant were wheat and other grains.[21] The Hanse cities of Bremen, Lubeck, and especially Hamburg were significant as suppliers of iron, *fer-blanc*, of which they seem to have had a virtual monopoly, and German, Polish, and Danish wool, the *laines du Nord*.[22] The trade with Great Britain remained significant in spite of the sanctions that encumbered it. Of special importance were the *salaisons*, salted beef, pork, and butter imported from Ireland for the sustenance of colonies and seamen. This was a branch of trade that, mercantilist principles notwithstanding, France could not forego.[23]

The most important branch of the international traffic of Rouen and Le Havre, in which both imports and exports were large was that with Spain, especially Cadiz and Bilbao. The Spanish export staple was unworked wool, Bilbaoan being the best. This arrived in enormous quantities to supply the Norman textile industry.[24] The principal export to Spain was the above-mentioned variety of linen made exclusively for export from the flax of the region of St. Georges-du-Vièvre. It was bleached and packaged at Rouen and was sent to the West Indies via Cadiz to make shirts for the slaves employed in mines.[25] While the principal Rouen exports to England were gourmet foods such as cheese and *confitures*,[26] to the rest of Europe, principally by way of Holland and the Hanse towns, Rouen and Le Havre exported Norman textiles, blankets, and handkerchiefs.[27]

These were only the most important commodities that flooded the wholesale mart of the Halles de Rouen. East of the Palais des Consuls, up the Rue des Tonneliers and the Rue de la Savonnerie, the Halles were said to be "the finest in the universe."[28] They would have provided a visitor with a clear perception of the economic foundations of the region. But neither there nor along the quays would he have found evidence of a trade with France's colonies in 1729. This would have stood in sharp contrast to the conversations he might have heard were he lucky enough to gain admittance to the bourse; for by the year in which Dugard and Company was founded, the merchants had drawn the world beyond the Atlantic into the orbit of their considerations.

In the aggregate of Rouen-Le Havre foreign trade, that with the colonies was of very little importance in the early eighteenth century, constituting only four per cent by value in 1730. The export of linen to Cadiz and thence to Spanish America in Spanish ships was the region's most important link with trans-Atlantic markets. But in the 1730s the merchants of Rouen and Le Havre became serious contenders in the French markets of the West Indies and Canada. That proportion of trade carried on with colonies increased to 36 per cent by 1776.[29] An essential aspect of this trade was the re-export of colonial commodities to other European countries. The new trade was thus complementary to the old, permitting Rouen importers to build up credits abroad. The history of Dugard and Company is a part of this larger history of colonial trade. Bereft of the context of France's expanding maritime economy and, in particular, of the ebullient atmosphere of the enterprising city of Rouen, the company would seem a strangely misguided venture; and its founders would lose their credibility as men of business and men of history.

The man most central in the history of the Société du Canada is Robert Dugard, whose forebears were a part of the Protestant community that had flourished at Rouen before the Revocation of the Edict of Nantes. His father had abjured, become a nominal Catholic, and had had his son baptised in the Catholic Church, as recorded in the register of the parish of St. André de Rouen—"1704, 27 October baptised Robert Dugard son of Robert Dugard and of Françoise Porrée of the so-called reformed religion."[30] Eighteenth-century registers of *état civil* specify *nouveaux convertis* as such, or frequently, as above, as "de la réligion prétendue réformée" or simply R.P.R. Conversions were usually nominal and were so regarded.

The numerous Dugards of Rouen, Elbeuf, and the surrounding region had been members of the congregation of Quévilly-près-Rouen which was, until the Revocation, the region's one Protestant church. The earliest entry of the name Dugard in the congregation's records refers to a baptism of 18 May 1608.[31] Thereafter until the closing of the church, the baptisms, marriages, and burials of Dugards appear regularly in the congregational registers. One of the most commonly recurring Christian names in the family (surpassed only by Abraham) is Robert. The subject of the present study was at least the fourth in a direct line to bear that name and he so named his own son.

The earliest of the direct line are known only from the record of their son's marriage on 3 November 1639—"Robert Dugard, son of Robert and the late Catherine Viart, with Marie Le Plastrier."[32] Robert II died in the parish of St. André de Rouen on 6 October 1673, aged 60 years and six months.[33] He and Marie Le Plastrier had baptised one son Robert in 1644; and following his death, gave the same name to their next son, baptised 23 January 1650.[34] The *état civil* of this second son, Robert III, can be traced no further in the registers of Quévilly. There is no record of a marriage or of the presentation of children for baptism from the years of his youth until he reached the age of 35, the year of the Revocation and the closing of the church. The unsettled circumstances of the years that followed would seem an adequate explanation for the further delay of marriage. Thus it would appear that he was older than 50 when he finally put his bachelor days behind him, marrying the daughter of a Rouen merchant, Jonas Porée, according to the rite of the Roman Catholic Church.[35] Two years after their marriage, Robert IV, founding member of the Société du Canada, was born.[36]

The mercantile vocation was traditional in the Dugard family. Receipts attest that Robert II was a member of the *communauté des marchands drapiers en gros et détail* and the *marchands en gros de la bourse*.[37] Three bills of exchange drawn on him are extant. The earliest is dated London, 3 January 1658/59, and by it David Congnard and Actham request "Mr. Robert Dugard, Marchant In Roane" to pay Mr. Peter Congnard "the somme of two hundred sixty nine crownes at sixty souls y crowne."[38] The others date from 1664 and are drawn in Amsterdam and London payable in London and Paris respectively.[39]

The earliest record of Robert III's career as a merchant is his payment, on 18 June 1680, of the *droit de hanse* of Rouen, a special tax by which a merchant bought the right to trade in the city.[40] According to an intendant, "All merchants who came to trade at Rouen pay the first time a *droit de hanse* from which the income is divided between the hospital and the town hall."[41] This does not mean that Robert III did not begin his career until 1680. Sons appear to have been covered by the *lettres de hanse* of their fathers while they lived, and in general persons were not prompt in paying the fee.[42] Robert III may have weathered the Revocation with minimum difficulty. Certainly, in 1691 the drapers taxed him 200 livres *tournois*, a reasonably high assessment indicating an unimpaired or repaired fortune.[43]

In a permit allowing him to keep 15,000 livres for business purposes at his home, Rue de la Madeleine, St. Denis's parish, Robert III is described as a "Marchand commissionnaire," that is, as one who handles others' business on a commission basis.[44] The commission agent was one with international connections. Thus like his father, Robert III was a frequenter of the bourse, a man who received foreign cargoes and sent abroad the produce of the region. He was a man of reputation who in spite of his Protestant taint, the Intendant of Rouen described as worthy of trust and "a good Trader of this town."[45]

Robert Dugard IV disappears from written record from his baptism in 1704 until 1 February 1722. At just over 17 years of age, he started in business for himself, not in Rouen but in Amsterdam. Although lacking information on his schooling, from his well-kept accounts we can infer his sound grasp of writing, arithmetic, and book-keeping. That his father entrusted him with a capital of 159,116 florins suggests he was already well versed in the arts of the *parfait négociant*.

Two slim volumes reveal in detail the activities of the year 1722. These are the journal and ledger in which Dugard recorded the business transactions undertaken by himself at Amsterdam, beginning in February and ending abruptly and without explanation on 27 August.[46] Dugard describes his capital as "having been ceded to me by my father to trade with for my own account" and gives us a glimpse of the prudential piety characteristic of a French bourgeois by adding "in which traffic may God be pleased to bless me and preserve me from loss."[47] The capital was composed of Amsterdam real estate (how Dugard père acquired that would be a story in itself), an account at the Bank of Amsterdam, cash on hand, shares in the Dutch East India Company, bills of exchange, merchandise, furniture, and a one-eighth share in a frigate, the *Reine Marie*. A few accounts were turned over to him, and this entailed debts totalling 16,461 florins.[48]

Dugard's capital was not small, so it is not surprising that he quickly established business relations with 16 merchants in foreign cities and 14 more in Amsterdam. He bought very little in Amsterdam. From six merchants he obtained Dutch woollens, whale oil and whalebone, pepper, brandy, wool, cheeses, and spices. To nine he sold wool, pepper, indigo, linens, cotton, and other items of general merchandise.[49] From the northern towns came wool—from Danzig, wool of Thoorn; from Hamburg, Austrian gray and Pomeranian; from Altona and Bremen, German wool. Frederick Spiegal of Danzig also provided a shipment of Polish flour for the Amsterdam grain market. Blancards, indigo, cloves, nutmeg, and pepper were sent to Hamburg, from where some of the pepper reached Danzig.[50] His correspondent at London, Michel van Soetenou, bought from him nutmeg and the dyestuff madder root, selling him ink-producing gall nut. Wool of different kinds was sold at Dunkirk. At Morlaix, he found a market for silk, pepper, and fine Carmanian wool.[51]

Dugard had three correspondents in Rouen, one of them his father. There he sent the wools of the north together with the cotton of the colonial islands of St. Eustache and Guadeloupe, the pepper of the east, the gall nut of England, and the cheeses of Holland. From Rouen, he received the syrup of the sugar refineries, drinking glasses, blancards, furniture, *chardons* for wool carding, and *vaude* for yellow dye.[52] Two correspondents at Nantes bought the whalebone which he had procured in Amsterdam. From Elie Dupuis of La Rochelle he bought colonial indigo and Guadeloupe cotton, selling him gall nut. His supply of Portuguese wool came from Benjamin Leclerc of Lisbon to whom he sold woollen *drap* and cloves. Cadiz sent the wool of Segovia and took large quantities of linen from Brittany, Holland, and Rouen, woollen fabric from Leyden, and lace from Brabant.[53] This broad and varied commerce was made possible by a variety of financial operations. Commercial institutions of some development and sophistication had made barter unnecessary even in the Middle Ages. Dugard's commercial transactions in Amsterdam itself depended upon cash payments or transfer payments in the Bank of Amsterdam. For example, on 12 March Dugard sold to Pieter Rutgers six bales of wool.[54] When five days later Rutgers sold Dugard a quantity of whale oil, the two made no attempt to set off the two transactions insofar as values permitted. Rather, at the same time Rutgers paid for the wool by means of the bank, and on 22 April Dugard paid for the oil with cash. But Rutgers was the only man in Amsterdam with whom Dugard both bought and sold. To eight others he only sold and from five others he only bought.[55]

In international traffic, it might seem more desirable to buy from and sell to the same correspondent. Yet Dugard bought nothing from five of the 14 correspondents to whom he sold and sold nothing to two of the 11 from whom he bought.[56] Nor were his purchases and sales regarding a single correspondent ever nearly equal. Northerners had more wool than they had need for pepper; and La Rochelle could absorb only a limited quantity of gall nut in return for its sought-after cotton and indigo. International commerce, even intercity commerce, was therefore dependent for its smooth working on the use of the bill of exchange. It moved money from where it was idle to where it was needed. In its most elementary sense the bill of exchange or draft was a device by which a merchant could sell or exchange a distant credit for a domestic one, the purchaser being another merchant who could make use of credit in the distant place on which the bill was drawn. Originally, there were always four parties to a bill of exchange. The first two were the "drawer," let us say Robert Dugard of Amsterdam, and the "drawee," say his correspondent in Hamburg, who had to be someone on whom Dugard had a valid claim to credit. Secondly, the bill could only be given in exchange for the equivalent of its face value; that is, another Amsterdam merchant called the "taker" would have to pay for the bill. It would be made out to the fourth and last party, the "payee," a Hamburg creditor of the taker. In the eighteenth century the taker and payee were usually the same person; the taker purchased a bill payable to himself in another city and by having it made out "to order" could then sell it to any other party who might find it convenient to purchase his right of payment in Hamburg.[57]

There is no better way to understand the role of the bill of exchange in merchandise transactions than to follow some of them in Dugard's Amsterdam ledger. The first example is of the simplest kind. When Jan van Paarling of Hamburg sold merchandise that Dugard had sent for his own account, he attributed the proceeds to Dugard's account with himself. However, this did not provide Dugard with sufficient credit at Hamburg for his purposes, so the account also shows the arrival of a number of bills of exchange.[58]

Van Paarling's subsequent venture in the Cadiz trade shows not only the indirect means of payment made possible by drafts, but the intricacy of which the commission agent system was capable. Van Paarling asked Dugard to ship 150 pieces of blancard to Cadiz on his behalf. Since blancards were available only in Rouen, Dugard asked his father to take care of the matter. Dugard of Rouen then bought the blancards and shipped them to Cadiz for Van Paarling's account and risk. He debited the total to his son's account. Dugard of Amsterdam then recorded Van Paarling's account as debtor to his own account with his father. Finally Dugard of Rouen drew a bill of exchange on Van Paarling payable to his son at Amsterdam.[59] This settled accounts with Hamburg, but left Dugard his father's debtor.

Dugard purchased wool from Barthélemy van Schelde of Altona. Having no credits in that city, he could not have made the purchase had he not been able to draw on Van Paarling in nearby Hamburg by means of the bill of exchange.[60] The process was reversed in the case of Peter Tervoet of Bremen. He was paid for wool sent to Dugard by himself drawing a bill on Dugard payable to one of his own creditors.[61] If exchange rates were unfavourable, they could be avoided. Thus Dugard paid Genwith of Morlaix by drawing on Dupuis of La Rochelle, just as he drew on Van Paarling to pay Van Schelde.[62]

All of the above uses of the bill of exchange are related to transactions in merchandise. But drafts were also bought and sold to gain on exchange rates or as a means to obtain credit. Dugard did not attempt these speculative uses of the bill of exchange. Still a very young man, his every transaction monitored by a watchful father, he conducted his affairs with caution. Some years later, as director of the Société du Canada, he would make ample use of finance bills.

Another significant aspect of the workings of eighteenth-century commerce revealed by the Amsterdam ledgers and journals is the variety of accounts in company to which merchants from time to time had recourse. In general these were partnerships limited to a single venture in which the partners shared equally all profit and loss. If two partners were involved, the account was referred to as *à demi*, if three persons, as *en tiers*. Dugard participated in many such partnerships. Wool of Thoorn was bought from Spiegal of Danzig for a *compte à demi* with Samuel LeBlanc of Amsterdam.[63] It was eventually sold at Leyden for *compte en tiers* between LeBlanc, Dugard, and Dirk de Jager of Leyden.[64] Van Soetenou of London, Dugard, and his father participated in a *compte en tiers* for the sale of gall nuts in Rouen.[65] Dugard also had a *compte en tiers* with his father and Elie Dupuis of La Rochelle for the sale of cotton in Rouen.[66]

A young man like Dugard could gain considerably from the association with established merchants that these accounts afforded. For example, Dugard made his first contact with Frederick Spiegal by joining with Van Paarling in a *compte à demi* to send pepper to the Danzig merchant. His association with Van Paarling provided an introduction and as a final result left him with a credit balance and a new correspondent. This was the foundation of Dugard's later trade with Spiegal in wool and grain. By such means were merchants introduced to merchants and the web of correspondence extended.

One of the most interesting of Dugard's correspondences was that with Henrique de Haro of Cadiz, for this provides the first written record of Dugard's direct involvement in the trade to America.[67] Dugard sent woollens and linens valued at more than 14,000 florins to De Haro, who sold them, using the proceeds to buy wool that he sent back to Amsterdam. As Dugard still had a considerable credit with him, he bought a supply of lace and blancards that he put aboard the galleon *Le Grand St. François* to be sold in Spanish America for a *compte à demi* between himself and Dugard. The transaction tells us that the entry of the Dugard family into colonial trade was less abrupt than it might otherwise appear.

On 27 August Dugard made a trial balance of his ledger. This showed a net increase in capital of 7,803 florins, or a profit of five and a half per cent for the previous seven month period.[68] Thereafter, began a new ledger and a new journal both designated "B." The most interesting account in this second set is that of a ship purchased by

Dugard for *compte en tiers* with his father and Benjamin Leclerc of Lisbon.[69] The *Fortune*, a hoy 74 feet long, 17 feet wide, and 12 feet in depth, was purchased on 16 September for 5,450 florins, half payable immediately with a rebate of one and a half per cent, the remainder due in "the usual term" of six weeks. The hoy was purchased for the run between Amsterdam and Rouen and had a crew of six under Captain Cornelis Jansen. The first profit of 266 florins each was entered into the ledger on 15 October.[70] Twelve days later on 27 October, the ledger and journal end abruptly.

Some pages after the end of Journal B, Dugard began a third journal. The opening date was 16 October 1723, a full year later; the money of account was the livre *tournois*; and the profit centre was not Amsterdam but Rouen.[71] The principal of these entries, which continued until 15 June 1726, concerned a *compte à demi* with Marie Le Blanc of Amsterdam. Tea and handkerchiefs are exchanged for wool and tapestries. The scale of these transactions is inconsiderable when compared with those of the Amsterdam ledger. Values of less than 100 livres predominate. Dugard's personal trade had dwindled to what was most probably a gesture of merchantly solidarity towards a recently widowed *négociante*. Dugard had returned not only to his father's house, but to his father's business.

From all Dugard père's years of trade there is only one account extant. This is the current account of Mlle. Jeanne Verel, probably of Bilbao, with himself, 17 November 1725 to 16 November 1728. It concerns a *compte à demi* by which they sell Segovian wool from Bilbao at Rouen, Elbeuf, and Louviers. The account is signed, "R. DuGard for my father."[72]

The historian cannot know why the Amsterdam venture ended just as and when it did. Perhaps the level of profit was deemed inadequate. More probably, Dugard père may have felt the educative experience and the test of his son's ability had been sufficient. It is also possible that sickness, either of father or son, may have intervened. Whatever it may have been, the Amsterdam experience is significant in the present context because of what it tells us about the world that produced the Société du Canada. The company was heir to a thriving commercial tradition. Import and export, sales on commission, the trade in textiles, and shipowning constituted Robert Dugard's heritage. His *compte à demi* with De Haro provided an early opportunity to participate in colonial trade. The cession of the *Reine Marie* by his father gave him his first experience of shipowning; and with the purchase of the *Fortune*, he became an outfitter as well. His share in the *Fortune* also linked him with owners living in foreign cities; and his participation in his father's business after his return to Rouen, gave him connections with the community of foreign merchants at Bilbao. All of these were important precedents for the role he would play in the creation of Dugard and Company.

At the end of 1733, the Dugards made a significant move from the Rue de la Madeleine, St. Denis's parish, to the Rue des Charettes,.St. Vincent's parish. The lease of their new home was in the name of Dugard père but was signed by "Monsieur Robert Dugard his son also merchant in Rouen."[73] The back door of the house opened on the Rue des Ramasses just behind the wall of the open bourse. The Dugards had moved to the centre of commercial Rouen and there Robert Dugard père would die and Robert Dugard fils would continue to live as long as he remained a merchant of consequence.

Little information has been found on the family and business background of the other members of the Société du Canada. Two of these families were Protestants of the Quévilly congregation. One of them was the Laurens family, of which father and son, both named David, were partners in the company. Among the large number of Laurens mentioned in the registers of Quévilly are three Davids, baptised in 1666, 1667, and 1669. The man most likely to have known the Dugards and to have become involved in commerce on a grand scale was the David born in 1666 to a family of mercers, this being one of the powerful merchant guilds of the city. (The other families were artisans.[74]) This David was the son of Thomas Laurens and Judith Cougnard, who were married at Quévilly in 1661.[75] He acquired his *lettres de hanse* on 31 March 1700.[76] David Laurens fils was born to him and Madeleine LeTellier in 1707.[77] His sister Marie married Robert Dugard, strengthening a business relation with a family alliance.[78] Their son, Robert V, was baptised at St. Vincent's.[79]

The third Protestant family involved in the company were the Vincents, a less numerous clan than either the Laurens or the Dugards. The elder of the two Vincents interested in the company was Gédéon, born to Jean Vincent and Anne Ferrant of Fécamp in 1656 and married to Madeleine Dangicourt at Quévilly in 1680.[80] All that is known of his business activities is that he received his *lettres de hanse* on 8 January 1698.[81] His son and partner, Gédéon Samuel Vincent, was born in 1681.[82] He married Marguerite Bouffe; on 21 January 1744, they baptised their own son, Gédéon Samuel Vincent II.[83]

There is no evidence that the other partners in the Société du Canada had any Protestant background. One of these was a man of high social standing, Guillaume France. At different times, he was *con-*

seiller échevin of Rouen[84] and Second Consul of the Consular Jurisdiction.[85] He received his *lettres de hanse* on 22 February 1702[86] and he married Elizabeth Catherine Besard[87] by whom he had a son, named Guillaume, who became a partner upon the death of his father.

The remaining associate was Pierre D'Haristoy, described by Dugard as "my intimate friend."[88] A man of bubbling enthusiasm and great imagination, his prophetic interest in industrialization was to make him one of the fathers of the industrial revolution in Rouen, an honourable but profitless role in which he persuaded Dugard to share. D'Haristoy appears not to have been of an old Rouen family. He had many relatives on his father's side at Bayonne, and those on his mother's side lived in Paris.[89] He did not receive his *lettres de hanse* until 31 July 1743; he then paid the full fee of 6 livres 2s 6d, indicating that his father had never received letters.[90] He was a director of the Manufacture du Plomb laminé established at Déville-les-Rouen in 1736 by the Parisian parent company, itself established in 1729.[91] He must have been connected with the parent company before 1736, for there are extant records of his sale of laminated lead roofing to the parish of St. Etienne des Tonneliers in 1733 and to the parish of St. Maclou in 1734 and 1736.[92] He was an inventor and entrepreneur with a lifelong predilection for industry over commerce.

Associated with these bourgeois of Rouen in the founding of the company that was eventually to become the Société du Canada, was one foreigner, Pedro Beckveldt of Bilbao; but he was to sell out his interest to the other partners in 1732. The other founders were six in number and are known from the signatures that appear on the minutes of the first formal meeting on 14 May 1732. The signatories were Guillaume France, père; David Laurens, père; Robert Dugard, fils; Pierre D'Haristoy and Gédéon Samuel Vincent.[93] The latter signed for himself and for his father, "Vincent père et fils." Aged 79, Dugard père was not involved in the new company.

Over the years, death was to change the membership. David Laurens père died at the age of 69; and the minutes of 18 January 1735 are signed, for the first time, "Veuve Laurens et Fils" in a wispy and blotchy hand. Those of 14 June are also signed "Veuve Laurens et fils," but this time in the sure handwriting of David Laurens fils, who from 29 November signs simply "D. Laurens."

Gédéon Vincent died in late 1736 or early 1737, aged 80 or 81, for the minutes of 30 January 1737, are signed "Ged. Samuel Vincent." Gédéon Samuel attained the age of 71; he was buried from St. Vincent's Church, Rouen, on 30 August 1752.[94]

The signatures of Guillaume France, Robert Dugard, and Pierre

D'Haristoy continue throughout the minute-book, which ends with the last known meeting, that of 9 January 1743. Guillaume France died in 1743 or 1744, and his interest devolved upon his son and namesake.[95] When Pierre D'Haristoy died in June, 1757, Robert Dugard was left the only founding member still alive.[96] He lived another 13 years,[97] but by that time the Société du Canada had long been dissolved. David Laurens fils lived to a venerable 77 and was buried in the Cimetière de la Rue de la Rose, 27 April 1784.[98] Guillaume France fils was perhaps still living at that date; but if so, he had long lost contact with the families of his father's friends and with the mercantile city of Rouen.

CHAPTER THREE

The New Company, 1729–1742

The history of Dugard and Company begins in 1729 with the building of a small brigantine, the *Louis Dauphin*, by Robert Dugard and five other Rouen merchants associated with Pedro Beckveldt of Bilbao.[1] The commercial connection between Rouen and Bilbao was well established, and the traditional business of the Dugard family was in part founded upon it. Similarly, the joint ownership of sea-going vessels by partners living in different and distant cities was common; Robert Dugard already had experience in such a proprietorship. There was nothing exceptional about the Société au navire le *Louis Dauphin*, as the partnership was called. Whether the members foresaw the considerable business enterprise they were setting afoot or had built their ship with Canadian trade in mind are questions that cannot be decided on the basis of known evidence. For its first voyage, they sent the *Louis Dauphin* from Rouen to Bilbao and back. Outward bound, it also stopped at La Rochelle, delivering a cargo of clay balls used in sugar refining; but this tiny cargo, valued at only 152 livres, would appear to be the only one carried for the owners.[2] The voyage was primarily a freighting venture; as such, it netted 429 livres.[3] But in 1730 the *Louis Dauphin* sailed for Quebec. It seems a bizarre adventure for a Bilbaoan dealer in wool and blancards and a radical initiative even for *Rouennais* merchants. But Canada was the object of a revived interest in Rouen. Peace in America and Europe and favourable economic conditions meant the safe prosecution of the Canadian fur trade, the *voyage de long cours* freed from the threat of privateers, and conditions suitable to the expansion of the European market. The *Louis Dauphin*'s westward course in 1730 stands at the very beginning of the period of Rouen's new interest in colonial trade; as such, it shares in the opening of a new chapter in the economic history of the city and of the French empire.

The partners limited themselves to a very modest cargo, 25,000 livres in value, for this first trial voyage to Quebec, but it was sufficient to show that they were thinking in terms of trade as well as freighting. The merchandise was entrusted to a supercargo, François Havy. He was young, Norman, and Protestant, coming from Beuzevillette near Bolbec in the Pays de Caux, a provincial obscurity that he was on the threshold of trading for a prominence no less provincial as the company's chief factor in Canada.[4] The captain of the ship had sailed it to Bilbao the previous year[5] and had been a captain sailing the Amsterdam-Rouen route.[6] He was named François Vangellikom Vandelle, bearing witness to a Flemish or Dutch ancestry and thus to Rouen's venerable relation with the Low Countries. His was an old Protestant family in Rouen, one that had suffered persecution in 1685.[7] François Vangellikom was born in 1699 and in 1727 married one Marie Anne Tessard at Rouen.[8] Until 1746, when he seems to have retired, he was master of whatever ship was deemed the company's finest.

The *Louis Dauphin*'s voyage of 1730 was triangular.[9] At Quebec, Havy sold all or the greater part of his cargo, about ten per cent of it on credit, sent bills of exchange and specie back to France, and made up a new cargo of Canadian produce for sale in the island of Martinique. Having reached the island, Havy appears to have left Vandelle and the ship, finding his own way to Cap Français, or "le Cap" as it was known, on the northern coast of St. Domingue. At Le Cap he purchased leather and indigo and in the spring of 1731 found passage on a ship bound for Nantes. He proceeded inland as far as Caen, where he received money and probably letters of instruction from Robert Dugard from the latter's brother-in-law, a local mercer. There was therefore no need for him to proceed to Rouen, and he set out immediately for La Rochelle, where he met the *Louis Dauphin*, already on its way back to Quebec with a second cargo.

The second voyage was not triangular. The cargo, twice the value of the preceding one, was sold; and Havy succeeded in embarking all the proceeds of the sale, somewhat over half in cargo, the rest in bills of exchange. In the parlance of eighteenth-century traders, he "made" a "complete return." The return cargo cost more than the total of receipts at Quebec, indicating the payment of some of the debt of the previous year. Havy again returned to France, signing the account of his administration at Rouen, 18 May 1732.[10]

The voyages of 1730 and 1731 served as the company's initiation to the Canada trade. They now felt that they had gauged its nature and possibilities; it was time for them to take another step. On 14 May 1732, the Rouen partners held the first meeting recorded in their *livre de délibération*, or minute-book.[11] They agreed to Dugard's proposal that the *Louis Dauphin* should be sent from Le Havre to Quebec fully laden with merchandise. But a second ship should be sent to Quebec from La Rochelle, where it would have obtained the wine, brandy, "& etc." needed for a well-assorted cargo. Having discharged its cargo at Quebec, this second ship would then pick up a Canadian cargo for the West Indies and proceed there immediately, returning to France early enough to be able to repeat the same voyage the following year. Free of the necessity of stopping at La Rochelle, the *Louis Dauphin* would shuttle between Le Havre and Quebec. This development would adjust the volume of shipping more exactly to the capacity of France, Canada, and Martinique, the three markets concerned, to absorb or provide merchandise as well as compressing the greatest possible sailing distance into the shortest possible season. The two-ship system would exploit "all the advantage that can be hoped of the Quebec trade."[12] Dugard offered not only the plan, but a ship. His proposition was accepted, and the 120-ton *St. Mathieu* under Captain François Le Provost, was sold to the Société au navire le *Louis Dauphin* for 9,000 livres.

The *St. Mathieu* had been purchased by Dugard, D'Haristoy, and the Vincents for 11,000 livres in 1730.[13] It had made one voyage to the West Indies for them, leaving Bordeaux in September 1731, and returning to Le Havre not long before the meeting in May 1732.[14] These members had thus carried out a separate but analogous venture to the Société au navire le *Louis Dauphin*. Its termination and the transfer of the *St. Mathieu* indicates a uniting of purpose among the associates. Their success and mutual confidence were such that an ephemeral trading venture was by stages being transformed into a company of long duration. The proposal and acceptance of this plan as recorded in the minutes also constitute the earliest documentary evidence of the preponderant role that Robert Dugard played in the company, probably from its inception.

According to Robert Dugard's rather unsatisfactory method of calculation, net profits on the first two voyages had been 12.5 per cent and 10.4 per cent, the former on the triangular voyage and the latter on the direct voyage.[15] Although these figures do not seem very high, the six merchants of Rouen were evidently satisfied with their experiment in trans-Atlantic trade. There was one associate, however, who was not; and that was Pedro Beckveldt. He intended to limit himself to the business of freighting and had no wish to participate in expensive cargoes. But as freighting propositions, both voyages to Quebec were failures. Apparently shipping without trading did not succeed in the Canada trade. The Rouen associates therefore agreed to buy out Beckveldt's share, and he was indemnified for his one-sixth interest in the *Louis Dauphin* by a payment of 3,595 livres, 6d.[16] Without Beckveldt, the company was more united in outlook and purpose.

The minutes of the company's second meeting, on 16 May 1732, confirm the pattern of the first. Robert Dugard explained what should be done, the problems involved and how best they should be met; the other members accepted his propositions. The question was one of insurance. The ships and cargoes for 1732, Dugard estimated, would be worth about 180,000 to 190,000 livres, a considerable sum that should be insured. The different insurance "chambers" (partnerships) in Rouen offered seven per cent for a return voyage, but insurance was to be had in Holland for five. Dugard was authorized to do business with the Dutch.[17] The decisions made, François Havy returned to Quebec with a third cargo, this time to establish a permanent *magasin*, or trading factory, for the company.

The third cargo to Canada was traded in the manner Dugard had proposed. The *Louis Dauphin* sailed directly from Le Havre to Quebec and back while the *St. Mathieu* went first to Quebec, then to Martinique, returning to Le Havre. No record states that it picked up its cargo at La Rochelle; but since this was the intended plan, the presumption is that it did.

The partners were not convinced that their tiny fleet of two sail was adequate for their purposes. Thus at the meeting of 28 January 1733, they agreed that "to render the navigation that we have undertaken for the Quebec trade more advantageous, it is advisable for our company to have a ship of from two hundred and fifty to three hundred tons."[18] Dugard and Vandelle were authorized to find such a ship in London. In March they returned, having bought a 300-ton vessel from the South Sea Company for 45,801 livres, 14s 2d. It was renamed the *Ville de Québec*, put under the command of Vandelle, and got ready to carry the fourth cargo.[19] The associates were plainly bent on expansion and long-term investment.

The continued extension and affirmation of Robert Dugard's authority is evident throughout the recorded minutes of 1733 and 1734. He was given greater discrimination in the handling and selling of merchandise, since being obliged to buy in a wide market that covered all of France and extended to Amsterdam and Hamburg made the soliciting of permission for every commercial operation a considerable nuisance.[20] Just as he had been authorized to purchase the *Ville de Québec*, he was asked to outfit it.[21] It was he who negotiated charter-parties when the need arose.[22] When tax officials at Le Havre attempted, contrary to the Letters Patent of April 1717, to tax wine and brandy the company was sending to Quebec, it was Dugard who sued them in the Cour des Aides.[23] Eventually, at the tenth meeting on 16 March 1734, the sale of all the company's furs was placed in his hands.[24] This was significant not only as an augmentation of Dugard's role, but also in the development of the company's independence.

Furs purchased in Canada had hitherto been marketed exclusively by La Rochelle middlemen. Dugard was granted this trade only because he could handle it at the same prices and conditions as they. The company thus snapped the second of two ties binding their Canadian trade to La Rochelle. On 11 February they had already agreed to send their first ship direct to Bordeaux and Mortagne, near the mouth of the Gironde, for wine, brandy, and Montauban woollens, having decided that it was best "to draw the necessary merchandise . . . from its place of origin whenever possible."[25] The 1734 voyage of the *St. Mathieu* from Le Havre to Bordeaux and Quebec, returning to Le Havre, marked the company's complete emancipation from the tutelage of the port that had traditionally handled the Canada trade.

In these two years, 1733–34, many principles of business operation began to appear in the pages of the minute-book in response to new problems and new situations. The definition of authority, the establishing of as direct as possible trade relations, the synchronization of expeditions involving more than one ship, were the most important of these, but there were others worthy of mention. Twice it is recorded that the risks on merchandise being carried from a place of origin to the company's ships were to be borne by all the members equally and not just by Dugard and his correspondents.[26] It was agreed that ships and cargoes should be insured, "all of it or the better part," and that insurance should be taken out wherever it could be had most cheaply.[27] When the risks did not appear great, a voyage was sometimes insured in only one direction.[28] Finally, cargoes sent to Canada after Havy's return there in 1732, were made up in conformity with his memoranda explaining what commodities were most likely to find a ready market in the colony.[29]

The third cargo had been the first attempt at Dugard's two-ship combination of direct with triangular trade; and it was not repeated in 1733, although the profits had remained steady.[30] This deviation from what appears to have been intended as a long-range policy is best explained in terms of the large investment represented by the purchase of

the *Ville de Québec*. The company had more ships than it could afford
to outfit and fill with cargo for its own account. This is at least one
possible explanation for the lease under charter-party of both the
Louis Dauphin and the *St. Mathieu* in 1733. They were to carry sugar
from St. Domingue at 19d per pound. Only a *pacotille* worth about
10,000 livres was to be placed in each ship for the account of the
owners.[31] The plan was not a happy one, ending with a substantial
loss, but it had the advantage of tying up little capital.[32]

The next year, it was the turn of the *Ville de Québec* to be let, this
time to the Compagnie des Indes. It carried sugar under the same terms
as the charter-parties of the previous year,[33] but realized a clear profit
of 65 per cent.[34] This brings into relief the startling comparison of the
Canada and West Indies trades—the one of only modest return but
reasonably stable year after year, something that could not always
have been said of it, and the other a trade of spectacular rise and fall, a
trade for speculators. Although Dugard and his friends were fully
committed to the Canadian market, they had thrown the dice in the
sugar trade and were not to forget that heady experience.

On 16 March 1734, the associates met in the home of David
Laurens to draft and set their names to an *acte de société*, or articles of
association, which formalized their relationship. In every way, from
the pious invocation imparting the sanctity of religion,[35] and the
paraphed signatures conveying legality *sous seing privé*[36] to this kind
of fundamental law of association,[37] even in their being retroactive to
1729,[38] the articles are representative and unexceptional.

The type of organization outlined in the articles classifies the company as a partnership. Although the company would henceforth have
the name Société du Canada, there is no mention of this *raison sociale*
in the articles; indeed, such titles were almost exclusively limited to
joint-stock companies (*sociétés de capitaux*).[39] Its absence from the
articles should remind us that the company existed in a business world
in which the corporate personality was a rarity and the business company was not regarded as more than the sum of its parts. In fact, in
certain instances, the company was broken down into its parts, the
associates each working for it under their own names. The articles
specify that although Dugard would act "in concert with us," he
would do so "in his name."[40] He bought, sold, and borrowed, all in
his own name in conformity with this formula. To take a somewhat
different example, when David Laurens interested a Parisian capitalist
in lending money to the company in 1742, he presented the other associates as his friends who wished to negotiate a loan and recognized

his own liability for repayment only in a secret document unknown to the creditor.[41]

The company was of the most common sort, the *société générale*, which lost its primacy as the almost invariable form of French business organization before the end of the century.[42] The fundamental characteristic of this sort of association, which rarely had more than four members, was, according to Henri Lévy-Bruhl, "la responsabilité solidaire et indéfinie des associés [the joint and several unlimited liability of the associates]."[43] This is expressed in clause six in which the associates agree "to reciprocally offer ourselves as guarantors, each for the other, of negotiable paper in notes and bills of exchange issuing from the capital of our said partnership."[44]

No amount of funded capital is specified in the articles or anywhere else, an omission which was not uncommon.[45] However, the division into five interests is specified, as was almost always the case.[46] The interest was usually proportional to the share of capital and from this it may be concluded that Dugard, D'Haristoy, France, and Laurens were each responsible for one-fifth of the capital and Vincent père et fils together for one-fifth.[47] They bore the risk of loss in this same proportion.[48] But in accordance with the principle enunciated in clause six, every member had unlimited liablity for the company's debts. As the company could be engaged by the actions of any individual member acting on its behalf, even if this action were without the approval of the other partners, this unlimited liability made partnership a risky business. It is thus not surprising that businessmen chose their partners carefully and often preferred members of their own families. This also explains the care taken by Dugard and Company to define all relations and responsibilities in the articles and in the pages of their minute-book.

No date of expiration was set. The absence of such a provision implied that the association would endure until the death of any one of its members unless renewed by the continued activity of the survivors and that it could also be terminated at any time by the renunciation of any or all of its members.[49] Clearly, the life of the company depended upon the lives and needs of its members. It could not outlive them; it was an extension of their personalities.

The object of the company was clearly stated in the articles—to outfit ships at Le Havre, send them to Quebec with cargo, and return them to Le Havre, and in general to send their ships with or without cargo wherever the partners might see fit.[50] Thus in 1734 Dugard and Company still saw the Canada trade as the foundation of their commerce, although the experience of the preceding four years had taught them not to reject the alternatives of Caribbean trade and freighting.

The articles prescribe the manner of handling return cargoes. To avoid the risks of fire, skins were to be divided between two warehouses. Hides used for leather were to be stored in Dugard's house and furs in Guillaume France's.[51] From the wording of clause three, the warehouses appear to have been in the merchants' houses. The provision that all merchandise of one kind should be in one place suggests that selling was conducted in the warehouses.

The partners were also concerned about their company's unity of purpose. It was agreed that none of them should have personal lots of merchandise, or *pacotilles*, in the company's or any other ships without the expressed permission of the company, the penalty of a fine of 500 livres payable to the Hôpital Général for the support of the poor being prescribed for the offender.[52] Ship captains were to be governed by the same rule to prevent their carrying their own *pacotilles* to the prejudice of the owners' cargo.[53] The company had progressed in solidarity from a point where half of its members saw no objection to their owning an entire ship, the *St. Mathieu*, as an additional private enterprise to that where it was regarded as prejudicial for any one of them to place a cargo worth only a few thousand livres in any ship.

Perhaps the most important provision was the naming of Robert Dugard as manager, this a confirmation of his role since 1729. The articles specified that he was to purchase outward cargoes, care for the company's interests in Canada, render accounts of sales and purchases at Quebec and remittances from there in bills of exchange, sell the return cargoes, be responsible for all accounts and papers, and give orders to the company's commission agent at Le Havre, Louis Le Vaillant. That is, he would undertake "in general all that should properly be done by a good manager."[54]

For his cares, Dugard was to receive certain commissions. These are described in the articles as one per cent on all merchandise ordered from the cities of France and Europe and two per cent on those commodities that he would be required to have cleaned, bleached, or otherwise processed. He would also receive one per cent on all sales of returned cargoes in the city of Rouen.[55] In practice, he also received one-half per cent on all sales made by his correspondents and one-half per cent on the total expenses of each expedition.[56] These provisions made Dugard's position within the company unique; his interest was more greatly advanced by expansion than was that of any other partner. This distinct point of view was combined with a very wide authority, although the associates would not have agreed with the eighteenth-century jurist Pothier that a manager could act "in spite of the others."[57]

Dugard was required not only to render accounts, but to communicate to the associates all letters received from foreign representatives, commission agents, captains, and merchants. The partners were to confer "all together by common consent on significant sales & before undertaking any voyage or cargo it will be resolved by the Company [and noted] in the minute-book."[58] Assemblies were to be held at three p.m. on the first and third Tuesdays of every month in the house of the eldest member, David Laurens père.[59] Dugard would keep the minute-book, each page numbered and paraphed, and the originals on loose sheets of paper would be kept by Laurens.[60] Thus the manager would be held in check by a system of collegiate decision-making. To encourage attendance at meetings, each member present at a session would receive two tokens of the Consular Jurisdiction, each worth 50 sols.[61] Such was the "Acte de société que Dieu veuille bénir," written in the minute-book and delivered on loose sheets to each member. The fruit of personal experience and of a long business tradition, it is fundamental to an understanding of Dugard and Company and stands as a model of the most common form of French business organization in the eighteenth century.

By the partners' own admission in a minute of 1742, the provision for the holding of regular meetings and the recording of their minutes was "poorly observed up until now."[62] There are only 34 meetings recorded, almost half of them in 1734–35. The assembly of the company played a significant part as a decision-making institution from mid-winter to spring in each of the years 1734, 1735, and 1736. Thereafter, it declined drastically, there being only two mid-winter meetings in 1737, no meetings in 1738, one in 1739, none again in 1740, then a marked increase in frequency for other than policy-making purposes, leading to a policy meeting in June 1742. At that time, the members resolved to meet more regularly, but thereafter only three additional meetings are recorded.

Most of the minutes that were written in the period 1737–43 provide little information on the company's history; for this reason it can be assumed that the absence of meetings, or at least of the records of meetings, does not greatly reduce the historian's understanding of the company's later history. It was only in the early years, 1732–36, when collegiate decision-making was very much a reality and the areas of decision new to all concerned, that detailed minutes answered the need of having a written statement of policies, responsibilities, and regulations for which minutes served as a legal record. The primary purpose of minutes was not to provide a running account to refresh the memory on day-to-day affairs. Hence in the later years the members were content to sign their names to laconic entries such as "Signed accounts," recording their acceptance of Dugard's administration. Minutes also exist that pledge their solidarity with regard to the repayment of loans, but they give no details of the transactions involved.

The atrophy of the assembly was paralleled by the growing trust of the members for one another and in particular for the manager, Robert Dugard. The usual formalities seemed unnecessary. However, the absence of meetings does not imply the absence of consultation or control over Dugard's actions. Rouen was a small community; the partners saw each other daily in the bourse on the quay as well as on many social occasions. When at a meeting of 27 June 1742, Dugard sought the written approval of his partners for many operations he had undertaken, they admitted that these were "certainly . . . known to the company." [63]

Of the company's later meetings, only the one of June 1742 merits extended notice in the context of the present chapter. According to the minute, "diverse business operations that he [Dugard] has undertaken to sustain trade at the level to which he has pushed it" [64] had never been approved by an assembly. One of these was the export of sugar, coffee, and indigo to London, Holland, and Hamburg. During the company's first ten years, its principal imports were Canadian furs and hides, and bills of exchange. Dugard's policy was to use the proceeds from the sale of these to buy this West Indian produce in the overstocked French market for resale abroad where demand was greatest. He continued to so convert Canadian cargo even when the company was importing its own sugar, coffee, and indigo. The company thus earned a double profit on peltries. Dugard had also had five ships built for the company at Quebec between 1737 and 1740. Such major decisions could not be left without written ratification, to become the prey of faulty memory as they receded into the past. This was even more true of his borrowings on the company's behalf, given the difficulty that prevailed of distinguishing personal from corporate affairs. Indeed, the problems that troubled Robert Dugard were largely questions of finance, which have been ignored in this discussion of the genesis, structure, and administration of the company. It is the object of the next chapter to trace the thread of the company's financial history from its beginnings in 1729 to this meeting of 27 June.

In retrospect, 1742 appears as the major turning point in the history of Dugard and Company. [65] Until then its investment in ships and its annual outlays in cargoes progressively increased. The expansion of these 13 years is mirrored in the growth of the company fleet from one in 1729 to eight in 1740–42, and in the increasing number of voyages undertaken each year, from one in 1729 to seven in both 1740 and 1742. The cutback that appeared in 1743 would not in itself be especially significant were it not that in view of the greatly reduced outlays of the years that followed, it marked the beginning of a reversal of the company's investment pattern.

While a glance at the graph of capital outlays in appendix D shows that until 1740 almost all of the company's money was being channeled into the Canada trade, the company was not without a Caribbean presence in the entire period. By 1739, it had singled out Martinique as the West Indian colony of greatest interest, sending two ships in that year to the island and having a third stop on its maiden voyage from Quebec to Le Havre. Another was sent on a rare expedition to Guadeloupe, which might be described as a colony of Martinique, whereas only one ship was sent to St. Domingue. Indeed, in 1742 outlays for the Caribbean trade, most of it at Martinique, were greater than those for the trade to Canada. Dugard and Company was in that year a business enterprise at its zenith, with extensive investments in ships and merchandise at many points around the rim of the Atlantic. Its principal weakness was this wide dispersion and the non-liquid character of its capital.

CHAPTER FOUR

Questions of Finance, 1729–1742

The increase in the number of ships and voyages, the mounting investment, and the steady run of good profits up to 1742 combine to lend an appearance of enviable good management and good fortune to Dugard and Company. The validity of such an impression depends entirely upon how this expansion was financed. Was it justified by the partners' contributions to the capital fund and the rate of return on this investment?

By cash payments, the endorsement and issuing of bills of exchange and promissory notes, and the furnishing of merchandise for ships and cargoes, the members all contributed to the company's capital. Dugard recorded all of these transactions in his partners' current accounts with himself; all manner of affairs, some of them related to the company and some not, are mingled in the pages of debit and credit. The capital fund was set at no specific amount. Dugard prevailed upon his partners for what he needed, and they did their best to provide their share.[1]

By the end of 1738, France, D'Haristoy, Laurens, and the Vincents had in this way contributed some 188,320 livres, an average of more than 47,000 livres per share.[2] From time to time, Dugard obliged his friends with money or credit, but these were always regarded as drawings against their capital. The profits were left to compound themselves into new profits.

As the company grew and its operations became more complex, this informal arrangement became increasingly unsatisfactory. On 1 January 1739, Dugard began separate books for the company "in order to be able to calculate shares from that day with exactness."[3] He balanced his associates' accounts to arrive at new balances with which to open the new books, and it is to extracts of these accounts and to a second set prepared at the close of business in 1759 that we owe our knowledge of the financing of the company.

The accounts reveal the amount invested in new ships and the outlays on cargoes for each year, the amount of paid-in capital contributed annually by Dugard's partners and the profit yielded by each cargo after the deduction of expenses not included in the outlay figure. With the help of these accounts, the process of capital formation can be traced, although only in an approximate way. This has been attempted in appendix D, where the many attendant problems are discussed. The sketch of the company's financial history given in the appendix is to be regarded as an approximation of historical reality, as the incompleteness of the documentary information must be compensated for with a number of assumptions based upon the business and accounting conventions of the time.

Table 33 in appendix D shows that the profits of one year were seldom sufficient to cover the investment and outlay of the following year. From 1738 to 1745 the finance required annually ran to six figures, with more than half a million livres required in 1740 and 1742. While the finance in excess of paid-in capital and profits needed by the company almost every year was impressively large, it was invariably paid back from the proceeds of the sale of return cargo. Large amounts of money or extensive credit were needed for short periods of time. The first year in which the gross profit on the sale of return cargo amounted to less than the initial outlay was 1748. This holds true even if a figure for depreciation of shipping is included, which is not the case, of course, in Dugard's accounts. The implication of this is that the profits of one year provided ample resources for outlay on the same scale the following year. Thus there are only two possible explanations for the company's large-scale borrowing. The first is that extra finance may have been needed because return cargoes were not converted into cash and credit quickly enough to cover the costs of the next year's voyages. This inconvenience probably had some importance, although return cargoes could be disposed of quite rapidly. For example, the provisional account of the return of the fourteenth cargo was signed within two months of the return of the ships to French ports.[4] The second and more fundamental reason for recourse to borrowing is that without it the company could not have sustained its program of expansion. The extensive use of credit was therefore a free choice motivated by ambition and not one imposed by any necessity. Some of the desired finance was undoubtedly covered by the short-term credit extended by suppliers, varying from six weeks to six months and more. By Dugard's own account, there was outside borrowing before the end of 1739, although he gives the impression that it was small.[5] If this was the case, finance must have been covered by suppliers' credit and Dugard's own advances, which he suggests were considerable in this early period and given free of interest.

Although the avoidance of borrowing from outsiders lessened the danger of a rigid and non-liquid position, that danger was still there. Capital was tied up year after year. Guillaume France was particularly uneasy about this policy of continued expansion and the ploughing back of profits. In 1738 he wrote to Dugard, "I also hope that you will restrain yourself with regard to our enterprise so that none of messieurs your partners will find himself in an enterprise beyond his capacities."[6] The company had grown beyond anything he had foreseen. It was unlike the usual, reassuringly finite *société générale* that lasted only a few years and terminated with a generous distribution of profits. "I would never have thought that our enterprise would have lasted for so many years without returning our investment," he complained. "I quit almost all business for our common enterprise."[7]

With the rationalization of the company's bookkeeping beginning 1 January 1739, the capital was set at 80,000 livres per interest, making a total of 400,000 livres.[8] This seems a reasonably accurate figure, in the same range as the figure of 442,162 livres calculated to have been the company's total wealth in table 33. Of all the members, Guillaume France alone made drawings against his capital after this date, reducing it below the minimum level of 80,000. France had his own problems. He was concerned with the social advancement of his family. The maintenance of a costly home in Paris and the provision of rich dowries for his daughters were matters dear to his heart. As he wrote, "My household is large and the cost of it heavy."[9]

Dugard makes much of the interest-free advances he made to the company, advances left in the fund and never repaid. In 1739, greater than usual demands were made upon him. Thereafter, expansion could not continue without accepting massive mobilization of credit as a basic feature of company finance. In Dugard's words, "The company's trade augmenting, the capital was increasingly inadequate."[10] Like one of their own frail craft leaving Havre de Grace for the gales of the mid-Atlantic, the company left the safe haven of private, almost familial, financing for the hazardous paper sea of the bourse. Apparently, "all the partners were agreed on it, and they all did their part in procuring money for the fund to the extent that they were able to find lenders."[11]

A sudden, steep climb in indebtedness in 1740–42 reflects the company's massive expansion into the West Indies trade on top of a more modest expansion of outlay in the established Canada trade. This expansion is sufficiently considerable to distinguish the early forties from the decade of almost exclusively Canadian trade, 1730–39.

Only occasionally can the mobilization of credit be glimpsed behind the operations of Dugard and Company. Each of the members borrowed for the company "were it by his signature or his endorsement." [12] In this, the negotiable promissory note, or *billet à ordre*, may well have played a role. There is no direct evidence of this although Dugard extended credit to Guillaume France on a number of occasions by providing him with negotiable notes against his capital. [13] There is evidence that Dugard and Company obtained considerable credit by means of the bill of exchange. As is shown in the work of Raymond de Roover, credit in medieval and early modern Europe was intimately linked with the international traffic in bills of exchange. The usance, or span of time to a bill's maturity, constituted the term of credit. The loss on exchange rates, which existed between two money markets using the same currency as well as between two currencies, was the equivalent of interest paid. [14]

Lenders preferred the bill to the note. Although promissory notes were legal and not generally held to be usurious, the scrupulous conscience might regard them so. More important perhaps, there existed a fund of money, or *provision*, in the hands of the drawee of a legal bill; and his acceptance written on the face of the bill was its guarantee. The acceptor was also one more person to go against in case of default. The legal proceedings were simpler than in the case of notes. The machinery of imprisonment for debt could be brought into play regarding bill defaulters of whatever social quality, whereas with notes it applied only to merchants and after a delay of four months. [15] Credit obtained from negotiating bills and notes was always short-term, always a matter of months. Given the limitations on promissory notes to order, the easiest access to credit, especially for a younger man, was via the bill of exchange. Credit on a large scale was most easily obtained by those able to draw on a farflung network of correspondents with whom they had credit. This throws into bold relief the importance of the youthful Dugard's season of trade at Amsterdam, his mercantile family background, and his connection with the Huguenot diaspora in the trading towns of Europe. It also explains why Dugard sent sugar, coffee, and indigo to London, Amsterdam, and Hamburg—if the company minute-book may be quoted—"to procure credits abroad" and how this was connected with a "circulation of credit." [16]

Command of a fleet, large deliveries of tropical produce, punctuality in meeting all financial obligations, honest dealing with correspondents, a confident, daily presence at the bourse: these built the reputation that made it possible for Dugard to negotiate his drafts. Similarly, the correspondents upon whom he relied had established their own reputations. But trust was sometimes misplaced, and our only evidence of the kind of "circulations" put in motion comes from the documentary detritus through which we can glimpse the spectacular, simultaneous bankruptcies of two of Dugard's agents, Antoine Clerembault and Son, remitters of London, and Luetkens Frères et Drewzen, commission agents of Bordeaux.

On 28 March 1742, the first of some 24,000 livres in Luetkens's drafts on Robert Dugard payable to Gabriel Da Silva, a Bordeaux banker, came due for payment at the Paris bank of Ridel Frères.[17] Ridel had in the meantime drawn a bill of exchange for Dugard's account on Clerembault and Son. The same day that Dugard remitted 1,200 livres to Ridel to pay the first draft due to Da Silva, Ridel's draft on Clerembault returned from London protested. Clerembault and Son were bankrupt. As a result, Ridel impounded what money Dugard had already deposited with him, leaving Dugard's acceptances to be protested, an action in Dugard's words, "which is extremely disgraceful to me & so much the more as Monsieur Clerembault's bankruptcy renders me liable for an immediate reimbursement of 80,000 livres."[18] In December 1741 and January 1742, Clerembault had drawn 14 bills of exchange on Luetkens, who were acting as Dugard's agents.[19] The bills were accepted by Luetkens, but shortly before their maturity Luetkens Frères et Drewzen followed Clerembault and Son into bankruptcy. There were no secure funds (*provision*) earmarked to honour any of these acceptances. These negotiations were for that reason not legitimate.

The situation seems obvious: bills were negotiated in Paris to raise capital; the bills were honoured in London by negotiating more bills payable in Bordeaux, where the circuit was completed by another issue to be paid in Paris. There a further issue on London was negotiated. Next time a circulation via Hamburg or Amsterdam might be tried. Perhaps it was being done simultaneously. The result was a few precious months of credit. If all of these drafts were at double usance (60 days) or more as were Clerembault's, the three sets overlap considerably, which would seem to shorten unnecessarily the term of credit obtained. This could result from the difficulty of communication or the exigencies of the bill market. But as the bankruptcies, and the documentation they have produced, have frozen a moment in history and cut it off from past and future, the impression could be deceptive. Ridel's drafts seem not to have been intended to cover the drafts to Da Silva's order, but perhaps to cover another upcoming issue. It may be that Luetkens was to negotiate still more bills to pay his acceptances from Clerembault and that the Da Silva drafts were part of an immediately previous circulation. These may be fragments of two consecutive, overlapping circulations. In any case, there is no doubt that circulation was in progress. Unfortunately for Dugard, his agents had become overextended. The most striking aspect of this sequence of events is that short-term credit should have required operations of such dubious legality, high risk, and great complexity.

The fragmentary remains of Dugard's and Luetkens's accounts with one another reveal a great variety of exchange operations that cannot be reconstructed. A list of the Luetkens's drafts on Dugard and his remittances to them from 10 January 1741 to 6 March 1742, totals 524,121 livres and includes a significant number of payees with Dutch and German names.[20] It is an indication of the scale and variety of these transactions. Although Luetkens Frères et Drewzen were regular merchants and Dugard's outfitters at Bordeaux and not specialists in banking, it may be observed of these accounts what De Roover remarked of those of medieval merchants, that they "contain many more items relating to bills than to dealings in commodities."[21]

The demand for drafts, of course, varied with the business seasons. As a result the prices fluctuated, and sometimes bills could not be negotiated at all. Finally, drafts were only as good as the credit of their authors; and if a merchant was suspected of issuing drafts without a sound base, his *tripotage* was decried and his credit vanished. It is an example of the sensitivity of the bill market that before his bankruptcy Luetkens was forced to sell a consignment of indigo that belonged to Dugard at a low price in order to raise enough money to outfit the *Alçion*, his drafts on Dugard "by the great quantity no longer being regarded favourably."[22] Similarly, in Paris the bankruptcy of Clerembault and Son gave rise to very grave rumours regarding Dugard's credit.[23]

As outlined above, the bankruptcy of his agents caused the collapse of Dugard's credit and the immediate necessity to pay some 80,000 livres. He could interest no one in accepting his drafts, partly because of the business climate at the moment. In a letter to Da Silva, Dugard referred to a "discredit which is general & which absolutely prevents all negotiations."[24] The letter reveals that the company, although endowed with impressive assets, had little liquidity in such a situation:

I was forced to cover at my own expense being thank God well able to stand the shock, but not able to satisfy all and several in the same instant with cash because the capital of our company consisting in 8 ships and cargoes is dispersed on all sides.

To meet its engagements the company had recourse to a more expensive and increasingly outmoded method of raising money, the *prêt à la grosse aventure*, or bottomry loan. By this means they could avoid asking for time, "une extremité disgracieuse."[25] Bottomry contained an element of risk for the lender, since if the ship and cargo should perish, the contract was nullified; and because risk was involved, the interest rate was high. It was to propose such a loan that Dugard wrote to Da Silva. A contract would engage the partners jointly and severally, and Da Silva was invited to investigate "the capacities of our company, they are today quite well known."[26] Da Silva was not interested, but promised to bring the proposal to the attention of his friends. One way or another, an adequate number of investors was found, and Da Silva was paid by 16 April.[27] On 3 and 4 April some 14 different parties took out contracts on the *Fleury, Alçion*, and *Imprévû* and their cargoes at 15 per cent maritime profit, the total of loans being 147,701 livres.[28] In May an additional 12,000 was obtained at 14 per cent, making a total of 159,701 livres.[29]

The latter contract may serve as an example. The taker, Valmaletie, was said to run all risks of the sea in place of the proprietors. Risks on the vessel finished 24 hours after it anchored at Le Havre and those on the cargo after it was entirely ashore. The owners were obliged to pay 13,680 livres in gold or silver specie two months after the return. For payment, they were liable in their persons and their goods, but in particular the *Fleury* and its return cargo were mortgaged to the lender.

The bottomry contracts yielded a significant sum, double the 80,000 livres which Dugard claimed he had to pay immediately. They were partly a supplementary expedient needed to boost the year's investment to its very high level, but primarily a stopgap, fulfilling the normal role of negotiable paper. The company had thus extricated itself from a difficult situation, but at a high price. The interest paid on a 15 per cent contract taken out 3 April on the *Imprévû*, the only one of the ships for which a return date is extant,[30] was 20 per cent *per annum*. But as proof that the lender really did run a risk, it should be noted that the *Alçion* sank on its return voyage.[31]

The unsettling experiences of the early spring set the stage for the company's important meeting of 27 June 1742. According to Dugard's

later recollection, the crisis made him realize how potentially dangerous to him were these negotiations that he conducted, for all practical
purposes, alone:

> This prodigious burden, sustained almost entirely by Monsieur
> DuGard, made him pay attention to the fact that men are not only
> mortal, but that they can change their minds, especially when
> business is not profitable; he thus proposed to his partners that
> considering the events that could happen & not because of any
> want of confidence in their rectitude, it was necessary that he not
> be left open to objections that might some day be made to him.[32]

Hence the meeting was called, and the members set their signatures to
a full approval of all Dugard had undertaken on their behalf, including
the negotiation of paper. To safeguard against any appearance that he
was acting for his own account, Dugard had written into the minute-
book that he took no commission on purchases of sugar, coffee, and
indigo or their sale, "as well as on the circulation of credit."[33] He
exacted only his expenses. These actions were "known to the company," but Dugard now demanded formal approval in order to protect
himself.

Nor had the associates approved all the construction of ships undertaken at Quebec or the sending of all the cargoes. Dugard also asked
for approval for the borrowing he had hitherto managed "on the market" and declared that he would no longer borrow without the participation of his associates. Finally, he asked approval for "everything
else he will do . . . for the greater advantage of the company, it not
being possible for him to protect himself with a special authorization
. . . in all the different cases."[34] Dugard's intention seems to have been
to combine the joint action and responsibility of all the partners on the
financial plane with his complete freedom to act on the administrative.
This was a freedom that the partners refused to give written sanction,
although most of the time they appear to have followed Dugard's lead.

The credit crisis appears to have shocked the company out of its
complacency with regard to expansion. The other partners fully
agreed with Pierre D'Haristoy's proposal, echoing the complaints of
Guillaume France in 1738, "That it would be appropriate to determine and fix the capital of our company in order to contain our
enterprise in just limits and to be able by this means to enjoy, each and
every one of us, an annual revenue proportionate to the capital that
each of us has in the said company."[35] It would be convenient,
D'Haristoy continued, if Dugard would balance the books to permit

them to establish the capital of the society after which they would be in a state to regulate the amount that could be spent on cargoes each year by means of which they would be able to enjoy an annual revenue, something they had never done up to this point, "because our common intention has been to carry our commerce to a point where it can be carried on with advantage, that which leads us to leave the profits with the capital in order to be able to arrive the earlier at the desired point." [36] Thus Dugard and Company's long period of expansion was at an end. The lower investment of 1743 bears witness to this decision.

The D'Haristoy proposal did not suggest that the company should be milked of all its profits. He agreed that there must always be money to meet unexpected contingencies, so they must settle for "an annual revenue less than the profits to be hoped for." [37]

The partners now keenly anticipated a division of profits. Unfortunately, there is no direct evidence to suggest whether or not any such division was made at this time. It is not surprising that they should have expected an imminent division of profits. As D'Haristoy's proposal reveals, the partners did not have a clear idea of the financial state of their partnership. They would balance the books and see. They were not accustomed to using accounting to provide themselves with a week by week, month by month, or even year by year diagnosis of the health of their business. Elaborate double-entry accounting procedures, as distinct from more primitive addition of outlays and cargo sales, were used mainly to keep track of operations so that at some terminal date the size of the partners' respective interests could be calculated. In this attitude to bookkeeping they were merchants of their own era. [38]

By 1742, Dugard, Laurens, D'Haristoy, France, and the Vincents had shown a willingness to extend their enterprise, to set aside immediate profits in the hope of long-term gains, and to mobilize credit in a bold and speculative way. Yet there was a sharp dichotomy between their capitalistic outlook in this regard and the inadequate institutions and methods (evidence of crosscurrents in their own mentality) employed to give form to their vision. The personal partnership was not suited to a company of long duration. The system of accounting was ill-contrived as an aid to administration. Financial institutions had to be strained to the limit and ingeniously exploited to yield sufficient capital. The archaic structures of the money market communicated their inflexibility to French trade and commerce, resulting in periodic crises of bankruptcy. Dugard and Company was not free of this brittleness; it escaped calamity in 1742 by a narrow margin and at considerable cost.

Under the circumstances the curbing of expansion was a necessary precaution. Since 1739 the company had carried on an extensive trade at Martinique while maintaining its trade at St. Domingue and in Canada. The West Indies trade was highly competitive, and market conditions were unpredictable. The company stood to gain or lose a great deal in sugar; and were losses to occur, the company's indebtedness would become a considerable burden. There had thus been a great element of risk in the company's determined entry into the sugar trade. It was a course of action characteristic of Robert Dugard's management, expressing that willingness to gamble that is applauded in success, but that in failure is unfailingly condemned.

CHAPTER FIVE

Cargoes Outward

I

When a tally is made of all the known departures of ships of the
Dugard and Company fleet, a rough pattern emerges.[1] The ships leaving earliest in the year went to the Caribbean in February and March,
but although these were the two busiest months, considerable activity
continued through July. From August through the following January
there were few departures. Ships began leaving for Canada a little later
than for the West Indies, departures being concentrated in April, May,
and June. It became impracticable to set out after July. Thus from
February through July, ports—and outfitters—were busy seeing off the
hundreds of merchant ships that crossed the Atlantic. The outfitting
itself had begun at least three months, and often six or ten months,
before the date of sailing. The historian can observe the preparations
of these busy months through the business records of 25 major voyages and a few other secondary ventures gathered together in four
cartons of the Dugard Papers.[2] These papers represent about one-third
of the total number of voyages undertaken by the company.

Ordering merchandise and outfitting ships may often have been
concurrent undertakings, but the ordering would seem to be the logical point of departure. The letters from Dugard's pen were carried to
the four corners of France, to Holland, Germany, and Ireland, but no
copies remain. The first papers in a cargo folder are the invoices that
accompanied the ordered merchandise. From these it is clear that cargoes were made up on credit, some orders being payable in as long a
term as six months.[3] The invoices contain the exact nature of the mer-

chandise, its value, and often expenses entailed in packaging and transport.

While Dugard was busy procuring cargo, the *armateur-commissionaire* at Le Havre or Bordeaux was undertaking the outfitting of the ship that he outlined in a *compte de l'armement et mise hors*. This included routine repairs, provisioning, the hiring of a crew who were paid a two month advance, and the obtaining of necessary clearance from the Admiralty and the Customs. For all this the agent was rewarded with a commission of two per cent. To give examples of what could come under the headings of outfitting, a ship might be careened (calked and scraped) and sometimes sheathed. New sails, ropes, tar, and other naval stores might be supplied; all manner of repairs were carried out, including the replacement of wooden curbs, pulleys, masts, yards, and even of sculptured pilasters. Powder was carried aboard, and the cannon were proved. Food and water were loaded, the latter requiring the services of a cooper. In certain cases where intermediaries were used to obtain commodities and services, brokerage fees had to be paid. One *compte de l'armement* contains an interesting reference to "brokers for shipping, piloting and long-boats,"[4] showing that brokers intervened even in the labour market.

The commission agent also incurred expenses in receiving cargo that arrived by river and coastal vessels. These were outlined in an *état des debours à la réception et disposition des marchandises*, those of Veuve Christinat of Le Havre being particularly lucid documents in which the arrival of cargo from the 32 points of the compass can be traced. These accounts also reveal the considerable costs that accrued to merchandise as it travelled from manufacturer to shipside. The cargo of the *Centaure* going to Quebec in 1743, part of the fourteenth cargo, is a good example.[5] First Christinat paid the freight cost on each item as it arrived, then cartage and warehouse fees, and then cartage and bateau charges when the merchandise was taken to the ship. She also paid the bateau captain his *chapeau*, or special consideration. Every shipment also occasioned a legal cost, the *décharge d'acquit*, always five sols. Movement of salt required the presence of an officer of the Gabelle and a measurer to remeasure the salt from Saintonge in the measures of Normandy. Numerous fees were paid for necessary papers, the largest being the *droit de présence* of the officer of the Gabelle, 211 livres, 10 sols. Bordeaux wines also required remeasuring. No less than three taxes were paid on Spanish iron as it passed through the port.

All of the goods that constituted a cargo were consigned to the captain, or in the case of voyages to Quebec, to the company's factors. They were listed in a *facture de cargaison*, or cargo invoice. It was

headed by a brief instruction to the consignee; for example, that of the
Ville de Québec to Martinique in 1735 is entitled, "to make returns as
well as possible." [6] If the captain were the consignee, before he left port
he and the agent, or sometimes Dugard himself, signed the invoice,
making it a legal document acknowledging the transfer of responsibility for the cargo. Invoices of goods consigned to Havy and Lefebvre at
Quebec had to be signed by them on arrival. [7] The cargo invoices carried away by the captains did not correspond exactly to the originals.
Among the papers for a *pacotille*, or small parcel of goods distinct
from the owner's cargo, carried to Léoganne by the *Ville de Québec* in
1736, there is an invoice on which for the benefit of auditors was
written the inscription, "N[ot]a. This invoice does not contain the true
purchase prices. It is the invoice for sales purposes at St. Domingue." [8]
The original invoice totaled 15,833 livres and the second one 16,563
livres. A similar second invoice exists for the *Alçion*'s voyage to
Léoganne in 1742. [9] Inflated invoices contained either approximate
F.O.B. prices or prices increased by a mark-up that had become customary.

The invoice had a counterpart in the *connaissement de cargaison*, or
bill of lading by which a ship captain acknowledged the receipt of
cargo in his capacity as ship's master and not as a sales agent to whom
the goods were consigned. There were always separate bills of lading
for cargo received from different parties or at different times. For
example, there are three extant bills of lading for the *Trois Maries*,
loading at Bordeaux for a voyage to Quebec, dated 22 and 23 May
1742. The first is for bales of textiles received from Rauly Père et Fils
of Montauban. The others, both dated 23 May, are for two separate
lots of wine and naval stores received from Dugard's Bordeaux agent,
Henri Goudal. [10] The bill of lading, like the invoice, lists the cargo, but
in terms of its volume and without reference to values. The number of
boxes, bales, barrels, and the like is listed with a very general description of contents. Each is identified by a bale mark and number. The
majority of merchandise for the Société du Canada was normally
marked SDC. But bales might also bear marks identifying the ship (LC
for *Le Centaure*), and it was common to identify goods destined for
particular colonial customers on the basis of orders sent (PG for Pierre
Guy of Montreal). *Pacotilles* were identified by the marks of their
owners (RDL for Dugard and Laurens; MRD for Manufacture Royale
de Darnétal). Cargo might also be marked RD if the bale had been
made up by a manufacturer and sent directly to the port of outfitting,
because it would not be repackaged and marked SDC. [11] It is thus impossible for the historian to identify bales with complete accuracy

from their shipping marks alone. The bill of lading also provides the name of the ship, its captain, the outfitter, the port of lading, the destination, the freight rate (company cargo was carried free), a date, and often the tonnage of the ship. It is a very valuable historical document.

Before the beginning of a voyage, a captain was given written instructions of which both he and Dugard kept copies bearing both their signatures. Seven of these are extant in the Dugard Papers. These were written instruments that assigned legal responsibility. They are also very useful to the historian, providing detailed information on the aims of an expedition and the methods that were to be employed to achieve those aims. Instructions also frequently stated the perquisites of the captain above and beyond the usual wages of 100 livres per month. Instructions to Captain Hurel for the voyage of the *St. Mathieu* in 1743 and those of Captain Fremont for the voyage of the *Union* in 1744, both to Martinique, permit the captains to carry their own *pacotilles* on the outward voyage free of charge. Both mention the possibility of a special gratification being granted by the owners at the end of a very successful voyage. Both also establish the captain's *chapeau* (a customary perquisite) at five per cent on all freight except the company's merchandise. Hurel was also granted two *tonneaux de port permis* "in return" (i.e. on the return voyage) and Fremont three *tonneaux*, these estimated at 300 and 400 livres value respectively. This meant that the captain was given an amount of the total freight earned equal to the freight paid for whatever number of *tonneaux* was specified. It was deducted before the calculation of the *chapeau*.[12]

If the captain's perquisites were not mentioned in the instructions or if there were none, as was the case when the *Centaure* was chartered to the Compagnie des Indes in 1748, then they were specified in a convention between the captain and Dugard. In this instance, for example, Captain Vandelle received 100 livres per month, a *chapeau* of five per cent (one sol per livre), and three *tonneaux de port permis* in return.[13]

Except where a resident factor might intervene, as at Quebec, a captain had full charge of freight payments. He collected the payments and paid himself his perquisites. Because freight was paid on delivery, the captain had ample time while at sea to calculate the amount of freight owing. The *état* of freight was compiled from the bills of lading. Two examples in the Dugard Papers bear marginalia in which the volume of cargo loaded is transformed from the *barils, barriques, futailles, balles,* and *ballots* into standard measures of volume. One converts into *tonneaux*, the most common measure, and the other into feet, inches, and *lignes*, presumably cubic measure.[14] The *état* of the *Centaure*'s voyage to Martinique in 1752 is an excellent example.[15] It is signed and dated by Captain Gosselin at St. Pierre de la Martinique and is in *argent des îles*. First the freight owed by 24 shippers (22,380 livres), the fares of five passengers (2,500 livres) and the freight cost which the company would have paid for its cargo were it being charged, (5,280 livres) are added, giving a total of 30,160 livres. From this the *port permis* is deducted, 800 livres for ten *tonneaux* at 80 livres each, leaving 29,360 livres. From this the *chapeau* of five per cent is deducted, leaving 27,892 livres. Perquisites having been calculated, the freight for the company's cargo is dropped. The resulting figure of 22,612 livres is the amount due to the owners from the captain for freight received. As noted in earlier examples, the value of the company's cargo was not always included in the calculation of the *chapeau*.

Every ship that sailed had its *rôle d'équipage*. These were registered with the authorities of the Bureau des Classes, which kept track of the records of sailors. There are some company crew rolls in the Admiralty archives at Bordeaux. Captains also kept copies of these lists, which they used as records of wages. The common desertions and deaths of sailors, and the hiring of replacements were all recorded. These are usually found in the papers of return voyages, since the accounts were closed at the voyage's end. Often they are called *décomptes de l'équip-age*.[16]

If a company ship was leased as a freighter or if the company itself was required to hire an entire ship, as sometimes happened, a charter-party was negotiated. This was often done by the *armateur-com-missionnaire*, acting upon instructions. Thus in 1744, Veuve Christinat negotiated a charter-party for the *Fleury* with the Compagnie des Indes, and the following year she negotiated Dugard and Company's hire of the *Thétis*, both *chartes-parties* or *traités d'affrettement* being extant among the voyage papers.[17] The charters stated the nature of the voyage, the freight rate, and the terms of payment. Hire for the *Fleury* was to be paid at the end of the voyage with an advance paid at the destination, Senegal. The *Thétis* was paid for by Dugard's draft, reaching maturity five months after issue. The *Centaure*, hired by the Compagnie des Indes in 1748, was to be paid for entirely after the completion of the voyage.[18] The latest possible date of sailing was always agreed upon, and sometimes a penalty was stated for a late start. The exact number of days that the ship could stay in any one port, *jours de planche* or lay days, for the benefit of either lessor of lessee was always stated, as was the price for extra days, *surplanche*.

The fully-laden ship could not leave port without its *congé et passeport*, a document permitting it to sail for a designated port "after visitation of the said ship will have been well and duly made & it will have made its submission to the registry of the Admiralty to go to no foreign island or coast, to undertake no trade there of the produce of the said Islands." [19] This involved making a *soûmission avant départ.* Many company *soûmissions* are to be found in the Admiralty archives at Bordeaux. They invariably state the number of *engagés* and guns carried to the colony. The name of the *armateur-commissionnaire* is inscribed as "pour caution," or standing bond.

Cleared of customs, with crew roll registered and submission made, the ship was free to leave with the first favourable wind. Meanwhile at Rouen, Robert Dugard would be busy with a final operation, the calculation of all his commissions. Three of his commission lists, those for the thirteenth, fourteenth, and fifteenth cargoes to Canada, are extant. [20] The items of cargo, the costs on merchandise and the outfittings of ships are neatly arranged under the headings of two per cent, one per cent, and one-half per cent. Even before the ships left their home ports, for Dugard, the commission agents, and a motley array of manufacturers, paid artisans, brokers, carters, sailors, and day labourers, many profits, the more modest tendered in specie, the handsomer still only credit entries in accounts, had already been generated by these outward voyages.

II

The story of men at sea, particularly in the age of sail, has been the subject of such romantic indulgence that it is easily forgotten that most ships were cumbersome, floating warehouses, their captains essentially men of business concerned with the safe delivery and sale of their cargoes. When this is remembered, the bread-and-butter expeditions too often become *The Romance of Commerce.* Some of the romance is genuine enough. Official reports of the testimony of Dugard and Company captains and sailors reveal exciting chases through tropical waters, ending in captures and sojourns in faraway, foreign colonies. [21] Others describe struggles against the sea: the *Astrée* shorn of all its masts by an Atlantic gale limping into the safety of Roscoff harbour; the *Union,* driven onto the rocks at Ile de Ré and broken in three, in spite of the crew having chopped down the masts to slow her speed; the *Trois Maries,* on a moonless, November night carried broadside into the rear of the enormous *Brillant,* the sailors leaping into the sea in a vain effort to save themselves. In the bobbing longboat that made its way from the foundered *Alçion* on 29 April 1743, to the island of

St. Marc near St. Domingue, were harboured so many dark suspicions and thoughts of mutiny against Captain Gautier, "always very severe towards his crews," that the scene and its long dénouement in the Admiralty courts are worthy of Nordhoff and Hall. Separated from the Duc D'Anville's armada of 1746 by a hurricane, Vandelle's crippled *Fleury* was blown helplessly from Nova Scotian waters to near Guadeloupe, carrying the remnant of its hungry, disease-ridden crew to eventual capture: Ulysses adrift. But most of the time it was business as usual.

On the outward voyage, the captain was almost exclusively a seaman; but unless he were sailing to Quebec, where factors would handle the sale of his cargo and supply the return shipment, he knew that when he made his landfall, his work would barely have begun. He would spend months on land selling the outward cargo and buying colonial produce. He and his bookkeeper would labour at the accounts, and these would provide extra work for spare hours during the return voyage as well.

The cargoes were the point of it all. There is no trade without merchandise. A history of trade that failed to consider cargo would err on the side of abstraction. A knowledge of cargo satisfies the same need for concrete re-creation of the past that leads the historian to enquire about the houses, clothes, and foods of past ages. Cargoes also reveal much about the economy and society of the colonies and about metropolitan industry. Those sent to the West Indies were not the same as those sent to Canada. The two must therefore be dealt with separately. The cargoes of the *Alçion* to Léoganne in 1742–43, the *Union* to St. Pierre, Martinique, in 1744, and two cargoes sold by Captain Renault during a long stay at Cul de Sac Marin, Martinique—those of the *Imprévû* and the *St. Mathieu* in 1743—are here taken as examples. Original cargo lists, taken from invoices in some cases and from sales records in others, have been condensed into a series of tables (1 to 4) designed to show the composition of Caribbean cargoes.[22] From these it is apparent that dry goods and provisions were the most important categories of cargo. The third category of goods, hardware, using the word in an extensive sense, fell far behind, ranging from 0 to 4.9 per cent of these cargoes by value.

The most significant items in the dry goods category were textiles, and the most important of these were common textiles. A large proportion of common textiles were manufactured in Brittany and Normandy. Many were of hemp, including not only sailcloth, but finer qualities for sheets, shirts, dressing gowns, and nightcaps. A blue and white check variety was used for mattress covering and to make shirts

TABLE 1.

The Alçion *to* Léoganne, St. Domingue, 1742–43; Breakdown *of Cargo. Total:* 122,734 Livres "Argent des Iles"

Common textiles	29670						
Finer textiles	24119		Common textiles	24.2%			
Table linen	2253		Finer and linen	21.5%		Dry goods	50.3%
Mercery	2839		Clothing	4.7%			
Hats	2217						
Shoes	684						
Tools, kettles, nails	4387		Metal goods	4.0%			
Guns and Shot	473		Glassware	0.2%		Hardware	4.2%
Glassware	247						
Wines	22808		Wine	18.6%			
Flour	12791		Foodstuffs	22.8%		Provisions	45.5%
Meats and butter	15297		Candles	4.0%			
Candles	4949						

Source: AN, 62AQ44, "Compte de Vente Générale et Achapts Provenant de la Cgn. du Navire [*Alçion*, 1742–43]."

TABLE 2.

The Imprévû *to* Cul De Sac Marin, Martinique, 1743; Breakdown *of Cargo. Total:* 115,076 Livres "Argent des Iles"

Common textiles	11929						
Finer textiles	9436						
Linens	1290						
Blankets	345		Common textiles	10.4%			
Shirts, *habits*	6383		Fines, linens, blankets	9.6%		Dry goods	33.7%
Mercery	6594		Clothes, etc.	13.7%			
Hats	2515						
Parasols	250						
Tools, kettles	2232						
Nails	1120		Metal	2.9%			
Shot and powder	1550		Other	2.0%		Hardware	4.9%
Paper	724						
Wines	13050						
Liquors	849						
Meat and butter	51254		Beverages	12.1%			
Flour	2395		Foodstuffs	46.9%		Provisions	61.4%
Pepper	331		Candles	2.4%			
Candles	2829						

Source: AN, 62AQ43, "Compte de Ventes des Marchandises Composant la Cgn. du Navire l'Imprévû, Capt. J. B. Renault, vendu au Cul de Sac Marin."

TABLE 3.
The St. Mathieu *to* Cul De Sac Marin *and* Fort Royal, Martinique,
1743; Breakdown of Cargo. Total: 32,840 Livres "Tournois"

Common textiles	2345	Common textiles	7.2%	Dry goods	15.4%
Finer textiles	2667	Fine, clothes	8.2%		
Clothing	24				
Wines	3640				
Liquors	435	Beverages	12.4%	Provisions	84.6%
Beef and butter	17689	Foodstuffs	68.5%		
Flour	4815	Candles	3.7%		
Candles	1225				

Source: AN, 62AQ42, "Facture des Marchandises chargées au Havre à Bord du Navire
le St. Mathieu, Rouen, 12 aoust 1743."

TABLE 4.
The Union *to* St. Pierre, Martinique, *1744; Breakdown of Cargo.
Total: 114,101 Livres "Tournois"*

Common textiles	13170	Common textiles	11.5%	Dry goods	21.8%
Finer textiles	7728	Finer and Linen	9.4%		
Table linen	2941	Thread	1.0%		
Thread	1049				
Kettles	453	Kettles	0.4%	Hardware	0.4%
Wine	11526				
Liquors	912	Beverages	10.9%	Provisions	77.8%
Flour	6170	Candles	3.9%		
Meats and butter	64888	Foodstuffs	63.0%		
Misc. foods	864				
Candles	4400				

Source: AN, 62AQ42, "Facture des Marchandises chargées au Havre à bord l'Union,
Rouen, le 25 janvier 1744."

for sailors and West Indian Negroes. The range of quality of flaxen
clothes was even greater. At the bottom were the *blancards* of the
Rouen region, used only as trunk lining and for the underwear of the
common people in France, but for which the real market was Spanish
America, where it was used to clothe slaves working in the silver
mines. Not surprisingly, it was also in demand in the French West
Indies.

Most flaxen cloths came under the heading of finer textiles, a category not far behind the common in importance. Linens from Maine,
Britanny, and Normandy, ranging from coarse écru bedsheeting to the

finest white linen of good shirts, were all exported to the Caribbean. Very fine *batistes* and lawns were sent from Flanders, Holland, and Beauvais. Textiles other than those of flax and hemp fibre were exported to the Caribbean only in small quantities. Among the most popular were *siamoise* of cotton and linen and light cottons. There were always some Lyons and Tours silks and even the occasional length of fine woollen suiting.

The essential accompaniment to these large consignments of textiles was the wide assortment of smallwares or *mercerie* needed for the sewing and ornamenting of clothing. Hundreds of pounds of thread came from Rennes, Lille, and Epinay. The most popular ribbon seems to have been the machine-made Dutch ribbon, although gold and silver French ribbon was also exported. There were laces of all kinds as well as gold, silver, and flowered gauze, gold and silver garters, *bourdalous* (buckled hat ribbons), and handkerchiefs. There were also knitgoods (*bonneterie*), especially bonnets and stockings. The most expensive stockings were from Lyons, those more reasonably priced from Paris. Shoes were an important item, including damask *mules*, a kind of high-heeled slipper for both men and women. Hats, still more important, came in black and white, various styles, and were either all beaver felt (*castor*) or made from beaver and rabbit (*demi-castor*). Items of ready-made clothing were uncommon and very expensive. The horse trappings that Dugard had made up to be sent to Cul de Sac Marin were of extravagant cost and slow sellers. The only other items that are to be classed with dry goods were parasols of waxed cloth and a few blankets.

The word "hardware" is used here to denote metals, glass, faience, and even paper. Although shipped in small quantity, these items were of great importance. Included were iron kettles, tools, nails, lead and shot, gun powder and muskets, the variety favoured in the West Indies called the *fusil boucannier*. Among the tools the most important were hoes, hatchets, spades, and bill-hooks, the latter a kind of machete used for cutting sugar cane. Files, planes, and saws were also exported. In terms of quantity, nails and iron kettles vied for first place among hardware exports. Faience, both from Rouen and Lille, also appears in the lists. In addition to writing and register papers, there were playing cards, playing cards, and more playing cards, testifying to the gaming habits of the planters.

Provisions were much the most important category of exports to the Caribbean, ranging from 45.5 to 84.6 per cent of the four cargoes shown in the tables. An obvious export in this category was wine, which was regarded as a necessary staple. Most of it was Bordeaux and it was shipped in *barriques*, each the quarter of a *tonneau*, the unit of volume measure. Red was a far more significant export than white. There was also always a smaller quantity of fine wines exported in bottle. Margaux and Frontignan, a dessert wine from a sandy coastal strip along the Mediterranean, were the common fine wines shipped. Two spirits were standard exports, *eau de vie* of grape origin but unspecified quality sent in small casks, and anisette measured in *paniers* of bottles. In spite of local substitutes such as manioc root, which fed the slaves, colonists wanted French wheaten flour. The quantities exported in the four cargoes in the tables varied from 60 to 378 *barils*. The flour was of two basic kinds, that of Normandy and that of Nérac. The latter is a small town upriver from Bordeaux today famous only for Armagnac and sandals. In the eighteenth century, its flour was highly esteemed. For example, in 1744 Nérac flour sold in France at 24 livres the *baril* compared with 18 livres 10 sols for Norman flour.

The most important foodstuff for the Martinique market was, by a wide margin, salted beef. Almost all of it came from Ireland.[23] In 1743, the *Imprévû* and the *St. Mathieu* carried 1,062 *barils* to Cul de Sac Marin. In 1744 the *Union* carried 1,747 *barils* to St. Pierre. Beef was never a very important item in the trade to St. Domingue, an enormous island, half of it sparsely populated by Spanish ranchers. Thus in contrast to the large beef exports to Martinique the *Alçion* carried only 38 *barils* to Léoganne in 1742. However, she also carried barrelled pork and ham as well as dried cod in quantities as significant as those that went to Martinique. The object, however, was not survival but variety of diet. In Martinique beef not only added a fraction of protein to the subsistence fare of slaves, but nourished all the lower orders of society. It is possible that freed from dependence upon imported beef for survival, the population of St. Domingue were able to spend more of their foreign exchange on other items. (The *Alçion*'s cargo to Léoganne carried not only a greater proportion of wine to other provisions than a comparable cargo to Martinique, but also a greater absolute quantity.) The only other meats that appear in the Dugard Papers as exports are goose thighs and sides of bacon. Both colonies imported a substantial quantity of Irish butter. Other items of food occasionally included in cargoes were olives, olive oil, capers, and pepper. Candles have been placed with provisions in the tables because most were of tallow and hence a byproduct of meat packing. Like beef and butter, most candles were from Ireland. They were an important item of cargo.

The two kinds of imports the islands needed were thus food and clothing. While France's inability to provide essential constituent items of the former category shows certain weak spots in her agricultural economy, the French textile industry amply met the demands made upon it. This serves as a reminder that textiles were the major European industry in the eighteenth century and that France was probably the leading industrial nation. The small quantities of other manufactures exported is explained by the lesser dependence upon industry of eighteenth-century populations compared with those of the nineteenth and twentieth centuries. The prime place of basic necessities (salt, meat, flour, common textiles, iron utensils) in the outward cargoes demonstrates the vital importance of these cargoes to the island colonies. This dominating dependence was the greatest weakness of the colonial economies, although it resulted from an attempt to exploit as profitably as possible the islands' one resource, the tropical climate that alone was hospitable to the sugar cane. The French tropical colonies all had staple-export economies. Because the staples were all luxuries of little use to the Creoles themselves and because they excluded from consideration the production of necessities, the island economy was totally dependent upon metropolitan trade and metropolitan naval strength.

It is worth noting that many of the food items on which Creoles spent so much of their foreign exchange were not really necessities: life goes on without wine, wheat flour, goose thighs, and olives. A traditional cuisine is a cultural trait not easily forgotten. This persistence of French diet is a reminder that the Creole was still a Frenchman.

The structure of island society is also evident from the cargoes. In that of the *Imprévû* to Cul de Sac Marin in 1743 six coats and breeches of silk contrast in nature and quantity with the 36 bolts of *St. Georges* and *blancards* for the work shirts of slaves, as do the six *castors point d'Espagne* at 89 livres with the 72 *chapeaux de negre* at eight sols. The *compte de vente* of the *Alçion*'s cargo in 1742 expresses social relationships in other terms: 89 hoes were sold, together with six muskets.

Detailed information on the nature of cargoes assembled for the trade to Canada exists only for the years 1742–44. The fourteenth cargo, 1743, is the most completely documented and has been chosen for detailed examination.[24] Each annual shipment to Canada by Dugard and Company was designated as a single numbered cargo, even though it was usually carried by two, sometimes three, ships. In contrast, each company ship that sailed to the Caribbean was viewed as a distinct venture and was referred to as a numbered voyage, for example, the first, second, or third voyage of the *Centaure* or *St. Louis*.

TABLE 5.
Breakdown of the 14th Cargo, 1743. Total: 168,002 Livres "Tournois"

Toiles, 30–36s 6d/aune	13726				
Toiles, 11s 6d– 29s/aune	11510				
Cotton, cot./linen	10835				
Various, incl. finest	10041	*Toiles*	27.4%		
Blankets	12742	Woollens	22.8%		
Etoffes de Montauban	10207	Luxury/decorative	6.9%	Dry goods	68.72%
All others	15386	Clothing and accessories	10.0%		
Siamoises	5544	Mixed invoices	1.7%		
All others	6083				
Mercerie/ bonneterie	12522				
Gloves, *mitaines*	685				
Hats	557				
Shoes	2733				
Mixed invoices (Textiles and clothes)	2874				
Tools	1754				
Stoves and stove plaques	6366				
Nails	1377				
Dinauderie	2905				
Bulk metals	7309				
All other	824	Metal goods	12.2%		
Marine cable and rope	5059	Non-metal "hardware"	6.3%	Hardware	18.57%
Paper	1425				
Dutch vermillion and *rasade* (beads)	1277				
Window panes	1060				
All other	1842				
Flour	4606				
Oil	1328	Foodstuffs	6.5%		
All other	4986	Beverages	6.0%	Provisions	12.46%
Wine and spirits	10008				
Unidentified items	431			Unidentified	0.25%

Source: AN, 62AQ41, 14ᵉ Cargaison, Aller, factures, nos. 1–160.

Thus a single Canadian "cargo" was always much larger than a single Caribbean "voyage." Hence the contrast between the value of the fourteenth cargo, which is broken down in table 5 and those of the Caribbean cargoes in the corresponding tables 1 to 4.

As was the case with the Caribbean cargoes, various kinds of *toiles* formed the largest single group of textiles in this Canadian cargo. They included an assemblage of hemp, linen, and cotton cloths varying in fineness and price, similar to that found in the West Indian cargoes. Woollens were almost as important as *toiles*, whereas they were virtually absent from the other cargoes. Included in the woollens were blankets in a variety of sizes, all measured by the point system. They ranged from one and one-half to eight points and most were from the Rouen suburb of Darnétal. The Canada trade was important for the Darnétal blanket industry. More than one invoice lists not *couvertures* but *canadasts*, most of them of two and one-half points. There were also numerous fine woollens for winter clothing and light serges for lining. There were heavy *camelots* of wool and goats' hair, including *baracan*, waterproofed by boiling and mangling and hence suitable for raincoats. The inclusion of many woollens in cargoes to Canada meant the purchase of more cloths from the wool-working areas of the Midi than was the case for Caribbean cargoes. There were several varieties from Niort and Montauban. The latter was the entrepôt for various woollen fabrics manufactured in Albigeois, the cheaper, nappy flannel-types known as *cordellateries*. The greater part of Montauban textiles in the cargo by value was *draperie* including *cadis*, light woollens in narrow widths, and *molletons*. The *molletons* in blue, violet, or red were thick, high quality stuffs of considerable importance in the Canada trade, corresponding to the English cloths, duffel and strouds. They were used by Canadians and Indians for *capots*, leggings, and blankets. The more decorative and luxury fabrics sent to Canada were the same as those sent to the West Indies.

The most important groups of textiles in the fourteenth cargo are easily singled out. First in importance were the hemp and linen *toiles* of medium price range, 30 sols to 36 sols 6 deniers per *aune*, totalling 13,726 livres. These were followed by blankets, most of them from Darnétal, valued at 12,742 livres. Third were the plain *toiles* of the canvas and sailcloth variety with a total value of 11,510 livres. The cotton and cotton-linen mixes in stripes and checks were next at 10,835 livres, followed by *draperies* and *cordellateries* of Montauban at 10,207 livres, the *camelots* and *calamandres* of Flanders at 6,306 livres, and Rouen *siamoise* at 5,544 livres.

The fourteenth cargo included articles of *mercerie* and *bonneterie* in greater quantity and variety than did the West Indian cargoes. In this category were thread, buttons, buckles, crosses, ribbons, appliquées, galoon, lace and gauze, ladies' headgear and collars, stockings and bonnets, hat plumes, and egret feathers. Many of these were lumped together in one invoice with bottles of perfume, swords and razors, gilt nails, and church candelabra, a processional cross, and an altar frontal, all under the heading of *articles de Paris*, a mixture of vanities, pious and profane. The cargo also included dozens of shoes, hats, and gloves. The "hardware" items in the Canadian cargo were also more varied and numerous than in the Caribbean cargoes, 18 per cent by value. Tools of all descriptions were included. Of special interest is a large shipment from the cutlers and gunsmiths of St. Etienne. This included knives of all kinds, among them a gross of medium "couteaux bucheron" with "ordinary" blades added to Dugard's order to fill the tonneau and of which the sender informed him, "All the other houses order the same from me for Canada."[25] Also included were trade awls, horse-pistols, iron compasses, "Siamese knives," steel forks, and flat-irons for pressing clothes. Perhaps the most bizarre item in this category was the Dutch stove. The sides of these stoves were cast with biblical scenes, the Mount of Olives and the Supper at Emmaus being favourites.

Reading through the invoices of the fourteenth cargo is like wandering through an old-time general store; it seems that everything imaginable is there: weights, locks, bridal mounts, roasting spits, shoe scrapers, combs, mirrors, window panes, plates, mugs, teapots, spoons, salad bowls, garden vases, foot warmers, paper, writing plumes, penknives, the ubiquitous cheap clay pipes, and playing cards, twenty-two gross of the latter.

Canadians of means were like Creoles in preferring not to survive without French foodstuffs. All manner of pleasurable comestibles were shipped from Rouen: pepper, cinnamon, nutmeg, cloves, bitter almonds, ginger, and jams. There was also *fromage de Prière* from Lyons, salt and vinegar from La Flotte, dried prunes and almonds from Bordeaux. There was even some Norman flour, although it was not an important export to Canada. Wines and spirits were well represented: 42 *tonneaux* of red Bordeaux and seven *tonneaux* of white, ten *panniers* of anisette, and 90 *demi-barriques* of *eau de vie*.

The fourteenth cargo did not contain an example of every kind of merchandise that Dugard and Company shipped to Quebec in 15 years. It is nevertheless representative and almost identical with the fifteenth cargo. More significant than the similarity of two successive cargoes made up by the same outfitter is the similarity of the fourteenth cargo to one proposed in an anonymous memorandum from La Rochelle which appeared in Savary des Bruslon's *Dictionnaire de Commerce* entitled, "List of different sorts of merchandise that compose the cargoes of vessels destined for the colony of Canada for the inhabitants' use." [26] The list could easily be taken as the description of a company cargo. It includes *siamoise, rouenneries* (cotton-linen mixes), and a great variety of other manufactures of the Rouen region, proving that their inclusion in Dugard and Company cargoes was not only a result of the company's being Rouen-based.

The list identifies the ultimate use of many cargo items. Lustrous black taffetas from Lyons sent to Canada were intended for the English colonials, presumably smuggled via Albany. The blankets of two and three points and "à berceau," the red and violet *dourgne* (a Montauban *cordellaterie*), and *molleton*, as well as inexpensive *toile de Saint Jean* from Roanne near Lyons, were all textiles for Indian use. The Indian market also absorbed its share of the muskets (*fusils de chasse*), short swords, bayonets, knives, and scissors of St. Etienne as well as large and small copper cooking vessels. Decorations sent for the Indians included gilt copper seal rings, buttons, lace, galoons, mirrors, combs, ribbons, Dutch beads (*rasade*), and Dutch vermillion.

When the Caribbean and Canadian cargoes are compared, the most striking contrast is the Canadian independence of France with regard to basic foodstuffs. Just as St. Domingue was less dependent than Martinique in this regard, so was Canada the least dependent. At the same time, the comparison shows the same determination to maintain French eating habits. A second striking contrast is the far greater variety of manufactures, particularly the inclusion of woollens and more smallwares and "hardware." This does not indicate that Canadian purchasing power was being directed from staple foods to appealing consumer goods. A large portion of the hardware and dry goods was destined for the Indian trade and, so far as the white population was concerned, filled an economic role similar to that of most of the barrelled beef exported to Martinique, which sustained the sugar export economy by feeding slaves.[27] The Indian fitted into the mercantile economy better than did the slave because he not only provided an export staple, but was a good consumer of manufactures, perhaps a better customer than a French peasant. Indian or white, the Canadian population showed the same dependence upon French manufactures that characterized the Creole populations. Only with regard to sustenance could the Canadians provide themselves with basic necessities. Like the Creoles, they were still Europeans, dependent for the mainte-

TABLE 6.
*Gathering the 14th Cargo: Percentages of Various
Goods Obtained in Rouen and Elsewhere*

	Rouen	Elsewhere
Toiles	44.4	55.6
Woollens	48.8	51.2
Fine and decorative	70.2	29.8
Clothing and accessories	35.3	64.7
Metals	34.5	65.5
Non-metal "hardware"	40.0	60.0
Provisions	16.9	83.1
Unidentified	100.0	00.0
Combined total:	39.8	60.2

Source: AN, 62AQ41, 14ᵉ Cargaison, Aller, factures, nos. 1–160.

nance of their civilization on economic links with the metropolis. Even the Indians must have been less at home in America than their ancestors, so much had they become prisoners of European technology.

Robert Dugard was able to buy almost 40 per cent of the fourteenth cargo in Rouen (table 6). Not all of this was manufactured in the city and its region, and Dugard's purchases reflect not only Rouen's role as a manufacturing centre, but as an entrepôt. Because of this facility, he was able to put together a large part of each cargo with considerable speed. Although some items, such as blankets from Darnétal, may have been ordered in advance, much of this 40 per cent was to be had at a moment's notice at the Halles de Rouen. Items that had to be ordered directly from distant points were easily and even quickly obtained because of the network of commercial relations, and the means and routes of transport that linked a great commercial city with other centres of production and distribution. The dates of Dugard's orders to distant manufacturers are not documented, making the invoices that came with ordered goods the earliest evidence of the commercial cycle. Most invoices for goods obtained in Rouen are dated May and so fall within the six-week period prior to the departure of the last part of the fourteenth cargo. Among invoices from more distant places, a large proportion are also dated April, but invoices with earlier dates (Bilbao, 16 February and Roanne, 23 March for example) are uncommon.

There are only a few references in the Dugard Papers to the routes

and modes of transport by which merchandise reached Le Havre and
other ports. On 23 March 170 bolts of *toile de Saint Jean* began their
journey down the Loire from Roanne. One month later they were sent
northward overland from the entrepôt of Orleans, leaving the river as
it began its westward course. Montauban was also an entrepôt. The
woollens from its hinterland were sent down the Tarn and Garonne to
Bordeaux. *Toile de Mesly* from Niort in Poitou was shipped out of La
Rochelle. It probably reached the port via the Sevre Niortaise River
and a small journey down the coast. These examples may be taken as
representative of the system—transport by river and sea wherever
possible and by cart when necessary, with extensive use of entrepôts.

To the 67,294 livres in merchandise obtained in Rouen, may be
added another 51,462 livres worth converging upon the city from different directions: 11,886 from the southeast, 5,480 from Paris, 16,706
from the northeast, and 17,390 from the northwest. An additional
30,009 livres worth moved directly to Le Havre from places as far as
Bilbao. Much of the cargo of the southwest, some 17,602 livres in
value, followed the rivers and coasts to La Rochelle and was there
embarked for Canada. Only 2,394 livres in merchandise was exported
directly from Bordeaux, although for other years Bordeaux was
an important point of export and La Rochelle was omitted. These
movements of goods, shown graphically on the flow map (figure 1),
indicate those regions on which the company's 15 Canadian cargoes
had their greatest economic impact. To the value of the merchandise
must be added the shipping costs, commissions, wages, warehouse
fees, and the like. If a similar flow map were drawn for Caribbean
cargoes, the movement from the regions of Niort and Montauban
would be missing. There would be no movement from Roanne and less
from St. Etienne. The other flow lines woud sacrifice some of their
thickness to a broad flow coming down from Cork.

At last the bales, boxes, and barrels assembled in the warehouses of
Robert Dugard's commission agents had to be loaded aboard ship and
committed to the hazards of the *voyage de long cours*.[28] For the fourteenth cargo, there were three ships and three ports of exportation.
The *Trois Maries*, a ship owned in part by some of the members of the
Société du Canada, left Bordeaux for Quebec on 12 April 1742. It
carried a small part of the cargo in soap and wine. But most of the
cargo did not leave until June. On 7 May Duroy et Fils of Montauban
sent to Henri Goudal in Bordeaux the shipment of textiles they had
gathered in Mazamet, Dourgne, and in their own city. A month later,
Goudal sent on these 12 bales to his own correspondent in La
Rochelle. Meanwhile, nine further bales of textiles and clothing were

FIG. 1. *The Fourteenth Cargo, 1743; Flow of Goods*

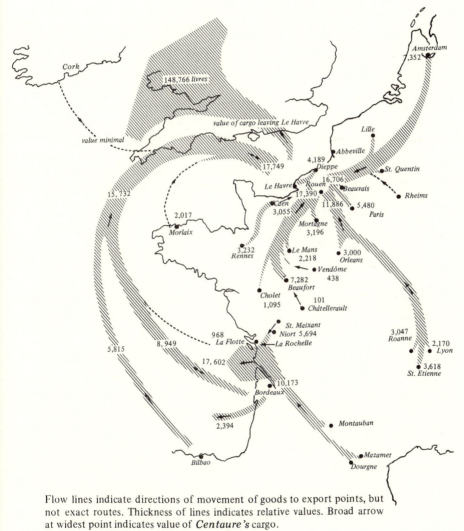

Cork

148,766 *livres*

value of cargo leaving Le Havre

value minimal

17,749

15, 732

2,017

Morlaix

3,232
Rennes

5,815   8,949

17, 602

2,394

Bilbao

Amsterdam
7,352

Lille

Abbeville

4,189
Dieppe

St. Quentin

16,706
Le Havre   Rouen   Beauvais
17,390

Rheims

Caen   11,886   5,480
3,055   Paris

Mortagne
3,196

Le Mans   3,000
2,218   Orleans

Vendôme
438

7,282
Beaufort

Cholet   101
1,095   Châtellerault

St. Maixant
Niort 5,694
968   La Rochelle
La Flotte

10,173
Bordeaux

Montauban

Mazamet
Dourgne

3,047
Roanne

2,170
Lyon

3,618
St. Etienne

Flow lines indicate directions of movement of goods to export points, but
not exact routes. Thickness of lines indicates relative values. Broad arrow
at widest point indicates value of *Centaure's* cargo.
Source : AN 62AQ41.14ᵉ Cargaison, factures.

being sent to La Rochelle from Niort. These shipments together with a few other items constituted the full consignment from the company loaded aboard the *Comte de Matignon*, which left for Quebec after 15 June.[29]

At Le Havre, Veuve Christinat supervised the outfitting and loading of the 350-ton *Centaure*, which carried the bulk of the cargo.[30] On 24 January arrived the first of 19 shipments that converged on Le Havre from all points of the compass aboard hoy, barque, and *navire*. The first vessel, the hoy of David Desmond from Rouen, brought only a few barrels of flour to be converted into hardtack for ship's provisions. Salt and vinegar, the first items of trade cargo, arrived on 15 February aboard the *St. Louis* coming from La Flotte. They were followed ten days later by a large shipment of wine sent from Bordeaux by Goudal aboard the *St. Charles de l'Ile Dieu*. On 16 February 13,500 pounds of iron bars had been put aboard the *Cézar* at Bilbao by Bonny and Hody. This shipment arrived at Le Havre on 1 March.

All of the above were early arrivals. Eight weeks then passed before a large shipment from Dugard in Rouen signalled that the loading was to begin in earnest. After that date, 28 April, a vessel arrived every few days—a hoy from Caen on 6 May bearing cargo from Rennes, another from Rouen on the 13th, the *Marie* from Cork on the 17th carrying ship's provisions. The *Heureux* arrived from Dieppe on the 20th, a barque bringing flour from Honfleur on the 22nd, another large shipment from Dugard on the 24th, the *Niger* carrying *toile de Morlaix* from Honfleur on the 28th, followed the next day by another barque carrying more flour. On 30 May, 6 June, and 8 June, three hoys brought large shipments down the Seine from Rouen. A final shipment of wine, brandy, anisette, and exotic foodstuffs arrived from Bordeaux aboard the *Triomphant* on 10 June. There were still a few odds and ends in Rouen to be added to the cargo, and these Dugard hurried off aboard the public *messagerie* on the 14th and 18th. The ship thus fully laden, there was no time to waste. On 20 June, the *Centaure* went out with the tide and the wind.

CHAPTER SIX

Quebec: A Colonial Trading Factory

I

It was mid-April when the Dugard ships left the coast of France bound for Canada. Beating about the prevailing westerlies, threading their way through processions of icebergs, they reached the estuary of the St. Lawrence, where, were they not too late, they were caught up by the spring easterlies and propelled against the strong river current to their anchorage before Quebec. Often it was mid-July when they reached the port; arrivals in August and even September were not uncommon. But the St. Lawrence navigation season was short; no matter how late the arrival, a November departure was mandatory.[1] By then the season of Atlantic storms had begun. "Booms and gusts, deafening, blinding, driving" is how Joseph Conrad remembered westerly weather.[2] Its one compensation was the speed of the return journey, sometimes completed in a month. The exigencies of time and weather meant that summer in Quebec was always a season of hurry.

Time and weather were important considerations when in 1732 Dugard and Company decided to put their Canadian trade on a permanent footing. Permanency meant freeing the business of buying and selling at Quebec as much as possible from the breathless schedules of seasons and ships. As a result, when François Havy brought the company's third cargo to Quebec in that year, he did not come as a supercargo to spend a busy summer in the port and then flee with the ships before the encroaching river ice of winter. He had been named factor, and his business was to establish the company's first colonial trading factory.

Quebec's merchant quarter was the Lower Town, looking as though it had sucked in its breath, making itself narrow and tall to fit between the black and jagged cliff and the river tidal flat. The whitewashed houses of rough schist, often three stories high, squeezed close together. "The streets," a traveller reported, "are narrow, very rough, and almost always wet."[3] Havy and his cousin, Jean Lefebvre, also a Protestant and a native of the Pays de Caux who had come as his assistant, spent the next 20 years of their lives living in the very heart of Lower Town on the market square that faced the church of Notre Dame des Victoires. Even today, a thoughtful traveller can recapture something of the flavour of those days by visiting the square. Louis Fornel's two-and-a-half storey house in which Havy and Lefebvre rented working and living quarters from 1735 and 1758 has been reconstructed.[4] The original storage vaults dug under the street, possibly for their use, are still there to be examined and to evoke the past.[5] The house was a much more lively place when Havy and Lefebvre lived in it with French, Indian, and Negro domestics, side-by-side with Louis and Marie-Anne Fornel and their five children.[6] The same was true of the square, far too busy with traffic then to make room for the Bernini bust of Louis XIV that occupies its centre today. The harbour was a short walk away, and almost all the important merchants in the city lived on one of the adjacent streets, Notre-Dame, St. Pierre, Sous-le-Cap, Sous-le-Fort, or Cul-de-Sac. There they resigned themselves to the colonial exile that had been the foundation of many a metropolitan fortune.

The most substantial Lower Town merchants were factors and consequently metropolitan Frenchmen like themselves. The traditional categories of *marchand forain* and *domicilié*, the seasonal trader from across the Atlantic and his settled counterpart, attached by the interest of property or family to the colonial community in which he lived, obscure the factors' situation. Some were little attached to the colony and were scarcely distinguishable from the *forains*. "They come here to spend two or three years or more," wrote the Intendant Bigot, who characterized them as "itinerant merchants who come and go."[7] But others stayed longer, marrying Canadians and founding families, although never cutting the transatlantic ties that were their *raison d'être* and that drew them back again to France. Men such as Antoine Pascaud in the seventeenth century and Denis Goguet in the eighteenth were *domiciliés*, but nonetheless Frenchmen backed by French businesses and aspiring to careers in France.[8] Havy and Lefebvre became a part of this inner circle of resident metropolitans who dominated the colony's import-export trade. While the retail business of Quebec might have been divided among more than 100 shopkeepers, most were super-numeraries in a very overcrowded profession. Those acknowledged "principal traders" of Quebec City who met at the *palais* in 1740 to elect a syndic numbered only 17, most of them metropolitans. François Havy was one of them.[9] *Forains* or *domiciliés*, the French traders in Canada constituted an enclave of considerable economic importance whose deepest affiliations were with the mother country.

Both Havy and Lefebvre were the salaried employees of Dugard and Company. Havy received 1,000 livres *per annum* until the end of 1736 and 1,500 livres thereafter, while Lefebvre was originally hired at 600 livres *per annum* and may have received as much as 1,200 in his later years in Canada.[10] It was probably an anomalous arrangement as far as Canadian trade was concerned. According to Havy, most companies were represented in Canada either by commission agents earning five per cent on sales of incoming cargo and two and one-half per cent on the value of the returns they provided, or by traders associated with their European suppliers for a one-third share, alternatives more lucrative than salary.[11] As Havy remarked in his later years, "My apprenticeship had its price."[12] But there were other benefits to being a factor: a measure of independence, the keeping of large amounts of money and merchandise, the enjoyment of influence and of a certain reflected prestige. Havy and Lefebvre would make the most of these as the years went by.

The appearance of the corporate signature, "Havy & Lefebvre," in 1743 announced that the two men had become business partners. At the same time, they remained salaried employees, their living expenses charged to Dugard and Company. To the modern mind, it was an anomalous arrangement. Under this signature they became involved in many enterprises for their own account. This was not uncommon among factors and finds a modest parallel in the captain or supercargo's *pacotille* carried free of freight. But as Havy later denied having had private ventures in Canada while working for the company, Dugard may have forbidden it.[13] If so, his decrees were without effect.

"Gallant & aimiable men . . . well liked & upright fellows" is how a fellow merchant described the two young bachelors.[14] Their letters to a well-loved friend and business connection in Montreal, Pierre Guy, reveal a ready humour and a refreshing forthrightness. They loved to drink, ever ready "de nous battre à coups de verre."[15] When Havy was unable to visit Guy in Montreal, he wrote that he regretted "that I am deprived of the personal pleasure that I would have had of drinking with you."[16] They probably drank too much, but is it not a failing to be expected of their little merchant circle, exiled in a small, rough frontier colony? If they regarded Quebec as "an enchanted place"[17] in comparison with Montreal, where the Parisian Guy found life dull and uninteresting, it was only a matter of degree. Even at Quebec, one drank "to divert oneself." [18] Perhaps they partook of the extravagant dress and dinners and the presence of ladies "as much adorned as if they were to go to court" noted by Kalm[19] that helped to paint colour on an otherwise drab existence.

Marriage was out of the question. Being Protestants, neither Havy nor Lefebvre could marry in the colony or bring wives and families from France. In most years, there were about a dozen Protestant bachelors like themselves in the colony, all of them clerks or partners of metropolitan merchants.[20] For the most part, they were not bothered on religious grounds, although there is record of the bishop himself trying on one occasion to convert a dying Huguenot.[21] Their faith was important to them, and their sometime profligacy implied no irreligion. In their uncertain lives, marked by war, famine and epidemic, there was ample room for God. One might piously ask Him for profits and receive instead the whiplash of war.[22] In either case, one submitted: "God above all. . . . Everything must be placed in the hands of divine providence." [23]

François Havy was a fervent admirer of education, but not himself a highly-educated man. His parents had provided him with the basic training for a commercial life rather than sending him to a college.[24] He is said to have prided himself on his polished manners, but they could not subdue a fiery temper or curb a sharp tongue. One day, when coming out of the Admiralty Court, where he was suing a ship captain, Havy remarked in a loud voice that he had overheard the captain tell his wife that he would cut short a voyage and return early to Quebec so as to beat her at his leisure over the winter. When the captain, who was also leaving court, replied that if he wanted to beat someone it wouldn't be his wife, Havy had him brought before the Superior Council on a charge of threatening assault. The council refused to waste its time with such a ridiculous affair, but it did produce the documentation providing this revealing glimpse of Havy's character.[25]

If there is a temptation—one unfounded by any evidence—to see Havy as small and wiry, Jean Lefebvre was definitely a man of ample proportions.[26] His handwriting, which so perfectly fulfills the writing-master's prescription of light on the upstroke and heavy on the downstroke, reflects the patience and the even temperament that made him the suitable companion to his cousin. Their complementary personalities were the true foundation of a partnership that ended only with Jean Lefebvre's death after a quarter of a century.

The Quebec merchants' busy season was framed by the arrival and departure of ships from France, Louisbourg, and the West Indies. The ships began to arrive in July and continued steadily through October. Furs from the hinterland as well as ships from France often came late to the town, and there was always a concentration of activity in the late summer and the autumn. In addition to cargo, the ships carried the mail, including letters and invoices for Quebec and Montreal merchants.[27] The mail was brought to town by messengers long before the ships arrived in port, some of it being forwarded to Montreal by freighters, travellers, or government couriers.[28] News of prices, shortages and oversupplies, prospective war, and political changes passed swiftly among the merchants. Much of the commercial news was of a confidential nature; and as Havy and Lefebvre passed it on to their Montreal correspondent, Pierre Guy, they enjoined the strictest secrecy, "not wishing to appear *auteurs de Gazettes de cette ville*."[29] They supplemented postal communication with France by frequent visits, one of them always remaining behind at Quebec.[30] Visits to Montreal during the slack season of winter and early spring were also essential to efficient business operations.[31] The merchant was always a writer and a traveller, a specialist in communication.

The cargoes sent from France and committed to the care of Quebec factors were transferred from merchantmen to small bateaux that carried them to shore or directly to Montreal. Portions of Dugard and Company cargoes intended for specific customers, frequently in Montreal, were baled and marked accordingly in France, thus reducing handling to a minimum. It was up to the factors to oversee disembarking and forwarding, to ascertain the condition of the merchandise, and to declare imports of dutiable tobacco, wine, and spirits.[32]

Each year the Montreal merchants descended upon Quebec when they had been informed of the arrival of the ships.[33] Money and merchandise began to change hands, and in the classic manner prices soon found their level in response to the market. Of course, the market required a little prompting to arrive at a suitable price. The French invoices upon which the Canadian wholesale prices were based were always slightly inflated. This was generally known, and buyers compared the invoice prices of different importers, refusing to buy where they found prices too enthusiastically increased. According to Gilles Hocquart, the Intendant of Canada, the invoices of Pascaud Frères of

TABLE 7.
Inflation of Invoice Prices in Canada 1743

Commodity	Price quoted in Canada	Original invoice	Per cent increase
Textiles			
Calamande rayé	29s	27s 6d	5.5
Calamande couleur	31s	29s 6d	5.1
Carisé	26s	25s	4.0
Beaufort	33–35s	29s	13.8
Blanket, 3 point	8#	7# 10s	6.7
Blanket, 8 point	20# 10s	20#	2.5
Toile d'Allemagne	11# 15s	11# 6d	4.0
Other			
Spiggots	9# 10s	7# 14s 6d	18.0
Plowshares	20# cwt	17#	17.5
"Bottes d'acier"*	50#	40#	25.0
Candles	340#	312# 16s	8.8
Wax	120#	117#	2.6

*Identity of this item is in doubt.

Source: SHM, Collection Pierre Guy, factures, especially item 24; AN, 62AQ41, 14e Cargaison, Aller, factures.

La Rochelle were always taken as the standard.[34] The level of inflation for the company cargo of 1743 can be measured because both the invoices sent to Robert Dugard by the suppliers of the cargo and invoice prices quoted to Pierre Guy for the same merchandise at Quebec are extant (see table 7). These increases ranged from two and a half per cent on eight-point blankets to 25 per cent on some metal items. The data also permit the calculation of an estimated increase of 5.88 per cent for the entire cargo.[35] The figure is low because the 1743 cargo, like all those of the company, consisted primarily of textiles. It corresponds to the five to six per cent estimated as normal by a prominent Canadian businessman of the time, François Etienne Cugnet.[36]

However anomalous the inflation of the invoice might seem, it had come to be regarded as a prescriptive right of the seller. The profit, or *bénéfice*, determined by the market at Quebec was a percentage calculated on this inflated base (see table 8). A normal peacetime *bénéfice* fell between 20 and 30 per cent. For a given season, the *bénéfice* was uniform throughout the city.[37] Each item in invoices made out for Canadian buyers was listed at the price of the inflated French invoice. As the *bénéfice* was usually the same for all kinds of merchandise, it

TABLE 8.
*Level of Profit in Excess
of Invoice Inflation
(Bénéfice), Quebec
1740–47*

Year	Per cent
1740	18–25
1741	25–30
1742	20
1743	20
1744	55
1745	
Jan.	60
March	60
Sept.	80
Oct.	80–100
Nov.	80–100
1746	
Aug.	100–120
Oct.	120
Nov.	100–180
1747	
Oct.	100

Source: SHM, Collection Pierre
Guy, factures; PAC, Collection
Baby, lettres de Havy et
Lefebvre, fols. 548–1102;
ASQ, Polygraphie 24.

was calculated on the total and added at the bottom. Practice sometimes deviated from this norm: different rates for certain commodities,
a sale based on the rate of some future date, or a special price resulting
from close bargaining (*à prix fait*).[38]

Wines and spirits were in a class apart. Neither were their invoice
prices inflated nor were they sold at the *bénéfice* that prevailed for
other merchandise. The prices Pierre Guy paid Havy and Lefebvre for
wines in 1743 exceeded those of the original invoices by 128 per cent
for red and 160 per cent for white.[39] These rates may have meant the
differences between profit and loss on outward voyages, given that
mark-ups on most cargo items (invoice inflation plus *bénéfice*) fell in
the modest range of 26 to 36 per cent. However, even in eighteenth-
century Canada, demand for wines and spirits was not infinitely elas-

tic. For example, these commodities constituted only six per cent of the 1743 cargo, which grossed a profit of no more than 33½ per cent. An anonymous "Mémoire sur la Domaine d'Occident en Canada (1736)" suggests that wines and spirits may have played a more significant role in the operations of other shippers, that they were "even at present the principal reason for the shipments made to the colony."[40] The memorial states that dry goods were usually included in *pacotilles* shipped for the account and risk of colonial traders, yielding only commission and freight to the metropolitan shippers, who reserved wines and spirits as *cargaison*—that is, to be shipped and sold for their own account. This distinction is not made in the accounts of Havy and Lefebvre and Robert Dugard, but it serves to underscore the crucial role of alcohol for all shippers.[41]

Havy and Lefebvre, like other Lower Town merchants, always stocked a wide range of goods that made it possible for a customer to satisfy all his needs at their warehouse. Failure to stock a proper assortment reduced a merchant's ability to demand the current *bénéfice*. Havy and Lefebvre recount how warehouses that lacked assortment lost any control over market prices and sold with less profit.[42] On one occasion Pierre Guy informed another Lower Town metropolitan factor, Jean-André Lamaletie, that he would only give him his business if Lamaletie could fill his order in its entirety.[43] By late winter nearly everyone in the Lower Town was usually *désassorti*, and the orders of Montreal customers could only be filled if the factors bought from each other.[44] The colony's capacity to absorb European goods varied according to economic and political conditions. Temporary shortages and gluts were common, and these had to be anticipated. The composition of their annual *mémoire*, or order for the following season's goods, may therefore be regarded as Havy and Lefebvre's most basic responsibility.

The credit system was closely linked with the practice of maintaining an assortment, in part explaining why the latter was so important for gaining customers. Credit was extended in return for volume purchase. It was necessary, in the words of Governor Beauharnois that the traders "find what is needed to make an assortment of all that is necessary."[45] Having been enabled to make a large purchase, the customer "often pays only half and is given credit for the rest." The Canada of Havy and Lefebvre was not a rich country. "Poverty prevails," wrote the Governor and Intendant. "One seeks to get out of it and procure a modest affluence."[46] To finance their fur-gathering voyages and other enterprises, many Canadian traders turned not unnaturally to the Lower Town mandarins of the import-export trade for needed credit.

The metropolitans, at once suppliers and creditors, clearly had the upper hand in such arrangements.

The debtor often signed a negotiable promissory note, or *billet à ordre*. In the case of fur trade outfits, this was not considered sufficient guarantee; and Havy and Lefebvre required that an obligation be drawn up before a notary. This was a security document with characteristics of both the modern mortgage and floating charge. Fourteen fur traders' obligations to the favour of Havy and Lefebvre are extant in the Quebec Archives.[47] They consist of a general encumbrance on the debtor's land and chattels "present and to come" and a special claim on the anticipated return of furs. While a specific date of maturity was agreed upon, the debt was considered due as soon as the fur canoes reached Montreal.

Taken together, the signers of obligations and notes accounted for no more than half of Havy and Lefebvre's total sales. Analogy with European practice suggests that considerable business was done by current account, a conjecture borne out by the fragmentary records extant. The Séminaire de Québec still possesses accounts showing the sale of agricultural products to Havy and Lefebvre and their purchase from them of French merchandise.[48] The accounts of Pierre Guy provide yet another example. But while there is an essential element of credit in the current account, it is not to be thought of in the same light as debts secured by notes and obligations. Credit by current account was short-term, being in principle settled on an annual basis; low-risk, being confined to stable business friends; and most important of all, it was reciprocal. Debit and credit transactions were continually cancelling each other out. In itself, the web of reciprocal accounts rendered Canadian business more efficient and stable rather than adding to its fragility. Of course, its outermost threads were invariably attached to the brittle twigs of a second or third party's own debtors, for example the fur traders outfitted by Guy at Montreal.

Credit was thus crucial and, next to the adjudication of the needs of the market, it was probably the extension of credit that most exercised the factors' judgment. While the misfortunes that befell their correspondents might have repercussions on Havy and Lefebvre's own business, the risks of credit can only be apprehended in the case of loans secured by notes and obligations. Only for the period 1730 to 1738 are the identities and liabilities of the total body of these debtors known.[49] Most of their loans were small, 80 per cent of them under 2,000 livres, although most credit extended by value was accounted for by larger loans above 2,000 livres. A mere four per cent (those above 5,000 livres) accounted for almost half of the credit extended.

Still, few of the debtors were remarkable for the large size of their
borrowings. Only four—Foucher, Gaudet, d'Auteuil, and Volant
d'Hautebourg (himself a front man for Havy and Lefebvre)—carried
the five-figure loans that were common and frequent among Europeans such as Robert Dugard and his circle. Over the years the character
of the debtor group changed such that the small debts were concentrated at the beginning of the 1730s and the larger ones at the end.
Extant obligations from the 1740s add five names to the catalogue of
men of substance—Monfort, D'Ailleboust, Texier, Auger, and Béner.[50] This tendency toward large figures would seem to be an indication of concentration and hence a reflection of the maturation of the
Canadian economic community.

Were all these debtors prompt in redeeming their notes, the advances made by the company in one year would be offset by the re-
demption of the previous year's debt. The extension of credit would
not interfere with the factors' ability to prepare a return cargo equal to
or greater than the value of the outward cargo sold in Canada. In the
jargon of the time, they would be able to make their returns. However,
a significant proportion of debts was paid very slowly. Of the 144
advances against notes and obligations made by Havy and Lefebvre in
the 1730s, 90, or 62.5 per cent, were redeemed within one year. An
additional seven per cent were redeemed within two years. The remaining 30 per cent were redeemed in various lengthy terms such as
one-half in six months and one-half in six years or one-third in one
year and another third in two years, with a final payment in three
years. One was outstanding for nine years, and many became lost
debts. Over the years the unpaid debts mounted and the percentage of
the total debt returned each year was usually much less than 62.5 per
cent (see table 9). Debt was thus a factor that served to slow the return
on investment in the Canadian trade and hence to reduce its profitability.

Havy and Lefebvre were persuaded that if treated leniently, their
debtors "would no longer be honest men."[51] They were indefatigable
in their pursuit of defaulters. In this Pierre Guy, who was in a much
better position to keep an eye on the fur traders, was a willing helper.[52]
The legal aspects of these pursuits were handled neither by Guy nor by
Havy and Lefebvre ("we who although Normans don't much understand the law"),[53] but by a Monsieur Poirier and a Monsieur Blanzy,
presumably the Montreal notary Danré de Blanzy. The managing of
these irregular barristers also required Guy's attention, "since they
have many affairs in hand, resulting in their always neglecting some of
them."[54]

TABLE 9.

The Accumulation of Debts Owing (Promissory Notes and
Obligations) 1730–38

Year	Debts owing paid	As % of debt owing	Debts owing carried	New credit extended	Total extended
1730				2835	2835
1731	2835	100	0	3025	3025
1732	1603	53	1422	22652	24074
1733	18831	78	5243	43208	48451
1734	26426	55	22025	27501	49526
1735	22061	54	27465	46837	74302
1736	33393	48	40909	23707	64616
1737	37496	58	27116	37818	64934
1738	16974	26	47960	57171	105131

Source: AN, 62AQ40, "Comptes de gestion à Québec 1730–38."

In their attitude towards money and interest, Havy and Lefebvre
were pragmatic but thoroughly traditional, expressing themselves in
an analogy of hoary pedigree. "What are a merchant's tools [?],"
they ask. "Money. If he hasn't any he can't work."[55] They explain
that they charged the common French mercantile rate of six per cent
for their advances,[56] using the above analogy of money with tools: "If
someone keeps a craftsman's tools and that prevents his exercising his
craft, ought not the one who is the cause pay for the delay?"[57] Usually,
as Hocquart put it, "these debtors [made] satisfaction little by little."[58] In 1759, 11 years after Dugard and Company had withdrawn
from the Canada trade, there still remained at Quebec 10,539 livres in
bad or doubtful debts, but considering the volume of company business in Canada, this was not a large sum.[59]

As the trading season advanced, Havy and Lefebvre's warehouse
filled with return cargo. The most important single item was, of
course, fur. A third area in which they were called upon to exercise
skilled judgement was therefore the appraisal and pricing of furs. All
furs other than beaver were sold on an open market. The manner in
which quantities and prices are entered into accounts suggests that
once the price of a good-quality pelt was determined, a specific lot was
examined for quality. If the furs were inferior in whole or in part, the
lot was regarded as equal to a lesser number of perfect pelts and their
total value was computed on that basis.[60] Sometimes the valuation
might be decided by arbitration.[61] In any case, it was a buyer's market.

Jean-André Lamaletie's adviso to Pierre Guy, "I have priced your mar-
tins at 40s ... as for the scraps I have not yet made a price" shows
how little say the seller had in price determinations.[62] All extra charges
were passed on to him, just as all those on incoming French merchandise had been assigned to him as purchaser by the adjustment of the
bénéfice. In another letter Lamaletie explained to Guy, "It wouldn't be
fair to have to pay you the same price as in previous years since freight
and insurance costs have considerably increased."[63] That the Canadian trader rather than the ultimate metropolitan purchaser of fur
goods should have borne the brunt of these charges indicates that the
colonial fur sellers were unable to curb supply or otherwise influence
the market in their favour.

Bills of exchange were another important export. A large part of
these was given to Canadian traders in exchange for beaver pelts by
the Compagnie des Indes, which held a monopoly on their export.
These bills thus represented purchasing power gained in return for a
commodity export. Other bills drawn on the French government and
received in exchange for Canadian paper money were exported because Canada could not provide sufficient exports to balance its
foreign trade. As their continued use was a measure of Canadian economic underdevelopment, it is significant that the proportion of Havy
and Lefebvre's "returns" constituted by bills of exchange declined
from between 37 to 44 per cent in the period 1730–32 to four to 13
per cent in the years 1741–43 (see table 10). The quantity and range of
Canadian export items was increasing.

Many private merchants' bills also passed between Canada and
France. The quantity and importance of these instruments has yet to
be determined. Canadians did write drafts on metropolitan merchants
with whom they had established credit by the sale of furs. Havy and
Lefebvre occasionally drew on Dugard to the credit of some Canadian
merchant's French correspondent. Most of the private bills were
drawn to pay freight costs on company ships. Customers sending furs
or other items to France for their own account delivered in payment
their bills of exchange to the order of Robert Dugard. When the company freighted from France to Canada for the account of customers in
Canada, Dugard himself drew bills on the receivers to the order of
Havy and Lefebvre.[64] Bills sent to France that were not honoured were
returned protested. Judgements were then obtained from Canadian
courts.[65]

All these operations of receiving and sending cargoes occasioned
extensive administrative work. Cargoes in both directions had to be
declared at customs, and duties on incoming tobacco and alcohol paid.

TABLE 10.
*The Declining
Importance of Bills
of Exchange in
Returns from
Quebec, 1730–44
(Percentage of
Returns Constituted
by Drafts)*

Year	Percentage
1730	37
1731	44
1732	38
1733	19
1734	24
1735	24
1736	13.5
1737	10.5
1738	10.5
1739	11.75
1740	9.5
1741	5
1742	13
1743	4
1744	44

Source: AN, 62AQ40,
"Comptes de gestion à
Québec, 1730–44";
"Compte de balance de
Havy et Lefebvre,
Québec, 15 juillet
1746."

Incoming freight was distributed while outgoing freight was solicited. Crew rolls were registered with the Admiralty and *congés* and passports were obtained for departing ships. The enormous bulk of invoices, accounts, and letters were prepared in triplicate.[66] When the last ships had left, hundreds of entries in daybooks were transferred meticulously to the ledger and condensed into current accounts sent to all business correspondents. Some part of the cargo always remained unsold, and this together with the time-consuming nature of the paperwork meant that final accounts for the cargo were not closed and signed until between mid-July and mid-August of the following year.[67] But by far the greater part of the cargo had been disposed of by November, and the season of feverish activity was over. "I wish it was never autumn at Quebec," was Havy's reaction late one October.[68] But soon the snow would be flying, the beginning of the calm and indeed the boredom of the long winter that made the return of merchant sails to the St. Lawrence an ever-welcome sight.

The fur trade had left behind those crises of oversupply that had characterized it in the seventeenth century. The growing market for a variety of furs compensated for the declining demand for beaver, making the trade a relatively stable sector of the economy. But it was the newer trades in agricultural and forest products suitable to the markets of Louisbourg and the sugar islands, that held the promise of commercial expansion. Customs house records show a diversification of export items at least as early as 1732, with volume in many cases peaking in the middle of the decade.[69] Indeed, in 1739 Hocquart was able to report to his chief Canada's first favourable trade balance, reflecting increased exports of flour, biscuit, vegetables, cod, seal oil, and furs other than beaver.[70] It was doubtless this expanding trade, later stimulated by their own investment, that first attracted Dugard and Company to Canada. They exploited the full range of new trade commodities, and to the extent that it was feasible, linked their Canadian with their Caribbean trade, using Louisbourg as an intermediate entrepôt. Thus Havy and Lefebvre also prepared cargoes for colonial ports and occasionally received exotic cargoes of rum and oranges.

In 1740 and 1741 the company's *Centaure* and *Imprévû* carried what were probably the earliest significant shipments of Canadian wheat and flour to France.[71] The accounts of Havy and Lefebvre with the Séminaire de Québec, a major supplier of agricultural and forest products, show that the 2,020 *minots* of wheat they provided for the trial export of 1740 had all been prepared with extreme care, a necessary precaution when competing in an export market, but one that Canadians, with their lax colonial standards, had been slow to take.[72]

This attempt to sell Canadian wheat in France was an isolated event occasioned by excess shipping capacity.[73] But even the promising Louisbourg and West Indian markets were not to be taken for granted. Both had alternative sources of supply; and in 1740 the Intendant of Martinique reported to Hocquart that while Canadian flour was good, it was still inferior to French flour, which the islanders could buy at the same price.[74]

The diversification of Dugard and Company activities in Canada went beyond trade to include an industrial activity, the building of ships. Between 1736 and 1746 Havy and Lefebvre launched six ships having a combined value of nearly 300,000 livres.[75] The high costs of the industry, pioneered by Talon but virtually abandoned between 1688 and 1713, together with the straitened circumstances of the local merchants stood in the way of flourishing development. In the 1730s shipbuilding was greatly stimulated by the combination of royal bounties and a steadily improving economy.[76]

It is probably no accident that woodcutting for the company's first Canadian-built ship, the *Alçion*, began in 1734, the year after encouraging revisions had been made to the bounty system. In the spring, small rafts of the wood were floated down the swollen Richelieu and over the rapids at Chambly; the small rafts were then combined into larger ones that were floated down to Quebec.[77] In October, the Governor and Intendant informed the King that the ship was already on the stocks.[78]

Royal bounties, equal to about two and a half per cent of the value of a ship, could by no means have offset the increased cost of building them in Canada rather than in France, once estimated by Marine officials to be roughly 15 per cent.[79] In spite of this, the launching of the *Alçion* was followed by the building of five more ships for the company, and it is difficult to quarrel with the logic of Hocquart's observation that Havy's construction of several vessels was "certain proof that he found profit in the first."[80] The most probable explanation for so extensive a program of shipbuilding resides in the fact that a Canadian-built ship was itself an item of return cargo. The general argument of Marine officials that the colony required new industries if it were to improve its balance of trade applied equally well to the needs of a single trading company intent on balancing its own trade. Instead of being converted into furs, bills of exchange or grain, French manufactures were being converted into ships. The profit made on the manufactures together with the bounties, was more than ample to cover the cost of the ships. Had there been a greater supply of profitable Canadian export items, and a complementary demand for them in Europe, shipbuilding might not have attracted company capital.

The contract for wood supply for the company's second ship, the *Fleury*, is extant as well as that for building a small vessel in 1741. In both cases Havy and Lefebvre made their payments half in merchandise, the second document specifying at the wholesale rate.[81] *Faux-sauniers* (transported salt smugglers) were engaged to cut wood for the *Fleury* at 200 livres per year plus food and lodging, the latter responsibilities then being transferred to the contractor. Thus they were paid considerably less than the 50 sols per day that was the going wage for day labourers. In addition, they were required to take half their pay in merchandise, but at the retail rate.[82]

The year 1739, in which the *St. Louis* was launched, was the last in which bounties were granted. In spite of this, three more company ships were launched: the *Centaure* and the *Imprévû* in 1740, and the *Astrée* in 1745. But although shipbuilding met the needs of the company, Havy and Lefebvre admitted in 1743, when the *Astrée* was still on the stocks, that "the vessels that we have built in this country come at a high price."[83]

The *Astrée* was the last vessel Havy and Lefebvre built for Dugard and Company in their makeshift shipyard on the St. Charles River, where they had blocked off St. Charles Street.[84] They built a number of smaller vessels of 60 tons or less for their private trade. This extended to Montreal, Louisbourg, the West Indies, and most important of all, sealing stations on the lower St. Lawrence and the Labrador coast in which they had begun to invest as Quebec entrepreneurs in their own right.

II

If none of the voluminous correspondence that passed between Robert Dugard in Rouen and Havy and Lefebvre in Quebec is extant, nonetheless there remain many accounts that provide an outline history of the Quebec factory.[85] The company's volume of trade in Canada may be judged from the accounts recording Havy and Lefebvre's receipts for each year from the sale of French cargoes and the payments made by customers moving freight on company ships and from the value of their annual "returns," meaning what they sent to France in the form of cargo, bills of exchange, paying freight, and newly-built ships, to which was added the year's expenses to satisfy the demands of the accounting system (see table 11). Dugard and Company's commitment to the Canada trade, indicated by the establishing of the factory in 1732, was reflected in the increased receipts of that year. For the next seven years receipts clustered around the 200,000 livres mark. The next notable change occurred in 1740, when they were boosted to the level of 300,000 livres, there to remain until suddenly reduced in 1742 to what they had been prior to 1740. If these figures are compared with those very rough estimates of the value of French merchandise annually imported into Canada prepared by the Canadian intendancy, the relative importance of Dugard and Company's Canadian trade becomes apparent.[86] From 1733, it usually ac-

TABLE II.

Receipts and Returns of the Quebec Factory, 1732–45 (Numbers Rounded off to Nearest Whole Livre)

Year	Receipts	Returns
1732	150,081	109,370
1733	225,148	211,785
1734	153,513	130,283
1735	203,091	205,395
1736	195,535	199,200
1737	220,212	217,578
1738	276,589	217,885
1739	234,673	213,414
1740	334,563	329,800
1741	362,570	410,257
1742	193,666	155,000
1743	232,684	215,931
1744	104,357	118,571
1745	119,275	212,593

Source: AN, 62AQ40, "Compte de balance de Havy et Lefebvre, Québec, 15 juillet 1746."

counted for an eighth or a tenth of the colony's import trade, rising to a sixth in 1738 and a fifth in 1741, having fallen to a seventh in 1740.

In its essentials, the task set Havy and Lefebvre was to receive and sell the cargoes sent by Dugard as advantageously as possible and to provide the best possible returns. Their performance may thus be judged by how well they succeeded in providing returns equal or superior in value to their annual receipts. Figure 2 illustrates this for the period from 1730, when Havy first brought a cargo to Quebec, to 1743, year of the last cargo received before the War of the Austrian Succession radically changed the conditions of Atlantic commerce and the fortunes of Dugard and Company. Specifically, it shows by what percentage returns exceeded or fell short of the factory's receipts for a given year; for convenience, it may be termed the curve of returns. It is an index of the performance of a business house as well as an indicator of the fortunes of the Canadian economy, reflecting its capacity to support an export trade and to pay its debts abroad. As the economic history of this period has been interpreted in terms of the vicissitudes of the money supply, the fur trade, and the production of wheat, the curve of returns will be compared with them.[87] The close corre-

FIG. 2. The "Curve of Returns" 1730–43

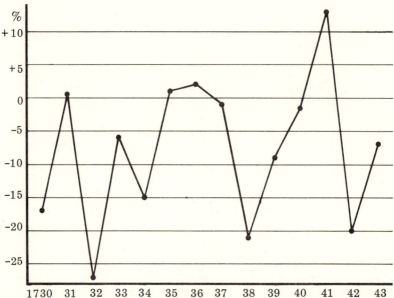

spondence that will be shown between the curve and these economic indices lends credence to all. The curve's similarity to or tendency to indicate greater buoyancy than these indices can be taken as a demonstration of the competent management of the Havy and Lefebvre-Dugard business, reflecting the maximization of possibilities. The nature of the articulation of the import-export trade to other economic sectors will also be illuminated.

Although France's monetary policy with regard to Canada was never satisfactory and both local officials and merchants continually clamoured for an increase in the money supply, sound money was probably more available in this period, especially the later 1730s and the 1740s, than in any other time in the colony's history.[88] It is, however, possible that the drop in returns evident in 1732 and 1734 is related to the inadequacy of the supply of bills of exchange on France. In each of these years Havy and Lefebvre were left at year's end with substantial sums of money in the cash box and owing by current accounts. There were 19,909 livres listed under this heading in 1732 and 29,044 livres in 1734. These balances were responsible for the significant drop in returns in those years.[89] The relation between the balance in 1734 and the inadequacy of the bill market, in the colonial setting largely dependent upon government redemptions, would seem to be confirmed by Hocquart's report to Maurepas that in that year he could not provide bills to redeem all the local government's fiduciary paper brought to him and was forced to return one-fifth of it to the merchants in the form of card money.[90]

Yet if capital was in short supply and hence a brake on economic expansion, the want of it was at least a constant. After 1734 the unavailability of metropolitan exchange appears to have caused no annual variation in the returns of Havy and Lefebvre. Returns were articulated to the possibilities offered by the money supply; what is chronic can at least be depended upon.

Fur holding pride of place among Canada's exports, it is to be expected that there would be a notable correspondence between the ability of Havy and Lefebvre to make returns and the fortunes of the fur trade. The latter may be traced by means of tables of the amount of beaver in pounds accepted by the Compagnie des Indes from 1729 to 1745, and the value of *menus pelleteries* (furs other than beaver) entering La Rochelle in livres *tournois* for the years 1729 to 1741, both long since compiled by Jean Lunn. These have been used as an index of the vicissitudes of the fur trade.[91]

Although there is no correspondence between the fortunes of the trade and the first three years of company operations in Canada, it is very marked for the next five trading seasons, 1733–37. For 1738, the correspondence is broken and the relation even inverse. Although beaver is down in 1739, other furs are up, maintaining the similarity. The trends compare in 1740 and perhaps in 1741, although the fortunes of fur in the latter year are by no means clear. There is no figure for pounds of beaver accepted; and the drop in the value of all furs imported to La Rochelle may be so great because of large exports to Le Havre for Dugard and Company, 1741 being the year of Havy and Lefebvre's greatest return, both in absolute terms and relative to sales and freight payments received. However, the definite increase in pounds of beaver delivered in 1742 is not at all paralleled by the curve. Indeed, in that year returns are in complete disarray. The continued rise in pounds of beaver delivered in 1743 and 1744 conforms to the rise of the curve of returns.

The third index, the state of the harvests, is reflected in the curve of the price of wheat established by Jean Hamelin, a price rise reflecting the poor harvest of the previous year.[92] The general downward trend in the price of wheat in 1730–35, parallels the general upward trend of the returns. The price of wheat in 1739–41, which is indicative of an adequate supply, corresponds with another upward trend. But the outstanding correlation is between the plummeting returns and the skyrocketing wheat prices of the years 1737–38 and 1742. The crop failures of 1736, 1737, and 1741 have completely upset the steady upward trend of the curve of returns.

Havy's returns for 1730 and 1731, years before the founding of the trading factory marked by a very small investment, demonstrate no correspondence with the indices of money supply, fur, and wheat. The failure to make a full return in 1732 is most easily explained in terms of a shortage of bills of exchange. But once the factory had been established and the regular expansion of the money supply assured (after 1734), the ability to make returns closely paralleled the fortunes of the colony's twin economic foundations, fur and wheat. The importance of wheat to the well-being of a large trading company is unexpected. So significant were the setbacks of 1738 and 1742 and so long was the period of recovery, that regular crop failures were the single most important factor retarding the orderly growth and profitability of the company's trade. This can be shown in yet another way. The percentage of debts owing to the company as of 1738 that were paid in that year was only 26 per cent, the smallest for any year of the decade (see table 9). The business undertaken for Dugard and Company in Canada by Havy and Lefebvre was obviously not confined to fur. By themselves, modest exports of grain, flour, and biscuit to Louisbourg and the West Indies do not explain the role of wheat. The twin disasters reflect the importance of the consumer demands (and the trade) of the mass of Canadians and of the religious orders. Havy and Lefebvre were merchants to an agricultural colony as well as a trading post. The trick was to make their returns to France in money and merchantable goods.

III

In 1743 François Havy was 40 years old, Jean Lefebvre probably younger.[93] They had lived in Canada for 12 years and had handled incoming and outgoing cargoes for Dugard and Company valued at more than 5,000,000 livres.[94] The company ships plying back and forth between Quebec and Le Havre, Honfleur, or Bordeaux, the welcome visits of their captains, the thick packets of letters and accounts to and from Rouen, constituted so many palpable links with the world beyond the St. Lawrence, keeping green their memories of France and nourishing their aspirations for a life beyond colonial obscurity.

On neither side of the Atlantic was the mercantile world of Havy and Lefebvre or Robert Dugard divorced from the empyrean of the Court and the bureaucracy. Gilles Hocquart, for example, reported that he talked to the merchants nearly every day.[95] On many occasions company ships carried Canadian despatches for Versailles.[96] The *Centaure* took to France the specimens of iron from the forges of St. Maurice that were sent to the Minister, and on many occasions carried plants for the Jardin du Roy that the Intendant at Le Havre forwarded to the Comte de Buffon.[97] With every packet of despatches forwarded to the Minister of the Marine, Robert Dugard always enclosed a covering letter outlining the extent of his company's activities in Canada and the West Indies, just in case colonial officials had not made a full report. He also included his complaints about the difficulties of colonial trade and the competition of smugglers at Louisbourg.[98] In reply Maurepas offered expressions of satisfaction at the building of yet another ship in Canada or at the extent of the company's trade, promising at the same time to look into complaints. He repeatedly encouraged the shipping of horses from Canada to Martinique, always making it seem the simplest of operations.[99]

The government valued the Société du Canada. In 1738 Maurepas assured Robert Dugard, "I am informed of the trade that you do in this colony [Canada]. You will always find me disposed to accord it what protection I can in those occasions where you will have need of it."[100] On many occasions Dugard was exempted from the regulations that required a ship to discharge its return cargo at the port where it had taken on its outward cargo. If the exemption were accompanied by a ministerial scolding, it was nonetheless useful.[101] Both in Canada and in France, the control exercised by government officials and their power to award supply contracts and favours made it important to be thought well of by them. Thus, behind the day-to-day operations of commerce lay this persistent lobbying and the ambition of being raised above others by the extended hand of royal favour.

By 1743 the fortunes of Dugard and Company had reached their zenith. The company's investment in trade was enormous both in Canada and the West Indies. Drafting a letter to Dugard for the signature of Maurepas, someone in the naval ministry was sufficiently enthusiastic to write that, "Satisfied with your zeal, I will gladly give you the help that I can in occasions of need."[102] But either clerk or minister prudently crossed out the sentence. At Quebec, Hocquart was equally appreciative of the company's efforts. In October he was forced to commandeer the crew of the *Centaure* to man the annual naval vessel, but he did everything in his power to help Havy and Lefebvre find replacements. His intention was "to favour a company that for fifteen years has maintained considerable enterprises useful to the Colony."[103]

Given these testimonials of governmental favour, it is surprising that the most coveted reward, the contract to supply the King's warehouse in Canada, should have escaped Dugard and Company. They were a serious contender for the award, but were ruled out by an old and seemingly defeated enemy, geography, and probably by the exigencies of Hocquart's system of clientage. The contract went to La Rochelle. As Hocquart explained, "Messrs. Pascaud would merit preference. They are in a better position than Monsieur Dugard to fulfill their engagements to the King to your satisfaction because of the proximity of La Rochelle to the Port of Rochefort and because of the relation that these traders must have with Monsieur de Ricouart" (Intendant of Rochefort).[104]

Failure to win the supply contract left little reason for optimism in the house on the market square. Business in Canada had been poor in 1743, as the misfortunes of agriculture reverberated through the economy. The prospect was equally dismal. The crops had failed for the third time. It now seemed certain that there would be a war between Great Britain and France, and both shipping and sealing stations would be exposed to privateers. But at least a crew had been patched together for the *Centaure*. On 5 November it finally set sail. François Havy was aboard, returning to France for the winter as either he or Lefebvre did from time to time.[105] As Jean Lefebvre watched the *Centaure* diminish and then disappear beyond Pointe Lévis, he was perhaps aware that he was witnessing the departure of the last merchantman of a long era of peace and commercial prosperity. He could not have foreseen that the war to come would be a turning point in the history of the colonial empire and in the destinies of private men like himself, Havy, and Robert Dugard.

CHAPTER SEVEN

Trade in the West Indies

I

In their hundreds the French ships of trade descended annually upon the islands of the French Antilles, a motley fleet ranging from 100 to 350 tons burden.[1] These "floating warehouses . . . enormous machines," as one government official called them, were built for capacity rather than for speed or manoeuvrability. The buffeting of heavy seas sent many of them to the bottom in spite of the best efforts of their crews, and condemned the remainder to short lives.[2] Outward voyages of between seven and nine weeks were usual for ships of the Dugard and Company fleet.[3] Their return voyages were longer, from seven to 12 weeks, and there is even record of a voyage of five months!

The ships arrived in the islands steadily from November through June; arrivals then dramatically dropped as the hot and humid south winds announced the season of the *hivernage*, culminating in the autumn hurricanes.[4] In a climate where provisions would not keep, the season of scarcity had already begun when the first winter ships arrived.[5] They received good prices, but were forced to wait several weeks for their return cargoes. Not until January were the first sugar canes ready to be cut and taken to the cattle- or wind-driven crushing mills.[6] A greater concentration of ships arrived in the spring, bringing the new wine of Bordeaux and finding return cargoes of sugar already waiting for them.

The trade winds carried the ships to the port of St. Pierre, Martinique. This first landfall on the route to America, thus described by Columbus,[7] was an open roadstead before the town a ship could enter and leave "by all winds and at all hours."[8] More than 10,000 people were crowded into St. Pierre, a parade of houses along the Martinique shore, one-third of a mile long by 100 feet wide.[9] Here was a seat of admiralty and the residence of the intendant, although the capital was some miles further down the coast at the bottom of the deep and safe harbour of Fort-Royal.

The whole trade of the lesser Antilles, the Iles du Vent, was centred at St. Pierre, where it was controlled by a caste of powerful merchants, known because of their modest origins as the *commissionnaires*, but who while being technically agents were the masters of the trade.[10] Planters from outlying islands such as Guadeloupe as well as those of Martinique were obliged to get their produce to St. Pierre themselves, but they were able to buy most of their supplies on credit at the *commissionnaires'* warehouses in all seasons. Metropolitan captains were spared considerable effort and their turn-around time was shortened. Pannié D'Orgeville, Intendant, 1728–38, found it difficult to see how either ship's captains or planters could do without the *commissionnaires*.[11] But to the Marquis de Caylus, the Governor from 1749–50, they were "a species of bloodsucker that swarms there that are called commission agents, avid fellows of bad faith."[12] Evidently, like most middlemen, they were at once disliked and found indispensable.

Charting a more northerly course to the younger colony of St. Domingue, the first French town encountered by a ship from Europe was Cap Français, or simply "le Cap." It was the scene of half the trade of the island, where on a single day there might be 60 or more ships in the harbour.[13] But the St. Domingue trade of Dugard and Company was concentrated in the remote, western part of the island at Léoganne, commercial centre of a wide region of fertile plains.[14] Here, in addition to the sugar of the great plantations, were to be found the cotton, tobacco, and slabs of smoked meat brought in by poor colonists descended from the buccaneers, and troops of cattle driven by Spaniards from their distant half of the island.[15] Like St. Pierre, Léoganne was built on an open roadstead, with no protection from hurricanes, pirates, or enemy ships.[16] It was set half a league back from the shore, and the transport of cargo across this torrid stretch of sand regularly caused the death of labourers. The proximity of rich plantations had made a trading town in this most inauspicious of places.

Dugard and Company was interested in the Caribbean trade from the year of the company's foundation. The *Louis Dauphin*'s voyage of 1730 had been triangular, from Le Havre to Quebec and Martinique, returning to Le Havre. But it was immediately apparent that this was as inefficient in practice as it was tempting in its logical simplicity. Canadian exports served two markets, one French, the other West Indian, and in both cases merchandise had to be brought to market as quickly as possible. By 1733 a more sophisticated plan had therefore been worked out whereby one ship made a direct passage between Le Havre and Quebec, and another followed a triangular route to Canada and Martinique via La Rochelle, where it loaded wine and other southern goods. Dugard desired, as much as any minister of marine, to knit together the Canadian and West Indian trades. To buy a bolt of cloth in Normandy, trade it for grain or cod in Canada, in turn trade this for sugar in the West Indies, and finally sell the sugar in Europe, thus making three successive profits on the initial investment—this was the dream of the French exporter. The problem was to make such exchanges in sufficient volume and at high enough prices that the profits were not exceeded by the high costs of long and complex voyages.

The ideal of triangular trade, on the evidence of the first voyage, was seen as part of the *raison d'être* of the company at the time of its formation. While it was never forgotten, the company soon became involved in the pursuit of the West Indies trade as an independent branch of commerce. The leasing of the *Louis Dauphin* and the *St. Mathieu* to freight sugar in 1733 and a similar lease of the *Ville de Québec* in 1734, all three expeditions carrying small cargoes or *pacotilles* for members of the company, were the first instances of this diversion.[17] The 1730s marked the company's apprenticeship in the Caribbean trade and were necessarily a decade of experimentation. It was characteristic of the company's voyages in the period 1735–38 that a given ship stopped both at St. Domingue and Martinique.[18] The company was without permanent links in either colony and conducted its trade in an interrogative fashion, probably stopping at ports not recorded, the sole rule being to seek markets wherever they could find them. Whenever possible, the same ship and the same captain were sent year after year to the same port, thereby establishing personal links and the reputation of the ship. The company's trade in the Caribbean was largely initiated by their senior captain, François Vangellikom Vandelle, aboard the *Ville de Québec*. Captain Mollard took the *Alçion* on its maiden voyage from Quebec to Léoganne in 1736; thereafter it returned annually to the same port.

The company would have found it considerably more difficult to establish themselves in this new trade were it not for the advice and

assistance of local commission agents. Raymond Lallement was for a
time their agent at Léoganne. The information he passed on to Robert
Dugard and the experience of trade at Léoganne were of crucial importance to the company's expansion of their West Indian trade in the
1740s.

Lallement insisted that ships must arrive as soon after the *hivernage*
as possible and disapproved of retarding arrival by visiting two desti-
nations.[19] He warned that cargoes should always be well assorted and
the merchandise of the latest fashion. As the arrival of a single ship
could decisively change market conditions, the shipper must always be
in receipt of recent *mémoires*, specifying needs at a given port. Having
an agent arrange a certain amount of return freight was a good precaution, as the returns from one's own outward cargo could not always be
collected in a reasonable time and other freight was sometimes hard to
find.

By 1739 Dugard had formulated a scheme by which he would keep
two or three ships in constant circulation between France and Léoganne, the company never being without a presence in the port.
"No better set-up," was Lallement's judgement.[20] He added that it
would be particularly advantageous if each departing captain passed
on the remains of his cargo to his successor so that the public would be
under the impression that it was new merchandise. Otherwise it would
be difficult to sell. The coming and going of company captains would
also facilitate the prompt dispatch of *mémoires* back to Rouen.

Dugard also asked Lallement's advice on the possibilities of the
trade between Canada and Léoganne. The latter judged that it might
be very profitable, as it apparently was at Martinique, but cautioned
that one ship of 120 to 150 tons would be adequate for this trade, that
it should come at the beginning of Lent with salmon, dried and green
cod, flour, and lumber, and that care should be taken that no other
ship was coming from Canada at the same time. Apparently, Dugard's
plan was to return such a ship to Canada or Ile Royale, for Lallement
added that the captain should bring along his own casks for a return
cargo of molasses and rum, commodities not carried to France.

In 1739, while Dugard and Lallement were exchanging corre-
spondence on these questions, the company had five ships in West
Indian waters, more than at any previous time. The *Louis Dauphin*
and the *St. Mathieu* had been sent to Martinique, the *Fleury* to
Guadeloupe, and the *Alçion* was making its customary visit to
Léoganne. One new ship on its maiden voyage from Quebec, the *St.
Louis*, visited St. Pierre. Thus while the company was maintaining its
trade at Léoganne, it was demonstrating an even greater interest in

Martinique and the Lesser Antilles. The only ready explanations for this are that Dugard and Lallement were already quarrelling, and that the trade at Léoganne had not answered expectations. In the next decade the trade to Léoganne was continued, but plans for its augmentation were dropped.

By the end of the 1730s Dugard and Company had developed a policy that was the basis for their West Indian trade in the following decade. It had been learned that ships should not be sent from island to island, but that individual captains and ships should build up clientele at particular points. Having chartered out their ships and dabbled in freight, the company still concentrated on carrying cargoes for their own account, although they were interested in ancillary freight. They determined to avoid the major colonial markets of Cap Français and St. Pierre and to seek the higher profits of out-of-the-way points such as Léoganne, where Lallement estimated profits at 20 per cent more than at Le Cap. Although commission agents had been invaluable allies and preceptors, the company was now resolved to do without them and to commit its cargoes solely to its captains, thereby saving the commissions. Dugard must therefore have believed that his own captains could provide the experience and shore contacts that were deemed an agent's principal assets. He was undoubtedly also swayed by a belief that his captains would prove to be more trustworthy stewards.[21] Finally, a plan of supply by a succession of ships with an appropriately scaled input of Canadian cargo had been formulated.

The resolution of the problem of triangular trade demands special comment. Two difficulties that prevented balancing the trade had always stood in the way. In the first place, Canada constituted a small market and could not absorb sufficient molasses and tafia to displace the English colonies in the trade with the French West Indies. By the same token, Canada constituted a small production unit and could provide neither the quantity of many foodstuffs required, the ships to carry it, nor the sailors to man the ships.[22]

The second problem regarded relative cargo volumes and values. A given volume of Canadian cargo was worth only about one-quarter as much as an equal volume of West Indian cargo. A Canadian exporter therefore had to "enrich" his outward cargo or return home with a shipload of ballast and the fear that the season's trade might not be worth the trip. By the 1730s, however, Louisbourg provided a way out of this difficulty. The West Indian market accepted only the finest flour, but coarse wheat, flour, and biscuit that were not to the taste of planters were perfectly suitable to the fisherman-soldier market of Louisbourg, where they were taken in exchange for dried cod. Thus as

Hocquart explained, "The trade of the islands with Canada can only be balanced by the shipments of flour and biscuit sent to Ile Royale to be converted there into cod that is sent to the islands or to France."[23]

In 1735, the *Louis Dauphin* made a shuttle voyage from Quebec to Louisbourg and back to Quebec before loading its return cargo for Le Havre. This is the company's first reported use of the port of Louisbourg. The purpose of the voyage is nowhere explained, but it may have been to explore the possibilities of trade at Louisbourg and to earn credits there in preparation for commercial operations in the following year. In 1736, the *Alçion* made its maiden voyage from Quebec to Léoganne, stopping at Louisbourg, becoming the first company ship to execute a triangular voyage including that port.[24] The company abandoned the West Indies trade in 1737; and when it resumed Caribbean voyages the following year, it provided for the Canada-West Indies connection by sending the *Louis Dauphin* from St. Pierre, Martinique to Quebec. But Louisbourg was not forgotten, and the *Ville de Québec*, under the command of the company's senior officer, François Vangellikom Vandelle, stopped there on both his outward and return journeys. Vandelle's mission was to find an agent who would take in hand the complex entrepôt business that the exchange of northern and southern cargoes entailed and leave substantial cargoes in his hands. His choice was Léon Fautoux, a young man from Bayonne who had become well established at Louisbourg and married into the prominent Lartigue family.[25] The port of Louisbourg at last became fully integrated into the company's trade. This new departure was the direct result of the company's decision to prosecute the West Indies trade in earnest.

The one triangular voyage of 1739 included Quebec as well as Louisbourg only because the Quebec-built *St. Louis* was used on its maiden voyage. From 1740 to 1743, the north-south link was executed by ships sailing from between Martinique and Louisbourg, while the northern connection was completed by ships sailing between Louisbourg and Quebec. In 1740, the *Imprévu* provided this service, shuttling back and forth until frozen fast in the ice at Kamouraska. The *Union* did duty in 1741. Havy and Lefebvre sent cargo aboard their own small ships, the *St. Charles* and *Marianne* in 1741; and in 1744, Fautoux bought the schooner *Eleanor* for the company together with its West Indian cargo and sent it to Quebec. Ships that were strangers to the company brought cargoes from Dugard in 1739 and 1740 while the *St. Louis* made a direct voyage from La Rochelle to Louisbourg and back in 1741. The most unusual voyage was that of the *Trois Maries*, which carried company cargo to Quebec in 1742 and on its return stopped at Louisbourg, where it loaded dried cod for Bilbao.

Without Fautoux, these complicated exchanges would have been impossible. Outgoing cargoes had to be ready for ships arriving on tight schedules. Incoming cargoes had to be stored. While the proceeds from their sale might not be realised for months, outgoing cargoes had to be paid for. As the trade between north and south never balanced, multilateral adjustments were made using the bill of exchange. Fautoux drew considerable sums on Dugard's debtors and made remittances to Dugard or his Bordeaux agents. By 1744, the entrepôt facilities of Louisbourg had enabled the company to perfect the integration of its Canadian and West Indian trade. But the last company ship to visit Louisbourg was the *Fleury*, sailing home from Canada in that year. The admirable system of interconnected sailings did not survive the capture of Louisbourg in 1745 and the War of the Austrian Succession.

There were two deficiencies of supply that the foundation of Louisbourg did nothing to improve. With regard to shipping horses to the Caribbean, a pet project of Maurepas, distance appears to have been the principal obstacle. Yet no one tried using Ile Royale as an entrepôt in this trade or as a site for horse ranches. The long voyage from Quebec, much of it against the spring northeast winds of the St. Lawrence, had a disastrous effect on the animals and occasioned enormous transport costs for fodder and fresh water.[26] It was difficult to protect the rest of the cargo from manure and urine. The minimal headroom between decks in any of the merchantmen of the time made it impossible to construct proper stalls on board. The horses had thus to be left lying down in the darkness of the hold for weeks at a time while the ship pitched and rolled to its island destination.[27] As an experiment, the *Alçion*, at 250 tons not a small ship, carried two or three horses in a hold only four and a half feet high on its maiden voyage. The horses died, and the company did not repeat the attempt.[28] Shippers in the English North American colonies had the advantage of much shorter sailing distances and times to the French West Indies. They were able to send horses on the main decks of their 90-ton vessels with a survival rate sufficient to maintain a profitable trade.

Entrepôt facilities were irrelevant to the solution of the second problem, the precariousness of the Canadian wheat economy. Although in good years Canada was capable of supplying a considerable quantity of grain for export, recurring bad harvests made it impossible to establish a regular supply of wheat and hence cod for which much of it was traded, or to acquire regular customers and a good reputation.[29] Even without Anglo–American competition, which the existence of Louisbourg also facilitated, the technical and volume deficiencies considered above made it impossible for Canada to fill its anticipated role in the French trading system. Havy and Lefebvre and Robert Dugard all concluded after many years of experience that the trade between Canada and the West Indies would remain marginal.[30] But if only ten of the company's 68 colonial voyages were triangular, this was over a quarter of the North American voyages. Because of the use of Louisbourg as an entrepôt, the importance of the Canada–West Indies trade is better expressed in terms of the number of voyages to the entrepôt. Louisbourg was a port of call for fully one-third of the company's North American sailings. In the period of the company's greatest activity, 1738–44, the proportion rises to 48 per cent.[31]

A remarkable phenomenon closely connected with the development of Dugard and Company's West Indian trade in the 1730s was its use of the port of Bordeaux. As described in chapter three, the first company ship to take on cargo at Bordeaux did so as part of an attempt to liberate the company's Canadian trade from the tutelage of the La Rochelle merchants, the company policy being "to draw the necessary merchandise . . . from its place of origin whenever possible."[32] The early triangular voyages and freight charters were all from Le Havre. But in 1735 and 1736 the *Ville de Québec* accomplished the company's only Caribbean voyages from Bordeaux. When the *Louis Dauphin* was committed to the sugar trade in 1738, replacing the *Ville de Québec*, which returned to the Le Havre–Quebec run, it too was sent via Bordeaux. But it returned from that voyage to Le Havre and made further West Indian voyages from there in 1740, 1741, and 1743. Between 1739 and 1741 the *Saint Mathieu* and the *Fleury*, having made outward voyages to the Caribbean from Le Havre, to which they had brought Canadian cargoes, were returned instead to Bordeaux, sent again to the islands, but ultimately returned to Le Havre.[33] In the period 1735–39 the company thus showed a special but shortlived predilection for Bordeaux. Of the 11 West Indian voyages begun between 1741 and 1743 inclusive however, only two began at Bordeaux, one of these returning to Le Havre and the other ending in shipwreck.

One possible explanation for the company's attraction to Bordeaux is that it was there that they loaded flour and wine, among the bulkiest constituents of their cargoes.[34] Wine was also liable to considerable damage in transshipping. But Bordeaux's advantage in this regard was probably offset by the fact that the greatest constituent of many

cargoes by weight and volume was Irish salt beef, another bulky commodity that was more cheaply delivered to northern ports. That the
voyages of the *Alçion* to Léoganne, a market requiring little or no salt
beef, continued to be sent from Bordeaux, gives some weight to an
explanation in terms of cargo.

Another possible explanation is that there were well-established
marketing facilities for sugar at Bordeaux. The shift back to Le
Havre–Honfleur in 1740 could be regarded as indicative of the development of the necessary knowledge and connections for sugar marketing. Viewed in this way, it would constitute a parallel to the company's emancipation from La Rochelle in its trade to Canada. This is a
plausible explanation in the light of the histories of the port of Bordeaux and the port complex Le Havre–Honfleur–Rouen. The former
began the spectacular development of its colonial trade in the time of
the Regency, whereas the latter became conspicuous in the Caribbean
only about 1736. They thus caught the second wave in the revitaliza-
tion of French colonial trade, Bordeaux having caught the first, the
two separated by the trough of the late 1720s and early 1730s.[35]

II

Throughout the 1730s Dugard and Company's investment in the West
Indian trade equalled only a fraction of its investment in the trade to
Canada. But it was a trade that was growing—from about 22,000
livres in 1733 to nearly 140,000 livres in 1739. Profits declined percep-
tibly over the period, but the island trade was known to be one of ups
and downs. Its profit range of ten to 56 per cent was still better than
that of the Canadian trade. The company was so confident in the
prospects of the new trade that in 1740 it nearly trebled its Caribbean
investment; it was a decisive reorientation.

Dugard and Company's island trade reached its apogee in 1742–43.
The arrangements of those years constitute its trading system at its
most mature. The *Alçion* continued its annual voyages to Léoganne,
but each year three ships were sent to Martinique from France on a
staggered schedule, while a fourth arrived on the triangular route from
Louisbourg. One of the ships sent out in 1742, the *Imprévû*, avoided
the entrepôt of St. Pierre and anchored instead at Cul de Sac Marin, a
harbour little used since the rise of the *commissionnaires* of St. Pierre
to a position of power, but one that provided access to a flourishing
agricultural region. Here was a market distant from competitors that
was to Dugard's liking. It is therefore not surprising that in 1743 all

the company ships destined for Martinique sailed directly to Cul de Sac Marin.[36]

In February or March the *Louis Dauphin* left Honfleur; the *St. Louis* sailed from Le Havre bound for Louisbourg. The *Imprévû* did not sail until the end of May, and the *St. Mathieu* until near the end of August. "The intention of our company," Dugard explained to Captain Renault of the *Imprévû*, "is to establish our trade at Cul de Sac Marin on a firm and stable footing."[37] There would be no interruption in the trade at Bourg Marin.[38] Since there was some doubt as to the amount of merchandise that the quarter could absorb, Dugard allowed that in the case of market saturation, excess cargo could be sold at St. Pierre and Fort Royal.[39] Captain La Roche Couvert of the *St. Louis* had been instructed that Léon Fautoux would have a cargo of cod ready for him when he reached Louisbourg. La Roche Couvert was expected to take this cargo to Bourg Marin with all possible speed, consign it to whatever company captain was there, return to Louisbourg with molasses and rum, and trade it for marine oil to be carried home to Le Havre.[40] As was often the case with shuttle voyages, the ship could not meet the breathless schedule; the second voyage to Louisbourg had to be omitted.

By trading at Bourg Marin, Dugard not only anticipated less competition and higher profits, but also circumvented and thereby challenged the *commissionnaires* of St. Pierre. He thus cautioned Captain Renault to remember that "Messrs. the commission agents of St. Pierre, not being favourable towards our enterprise, he must be careful to whom at St. Pierre he addresses the letters he will send me by that way."[41] If the company earned disfavour in one quarter, it apparently derived protection from another. The commander at Bourg Marin, a Monsieur Nadeau, supported their project. "He appears to me a gallant man, he must be suitably managed," Dugard wrote of him. "He uses his authority to make the inhabitants pay."[42]

The captains at Bourg Marin were expected to push their sales so that the greater part of their cargoes would be sold before the next company ship arrived in port.[43] They were not to reveal that they were expecting subsequent ships, as this would retard sales, the planters becoming less anxious to buy in their anticipation of abundance. Captains had little manoeuverability with regard to their selection of returns. As they dealt directly with planters, they were confined by a system of barter. They did control the make-up of their return cargoes, within limits, being guided by current demand in France. Cotton was considered the best return, but it was so much in demand that it had to be paid for in cash, an exception to the barter system. Coffee was overpriced. Semi-refined sugars were preferable to raw sugars because they had better value to volume ratios and the ships sent to Bourg Marin were small.

Each captain did everything in his power, including advancing money, to ease the departure of his predecessor. Whoever remained behind took over the remaining cargo of the departing ship and the pursuit of the cargo debtors. There was to be no possibility of captains competing with each other, something Dugard must have had in mind while penning repeated injunctions that they should work together. They were all expected to write to him as often as possible and to maintain a steady stream of informative *mémoires* arriving at the house on the Rue des Charettes.

Dugard was following the custom of the Caribbean trade in consigning his ships' cargoes to their captains. Indeed, Richard Pares quotes a New England shipper's complaint, "It is now call'd sneaking to consign a sloop to any but the M[aste]rs." [44] In spite of its orthodoxy, the system did not fully satisfy Dugard. In 1744 he solved the problem of combining trustworthiness with local experience and continuity by instructing Captain Fremont of the *Union*, bound for St. Pierre, to remain on the island and send the ship home under command of the first mate. At the same time he wrote to Captain Renault, who was already at Bourg Marin, that he should similarly remain there while sending the *Imprévû* home. [45]

The accounts kept by Renault during his long sojourn at Bourg Marin give some impression of the daily life and work of the ship's officers, who constituted the local sales force. [46] After seeing to the inevitable repairs to the ship and the hospitalization of some of the crew, their next concern was to rent a warehouse and to stock it with a few chairs and a keg of beer. A cabin boy acted as watchman, and he and a rented Negro slave took care of errands and light duties. The ship's company kept their own chickens and appear to have eaten together.

The most frequently encountered expense in the account is for travel. Officers made frequent trips to the countryside, buying, selling, and collecting debts. Visits to St. Pierre and Fort-Royal were essential both for strictly commercial purposes, such as conferring with Captain Fremont or attending the interrogation of cargo debtors by the Governor, and for the filing of declarations and the payment of duties.

Once the *Imprévû* had left Cul de Sac Marin, Captain Renault found room and board in the bourg and rented a less spacious warehouse that was adequate to shelter the remains of the half dozen cargoes left in his care. From 10 September 1743 until 31 August

1748, he rented a horse to facilitate his long journeys for the recovery of debts. As return cargo collected, he freighted it back to France on whatever ship was available. Renault remained in the company's service at Martinique until 8 October 1748, when he accepted command of a ship then at St. Pierre named the *Aimable Raechal*.

Captain Fremont's accounts tell a slightly different story, as the conditions of trade at St. Pierre were different from those at Cul de Sac Marin.[47] Travel was not so important to him, as most of his business was done in the town. It is interesting to note that the only way he was able to obtain a warehouse in that busy centre was by buying the remaining stock of another captain, thus freeing the building he was using. Fremont did not leave St. Pierre until 8 January 1747, a little less than two years before Renault's departure from Cul de Sac Marin.

The determination of prices was a source of constant complaint from captains and planters alike. Once ensconced in his warehouse, the captain posted a list of his cargo on the door, then sales began.[48] Prices of French cargo and colonial produce were determined by the market. The numbers of ships involved in the island trade increased throughout the period, lowering the prices of European goods and raising those of colonial produce. It was a trend already apparent in 1729.[49] The planters were able to profit from the competition of captains just as the French often enough profited from local scarcity and even famine.

If the captain was the first to part with his goods, he received the planter's note payable in sugar or other produce. But when the sugar was made, cured, and presented in payment, it was the Creole seller who stated its price, the opposite of the practice prevailing in Canada.[50] A captain who had arrived early and sold his cargo before the sugar crop was in, might lose the benefit of his scarcity profits if the price of sugar turned out to be high. On the other hand, if he waited until the price of sugar had been determined, or if he did not arrive before that time, he lost the advantage of higher November-December prices and found himself competing with other captains for return cargo, having no special claim to anyone's sugar. It was a difficult business, particularly in the larger centres.

From 1736, it was required by law at Martinique that buyer and seller agree on the price of finest quality sugar at the time of their transaction, leaving the price of the actual product to be estimated in terms of this standard by themselves or by arbiters.[51] Martinique practice, with every grade of sugar having its own price, was looked upon as a model by administrators in the more recently settled and more chaotic colony of St. Domingue. There all sugar sold at the same price, no matter what its quality.[52] That French traders tolerated this is evidence of the strong position of the seller of sugar, both in the islands and in Europe.[53]

As was the case in Canada, the market mechanism did establish a fairly uniform price at a given time and place. De Fayet, Intendant of St. Domingue in 1734, wrote of a formal "opening of sugar prices" at Léoganne by an assembly of merchants and planters. As ill health prevented him from presiding over the meeting, he was represented by subaltern officers who used their influence to keep the price of sugar high. They were themselves married to Creoles and were beginning to identify their interests with those of the island community.

In their own effort to keep profits up, the captains and commission agents sold their merchandise at different prices, depending upon the means of payment—in money, in notes payable in money, and in notes payable in produce. They even had a special price for produce given in payment for old debts. The Intendant of Martinique was shocked by this price variation, which was as much as 40 per cent on some items, although it could be argued that this represented the longer delay or the greater expenses in realizing profits when payment was not in cash.[54]

Mingled with complaints about price were those concerning fraud in weights, measures, and qualities. French merchants were said to cheat on all weights and measures and to send substandard merchandise to the islands.[55] Even as late as 1742, when many flagrant abuses had been overcome and the bargaining position of the planter was considerable, the Governor and Intendant of St. Domingue were able to complain that barrels of flour and beef often contained a quarter less than their supposed weight and that "l'avarice provençale" had produced an olive oil flask that held only one-half of what it appeared to hold.[56] Creoles were equally susceptible to temptation. According to a memorialist, in the New World "infidelity and bad faith are, it is said, contagious."[57] Only the planters had scales to weigh their sugar barrels—which were of all different shapes and sizes—and their declarations had to be accepted.[58] Furthermore, some planters were not above wetting their cotton, which increased its weight but ultimately caused it to heat and rot.[59] Although the collected correspondence of the colonial governors and intendants fairly bristles with projects to regulate the determination of prices and the accuracy of measures, little was accomplished. In spite of warm recommendation from the scene of action, the close regulation of commerce was gradually falling into disfavour in Paris, where reform was coming to be seen in terms of *laisser-faire*. In any case, it was a task quite beyond the organizational capacity of the absolute mercantilist state in even its most ardent phase.[60]

Almost every transaction of maritime commerce was burdened and slowed by the barnacles of colonial indebtedness. Not surprisingly, it was a question that particularly exercised Robert Dugard. His captains were always cautioned to find solvent buyers and to report to each other on the solvency of potential customers. Accepting lower prices or failing to sell at all were, he thought, preferable to acquiring suspect debtors. On one occasion he suggested that the captains should reverse roles with the planters if possible and make the company debtor, purchasing their return cargoes before providing the planters with merchandise.[61] The company's system, which may not have been representative of French methods in general, was thus strikingly unlike that of the British, which tended to encourage Caribbean debt. In the British system, debts that the planters could scarcely hope to make good tied them more or less permanently to their London or Bristol factors.[62] But if Dugard intended to put his trade on a stable footing, he was also concerned not to lose the initiative and find himself tied to a given trade. The company was to be maintained "in a state to be able to leave this trade if the advantage drawn from it does not merit its conservation."[63]

In dealing with their debtors, Dugard and Company as well as other metropolitan traders were very much dependent upon colonial officials. In the case of officials who were themselves Creoles or who had married into local families, the exporters were, rather, at their mercy. Obtaining judgements favourable to creditors from courts staffed by Creoles was generally regarded as unlikely: "It is in this circumstance that the aunt, the nephew and the cousin intervene so that hard justice is not done."[64] According to a *règlement* of 12 January 1717, which applied to Canada as well as the West Indies, debts arising from the purchase of ships' cargoes were of Admiralty jurisdiction. The *règlement* empowered Admiralty courts to judge cases summarily, order execution although an appeal was filed, order the judicial sale of a debtor's assets and even his imprisonment. In some cases provisional execution in advance of a final judgement was allowed provided the plaintiff posted bond. But the relevant clause referred to ships "ready to sail," leaving in doubt jurisdiction over the cargo debts of departed ships. The loophole was crucial because if jurisdiction over these debts were transferred to ordinary courts, shippers would lose the advantage of speedy remedies. At Martinique, where practice was more regular than at St. Domingue, this second category of cargo debts was regarded as of Admiralty jurisdiction; but if the formal legal claim had been drawn up after the ship had set sail, the creditor's right to summary proceedings was somewhat curtailed.[65]

A declaration of 12 June 1745, confirmed that the cargo debts of departed ships were of Admiralty jurisdiction and that summary proceedings were to be applied to their full extent after a ship's departure. At St. Domingue claims filed after a ship's departure had hitherto been considered within the jurisdiction of the ordinary courts, which the merchants of La Rochelle pointed out "opens a vast scope to debtors of bad faith."[66] They sighed for the simpler proceedings of earlier times, when in a "brief and natural way" the colonial officials simply forced planters to pay their debts. Scope for the use of force was limited by the immunity of land and slaves from seizure. Intendant D'Orgeville of Martinique, a true man of the robe, noted his distaste for such "brief and natural" justice in a memorandom of 1735. Executive action was quick and efficient, he observed, but it had not the sound rules and limits of the courts. In a colony, far from central control, it could be dangerous. As a result of his own reforms, he and the commandants limited their use of authority to "lending a helping hand to justice, to conciliate parties without doing them violence."[67]

D'Orgeville probably set the pattern for his successors, although the question cannot be regarded as settled. Certainly, especially if judged from the rather spotty result, an appearance of Captain Renault's debtors before the Governor to explain themselves, mentioned in Renault's accounts, must have been the occasion for paternal harangues rather than threats of violence.[68] In 1751, eight years after Renault had first taken the *Imprévû* to Cul de Sac Marin, he wrote Dugard from Le Havre that Commandant Nadeau was going to make the old debtors pay, having received orders from the Governor.[69] But even as late as 1763, 20 years after the *Imprévû*'s voyage, Dugard received a bale of cotton from a debtor. All the others, his agent reported, were insolvent.[70]

The experience of Dugard and Company confirms the accepted notion of the planter as being heavily burdened with debt. But as D'Orgeville explained, "These debts do not result from their luxury or foolish expenses, it is the cost of their plantations that they owe."[71] The causes of French colonial indebtedness cannot therefore have been very different from those ascribed to English planters by Richard Pares, the foremost being the advances made them for the purchases of their plantations and slaves.[72] Although Dugard and Company did not lend, it sold to customers already burdened with an overhead of debt. Ultimately, the company wrote off a debt of more than 66,000 livres in the Caribbean. Given the overhead problem of the plantation economy, it did well to lose so little. But the situation compares unfavourably with the record of the company's trade to Quebec.

In the trade to the French sugar islands, no single company could claim the pre-eminence that belonged to houses such as Dugard and Company or Pascaud Frères in the trade to Canada. To attempt to calculate the company's exact share in the Caribbean trade would be to perform an Herculean task with a result as unimpressive as it would be inaccurate.[73] The magnitude of the company's island trade may best be appreciated by comparing it with its Canadian trade.

From being a mere speculation in the earlier 1730s, the island trade accounted for an outlay of 138,721 livres in 1739, about a quarter of the total outlay of that year. In 1740 it shot up to 43½ per cent; it sagged a little in 1742, but climbed to a commanding 61 per cent the year after. In 1743 the two trades were even, Caribbean trade being 404,783 livres or just above 49 per cent of the total. The early 1740s were therefore a time of major reorientation in the company's trade as sugar came to equal, and for a time to surpass, the importance of fur.

The ships and captains of Dugard and Company became familiar names at St. Pierre, Cul de Sac Marin, and Léoganne. The company was sharing in a period of great prosperity for the French empire as a whole. But imperial prosperity was as much a political phenomenon as an economic one, and the colonial foundations of the commercial economy, which had been fostered and protected by political means, were to be rudely shaken by them. When Robert Dugard sent the *Union* to Martinique at the end of January 1744, he warned Captain Fremont of the critical state of affairs in Europe. At first, Dugard warned, Fremont should not push his sales. Should a war break out between France and England, "the inhabitants would be obliged to buy everything at very high prices."[74] His own estimate was that the outcome should be known in about two months.

III

The level of profits on outward cargoes sold in Canada was considered in chapter six. Caribbean profits and those on cargoes in return, both from Canada and the West Indies, now require the same attention. There is difficulty in comparing prices from voyages to different locations on two islands where market conditions were seldom alike. There was necessarily less uniformity of prices than in Canada, where

TABLE 12.
Sale of Outward Cargo, Alçion *to Léoganne and Region,* 1742–43

Class of Merchandise	Bought in France (*tournois*)	Sold (*tournois*)	Per cent Profit
Common textiles	11764	17920	52.3
Finer textiles	8987	12464	37.5
Fancy textiles, mercery, and clothes	10193	15236	49.4
Hats	1136	1663	46.4
"Hardware" incl. glass	2028	2751	35.6
Provisions	18573	24094	29.7
Wine and spirits	11327	17106	51.0
Totals	64008	91234	42.5

Source: AN, 62AQ44, *Alçion* à Léoganne, Aller et Retour, 1742–43, original invoices and sales account.

all trade centred at Quebec. A second problem, that the typical and the extraordinary cannot be separated without the aid of long chronological series of prices, is particularly acute because of the known annual variation in the Caribbean trade. The calculation of profits is further complicated by the exchange rate between the livre *tournois* and the livre *argent des îles*.

In an effort to attract specie to the colonies, the Creoles had 1⅓ livres of their money declared the equivalent of a single livre *tournois*. That is, the livre *argent des îles* was devalued; it corresponded to a smaller amount of silver than did the French livre. This was not then clearly understood, and the contemporary belief was that silver was being given a higher price in the colonies. But it was silver that gave value to the livre and not the livre that gave value to silver. Devaluation was as ineffective a measure as it was misguided; prices of French goods were simply raised to take it into account. It could do nothing to stop the flight of specie, a phenomenon related to the perennial colonial problem of the balance of payments.

Devaluation itself would not be an obstacle to research, but the livre *argent des îles* also suffered considerable depreciation as the years went by, and the depreciated value is difficult to establish for any given year. According to R. Richard, the livre *tournois* was worth 50 per cent more than the livre *argent des îles* as early as 1749, that is, conversion of the colonial currency to French currency entailed a loss of one-third. This is also the value assigned to West Indian currency by

TABLE 13.
Sale of Outward Cargo, Imprévû *to Cul de Sac Marin,* 1743

Class of Merchandise	Bought in France (*tournois*)	Sold (*tournois*)	Per cent Profit
Fancy textiles, mercery, and clothes	7863	13049	66
"Hardware"	1646	3379	105
Provisions	22165	42572	92
Wines and spirits	4493	9056	102
Totals	36167	68056	88

Source: AN, 62AQ43, *Imprévû* à Cul de Sac Marin, Martinique, 1743, original invoices and sales account. All original invoices for common and many better textiles are missing, but the above represents 82 per cent of sales.

the Bordeaux merchant Samuel Ricard in his *Traité général du Commerce* (Amsterdam, 1781).[75]

The Dugard Papers do not provide a consistent aye or nay to any exchange rate. For the year 1744 alone, the accounts of the *St. Mathieu* and the *Imprévû* provide depreciations of 15½, 20, and 25 per cent, this last the official rate. Richard and Ricard's rate is first mentioned in a letter of 1754, while in 1751 Robert Dugard twice used a depreciation of 30 per cent, in one instance correcting Captain Renault's figures based on the official rate.[76] A remarkable promissory note provides the best insight into these variations, linking them to the balance of payments by referring to a sum owed in Martinique currency, "which sum will be evaluated in France according to the losses or profit that will have been made on the returns of American produce in France. ...."[77] It is also possible that specific exchange rates included dissimulated interest or favours and that there was a lag between the bill market and the reckoning of exchange in merchandise transactions. It would thus seem the safest policy to calculate in terms of the official rate. However, the marked difference of the two rates quoted in 1751 and 1754 would seem to confirm Richard's view that circa 1749–50 was a dividing point, after which the livre *argent des îles* underwent a more considerable depreciation. Because of this, for the years after 1749, Robert Dugard's depreciation rate of 30 per cent has been used.

Tables 12 and 13 show the costs of purchasing the cargoes for the *Alçion* in 1742 and the *Imprévû* in 1743, the prices at which the cargoes were sold converted to *tournois* at the official rate, and the per cent profit on different classes of merchandise.[78] The wide divergence of profit in the two sales is remarkable—42.4 per cent for the *Alçion* and 88 per cent for the *Imprévû*. The sales were on two different islands, but both were in similarly out-of-the-way places and took place within one year of each other. It is unlikely that the *Imprévû*'s higher profit level was greatly affected by impending war, because no such price rise can be detected in sales in Canada in 1743. The difference in prices probably resulted at least in part from Dugard and Company's monopoly at Cul de Sac Marin, Martinique, but it is difficult to estimate the importance of this factor.

The breakdown of prices and profits for selected commodities (table 14) shows that certain items of the *Alçion*'s cargo were obtained at very high prices.[79] In these cases, *Alçion*'s profit margin was considerably narrowed. It appears that increases in French prices could not always be reflected in the price of the sale of cargo; there is much greater uniformity in the sale price of wine, for example, than in its original purchase price.

The effect of war on prices can be appreciated to some extent by comparing the profits of the *Imprévû* in 1743, with those of the *Union* at St. Pierre in 1744 and 1746. The price ranges from the sale of the *Imprévû*'s beef and flour represent a low price when the ship first arrived and commodities were abundant and a higher price as the months passed and the two perishables became more and more scarce. The *Union* arrived at St. Pierre on 23 March 1744, in expectation, as Robert Dugard suggested, of gouging the planters. However, the ship came in convoy, and the result of convoys was that a very great amount of merchandise arrived simultaneously. Thus the early sales of the *Union* were at rather low prices, and only with the passage of time did prices of beef and Nérac flour reflect the impact of scarcity. The scanty evidence provided by the sale of the *Union*'s next and atypical cargo (mostly bricks and slates) in 1746, the middle of the war, shows that by that time the colony was under much greater stress, with profits of 112 and 110.6 per cent earned on flour and cloth respectively. There is no evidence here of the astronomical profits sometimes reported by colonial officials. The price of beef at St. Pierre quoted by Champigny in November 1744, as 450 livres the *baril* must have been most exceptional and short-lived, marking a hiatus between the substantial sale of the pre-hurricane cargoes of 1744 and the arrival of new cargoes in 1745.[80] Such profits would accrue to local speculators, an earlier sale and speedy return to France before the hurricanes struck being the rule amongst captains responsible for expensive crew rolls and hulls rapidly perishing in tropical waters.

TABLE 14.

Profits on Selected Commodities: Beef, Flour, Red Wine, Kettles, Toiles, 1742–46

Voyage	Beef (livres per *baril*)				Flour, Norman (livres per *baril*)			
	A	B	C	D	A	B	C	D
ALÇION (Léoganne, 1742)	45+	av. 54.4	40.8	−9.3	—	—		—
IMPRÉVÛ (Cul de Sac Marin, 1743)	26.3#	60–80 av. 79.3	av. 59.2	125.4	16.3	—		—
UNION (St. Pierre, 1744)	28.7#	Early sales 56–60 av. 57 — Later sales 70–105 av. 82	42.75 — 61.50	48.9 — 115.2	16.28	35–38 av. 35.8	26.85	64.
UNION (St. Pierre, 1746)	—	—	—	—	—	—	—	—

Legend

A Purchase Price (*tournois*); B Selling Price (*argent des îles*); C Selling Price (*tournois*); D Per cent Profit; + French beef; # Irish beef.

Sources: In addition to sources of Tables 12 and 13, invoices and sales accounts of *Union*, 1744 and 1746, AN, 62AQ42.

In the inter-war period 1749–56, profits at Martinique never fell to the level of profits in Canada or to the level of those of the *Alçion*'s voyage to St. Domingue in 1742, perhaps suggesting that they never had been so low. In 1750, the *Astrée* sold a cargo of French merchandise for a profit of 82 per cent, and the cargoes of the *Centaure* in 1754 and 1756 yielded profits of 54 and 77 per cent respectively, all computed on the basis of the more greatly depreciated colonial livre.[81]

There are two good examples in the Dugard Papers of the sale of Canadian or Louisbourg cargoes at Martinique. The *St. Louis* in 1743 sold its cargo for a profit of 143 per cent (*argent des îles* depreciated by 25 per cent) and the *Astrée* in 1749–51 sold its northern cargo for a profit of 307 per cent (*argent des îles* depreciated by 30 per cent).[82] These extraordinary profits, especially surprising in view of much

our, Nérac (livres per *baril*)				Red Wine, Bordeaux (livres per *barique*)			
A	B	C	D	A	B	C	D
7.17	48.8	36.6	34.7	70.4	av. 142.7	107	52
3.1	45–55	38.2	65.3	45.77	150	112.5	140.5
4.6	48–91.5	39.53	60.6	64.75	150	112.5	73.7
our, Saumur (*le baril*)							
v.	36–48	27.45	112.1	—	—	—	—
9.94	av. 36.6						

lower profits on French cargo, resulted primarily from the sale of wood, although cheap Canadian flour also made a good profit, underscoring the point that the small proportions of Canadian-Caribbean trade did not result from want of a West Indian market. It is nevertheless possible that these profits were exceptional and due to momentary lapses in the trade with the English North American colonists.

The most remarkable thing about profits on outward cargoes as revealed by these few data is their low level. They do not correspond very well with the notion of colonial, and especially West Indian, traffic as the agency by which such ports as Le Havre, Nantes, and Bordeaux achieved a gilded prosperity by the mid-eighteenth century. This raises the question of whether the sale of return cargo, both from Canada and the West Indies, netted profits sufficient to eclipse the im-

TABLE 14. (*continued*)
Profits on Selected Commodities: Beef, Flour, Red Wine, Kettles, Toiles,
1742–46

Voyage	Kettles (sols each)				Toile, Vitré			
	A	B	C	D	A	B	C	D
ALÇION (Léoganne, 1742)	15	av. 39.8	29.85	99	pièce 51.61 (10s/au.)	pièce 87	65.25	26.4
IMPRÉVÛ (Cul de Sac Marin, 1743)	13.1	av. 41.9	31.43	139	?	22.3–24s av. 22.8s per au.	17.1s	?
UNION (St. Pierre, 1744)	13.7	av. 44.3	33.2	142	13.5s/au.	22.3–28s av. 26.6s per au.	20s	48.1
UNION (St. Pierre, 1746)	—	—	—	—	—	—	—	—

portance of the outward cargoes, as is said to have been true of the
British sugar trade.[83]

Table 15 shows the profits yielded by the return cargoes, or portions
thereof, of six voyages to the West Indies and one to Canada. The
figures for profits on gross sales are comparable to the percentages in
tables 12, 13, and 14. The *Union*'s profit on colonial produce is much
superior to the very good profits realized by the outward cargo. The
gross profit on furs is superior to that of the outward cargo to Canada
in 1743 (40 per cent compared to an estimated 33 per cent); but high
costs, including stiff taxes, reduce this considerably. In all other cases,
profits are less impressive than those on French merchandise sold in
the colonies. Evidently, profits on outward cargoes were just as important as those on return cargoes.

oile, St. George			
A	B	C	D
—	—	—	—
	34s/au.	?	?
v. 7.15s	30–40s/au.	27.75	61.8
7s	46–50s/au. av. 47.7	35.8	110.6

The papers of the *Union*'s voyage to Martinique in 1744 are sufficiently complete to permit an accurate comparison of the value of an outward cargo to all the costs incurred in sending the cargo to the colony, selling it, and disposing of the return cargo. The data are shown in table 16. Costs equal 80 per cent of the value of the outward cargo. It follows that a profit of 80 per cent was necessary for the venture to break even and that a reasonable profit of 15 per cent could only be made if overall gross profits were 95 per cent of the value of the initial cargo. Given the information in tables 12 to 15 such a profit level could usually have been reached only in two steps, by earning reasonable profits on the outward cargo sold in the colony *and* on the return cargo sold in Europe. Table 17 shows a number of combinations of profits that would have produced a net return of 15 per cent

TABLE 15.

Profits on Return Cargoes, 1742–55

Year	Cargo	Cost FOB†	Gross Sale	% Profit	Net Sale	% Profit
1. *Voyage of the* Alçion *to Léoganne, 1742–43*						
1743	cargo via					
	Le Triton	33171	42537	28	39680	20
	L'Utile	19817	22339	13	19908	0.4
	Le Victoire	865	1583	83	1205	40
	Le Catherine	6220	8175	31	7146	14
	Le Vigilant	3328	3340	0.3	3050	−8
	Totals	63401		22	70989	12
2. *The Fourteenth Cargo to Canada*						
1743	Furs	13741	19289	40	17454	27
	Oil	87593	?	?	111764	27
3. *Voyage of the* Union *to Martinique, 1744–45*						
1745		87267	217541	138	199748	129
4. *Voyage of the* Astrée *to Quebec and Martinique, 1749–51*						
1751	Sugar	13524	19681	45		
	Sugar	3467	4120	18		
5. *Three Voyages of the* Centaure *to Martinique, 1750–55*						
1750–51	Cotton	31504	38961	23		
	Sugar	4018	6035	50		
1752–53	Sugar	22938	23889	4		
	Coffee	4540	5492	21		
1754–55	Sugar	44310	67509	52		
	Coffee	10868	13347	23		

†West Indian prices are reduced by 25 per cent before 1749 and 30 per cent thereafter.

Sources: Accounts of sales in voyage-in-return papers in AN, 62AQ41, 42, 43, 44.

for any voyage in which costs equalled 80 per cent of the outward cargo, as was the case with the *Union*'s voyage of 1744.

While all of these figures suggest that the *Union* made a very successful voyage to St. Pierre, amply fulfilling Robert Dugard's expectations, the voyage of 1744 in fact resulted in a deficit, as is shown in table 30 in appendix D. One reason for this was that a part of the outward cargo was burned in a warehouse fire at St. Pierre. But a more important reason was the burden of wartime insurance premiums. Omitted from table 16, which includes only premiums on insurance taken out before the declaration of war, these premiums are included in the costs in table 18, where it will be seen that they almost doubled the voyage costs. If the burned cargo, valued at roughly 11,000 livres and almost all textiles, had earned 60 per cent at Martinique and the return cargo purchased with this had netted 129 per cent in France, the result would have been to have increased earnings by 22,704 livres. This is still less than the voyage deficit of 31,363 livres. The high insurance premiums were thus a vital factor in rendering the voyage unprofitable. The burden of premiums can be presumed to have contributed significantly to the company's string of wartime deficits. Perhaps most French voyages between 1744 and 1748 were unprofitable. The merchants cannot be expected to have foreseen such a possibility, so remote had experience with wartime trading become by 1744.

There can be little doubt regarding the accuracy of the data upon which the above calculation of percentage profits is based. Figures are drawn from records of first instance—invoices from manufacturers, books of sales and purchases written by captains or their *écrivains*, and the accounts rendered by commission agents responsible for selling return cargo. The profits reflect the experience of a major trading company in the period 1742–55. It is most unlikely that the voyages considered were uniformly more or less profitable than those for which data are unavailable or that the experience of Dugard and Company was wildly at variance with that of other companies. The limitations imposed on these data are nevertheless very real. The profit levels of the 1730s cannot be inferred from them, the implication of the global profits recorded in table 30 in appendix D being that the earlier Caribbean voyages were more lucrative. Secondly, the calculation of profit on return cargoes from Canada is based exclusively on a portion of the fourteenth cargo. Thirdly, the typicality of profits on the two Canadian cargoes sold at Martinique is in doubt; and finally, the sole voyage of the *Alçion* in 1742 provides insufficient data for making valid generalizations regarding comparative profits at St. Domingue and Martinique.

The above data do suggest that profits in colonial trade were modest and that in extending research in this area historians should not expect to find exorbitant earnings. They confirm the modest level of profit recorded in Robert Dugard's final accounts and the interpretation given them in appendix D. The importance of both outward and return cargoes in earning these profits suggests that eighteenth-century merchants or twentieth-century historians who have held that with regard to profits "les retours gardent une place prépondérante" have been in error.[84] The data point to the conclusion that modest profits made often enough make poor men rich and rich men richer.

TABLE 16.
Cargo Versus Costs, The Union *to*
Martinique, 1744

Outward Cargo	115,639
Costs	
In France (out and ret.)	66,535
At Martinique (*tournois*)	22,660
Depreciation	3,816
Total Costs	93,011

Costs equal 80 per cent of value of outward cargo. Therefore, 80 per cent profit
on net sales is needed to break even, 95
per cent to net 15 per cent.

Source: AN, 62AQ42, Papiers de cargaison, l'*Union*
en retour de la Martinique, 1744–45.

TABLE 17.
*Possible Combinations of Profit on Outward and Return Cargoes
Yielding Net Profit of 15 Per Cent (Outward Cargo Equals 100)*

Outward Cg.	% Profit	Return Cargo	% Profit	Gross Profit
100	20	120	62	195
100	30	130	50	195
100	40	140	39	195
100	50	150	30	195

Source: AN, 62AQ42, Papiers de cargaison, l'*Union* en retour de la
Martinique, 1744–45.

TABLE 18.
The Impact of Wartime Insurance Premiums, The Union *to Martinique, 1744*

	Debit	Credit	
Outward Cargo	115,639	Sales of return cargo, net	199,748
Costs		Sale of cargo never sent	3,498
In France	66,535	Return freight	29,708
At Martinique	22,660	Insurance rebate	163
Depreciation	3,816	Estimate, sale of	
Additional Insur.		additional return	
premiums for return	82,886	shipment	27,056
	291,536	Total	260,173
		Debit to balance	31,363
			291,536

Source: AN, 62AQ42, Papiers de cargaison, l'*Union* en retour de la Martinique, 1744–45.

CHAPTER EIGHT

Destructions and Diversions

I

The war between France and England declared on 15 March 1744, transformed the orderly trade of the Atlantic into a lottery. If colonial prices for European merchandise and provisions were bound to rise to spectacular heights, it was also true that French shipping became a prey to the Royal Navy and English privateers. The company entered the war with a reduced fleet, the *Alçion* and the *Louis Dauphin* having been lost to heavy seas in 1743. The *St. Louis* and the *Centaure*, the latter stripped of its cannon by the Navy commissary,[1] were trapped in the channel port of Le Havre, where they were surprised by the declaration of war. The *Fleury* had been chartered out to the Compagnie des Indes and was bound for Senegal. The *St. Mathieu* and the *Imprévû* were still at Cul de Sac Marin, and the *Union* had just arrived at St. Pierre.

In spite of risk, the company felt compelled to keep its ships working. Being built of wood, they deteriorated rapidly, especially when left idle, and they earned nothing to offset this depreciation. Furthermore, no company, in particular one that leaned heavily on credit, could afford to leave a considerable investment idle in the colonies.[2] In 1744 the *Trois Maries*, a ship owned by Dugard, D'Haristoy, and some friends, was sent to Canada as it had been in 1743. It carried flour that the company had contracted to supply to the famished colony for the King's account.[3] The bulk of the fifteenth cargo was sent out on the *Andromède* and the *Sultanne*, two ships of La Rochelle. As the year approached its end, the anxious partners counted the days as they awaited the return of six ships across the dangerous sea lanes.

No sooner had news of the war reached the colonies than the prices of European goods rose sharply. For example, a barrel of beef that had probably been bought for less than 25 livres was said to be selling at St. Pierre for 450 livres.[4] But the price to the producer of West Indian sugar and indigo or Canadian furs was severely depressed because the selling price in Europe, which was not infinitely elastic, had to include wartime increases in freight and insurance. By August 1744, the price of sugar at St. Domingue had fallen from 26 livres 10 sols per quintal to 10 livres.[5] In Canada, many owners of furs simply set them aside for a better day—if they could afford to.[6] There the war was merely the capstone of a long succession of misfortunes. Three years of poor harvests had destroyed the provision trade with Louisbourg as well as the incipient hemp industry.[7] By the middle of the war, the mobilization of the Indians threw the fur trade into complete disarray.[8]

Havy and Lefebvre were cynically resigned to this disruption of their lives "for almost nothing." It was the way of princes.[9] The cargo they received from Dugard was pitifully small; apparently, high wartime prices were not seen as sufficient to offset the high risks of navigation and the derangement of the fur trade.[10] By the end of the trading season, three-quarters of the cargo remained unsold, and Havy and Lefebvre wrote Dugard that if the war continued, he should send no merchandise in 1745.[11]

The Department of Marine did its best to put French maritime commerce on a wartime footing. Peacetime regulations that had become a hindrance, the rule that ships bring their return cargoes to the ports from which they had set out and the time limit on the entrepôt of merchandise destined for the colonies, were suspended.[12] But the Ministry was woefully unprepared for the protection of merchant fleets and hampered by a niggardly budget. Two warships were sent to each of Martinique, St. Domingue, and Ile Royale to convoy back the merchantmen, small protection under the circumstances.[13]

On 3 December Captain Escallier brought the *Fleury* safe into the port of Lorient, but his fellow captains were less fortunate.[14] Three weeks later news arrived that the *Imprévû* had become separated from its convoy, captured, and taken to Exeter.[15] The partners had barely absorbed this blow when they learned of the sinking of the *Trois Maries*, which a violent storm had carried broadside into the stern of the Compagnie des Indes's much larger *Brillant*.[16] Three days later, it was reported that the *St. Mathieu*, like the *Imprévû*, was a prize in England.[17] There remained only the *Union*, which happily arrived at Nantes in March.[18]

The events of 1744–45 did not break the company's nerve. They were, as Guillaume France put it, "events more rare than one can say."[19] Thus in February 1745, they attempted to fill the gap left by captures by chartering the 160-ton *Thétis* to carry 560 barrels of Irish salt beef to Fort-Royal.[20] But misfortune followed misfortune. Early in June letters arrived from Captain Fremont and Captain Renault relating the destruction of merchandise worth more than 30,000 livres in a fire at St. Pierre.[21] The first letters of July revealed that the *Thétis* had been captured on its outward voyage. "We must be patient," France wrote to Dugard, "and offer this new loss to the Lord."[22]

The strain of war was also a financial calamity for the Department of Marine. The minimal protection of two or three ships for each convoy of merchantmen could only be financed by means of an agreement whereby the merchants taxed their incoming cargoes eight per cent and turned the money over to the Minister.[23] Maurepas's plans for the husbanding of his slender resources had been set awry by a revolt of the garrison of Louisbourg and the subsequent attack on the town by New England forces. The siege also halted Dugard's preparations to send a modest cargo to Canada, and for want of a safe escort it was left in the warehouses of La Rochelle.[24]

At least grain was abundant![25] Canadians entered the year 1745 apprehensive but without hunger. The *bénéfice* on French goods had, however, already risen to 60 per cent.[26] In spite of modest abundance, the cautious Hocquart refused permission for Havy and Lefebvre to send a schooner with provisions to Louisbourg as he feared its possible capture. Although greatly impatient of his paternal advice,[27] they too became less optimistic as the little community received no news from the outside world: "Nothing either from Ile Royale or France in spite of the N.E. wind that has blown for several days, however it begins to disquiet."[28]

The news of events at Ile Royale came in fragmented form. In June the grand battery at Louisbourg was reported captured, and a local captain named Lagroix brought back news in July that he had sailed within a league of the town under cover of fog and found it in a state of siege.[29] Toward the end of the month Abel Olivier, captain of Havy and Lefebvre's schooner, which had ultimately been permitted to sail, brought back the news of Louisbourg's surrender, having remained 21 days hidden in a nearby bay in order to know the outcome. Fear of an Anglo-American assault on Quebec ran through the population. Many merchants began baling up their goods in preparation for flight, an example Havy and Lefebvre refused to follow, believing, "The King will not thus abandon New France."[30]

By September, the *bénéfice* at Quebec had risen to 80 per cent, and

Hocquart was buying up all available dry goods for the King's account.[31] Even the wine found its way into royal storehouses, so much so that Havy and Lefebvre feared they would soon be reduced to drinking beer.[32] To Pierre Guy, they expressed their desire that the ships would soon arrive. Even though they might gain from high prices, they protested that "the general good is more to be hoped for than our own."[33] As early as the end of August, the invasion scare had been dissipated, and the merchants had unbaled their merchandise. The militia no longer mounted guard.[34] It was not the feared appearance of an English fleet that now caused concern, but the absence of a French one:

> A continuation of a fine wind from the N.E., the end of September and no news of ships, something that leads to no longer doubting that we will have none this year. This will do great harm to the Colony because almost everything will be wanting and we will remain without any news and nothing to drink but beer to pass the time.[35]

The dearth of shipping made 1745 a favourable time to launch the *Astrée*, which had long lain on the stocks for want of cargo.[36] The labours of outfitting it, finding a crew, and preparing its cargo sent Havy to his bed for several days.[37] But at last it was ready. A little flotilla sailed from Quebec with what protection a lonely frigate could give. The last ships, including the *Astrée*, left the harbour on Sunday, 14 November. "Finally," Havy and Lefebvre wrote, "here we are, prisoners without news from any side."[38]

By this time the first refugees from Louisbourg had begun to arrive in France, and among them was Léon Fautoux. Owed more than 5,000 livres by the company, he presented himself at Rouen, where he received a cash settlement, some company merchandise at Louisbourg, and all rights to the company's debts there.[39] No doubt all the partners agreed with Guillaume France that "this man is worthy of pity."[40]

The company still did not know whether the *Astrée* had been launched. As there was no way of finding out, the partners decided not to insure it, but to leave matters to take their own course. The letters of Guillaume France give the impression that he was exhausted by their attempts to prepare for all eventualities. After so many misfortunes, they deserved some luck. After all, he reasoned, "Life is a composite of good and evil that normally succeed each other."[41]

It was the third week in December before news was received that the *Astrée* was coming, and not more than two-thirds of the desired

160,000 livres in insurance was subscribed by the time Captain Olivier brought his ship, limping, without any masts and wildly off course, into the port of Roscoff on the coast of Brittany. Needed repairs were especially costly, and the cargo, mostly oil, was neither easy to sell nor profitable.[42]

"Fortunate are we that in our misfortune we are insured," Guillaume France wrote when he had first received word of the loss of the *Imprévû*.[43] Without adequate insurance the French ports could not have risked a single ship to the trade winds. In many European trading towns brokers simply brought the policies of their clients to the exchange, where they collected the signatures of sufficient insurers to provide the required sum. In other towns, of which one was Rouen, there were more reliable insurance companies, or chambers, the members of which were jointly and severally liable for policies they underwrote.[44] Over the years Robert Dugard belonged to four chambers each with 12 to 24 members, and there are references to the memberships of D'Haristoy, Laurens, Vincent, and the younger France as well.[45]

As insurance companies usually limited their liability for a single ship and cargo to 75,000 livres or even 30,000, several policies were usually necessary. The chances of obtaining enough insurance and of avoiding the risk of underwriters' bankruptcies were improved by making up the insurance for a single voyage in a number of towns, frequently including many outside France. For example, the return voyage of the *Union* from Martinique in 1745 was insured at Marseilles, Bayonne, La Rochelle, Nantes, St. Malo, Amsterdam, Cadiz, and Pantaleo, Italy. Nor did the company shrink from insuring in the enemy capital of London.[46]

Peacetime rates were reasonable, three and four per cent on the *Alçion* in 1742 and six per cent on the *Centaure* in 1743. Even in the midst of the war, rates were not high for the coasting trade, half of the *Astrée*'s cargo of oil being insured from Brittany to Amsterdam for three per cent. But rates for ocean-going voyages rose quickly and sharply. In April 1744, a month after the declaration of war, the *Trois Maries*'s voyage to Canada was insured at 16 per cent. In May and June, cargo on the *Andromède* could only find underwriters at 20 and 25 per cent. Policies on the ill-fated return voyages of the *Imprévû* and *St. Mathieu* ranged between 26 per cent and 36¾ per cent. Those underwritten between December 1744, and February 1745, for the return voyage of the *Union* from Martinique were mostly at 40 per cent, although two were at 30 and 30¼ per cent.

Rates at different centres are difficult to compare because of the varied terms offered. In the case of total loss, some policies specified payment of 98 per cent of insured value; others augmentation of the premium by five per cent. Although London rates are thought to have been generally lower, the policies in the Dugard Papers do not confirm this. The four English policies extant are higher than most others taken out on the same voyages in other cities. The rate on the *Union* from Martinique, 1745, was 3 6¾ per cent at London compared with 30 per cent at Marseilles and 34½ per cent at Cadiz. It was lower than the 40 per cent demanded at Amsterdam and in most French cities. Amsterdam, however, gave a ten per cent rebate for convoy, while London offered only five and a half per cent, making the premium actually paid at London in this case one and a quarter per cent higher than the Dutch premium. Insurance on the *Union*'s return in 1747, rate with convoy, was 16 per cent at London compared with 12 per cent at Nantes. But the French insurers exacted a further five per cent for prompt payment. The nominal *Nantais* rate on the return of the *St. Mathieu* in 1744 was also the lower, 26 per cent compared with London's 3 6¾ per cent. But the Nantes rate was augmented by one per cent because the ship left Martinique late and a further five per cent because the ship was taken. If a guarantee for prompt payment were exacted in 1744 as it was in 1747, then the French rate would have been one quarter per cent higher than the English. The comparison at the very least casts doubt on the notion that it was the cheapness of English insurance that drew foreign shippers to Lloyd's. The solidity of English insurers and their reputation for prompt payment were probably more important. Almost all of the company's insurance was in fact paid promptly, no matter from what city. As at Nantes, payment could often be guaranteed for one per cent. Ultimately, bankrupt underwriters, mostly from La Rochelle, left a debt to the company of 7,500 livres. But that is a very small percentage of the total amount insured. As explained in chapter seven, wartime insurance was nevertheless a heavy charge against a successfully completed voyage and a poor substitute return for a lost ship and cargo.

In the insuring of ships and cargoes, Guillaume France fils was a willing and able helper, although this was by no means the extent of his services to the company. His father had brought the family from the realm of business to that of finance, buying his son the office of *secrétaire du Roi*. In October, 1745, France became part of a company of the Ferme des Domaines de la Ouest Flandres, a fresh conquest.[47] So divorced was he from the family's mercantile origins that he confessed himself "very ignorant of business matters."[48] His participation

in the Société du Canada was an accident of inheritance, a kind of re-
cessive social gene.

France was able to use his *entrée* at Versailles to find out in advance
the dates of convoys, to have a petition for the return of the *Centaure*'s
cannon delivered to Maurepas by one of the Minister's friends, and to
obtain the services of scarce sailors for the company's ships.[49] Con-
veniently located at Paris, he also undertook the negotiations with the
Compagnie des Indes for compensation for the loss of the *Trois
Maries*, receiving the award of 50 per cent damages in July 1746.[50]
Altogether, he was a man of wide connections and a valuable partner
in troubled times.

By the third year of the war the cumbersome convoy system had produced a situation of feast or famine in the sugar islands. Instead of
reaching the islands at all seasons in a fairly steady stream, merchandise arrived in great lots at unpredictable times. Provisions that remained any length of time soon spoiled in the tropical climate; scarcity
rapidly replaced overabundance.[51] The flotilla that left Ile d'Aix at the
end of April 1746, under the escort of three warships and one frigate
totalled well above three hundred sail, of which the *Union*, destined
for St. Pierre, was one. It was no wonder that France was apprehensive
about the large size of the convoy that extended for two leagues. He
and his partners must have been relieved to hear of its safe arrival at St.
Pierre on 15 June.[52]

Although Fremont and Renault had written that French merchandise had become extremely scarce in Martinique, the *Union* carried a
cheap, almost a ballast, cargo of bricks, slates, planks, and window
panes that might find a market in the burned-out town of St. Pierre.[53]
The voyage shows very clearly the problems of trading in wartime. A
full outward cargo was usually exchanged mostly for sugar, a commodity that because of its bulkiness paid a good deal of freight and
often required more shipping than had the outward cargo. But in wartime, shipping was scarce and freight rates were high. To get around
this problem a shipper either had to reduce his outward cargo or resign
himself to leaving a large outstanding credit in the islands until the end
of the war.[54] The company's decision was to reduce the cargo.
Dugard's purpose in sending such a large ship as the 350-ton *Union*
appears to have been to provide Fremont and Renault with the necessary capacity to ship back returns from earlier outward voyages and
perhaps to take on freight, capitalizing on the same high rates that
discouraged him from hiring freight on other ships. Many captains
were demanding payment for their outward cargoes in gold and silver

to reduce their own need for freight space and make it available to customers.[55]

The company was no more interested in sending large amounts of goods to Canada than to Martinique. Only merchandise worth about 20,000 livres was sent from La Rochelle in May 1746, the intention being to sell out everything in the Quebec warehouse.[56] This restraint might in part have been related to the King's commandeering of the company's last operational ship, the *Fleury*. In vain did they wish he had chosen the *Centaure*, idle and useless to them, but they had to accept the fact that, as France put it, "We are not the strongest and we must obey."[57] The ship had been taken under a regular charter-party as had many others and was to form part of a fleet that was gathering at Ile d'Aix to be taken by the Duc d'Anville to the relief of Louisbourg.

By the spring the people of Quebec were starved for news, and what little they got was bad. From the first meridian to the coast of France the sea was filled with English corsairs; not even a fishing shallop could put out.[58] For those who could afford it, at 300 livres the *barrique*, there was still wine in the colony. Havy was making the time pass somewhat incongruously by reading Pufendorf's *The Law of Nations*.[59] On 7 May a cipher dispatch arrived from the court. The announcement that there was civil war in England and that a great fleet was coming to Canada gave heart to the whole population.[60] But as the summer passed, only a few ships arrived, and the *bénéfice* did not fall below 120 per cent.[61] In spite of this, consumption was not flagging, especially amongst artisans, because of the considerable fortifications and other military works being built.[62] This put a great deal of money into circulation; it gave a superficial air of prosperity, but one that did not deceive Havy and Lefebvre. "We need a good peace," they advised Pierre Guy, "in order to be able to work solidly at increasing the trade of this country. It must be hoped that God will give us the grace soon to see the end of the war."[63]

Any hope for a "good peace" rested on the success of the mysterious expedition that never arrived and which Havy and Lefebvre thought would bring Captain Vandelle, the *Fleury*, and a great cargo.[64] It was October before it was known that the fleet's destination was Chebucto Bay.[65] Given the enormous purchases of the King, the modest amount of new merchandise entering the colony, the lack of assortment, and the uncertainty about whether a large merchant fleet was coming to Quebec, trade was at a near standstill.[66] Available shipping was so inadequate that only the previous year's beaver was exported.[67]

While Quebecers were still wondering whether D'Anville would arrive or not, the admiral was already dead, his second-in-command had attempted suicide, and the remains of the fleet, which had been mauled by a stormy three-month crossing, had left North American waters in failure. On 29 October the *Fleury* lost some of its masts in a storm; and the understrength and sickly crew, being unable to control the ship, allowed it to drift south to the calmer waters around Martinique, where it could be refitted. But the crippled vessel was set upon by the *Greyhound* and in spite of assistance from a French ship was captured near Guadeloupe, taken to New York, and there adjudged a prize on 19 February 1746/47.[68] Within a few days, perhaps hours, of learning of the fate of the *Fleury*, Dugard also received word of the shipwreck of the *Union*, which on the night of 27–28 February 1747 was carried onto the rocks off the coast of Ile de Ré in spite of the captain's having ordered all the masts to be cut down.[69]

It seemed impossible. In the short space of four years Dugard and Company had lost to shipwreck and capture the *Alçion*, the *Louis Dauphin*, the *St. Mathieu*, the *Imprévû*, the *Fleury*, and the *Union*. The *Trois Maries*, carrying company cargo and owned in part by some members, was also lost. The *St. Louis* and the *Centaure* had been perishing at Le Havre since 1743; repairs to the *Astrée* had taken two years to complete, and a large stock of merchandise had been burned at St. Pierre. There was no way to rationalize such devastation but to put it in the larger context of the Divine Will: "We must adore the hand of God that strikes us." [70] At the same time, Dugard, D'Haristoy, Laurens, and the Widow Vincent must have agreed with France that it was time "to liquidate all our business and cease this trade that is so declared against us." [71] Certainly, France extracted a promise from Dugard to engage in no new enterprise for the company until they had regulated their accounts and understood their situation more clearly. It was not a difficult promise to extract from a man who had just lost his wife in addition to sharing in these common misfortunes.[72]

In 1747 there was little rejoicing in any of the Atlantic trading towns or in the colonies. The system of West Indian convoys had broken down completely; and although most of the ships had reached the islands, there was no safe way of either getting them back or sending out another fleet.[73] At St. Pierre, however, Captain Fremont had at last finished his affairs and was able to return to France, leaving Captain Renault to coax payment from their many debtors. In Canada, scarcity was eased by the arrival of a number of ships, as reflected in the falling of the *bénéfice* from 180 to 100 per cent. But a hoped-for fleet that was

to bring many more merchantmen, several warships, and a new governor had been stopped by the English. The colony was again fearful of
invasion.[74] Havy and Lefebvre received very little merchandise from
Robert Dugard that year.[75] They did receive a letter of great importance, one that they must have read with sinking hearts. Dugard
and Company had made its decision. Its trade to Canada was ended.
From 1 November 1747, the company would cease to pay the rent of
the warehouse, and the room, board, and wages of its former factors.[76]

The immediate plans of the company were to sell the repaired,
sheathed *Astrée* to either the King or the Compagnie des Indes, a task
left to Guillaume France. Knowing that "It's the devil to get money
out of the King," France favoured a sale to the company, although the
same persons he had paid to ensure that the King gave compensation
for the loss of the *Fleury* would again sell their services.[77] But on 5
May 1748, news reached Paris of the capture of Maastricht and the
end of hostilities. With the seas once again open, the earliest arrivals in
the colonies would find a fortune in return freight. Instead of being
sold, the *Astrée* was to be outfitted to leave as soon as possible for
Martinique.[78]

"It seems to me that in the present circumstances the Frenchman,
always extreme, will breathe nothing but maritime trade. All Paris is
seeking an opportunity for it," wrote Guillaume France from Paris on
24 May 1748.[79] He was convinced that the initial voyage of a ship
already prepared to sail would be fortunate, although in the scramble
that would be sure to follow many would "break their necks." In October the *Astrée* left Bordeaux on its search for freight at Martinique,
and the *Centaure* sailed from Le Havre bound for Léoganne, chartered
out to the Compagnie des Indes.[80] It was the decision of the company
to consign the *St. Louis* to the cod fishery.[81] These activities constituted not a vigorous continuance of operations, but the reduction of
the Société du Canada to the status of a caretaker operation. The
partners were agreed, although in this Guillaume France required con-
vincing, that they would sustain a considerable loss in selling their
three remaining ships. They therefore intended to sail them as long as
they would last. By limiting cargo for their own account to modest
pacotilles, they would tie up very little capital.[82] Guillaume France
even argued that the original company was destroyed by the war and
that post-war operations were "a species of resumption of accounts
... that ought *not* to be confounded with the preceding ones and
whose nature requires an accounting at each return with a prompt
division of profits."[83] He never gave up the notion that what he de-

cided should be true was true although no one else was of his opinion and Dugard attempted no prompt division of profits.[84]

In spite of war losses, Dugard and his friends were still optimistic about their company. In February, 1744, they had assembled to sign accounts and had either established or received from Dugard an "état estimatif" of the society that gave its worth as 894,705 livres.[85] In August 1750, Dugard had paid D'Haristoy, Laurens, and Vincent a dividend of 6,000 livres each. (Because France père's drawings against capital had left his investment in the company deficient, there was no payment for France fils.[86]) The war with the English had destroyed a magnificent commercial undertaking just at the moment when it had ceased to require the reinvestment of every *écu* it earned and was expected to begin paying handsome annual dividends. No one had the heart to rebuild it, but the company still had considerable capital invested in cargoes and debts. Robert Dugard was tending to the liquidation of these old affairs and drawing up the final accounts. The presentation of the balance sheet and the fivefold split of the company's wealth could not be far off.

II

At Rouen, other enterprises had already diverted considerable attention and capital away from the Société du Canada. Pierre D'Haristoy, described by a contemporary as "a very well-informed businessman with a genius for mechanics,"[87] was one of a group of Rouen and Paris entrepreneurs who had developed a machine based on an English model for the lamination of lead sheets. In the 1740s he lent his talents to the solution of another technical problem, that of duplicating a permanent red dye called Adrianople red. It had for years been an object of French government policy to discover this closely-guarded secret of the Turkish Empire.[88] As has so often occurred, the discovery was made simultaneously by another experimenter working independently, an impecunious textile manufacturer named André Fesquet. To avoid costly competition, Fesquet was taken into a company founded to exploit the discovery, even though he could only deposit a promissory note against profits as his share of capital. D'Haristoy was able to persuade Dugard, his intimate friend, and two other Rouen businessmen, Louis Paynel, a former judge consul, and his brother-in-law, Jean Joseph Louvet le jeune, to each take a one-sixth interest in the company, which was capitalized at 100,000 livres and was to last from 1 January 1747 to 1 January 1757.[89] The two inventors, with

one-quarter share each, took charge of the dyeing; Louvet purchased
the required cotton and Dugard the required chemicals, while Paynel
sold the product.

D'Haristoy and Fesquet next travelled to Paris to visit M. de
Montaran, Intendant of Commerce specializing in cotton and linen
cloth, with the intention of obtaining the backing of the state.[90] They
were soon introduced to the chemist Jean Hellot of the Académie des
Sciences, a regular adviser to the government on dyeing, who prepared
the official report of the demonstration of their process.[91] He became a
consistent supporter in the years that followed. To their surprise,
D'Haristoy and Fesquet learned that they had been preceded in their
discovery by two years by François Gaudar, a manufacturer of Aubenas in Languedoc who had already asked for permission to establish
a dye works at Rouen. However, at the insistence of Rouillé de Jouy,
the Director of Commerce, all three discoverers were associated in one
company, Gaudar receiving a one-sixth share without investment for
his primacy of discovery. As both Rouen and Aubenas samples
withstood trial bleaching at Beauvais, something which no formulae
smuggled back from Greece had done, there was good reason to believe that this was a discovery of the highest importance.[92] On 26 August 1747, the Conseil d'Etat declared the company the "Manufacture
royale de teinture de coton et de fil en rouge façon d'Andrinople,"
which entailed the right to exclusive use of the dye process for twenty
years and a government subsidy of 30,000 livres payable over ten
years. In return the company was required to fence its property, dis-
play the royal arms, and conduct its work in secret.[93] By the end of the
year the dye works had been built in a disused charterhouse at Darnétal outside of Rouen. In 1748 dyeing began.[94]

The commencement of operations and the exhaustion of the company's capital were simultaneous. A decision was therefore made to
borrow 45,000 livres, this being equal to the paper shares of Fesquet
and Gaudar. The first loans were private advances from Dugard and
D'Haristoy, but on 8 June borrowing from the public began, backed
by promissory notes or bills of exchange signed by Dugard, D'Haristoy, and Paynel.[95] The bills of exchange were drawn on Dugard and
accepted by him to make them more attractive to lenders and were
negotiated as "acceptances." At the same time, Louvet, who was not
endowed with a large fortune, declared himself incapable of continuing the purchase of cotton until the company had paid him his
advances. Dugard therefore agreed to take this task upon himself and
became a permanent creditor of the company.[96]

Financial problems were soon compounded by the company's failure to sell its product. Both the hostility of the guilds to this monopoly factory established outside the city limits and dyeing its own thread rather than accepting cotton from the public, and the imperfection of the dyed product itself were responsible for this. By the end of the year the company therefore decided to hire its own weavers to use up its growing stock of red cotton in striped cloths in which imperfections were not noticeable. The decision seemed unavoidable and it meant the expenditure of more money, consequently more borrowing and even greater financial commitment on the part of Pierre D'Haristoy and Robert Dugard.[97]

The necessity of government permission for the manufacture, undertaken by the poor cottage weavers of the district, was the occasion for more visits to Paris and the distribution of ten dozen red handkerchiefs throughout the various levels of administration.[98] (Such *pots-de-vin* were routine. Hellot had in the past been the recipient of Canadian martin pelts and several highly-placed officials would in the future be regaled with baskets of fancy meats.[99]) Special workers were brought in from Cambrai to teach the cottage workers the art of making cloths without knots or imperfections that would spoil the dye.[100] For it was at least in part the poor quality of thread and cloth that had made production dyeing less successful than the original experimental demonstrations. It seemed necessary to create "a metamorphosis in changing French hands into those of Indians as much for the spinning of the cotton as for fashioning the work [ie. cloth]."[101]

The pressing need for money continued. Since the company had already saturated Rouen with its paper, an issue of 90,000 livres in notes, made out by Dugard for value received from D'Haristoy and endorsed over to Paynel, was negotiated in Paris in November 1749. Louvet offered to place the notes with his friends in Paris, and D'Haristoy accompanied him to attempt to borrow money from his own opulent relatives in the city.[102]

From Paris D'Haristoy reported that "the common feeling is that our enterprise is pure gold."[103] He was not only well received by Montaran, Hellot, and Daniel-Charles Trudaine, successor as Director of Commerce to Rouillé, who had replaced the disgraced Maurepas at the Marine, but acquired the protection and sponsorship of the Governor of Normandy, the Duc de Luxembourg, with whom he seems to have lodged.[104] It was Luxembourg who obtained for him an "entrée to Mme. de Pompadour's while the King was there and with his permission."[105] He was charged with providing flowered cloth brocaded with Darnétal red cotton for a new château being built for *la maîtresse en titre*. Three weeks later, when D'Haristoy visited the court at

La Muette, he found himself beset by admirers who waved their hand-kerchiefs of the Darnétal cotton that had won La Pompadour's favour. "God but men are fools," was his reflection. "But never mind, let us profit from it." [106]

It was a favourable time to solicit payment of the 30,000 livres grant, badly needed but difficult to obtain given the state of the royal treasury at the end of the war. [107] After an hour's conversation with De la Bourdonnaye, the Intendant of Rouen, at his Paris home, "tête à tête by his fire," which included much bravado on D'Haristoy's part, he extracted an admiring "Vous êtes notre homme" from the Intendant, which was as close as he could get to a promise of payment. [108] He was more successful with his family of which he at first unhappily reported that "the scruple is beyond imagination." [109] They were eventually won over by his plan to issue *actions*: These may have been *actions intéressées*, combining fixed interest and the possibility of a dividend in the manner of those issued by John Law, or *actions rentières*, which were more like bonds. It is not clear whether *actions* of any kind were held to confer ownership or simply to be loans with varying degrees of risk. In any case, their issue depended upon government authorization and they were probably free of the taint of usury. Those of the company bore coupons bearing interest that varied from five per cent to ten per cent by their fifth and final year. [110] Financing by *actions* was sufficiently uncommon that D'Haristoy felt called upon to explain to Dugard the nature of "what are called coupons," the manner in which the printed forms were to be signed, and the way in which interest was paid. [111] Ultimately, he appears to have gained about 85,000 livres from his family, but only by making over to them half his interest in Darnétal. [112] This tendering of collateral suggests very strongly that D'Haristoy's *actions* were proto-debentures rather than shares.

As the needs of the company surpassed the ample means of Dugard and D'Haristoy, however, they found themselves slipping beyond the limits of legitimate paper negotiation into the penumbral zone of doubtful but all too common practice. The basic understanding of the trade in bills and notes was that each was founded in a commercial transaction and represented a well-founded credit, that the paper had been issued "for value received." In the case of bills of exchange it was also held that the "value received" had been given over in payment for a fund of money which existed at another place. The practical result of these restrictions was that bills and notes represented genuine claims, and were not mere paper promises. To issue them without receiving value, or to draw a bill on someone not really a debtor, was to issue fictional paper. The engagements so contracted could only be met by still more issues of paper until at last, it was hoped, the profits of enterprises so financed would be sufficient to bail the authors out of such dangerous operations. It was to such expedients that the company of Darnétal surrendered.[113] "I scarcely refuse myself for the common interest of our company," Dugard wrote, "for I am going in over my head & probably no one could be found to do what I am doing in this occasion."[114] D'Haristoy was equally worried, especially about the results of having second and third issues appear on the market.[115] But like Dugard, he was willing to accept the money realized by this *tripotage* provided he did not have to become involved in Louvet's operations: "As it's not to my taste I leave it to him."[116]

Louvet worked slowly and with patience. "Time is needed for everything," he explained, "& especially in this business where one cannot be too circumspect. Social visits, visits to sound out dispositions, and other visits to operate."[117] But Louvet "operated" on his own terms. The capital from the paper which he negotiated, mostly through a Paris banker named Alexandre Le Leu le jeune, was made available to Dugard by his drawing on Louvet or by Louvet's remittances. It was best explained by Dugard himself:

> [Louvet] certainly took the precaution of asking that the money
> that would be negotiated at Paris passed through his hands. . . .
> He always has our money in his hands; if he has it for only
> 8 days, 15 days or 3 weeks, it is always of very great usefulness
> to him while I am continually advancing my funds & on the
> due dates of my notes and acceptances I most certainly have to
> find some, something which very strongly disrupts . . . my other
> business.[118]

There was the ever-present possibility that while Dugard and D'Haristoy were sacrificing their fortunes the end result might be to aid Louvet, "who hasn't the resource of a thousand *écus* in case of need,"[119] rather than to sustain the enterprise at Darnétal.[120]

In 1750 the company had 180 looms weaving cotton in the Rouen region. There were never profits sufficient to meet its engagements, yet the only hope of meeting them lay in continuing to use up the stocks of poorly-dyed cotton and in persevering in the attempt to produce a perfect product: "we were in a vicious circle and forced to follow it."[121] Promissory notes then due could only be paid by a second issue of 90,000. True to worst expectations, Louvet had abused the trust in him by employing notes and dependent bills for his own purposes, so that Dugard and D'Haristoy personally took over the negotiation of

paper, although they found themselves obliged to make use of the
channels opened for them by Louvet.[122] Bills of exchange replaced
notes in further negotiations as they were more easily negotiated. Acceptances given to Jacques Vasse, a young Dieppe merchant introduced by Louvet, were used by Vasse to parry his own creditors before
he succumbed to bankruptcy following the discovery of a large-scale
smuggling enterprise that Louvet had persuaded him to join. The
vastly over-extended Le Leu was forced to stop payments upon the
death of one of his correspondents, the Paris banker Pictet. Louvet
managed to trick Dugard out of still more acceptances before himself
ceding his interests at Darnétal to his partners and seeking refuge as a
smuggler in England.[123]

As Ridel, the Paris banker with whom the company's paper was
domiciled, refused to indulge in the *cavalerie* that had been acceptable
to Le Leu, the desperate associates found they must, in Paynel's words,
"work every conceivable angle to save that which is more precious
than gold."[124] Claude Torrent, director of the Compagnie du Plomb
laminé, now lent his signature to the company in exchange for a large
shipment of Darnétal merchandise as well as D'Haristoy's interest in
his company, these constituting the *valeur reçue* for legitimate bills of
exchange.[125]

But the troubles of Darnétal were not only financial. From 1749 the
associates had quarrelled with André Fesquet, who without having
found money to pay for his capital share had nevertheless managed to
establish more than a score of looms for his own account, all weaving
Darnétal red.[126] In 1753 he broke with his partners and in the next few
years led a public campaign against them, alleging bad treatment and
offering to dye for the general public should the government authorize
him.[127] This last argument was calculated to win the support of
Trudaine, who was disposed against privilege. For a time it seemed
that the government might even divulge the secret formula of Darnétal
red, and they were probably prevented from doing so only by the fear
that it would reach foreign eyes "as promptly as the gazette."[128] As
D'Haristoy reflected, "The spirit that reigns always will reign; the per-
suasion is that privileges are inimical to emulation."[129] With this he
entirely agreed, except that there were always exceptions, of which the
teinture de Darnétal was one "without contradiction." Bowing to
necessity, in 1755 Dugard promised on the company's behalf to accept
cotton for dyeing from the public.[130] The relation with Fesquet was
ultimately dissolved without the company's losing the favour of the
administration.[131]

Of Daniel-Charles Trudaine, D'Haristoy wrote that "all the days of this lord are counted and allotted" and that "this lord is considered hard."[132] Of all the eighteenth-century administrators, it is he who most closely resembles Colbert. He was the moving spirit behind projects of industrial renovation and a disciple of economic liberalism, which had become the focus of national economic aspirations that a century before had been identified with the very different notions of Colbertism. The support and friendship that Trudaine extended to Pierre D'Haristoy surprised those who knew him and were not considered empty gestures.[133] In January 1753, he revealed to D'Haristoy that he had a new project in mind for him, the establishment of a factory to imitate English cotton velour and fustian.[134] The Inspector of Manufactures, Morel, had met an expatriate Englishman named John Holker at Rouen in 1749, and Holker had offered to import English Catholic workmen and to supervise the installation of English machinery if financial support for such a factory could be found.[135]

D'Haristoy accepted the challenge and set up an experimental arrangement at Darnétal, for which he was granted 5,000 livres, to determine the technical and financial requirements.[136] M. de Montigny of the Académie des Sciences negotiated suitable terms for the formation of a company, including a royal grant and the inclusion of Holker without his contributing capital.[137] De Montigny was specifically instructed to entertain no "propositions tending to obtain an exclusive privilege, the intention of the King being to render commerce very free."[138] This new *manufacture royale* was to be the object of emulation. By the final agreement the associates were to receive 60,000 livres over ten years and 10,000 livres immediately for the building of essential machinery.[139] On 28 September 1753, the articles of association for two companies were delivered to de Montigny, one for a *manufacture de velours de coton façon d'Angleterre* and another for a *compagnie des calandres à l'anglais*, the calandres being machines required to give finish to the woven cloth.[140]

By means of these new enterprises located in the Rouen suburb of St. Sever, it was hoped to renew the sagging cotton industry of Rouen and compete in world markets with the English.[141] To finance these enterprises, various new partners were brought in, the most notable being Claude Torrent. *Actions* were sold and promissory notes negotiated. Based upon tried and true models, the enterprises of St. Sever did not repeat the financial catastrophe of the experimental undertakings of Darnétal.[142] Darnétal and St. Sever together constituted an absorption of capital that precluded any further expansion of the Société du Canada, even had it been desirable. In making this choice of industry over maritime trade, Dugard and D'Haristoy illustrate a movement general among the bourgeoisie of Rouen, who progressively lost their links with ocean traffic, which was consolidated in the hands of the outfitters of Le Havre.[143]

The calamitous history of the Darnétal enterprises is of particular relevance because it demonstrates even more clearly than the financial machinations undertaken to support the Société du Canada in 1742, the extreme difficulty under which French merchants laboured with regard to the mobilization of capital. To realize their undertakings the Dugard group was constrained to violate both law and conscience and confide their fortunes to a man whom D'Haristoy qualified as "a big beggar and the most notorious swindler and even thief that I know; he has neither faith nor religion and even less honour."[144] If it is true that there are Louvets at all times and in all places, it must nevertheless be conceded that the institutional limits of this particular time and place made him the common companion of honest men.

Just as the entrepreneurs of the Société du Canada were being drawn into many other enterprises, so too were Havy and Lefebvre at Quebec. The most important instance of this was their involvement in the sealing industry. Almost all of the more than twenty sealing stations on the lower North Shore and the coast of Labrador were established in the eighteenth century, more than half of them after Utrecht. The greatest number of new foundations was in the 1730s, the decade of Havy and Lefebvre's earliest investment.[145]

Sealing was undertaken primarily for oil, and seal oil, unlike wheat and lumber, was an export for the European market. The required buildings, ships, and hired labour were expensive. There was a high element of risk resulting from the vagaries of migrating seal, the depredations of Eskimos and, in wartime, of Anglo-American privateers. Even in good years the profits were not inordinately high. But sealing was an exploitation within Canadian means. And barrels of oil did fill the holds of ships that would have returned to France mostly in ballast; oil did earn precious credits to help pay for Canada's imports.

From 1737 to 1748 Havy and Lefebvre held a lease on a post at Mingan. It was exploited on their behalf by Jean-Louis Volant d'Hautebourg, to whom they advanced 37,500 livres in merchandise on credit in 1737 and 1738.[146] In other words, it was an advantage of their position that as representatives of Dugard and Company they were able to extend credit to themselves. They also sold oil to the company, although their own names never appeared in the accounts.[147]

In 1737 they and their friend and landlord, Louis Fornel, acquired a two-thirds interest in an undeveloped sealing site at Baie des Châteaux on the Strait of Belle-Ile from its concessionaire, Louis Bazil. Fornel, Havy, and Lefebvre provided all the capital, including Bazil's one-third share, for what proved to be a costly undertaking.[148] In spite of Bazil's inability to make any financial contribution, Hocquart prevented his being squeezed out of his own concession by his solvent partners.[149] During the war the Intendant quite legitimately left the matter in abeyance, and an order from Maurepas to settle the question was simply ignored.[150] The war cut off the Quebec merchants from the gulf and their sealing stations, where buildings, equipment, and oil perished. A third of the 100,000 livres invested in Baie des Châteaux was lost.[151] Although Hocquart's successor granted the post to a new concessionaire in 1749, Havy and Lefebvre appear to have retained some interest there until 1754, when the post's ship and equipment, all described as belonging to them, were sold at public auction at Quebec.[152]

In 1740 Havy and Lefebvre sublet a two-thirds interest in the concession of Grand St. Modet.[153] The original lease ended in 1747, but there is evidence that they sent a ship there in 1758, that being their last known sealing venture.[154] These interests in sealing-trading stations proved to be of great importance to Havy and Lefebvre as they constituted an economic base that withstood the severance of their relation with Dugard and Company. Indeed, in 1748 their most ambitious Labrador ventures were still before them.

In the half decade from 1745 to 1750 war and accident destroyed a great part of the investments of Dugard and Company, the colonial enterprises of Havy and Lefebvre, and even the modest fortunes of their captains invested in small lots of trade goods. Although three ships remained to the company and it had made reasonable insurance recoveries, the net loss was still considerable; and its days were numbered. The reinvestment of funds and the borrowing necessary to restore its vitality were not forthcoming. On both sides of the Atlantic capital and attention had been diverted to new endeavours.

CHAPTER NINE

The Lord Taketh Away

I

Havy and Lefebvre were on their own. In terms of their business, that was the principal result of the War of the Austrian Succession. The last strands of the tie with Dugard and Company were cut slowly, as for some years they continued to sell a residue of merchandise on the company's behalf, in addition handling some bales of handkerchiefs sent from Darnétal.[1] For a time in the 1750s they even owned a ship, the *Parfaite Union*, in company with Dugard, acting in his own right, and a fourth party who was probably Jean Jacquelin, whom Dugard had sent to Quebec to help them in the 1740s.[2]

Even at the time of the war, Havy and Lefebvre had had small interests of their own in schooners and bateaux sailing to Louisbourg and the West Indies.[3] Released now from their close liaison with the Société du Canada, they also acted as commission agents for at least two other metropolitan shippers, Jean Gardère of Bayonne and a Sieur Garisson of Bordeaux.[4] Much of their capital was invested in houses and properties in and around Quebec and in mortgages, providing them with some immunity against the fickle ups and downs of trade.[5]

In the aggregate of their affairs, investments in Labrador became increasingly important. In 1743, partly at their expense, Fornel had explored the mouth of the Kessessakiou River, the Baie des Esquimaux, the estuary today named Hamilton Inlet.[6] Fearing that a trading post, which was the inevitable adjunct to almost any sealing station, would interfere with the trade of the King's Posts, Hocquart had refused to grant a concession to the trio, but in 1749 the new Intendant, François Bigot, granted it to Fornel's widow, Marie-Anne

Barbel, and to Havy and Lefebvre, her business associates.[7] At the same time, the three partners under the name of Veuve Fornel et Cie, received a six-year lease of the King's Posts themselves.[8] In clearing the decks of substantial trade rivals, in this case the former leaseholder of the posts, François Etienne Cugnet, Bigot had incidentally made them his beneficiaries. Their gratitude must nevertheless have been shortlived, as they and the other independent traders stood only to lose by the new Intendant's elaboration of a network of patronage that soon enmeshed much of the colony's trade. At the expiry of their lease on the King's Posts in 1755, they surrendered them to the Crown because of their fear of incurring wartime losses, being the last lessees of the Old Régime.[9]

Havy and Lefebvre had thus taken full advantage of the many opportunities open to factors with large sums of money at their disposal. They had made a place for themselves in the Canada trade. But it was not the custom of the Quebec trading fraternity to think of settling permanently in Canada; and for Huguenots, neither free to marry in the colony nor to bring to it established families, it must have been unthinkable. It is therefore not surprising that Havy and Lefebvre should have planned to transfer their seat of operations to France. Their removal was a foregone conclusion; only the time and the manner were determined by the play of events.

The occasion for departure was the war that broke out at the forks of the Ohio in 1754, opening yet another chapter in the Anglo-French struggle for imperial supremacy. Under hazardous but potentially profitable wartime conditions, Havy and Lefebvre decided that one of them should return to France to supervise their export of merchandise to Canada as well as to prepare for the eventual transfer of their business from the colony. In January 1756, Havy arrived at La Rochelle, having "escaped the clutches of the English."[10] There was war without declaration of war. Mere English visitation of French merchant vessels had been superseded by a policy of seizing French shipping, resulting in the capture of some three hundred merchantmen. To François Havy it was certain that England, "this nation that talks of nothing but the law of nations entirely blackens itself by becoming the equal of pirates."

The arrival of Havy in France added one more voice to the chorus pressing for the rendering of the accounts of Dugard and Company. Shortly after his arrival, he made a long visit to Rouen, where Dugard gave him a warm welcome, assuring him that their accounts would soon be terminated.[11] In spite of this, he found himself constrained to remind his old chief two years later than in the 26 years since the company was founded, "there has been time to die many times and all things have an end." [12]

The British declaration of war did not come until 17 May 1756, four months after Havy's arrival. Just five days before, the *Centaure* had set sail from Martinique in company with a dozen ships bound for France. [13] Separated from its companions, it was captured on the seas by the *Nightingale*, taken to New York and there on 2 August declared a lawful prize. [14] "We must make a sacrifice of it and submit to the decrees of Providence," so wrote Guillaume France. [15] Still, it was a misfortune that he may have found had its compensation, for this was the very last of the company's ships. After so much procrastination, Dugard would at last have to agree with him, "There is an event that definitely puts an end to our company." [16]

Everyone connected with the Société du Canada must have had its impending conclusion continually in the back of his mind, even though the war took first place in his thoughts. Commerce was hard hit from the beginning. In 1757 two years' supply of Canadian fur remained unsold at La Rochelle, and money was of surprising rarity. "Isn't it terrible," wrote Havy, "that the Court gives no help or protection to trade." [17] The replacement of Machault by Peirenc de Moras at the Ministry of Marine gave no hope in this regard, the decided policy of government being to let French shippers take care of themselves while neutral shipping was depended upon to supply the colonies. [18]

In 1758 occurred the spectacular fall of Louisbourg. As soon as news of the siege reached La Rochelle, Havy prophesied the surrender of the town, the opinion of himself and others "who know the place." [19] Although he had investments there ("not for a lot but it is always too much when you lose"), he held that if it brought peace, loss of the fortress would be worth the price. [20] According to his report, most of his compatriots at La Rochelle would not believe the town was captured, even when the capitulation appeared in the *Gazette d'Hollande*; but it was difficult for someone like himself with knowledge "of the manner in which things are done by our navy" to be fooled. [21] By mid-September the arrival of the first refugees proved that in spite of the valour of the Troupes de Terre the worst had indeed happened. [22] As for Canada, where bad harvests and wartime needs made scarcity endemic, Havy pitied its poor inhabitants. [23] Remembering how in the previous war Hocquart so frequently complained, "Poor King how you are robbed," he wondered what superlatives of scorn could be applied to the profiteering that was of daily occurrence in Canada. [24] The issue of enormous amounts of government paper, already ten times greater than in the War of the Austrian Succession according to his estimation, was certainly cause for alarm. It would cause the ruin of many should it not be honoured.[25]

In September 1758, Havy announced his resolution to establish himself permanently at La Rochelle.[26] His marriage into the François family of Bordeaux, "a family both rich and highly respectable," had probably already taken place.[27] Unfortunately, this personal good fortune found no parallel in business and politics. The saving of trade and empire had become undertakings well beyond the means of private parties. By February 1759, there were few ships available, even fewer seamen and no insurers. Havy believed France to be lost in lethargy and feared the loss of Canada itself, "this big and beautiful colony," dragging in its train the collapse of the Marine and the loss of the West Indian colonies.[28]

Neither Havy nor anyone else was to find his war-dampened spirits raised when on 14 May the long awaited, frequently demanded accounts of the Société du Canada were at last presented. The accounts rendered were the current accounts of Dugard's four partners. Each began with a tabulation of the recipient's one-fifth share of the company's debits and credits and ended with a series of transactions between him and Dugard. Company and personal affairs were thus fused together.[29] According to these accounts, as explained in appendix D, the company had not made annual profits of more than 11 or 12 per cent in good years, losing more than six per cent per annum during the War of the Austrian Succession. Since the war the *Astrée* and the *Centaure* had earned a mixture of very high and very low profits, but the capital upon which these profits were earned was itself comparatively insignificant.

The partners had expected the company to be worth much more than it actually was. "It is true that this commerce has not been as fruitful as the great labours that it has occasioned would seem to promise . . . let us thank God for what he has left us," was Dugard's final verdict.[30] An *état estimatif* of the company's financial status drawn up in February 1744, on the eve of the War of the Austrian Succession, estimated profits at roughly 20 per cent, which was far too high, and made further unrealistic estimates of the value of return cargoes due to arrive before the end of the year.[31] In the decade after the war, the partners therefore presumed that they had ample credit with Dugard, and upon this assumption were based numerous financial operations between them. Dugard advanced money to associates to whom he assumed he owed.[32] Confident that Dugard was already his debtor, Laurens had been charging him interest for advances.[33] An astonished Guillaume France exclaimed to Dugard that he was "always deeply persuaded that it was you who owed me!"[34] For that reason he had kept a large part of the payments made by the Crown for the loss of the *Fleury*. When the final accounts were rendered, it became clear that with the exception of the Vincent estate, to which Dugard owed 8,000 livres, the partners had all used up their credits resulting from the Société du Canada and were themselves indebted to Dugard.

As Gédéon Samuel Vincent had died seven years earlier and his children were still minors, the family's financial affairs were in the hands of the widow and a Monsieur Lucas, the guardian required to represent the children's interest according to the Coûtume de Normandie. As required by law, Lucas examined all the accounts, finding only two important errors.[35] Everyone but Guillaume France was satisfied with this and completely trusted the bookkeeper, who had kept accounts for Laurens for many years and had audited the papers of both D'Haristoy and Vincent after their deaths.[36]

France, who had for years urged closing the books of the company and the liquidation of its assets, was outraged by what must have appeared to him a monstrous trick. All Dugard had ever done, he petulantly claimed, was inform him of the loss of all their ships. He insisted upon the validity of the *état estimatif*, which Dugard dismissed as necessarily vague.[37] At the end of July 1760, France engaged an auditor, Monsieur Barraguay, who continued his examination of the accounts until 1762. The job was then passed on to France's cousin, Monsieur Duperreux, who was still working on the accounts in 1764. He may not have finished until 1766, when France asked him to settle the affair by conciliation. Although France's letters give evidence of no disposition to pay the 13,773 livres asked of him, some reconciliation may well have been effected, as no further correspondence among the three men is preserved.[38] The 24,574 livres requested of the D'Haristoy estate was added to the 290,759 livres that Dugard claimed owing for the account of Darnétal and became the object of litigation. The debt to the Vincent estate was paid, but with difficulty. No evidence remains of any arrangement made between Dugard and his brother-in-law, Laurens.

The verdict of the final accounts thus came as a disagreeable surprise to everyone, including their author. There could be no greater condemnation of the company's accounting procedures than the fact that this was so. The tardy closure was, of course, the direct responsibility of Robert Dugard. In his defence the astonishing length of time required by Barraguay and Duperreux simply to audit the accounts should be considered. If the audit may be used as a yardstick of time required, it may be suggested that Dugard began to work on the accounts in 1756, possibly before. His failure to give earlier attention to them can undoubtedly be explained by his concentration on the great undertakings of Darnétal and St. Sever. This is yet another condemnation of the accounting system, for if the books were in order, it should not have taken the same length of time to produce current accounts as to conduct the audit. According to Dugard the final reckoning was so long in coming because his bookkeeper, Corroyer, had structured the accounts in such a way that it was impossible to tell how much was owing Dugard for his advances over the years without doing Corroyer's work all over again, this time with the bookkeeper who had worked for Laurens:

> Many persons other than me would have enriched themselves in such an administration but I have rather let my own wealth slip into it as appears among other things from the balances that each of the partners owes me and during that time I paid the interest on the borrowings I made. There Monsieur is how stupidly I have conducted myself, because the clerk that I had by his negligence in the accounts deprived me of my only means of seeing what I might be owed. I could not ask for money without producing the accounts and these accounts required an immense labour. A considerable time has been necessary in order to establish and correct them.[39]

It is also true that if the enterprises of Darnétal and St. Sever monopolised Dugard's time, they also required all the capital at his fingertips. If he believed that the Société du Canada had been much more profitable than it was, then he would have expected that on closing its accounts he would have to surrender considerable sums to his partners. For the same reason, it was essential for him to know exactly the amount of his advances *before* the accounts were rendered. Were this left to be settled after the disclosure of accounts and the distribution of capital, it is entirely possible that he would never have been paid for these advances. They would become the subject of litigation. As is evident from the Vasse, Le Mercier, and Luetkens bankruptcies in which Dugard was involved, the case could be immobilized in the courts for decades. Dugard's temporization with regard to accounts also suggests the possibility of dishonesty. This is a question that the documentary evidence cannot resolve. While it is possible that the accounts do not reveal the true financial history of the company, successful dishonesty in this case implies not only that Dugard was devilishly clever, but that his partners were dull-witted. It is a most unlikely possibility.

The accounts of 14 May did nothing to clarify the position of Havy and Lefebvre; they were in fact provisional pending the audit of their own accounts. With much complaint Havy accepted their position as salaried clerks in the trade in which almost everyone was paid on commission as the price of apprenticeship, although 22,000 livres for himself and even less for Lefebvre seemed a paltry reward for sixteen years of work that would have earned commission agents more than 160,000 livres.[40] Even before he had finished his audit of their accounts, Dugard was grumbling that they would prove short by more than 30,000 livres, an amount which Havy was quick to point out was scarcely one per cent and easily accountable in terms of theft, leakage, bad debts, and the like. No one would find it astonishing, he protested, "especially given the way business is done in Canada."[41] Nor did he think salaried clerks could be held responsible. Eventually Havy sent his power of attorney to a friend in Rouen who could deal with Dugard personally.[42]

Throughout a long period of epistolary fencing with Dugard, ending with receipt of the completed account at the end of June 1760, Havy was on the defensive, having left important account books in Canada with Lefebvre.[43] Depending upon memory, he thought the account correct. He once again explained the debit of 46,850 livres as a result of bad debts, a reason unacceptable to Dugard.[44] This account did not tell the whole story. At the time of its presentation, Dugard was still working on Havy's personal current account with himself. To this were credited all Havy's wages. The financial operations between the two men, each for his own account, were then tallied. This account was sent to Havy on 11 August 1760. It totalled nearly 80,000 livres and showed Havy as being indebted to Dugard for 10,746 livres.[45] Havy contended that it was really a joint account with Lefebvre and that the latter's wages should be credited to it as well, more than covering the debit balance. The letter containing this protest is the last item of direct evidence bearing on the financial relations of Dugard with Havy and Lefebvre. Ultimate reconciliation may only be inferred from Havy's description of Dugard in his last extant letter to him as one to whom he was "beholden for favours."[46]

It was difficult for Havy to find justice in the world about him. So many had been enriched in Canada, while he wagered that there had been no metropolitan merchant in the colony who had worked as hard as he.[47] Since his return to France in 1756, nothing had succeeded for him either there or in Canada. His fate, like that of every French mer-

chant, depended upon the war that he already regarded as lost. Fulmi-
nations against the government fill his correspondence. The death of
Ferdinand VI of Spain early in 1759 and the resulting prospect of a
Franco-Spanish alliance filled him with dread. "The death of the King
of Spain," he advised a Canadian customer, "will end up setting
Europe ablaze, and everything will be in flame. We are in an age of
iron in which unheard-of things are happening."[48] It was his pious
hope that, "finally God in His infinite goodness will want to give us
better days and preserve you as well as all poor Canada and particularly its brave and poor people."[49]

The Spanish alliance was long in coming, but the ruin of Havy and
Lefebvre was consummated before the end of the year. The Battle of
Quebec occurred on 13 September and on 15 October the government
suspended payment on all colonial paper. "The capture of Canada,"
Havy reported, "has taken from us, Monsieur Lefebvre and I, all the
fruits of our immense labours because we still had a lot in various
establishments of all kinds, especially seal fisheries, mortgages on
houses. All that has been destroyed and consequently all is lost and
since I have been [in France] I have only lost and nothing has succeeded for me. The bankruptcies in which I find myself, the Canadian
bills of exchange which are not paid & etc. All that leads to a desperate situation!"[50]

The siege of Quebec had left the town, in Havy's words, a heap of
stones and debris.[51] In the spring, Jean Lefebvre, like many other
townsmen, had found more comfortable accommodation in the countryside. He remained on the Ile d'Orléans until October in the company of François Levesque, a cousin of Havy and himself who had
earlier come to Canada to work with them. Leaving most of his account books with Levesque, the executor of his will and his attorney,
he then boarded the English warship *Trident*, bound for Portsmouth,
from which he planned to reach La Rochelle.[52]

From the middle of August 1760, until the end of the following
January François Havy struggled with a long illness. When fully recov-
ered, he was advised of the death of Lefebvre during his return to
Europe, news that had long been withheld from him. It was news that
he confessed had broken his heart. He had counted on the great pleasure of their being together again, but, he wrote, "God did not wish to
give us this satisfaction blessed be His Holy Name for ever."[53] Havy
accepted no new obligations of trade.[54] In 1762 or 1763 he and his
family moved to Bordeaux, where he could be advised and helped by
his in-laws.[55] There are indications that he was no longer mentally fit

for business.[56] It was at Bordeaux that he died, at the age of 63 on 12 December 1766.[57]

II

Shortly after the fall of Quebec, Havy had remarked to Dugard that "There is no longer either confidence or money and consequently those who have obligations are much to be pitied and most unfortunate."[58] Although Havy was still unaware of it, Dugard himself was one of the most unfortunate. The financial pressure caused by the failure of the Darnétal enterprises had been aggravated by the death of D'Haristoy, the intransigence of Guillaume France, and the failure of the syndics to terminate bankruptcy proceedings relating to Vasse, Le Leu, and Michel Lemercier, a cotton buyer who had stopped payment 17 years before. The inventory of Darnétal had been sequestered by the courts pending a settlement. Louis Paynel, himself in possession of some of the company's effects, had declared that Darnétal had really been a *société en commandite* and that as a *commanditaire* he enjoyed limited liability, thus ignoring his endorsement of thousands in bills of exchange, promissory notes, and bonds. The *ad hoc* system of robbing Peter to pay Paul by which Dugard then maintained his solvency became yet another casualty of the war as the financial difficulties of government had their repercussions in the world of business, both through the absorption of all available capital for government purposes and by the stop payment on all manner of government paper.[59] Dugard's Paris bankers, Ridel and Company, were obliged to diminish their advances to him as of June 1760.[60] "The Darnétal enterprise is going to be annihilated with a frightful loss," Dugard warned the Paynels. "That for velours will be prodigiously shaken by the cessation of the credit that it enjoys."[61] He seems to have met his obligations for the year with regard to St. Sever with money extracted from them and from another member of the company. But the catastrophe was postponed rather than averted.

Robert Dugard's creditors assembled the first Saturday in October 1761, at the home of his friend Pierre Godefroy, there to hear his announcement that he could not meet his engagements and to be shown the balance sheet of his affairs.[62] His career, begun at Amsterdam 40 years before, was at an end. "My design and my resolution," he reported to his correspondent at Honfleur, "are to continue no business and to retire far from the world."[63] His only concern now was to save what he could from his "naufrage" and to avoid an official declaration of bankruptcy and "the shame with which a declaration always stamps a family." [64] Mme. Dugard, his second wife, whom he had married in 1749 without community of property, had lost 40,000 livres in his affairs. She now agreed to exercise her rights as his creditor only if he declared bankruptcy, thus encouraging other creditors to accept a private agreement. [65]

Dugard's creditors met for a second time on 18 October. They were willing to settle for 40 per cent, deciding after careful study of his balance sheet that that was as much as could be hoped for. But as Dugard did not believe he could pay more than 20 per cent immediately and a further 20 per cent only after two years, this delay being occasioned by the liquidation of Darnétal, it was decided that only by the endorsement of his promises by his family could such an arrangement be accepted. [66] David Laurens, the brother of Dugard's first wife, appears to have accepted quite readily the family responsibility of supporting Dugard and even pressured creditors to sign the agreement by threatening to withdraw his correspondence from them. [67] Jean De Cuisy of Caen, husband of Dugard's late sister, also saw the need for united action and warned cryptically that being Protestants they had "in every respect more precautions to take." [68] But he was less amenable than Laurens, believing that in order to save something for himself Dugard was demanding unnecessary risks on his part.

The situation was complicated by the peculiar position of the country estate of Bonneval to the west of Rouen near the hamlet of La Haye-Aubrée. This had been purchased by Dugard in the prosperous year of 1743. [69] Bonneval was worth 75,000 livres, but its revenues were absorbed by legally privileged debts, a lifetime annuity paid to its former owner, and further annuities representing the fortune of Mme. Dugard and the inheritance of Dugard's two children by his first marriage, their *tiers coutumier*. [70] These credits privileged in law were all that made it possible for Dugard to withhold Bonneval from his creditors, possibly a well-conceived arrangement planned years in advance to protect the family from business reversals. But privileged or not, Bonneval was the only resource that remained to be offered to Laurens and De Cuisy as collateral for their signatures. The disagreement with De Cuisy revolved around the terms of such an offer. A visit to Caen by Mme. Dugard appeared for a time to have satisfied him, and on 23 March 1762, Dugard's creditors signed his agreement. [71] Although De Cuisy subsequently declared that he had come to no understanding regarding the guarantee, refusing to endorse Dugard's

TABLE 19.

Robert Dugard's Financial Position, 23 March 1762 (Simplified Balance Sheet)

ASSETS		LIABILITIES	
Easily realised Assets		Creditors privileged	
Capital, St. Sever	12,500	at law (includes	
Furniture, movables	12,000	mortgagees)	76,872,,11,,8
Interest in river craft	1,000	Creditors signatories	
Bills of exchange &		to agreement for	
trade balances owing	3,190	repayment	121,608,,3,,5
Houses, garden,			
small farm	26,000		
rentes	10,008		
Subtotal	64,698		198,480,,15,,1
Assets of doubtful value, Debts of doubtful value.			
Owed by G. France on c/c	11,018,,13,,0		
Trade balance, Luekens of Bordeaux (from 1742)	4,703,,11,,0		
Darnétal enterprises, estimated realizable	44,409,,0,,0		
(Capital is 16,666,,13,,4 and acceptances and advances of primary material total 234,635,,11,,4, but of this only 20,000 from inventory and 24,409 claimed from Paynel for his endorsement of notes seems realizable.)			
Subtotal	60,131,,4,,0		
Frozen Assets			
Terre de Bonneval, estimate	75,000,,0,,0	*Rente viagère* & family claims privileged at law	75,000
Assets total:	199,829,,4,,0	Liabilities total:	273,480,,15,,1
To balance:	73,651,,15,,1		
	273,480,,15,,1		

Source: AN, 62AQ31, "Bilan de Dugard."

promissory notes and endangering the settlement by his delays, he finally signed them in return for Dugard's procuration permitting him and Laurens to sell Bonneval without consulting Dugard should they be called upon to meet his engagements.[72]

Even before Dugard had signed the agreement with his creditors, he was faced with yet another problem. If his own financial situation were bad, it seemed unlikely that that of Louis Paynel could be much better. Were he forced into bankruptcy and his affairs placed in the hands of syndics, there would be no early conclusion of the affair of Darnétal, perhaps no conclusion at all.[73] The reality was even worse than Dugard had expected. On the morning of 30 November he learned "that Monsieur Paynel is visibly perishing and almost always remains in bed." [74] Before him opened a "dreadful perspective," a future burdened with legal disputes with Paynel's heirs in an affair that would be submitted to the Intendant and then appealed in the Conseil d'Etat, denying him for years the money that he counted on to make his second payment. By Christmas Paynel was dead.[75] His accounts were in a state of chaos, many of them being on loose sheets of paper.[76] From the audit of the accounts by Dugard, Mme. D'Haristoy, and the two sons of Louis Paynel, arose a series of disputes, charges, and countercharges laid out in a spate of printed memoranda, each a wedge to drive the disputants even farther apart.[77]

Bankruptcy, unofficial though it was, changed completely the tenor of Robert Dugard's daily life. He was still called to merchants' assemblies, to the nomination of the *juges consuls*, and he had successfully avoided a declaration of bankruptcy.[78] But his material situation was drastically altered. The fine house on the Rue des Charettes that he had rented since 1733 at 1,000 livres per year had to be abandoned. Beginning at Christmas 1763, he rented at 170 livres per year a suite of rooms where he could work at his accounts.[79] Mme. Dugard, "no longer being able to appear in town in a suitable style," had retired to Bonneval, where Dugard would follow as soon as business permitted.[80] The furniture, linen, and silver were sold,[81] as was Dugard's library of Protestant treatises, classical literature, and works of philosophy and history.[82]

If war was a natural occasion for bankruptcies, it provided no occasion at all for profitable liquidation. Dugard reported to De Cuisy that he was getting no good offers for his real estate and annuities, "the large amount of property being sold because of the general poverty and the considerable taxes to be paid," and "the bad situation of manufacturing because of the war" being the cause. Most of his houses were small, "which are only suitable for individuals of a certain class

& who at the present time have no money."[83] He did not expect more than 30,000 livres for property valued at 36,000.[84] A garden at Darnétal was not sold until 1769, apparently a result of the depressed condition of the market.[85]

Nor was the recovery of Dugard's credits easy and rapid. By 1769 the proceedings against the Vasse estate and the De la Rues, a family connected with the Le Mercier bankruptcy, were still in progress.[86] Paynel Frères declared their own bankruptcy; and although Dugard thought they would be required to settle their father's debts first, their own creditors signed their accord in March 1770, forgiving 92½ per cent of their debt.[87] All these affairs outlived him.

It is impossible to trace fully Dugard's payments under the terms of his agreement. The first 20 per cent seems to have been paid with only minimal difficulty, but in several instances Laurens and De Cuisy were called upon to render payment for notes they had endorsed for the second 20 per cent.[88] By endorsement much of Dugard's outstanding debt was thus transformed into a family affair. In return for this, neither Laurens nor De Cuisy ever called upon him to surrender Bonneval.

When the Société du Canada had been terminated in 1759, Robert Dugard had reminded Guillaume France that it was the Lord who giveth and taketh away according to his good pleasure and that they should thank God for what he had left them.[89] Under the stress of his bankruptcy, he bolstered himself with this same stoic advice. "It seems that heaven has arranged things in a very unfortunate manner for me," he wrote in 1761.[90] He had worked much and made no ruinous expense. When his commerce was destroyed during the war of 1744–48, he set himself to the new labours of Darnétal and St. Sever to repair his losses, but again what he built came crashing down. In this second and final calamity he was sustained "by the consideration that all events are directed by the hand of God and that we ought to submit to his will and to the trials that he sends us."[91] Yet these professions of the sustaining power of God's Providence, echoing sentiments expressed through the years by Havy, Lefebvre, France fils, and himself, do not appear in his correspondence after 1761.

The idea of Providence did not prevent Dugard's finding temporal reasons for his downfall. It was D'Haristoy "who always had big ideas," who first engaged him in the adventure of Darnétal, and it was this that caused his ruin. He had followed "unfortunately too vast ideas" with which D'Haristoy was always filled.[92] But this hint of his own too great ambition was overshadowed by the idea that it was his lack of self-interest and his foolish generosity to a visionary friend that had lost him his fortune.[93] Similarly, he found that Guillaume France still owed him for the account of the Société du Canada by reason of this same indifference "for all that is called self-interest."[94] "My lot has always been to be sacrificed," he concluded.[95] His major flaw was thus one that seemed eminently forgivable.

Dugard was not a man of deep spirituality, and bankruptcy, which threatened scandal, shame, and the loss of his family's honour, was not an experience from which he emerged with serenity. Having lost most of the external props sanctioned by his society, all but Bonneval to which he tenaciously clung, he found no peace within. His altered social position was not something with which he could come to terms. His complaint of 1761 that he merited the compassion "of all those who have known me, because I fall from a great height"[96] is a theme continued in his letters until as late as 1768, when he wrote of his "situation which is not gracious after having been one of the foremost traders of the Rouen market."[97]

From the first he hinted darkly of death, "a result that I desire more than I dread it."[98] He was distracted and complained that he was "little the master of his mind and his time."[99] He began to notice his age.[100] Retreats to Bonneval became long and frequent, inspiring the complaint that audit proceedings were thus greatly retarded.[101] Sickness, which made its appearance in 1761, became more of a problem, keeping him in the country from April to November 1768.[102] In January 1770, he complained of "the disorder and the derangement that my head & health undergo." He could scarcely walk two hundred steps without an attack which he described as "a cruel oppression that forces me to stop."[103] "For me death would be a happy deliverance," he proclaimed. "There is not a day that I do not desire it."[104] Nine years of altercations with debtor and creditor, of pleading for money and pleading for time, of appearances before courts, intendants, and councils, had drained him. His pilgrimage had been the opposite of Job's; God did not bless his latter end more than his beginning, and at the last he saw himself "absolutely face to face with nothing."[105] He died on 25 July 1770, at Bonneval.[106]

After Dugard's retirement from trade in 1761, his son, Robert V, had received the accounts of old family correspondents, Bansa Brothers of Frankfort, exporters of azure. But as it seemed irrefutable to them that "being young and being absolute master, one often takes false steps,"[107] they demanded a guarantee of his solvency, which was eventually given by his uncles Laurens and De Cuisy and by his father's friend, Pierre Godefroy.[108] This occasioned much avuncular advice from Caen to be active and vigilant and to never put off till tomorrow what could be done today.[109] But it was Rémy Bansa who dispensed the distillate of his experience most freely. When he learned of the death of the elder Dugard, he was quick to find a lesson in the life that had ended; and his exchange of letters with his young correspondent provides the epilogue to the history of Robert Dugard and his many enterprises:

> All the advice that I can give you, Monsieur, is not to get yourself into overly extensive ventures. It is better to keep a tight rein, especially today. Luxury must be avoided and you must never wish to imitate those who live a high life; that is the way to build a solid house and to remain always on your feet . . . those who give themselves up to luxury will feel it to their loss sooner or later, with wisdom we must gauge our expenses against our income and never consume our income, that makes us loved and honoured. What is the point of putting ourselves in difficult straits and into great risk to gain more wealth in order to spend even more; that makes us hated and results in our loss. I count on you, Monsieur, to measure your steps.[110]

The young Robert Dugard agreed with this and declared himself "definitely determined not to undertake any considerable business."[111] "I have the good fortune," he continued, "to be without ambition. I have neither wife nor family to maintain; thus my fortune suffices to sustain my business. I am more jealous to keep it than to run the risks of losing it while desiring too ardently to augment it. I am of your opinion. I like the simple life best."

From Business History to the History of Society

For the historian, Robert Dugard's life is not the empty progression ending "vis à vis de rien" that Dugard himself in his last year interpreted it to be. Neither can he regard it as the morality play of calamity wrought by a too-great ambition that it was for Rémy Bansa. Rather, it is the central, unifying thread in a fabric of many lives that together constitute an example of economic activity and assumptions in eighteenth-century France and her Atlantic colonies. The story of Dugard and Company, as is true of all business histories, occupies that middle ground where the economic sphere overlaps with the social.

In form, the company was typical of its time and place, a partnership drawing together like-minded men of intimate acquaintance in the pursuit of profit. Some degree of intimacy was essential. It was the safeguard of secrecy and mutual trust that were the foundation of a company of unlimited liability, bound by the action of any member, liable for the debts of a bankrupt partner, and capable itself of consuming their private fortunes.

The confident acceptance of growth as a major aim of the company, the ploughing back of profits, and the assumption of considerable risks in the use of credit mark the venture with the stamp of commercial capitalism. The financing of the company is a remarkable episode, vividly revealing the clumsy character of short-term finance by bills of exchange and the danger inherent therein, but also the surprising expansibility of commercial credit. If contemporary financial institutions and methods occasioned one major crisis in the company's history, they also enabled the company to achieve a considerable expansion. Without credit, and hence the costs and the risks involved, the company's rate of profit might have been higher, but the capital would have been so much smaller as to change the character of the business from that of a great to a petty trade.

Adequate, if dangerous, for the financing of a trading company, bills of exchange and promissory notes could by no means meet the needs of industrial undertakings with larger fixed capital, such as the manufactures of Darnétal and St. Sever. The only other traditional method by which partnerships could increase their capital was a form of partial limited liability known in France as early as the seventeenth century, the *société en commandite*. In a partnership of this form, certain members could limit their liability to the extent of their capital provided that the administration of the company was entirely in the hands of other partners with full joint and several liability. It was thus a means of tapping the capital reserves of wealthy retired merchants, financiers, or aristocrats who did not wish to dabble in trade themselves or to take the full risks of participation in the usual form. Like the bottomry loan, the bill of exchange, and the merchant's note, this was also clearly a device that permitted investment untainted by usury. Louis Paynel claimed to have entered the Société de Darnétal as a limited liability *commanditaire*. But as the company's funds soon proved inadequate and he was moved to sign its bills of exchange, he undermined any presumed limited liability status with the stroke of a pen.

The acceleration of the number of bills and notes subsequently issued to support Darnétal not only led Dugard and his partners to violate their consciences but to eventual bankruptcy. For large-scale undertakings other means of finance had to be found. Hence the recourse for the first time to *actions*: five-year proto-debentures, bearing interest that averaged 7.2 per cent per year. These loans to the company, placed only with difficulty in the absence of any real stock market, in no way tended to break down the personal character of ownership or administration. Those later issued for the Société de St. Sever were described by a member of the company as "confidential commercial paper that I can propose only to persons of my acquaintance."[1]

That secret, private character of the *société générale* characteristic of Dugard and Company was to some extent attenuated in the Darnétal enterprises because of the Crown's insistence on associating all inventors of Adrianople red in one *manufacture royale* of registered capitalization. The Société de St. Sever was more specifically the creation of the State, bringing together strangers and imposing terms of association on the entrepreneurs. Yet even St. Sever was a partnership. The step from the *société de personnes* to the *société de capitaux*, or joint-stock company, was psychologically a very long one. It was difficult to break out of the complex of interdependent ideas, practices, and institutions inherited from the past, even though these traditional structures were severely taxed by the necessities of these three companies. The progress of Dugard and his partners in these various enterprises towards such a liberation was nevertheless very real. In 1742 they were resorting to expensive bottomry loans and international bill negotiations that provide no clear evidence of discount. By the 1750s the international character of bill negotiations had been dropped, and the bills were being discounted in the modern sense of the term.[2] Finally, borrowing secured by *actions* makes its appearance, although limited to sales to acquaintances and to D'Haristoy's own family. This succession of organizational and financial structures marks a period of transition in the history of French business.

Eighteenth-century business histories are not abundant, but those that have been written suggest very strongly that in France and England, the individual, the family, and the partnership were the basic units of business activity.[3] Given that England is considered to have been the most advanced commercial nation of the period, the homogeneity of French and English structures is particularly instructive. Joint-stock failed to displace the partnership in eighteenth-century English business because of the reaction to the South Sea Bubble. Thereafter English courts refused to recognise the principles of limited liability and the transferability of shares, a situation that prevailed until well into the nineteenth century. In spite of this, the joint-stock idea persisted, and from time to time illegal, limited liability assignable shares were offered to the public. It was the inevitable answer to the demands for greater concentration of capital made by industrialization in the later part of the century.[4] Had the enterprises of Darnétal and St. Sever been English, it is doubtful that they would have been financed by joint-stock. A common trading business such as Dugard and Company would never have been organized as a joint-stock venture.

The situations of French and English merchants also seem to have been remarkably similar with regard to long-term loans. Although the English banking structure was more advanced and the royal finances more stable, venture capital was not always easily found. Credit for so short a term as two years was unobtainable.[5] That banks were not interested in speculative advances of capital is suggested, for example, by a maxim of Martin's Bank dated 1746, "Not to lend any money without application from the borrower and upon alienable security that may be easily disposed of, and a probability of punctual payment without being reckoned hard by the borrower."[6] The historian of the London private banks has found it difficult to judge how well they served English merchants, but concludes that the latter obtained working capital mainly through discount, which puts them precisely in the same position as French merchants.[7] But they did have the advantage of a lower rate of interest, which suggests more investment capital and perhaps a better bill market.[8] In sum, the structure and financing of Dugard and Company appears to have been typical of French business, although the latter was beginning to exhibit change; and French business does not appear to have been backward judged by the standards of the century.

In *The Wealth of Nations*, Adam Smith provided a guide to what business profits usually tended to be: "Double interest is in Great Britain reckoned, what the merchants call, a good, moderate, reasonable profit; terms which I apprehend mean no more than a common and usual profit."[9] While such a proceeding as the *prêt à la grosse aventure* was extremely costly, the usual French rate of interest for mercantile advances according to Havy and Lefebvre was six per cent. Interest on the first year of St. Sever and Darnétal *actions* was only five per cent. Discount on bills was presumably scaled to this level of five to six per cent. Alternatives to commercial investment usually earned less. Rents from land have been calculated at two to four per cent of capital value, while investment in venal offices, which absorbed so much French capital, sometimes earned no return at all or only as much as five per cent. From 1725 until 1766 the official rate of interest was set by the government at five per cent.[10] Using Smith's rule of thumb, ten to 12 per cent must have been "no more than a common and usual profit" for a French merchant. Dugard and Company's profits as shown in tables 30 and 33 recall another of Smith's dicta, "Profit is so very fluctuating that the person who carries on a particular trade cannot always tell you himself what is the average of his annual profit."[11] But if the average of company profits to 1743 is calculated on the basis of the figures in table 30, uncomplicated by depreciation or interest payments, the resulting 11.4 per cent fits nicely into Smith's range. When the average is reduced to take account of depreciation, on which Smith is silent, the resulting figure is 8.5 per cent. But greater refinement is possible. Smith further states, "In a country where the ordinary rate of clear profit is eight or ten per cent, it may be reasonable that one half of it should go to interest, wherever business is carried on with borrowed money."[12] From the data in table 33, where the cost of credit is taken into account to as great an extent as the data allow, clear profit for the same period can be calculated to have been 7.7 per cent. Given that the company seldom depended upon borrowing to provide as much as half of its outlays and often to provide much less, it appears that Smith is an impeccable guide to its profit history—or conversely, that the company's record of profits corroborates Smith's estimate.

Where they can be compared with the profits of other eighteenth-century businesses, those of the company appear to have been quite acceptable. William Braund, a London merchant, earned 10⅓ per cent in 1753,[13] when according to Smith "people of good credit" borrowed at 3½ to 4½ per cent.[14] English silk traders, working in a business that was certainly as risky as Dugard's, earned about ten to 20 per cent on turnover, which took two years, making 5 to ten per cent per annum.[15] Research into French sources has generally revealed lower rates. Profits per annum of the Maison Chaurand of Nantes for 1776–84 were only six per cent and dropped in the years that followed.[16] The voyages of the ships of the Maison Bouteiller, also of Nantes, varied between .9 and nine per cent![17] Indeed, Solier et Cie. of Marseilles seems to have earned as little as two to six per cent per annum on its West Indies trade after 1783.[18] Admittedly, these figures are all from a period when the West Indies trade was in decline. In the much better years of 1726–29 Jean Pellet of Bordeaux averaged 28 per cent on outward cargoes and 11 per cent on returns, indicating a profit level not very different from Dugard and Company's.[19] The profits attributed to Dugard and Company thus do not appear too low when compared to those of other traders that have been examined by historians and compare favourably with Smith's "double interest" except in time of war.

It has been argued cogently that the risks of trade were preferable to the security of *rentes* in spite of modest profits because of the speed of return on investment. The capital of most other investments could not easily be regained. Neither land nor offices were usually sold for cash. Many offices had to be held for 20 years to confer nobility permanently upon the family, the principal reason for buying them. The capital of an annuity was irretrievably lost, and annuities were difficult to transfer. But commerce quite quickly returned a good mass of working capital, even if a small part of investment was immobilized in receivables that remained unpaid year after year. Thus this capital could be reinvested and set to work again. Rapid turnover is then taken to be the explanation for the growth of trade in spite of the profit level and the absence of a large investing public.[20] But too often business histories have ignored the expansion of credit by the negotiation of commercial paper, which the history of Dugard and Company and of the Darnétal and St. Sever enterprises reveals to have been of such vital importance. It was not the profit but the large capital upon which the profit was made that was crucial. To once again quote Adam Smith,

"A great stock, though with small profits, generally increases faster than a small stock with great profits. Money, says the proverb, makes money."[21] As the strings of interconnected bankruptcies that punctuate the commercial history of the period suggest, one of the principal means by which a large capital was amassed in the eighteenth century was the negotiation of notes and drafts.

The union of shipping and cargo trading that characterized Dugard and Company appears to have been extremely common in the period, although by no means universal. It gave the company extra flexibility, permitting it to alternate between freighting and cargo trading expeditions according to its needs and the demands of the market. It ensured adequate transport for company cargoes at Quebec, a port not usually visited by freight seekers, who were unlikely to find a profit in their return journey. It also made possible the establishing of trade at out-of-the-way ports in the West Indies, opening the prospect of higher profits on cargo than was possible at the main centres of St. Pierre, Martinique, and Cap Français, St. Domingue.

Just as Dugard and Company was extremely dependent upon credit, so too were its colonial customers. There would have been no furs at Quebec had not a large part of the goods traded for them been given on credit the previous year. Thus the credit apparatus of promissory notes, personal bonds, mortgages, the taking of interest, redress through the courts, and imprisonment of commercial debtors was elaborated in Canada. Official correspondence from the West Indies reveals something of the tribulations of debtors and the evasions of which they were capable to confound their creditors. It is not surprising that Dugard wished to limit credit to the planters as much as possible, avoiding that permanent commitment to a particular market that debts owing would entail. But in maintaining the greatest possible freedom of action—and it is impossible to say whether or not this was typical of French merchants in general—Dugard did not gain that solid position in a highly competitive trade that was attained by British merchants in their own sugar empire by generously extending credit, chaining planters by links of debt, and eventually taking their plantations for payment.

The handling of the Quebec trade by factors and that of the West Indies by captains were typical of those two trades. It is clear from Havy and Lefebvre's letters to Pierre Guy and from many references in the correspondence of Canadian officials that the Quebec Lower Town trading community was composed primarily of the factors of La Rochelle, Bordeaux, and Rouen trading companies; they controlled the import-export trade of the colony and, by the near monopoly of credit that was the natural lot of metropolitan concerns in an underdeveloped colony, had considerable control over the trade of the hinterland. The division of the trade of Canada between two points, Montreal and Quebec, permitted a degree of specialization. The native Canadian merchants at Montreal dealt directly with fur traders, or were themselves fur traders, while Quebec merchants usually confined themselves to import and export and to the exploitation of a separate hinterland all their own, the "Kingdom of the Saguenay," the coast of Labrador, the island of Cape Breton, and the West Indies. The Montreal merchants were thus in a position similar to the *commissionnaires* of St. Pierre, who were the intermediaries between the scattered planters of Martinique, Guadeloupe, and lesser islands and the *capitaines-géreurs*. Only at these two points, Montreal and St. Pierre, links with hinterlands to which metropolitan agents (factors or captains) had no easy access, did independent merchant groups develop. The comparative analysis of the rise and character of these two groups, of their use of credit and of the laws that governed their economic activity is an area of colonial history that awaits its historian.

Business methods and institutions are themselves aspects of a total society. It is in a larger, more global understanding of society that historians frequently attempt to explain the specific character of French business, ascribing to it marked deficiencies in comparison with English business. According to the most widely-held views, the prestige of nobility and government service and the access to both by means of the system of venality in public offices drained both money and talent from the ranks of the merchant class, leaving it permanently impoverished and incapable of giving its own characteristic stamp to society as a whole. In England, on the other hand, throughout the seventeenth and eighteenth centuries trade increased in prestige, substantially sharing in government during the "Whig Supremacy" and producing in the end that "nation of shopkeepers" of which Napoleon spoke with such disdain.

Different members of the Société du Canada provide such divergent models of behaviour that the history of the company gives no clear affirmation of this dichotomy. The behaviour of the France family would seem to confirm the common interpretation, the merchant father being succeeded by a son who was a *secrétaire du roi*, tax farmer, landed gentleman, and avowedly "very ignorant of business matters." [22] A contrary destiny is represented by David Laurens who, according to his nephew, was "in business only to divert himself and make use of his money." [23] D'Haristoy was different again, an industrial promoter of great enthusiasm and an amateur of technology reminiscent of the Encyclopedists. Dugard himself showed no signs of attempting to leave the commercial life and evidently raised his son with a thorough knowledge of business. His purchase of a country estate in 1743 was no desertion of the middle class. The history of Dugard's bankruptcy shows clearly the role of land as a safe investment for a merchant the bulk of whose fortune was tied up in high-risk ventures. To invest a portion of one's capital in land was only good sense in the eighteenth-century context.

The great prestige attaching to land and hence a large measure of its attraction to the merchant cannot be denied. But it is important to remember that landed status was sought by merchants everywhere, except perhaps in Holland. An English historian writes that, "Generally speaking, the ambition of a London merchant in the eighteenth century was to make a fortune in trade and bring up his eldest son to live as a country gentleman on an estate bought with the profits of his father's trade," and that, "The business that was carried on in a second generation after a real fortune had been made was a rarity."[24] Clearly, it would be a distortion to single out the eighteenth-century Frenchman to the exclusion of others as having "an atavistic attachment to the soil."[25]

The difference between French and English behavioural patterns with regard to the aristocratic and business ways of life is perhaps to be found in the greater coming and going between the English country house and counting house. Even if an eldest son were landed, his younger brothers were likely to continue toiling in the city, possibly with his financial backing. Sons of the manor might be apprenticed to wealthy merchants. Caste lines were certainly less rigid than in France. England had had no Louis XIV to sap the aristocracy of its initiative and let them render sloth a model for society. But norms of behaviour are not by themselves sufficient to explain the divergent destinies of the English and French merchant classes. Not every case fits the model. Research on Nantes shipping, for example, has revealed that 6,300 of 10,277 trading voyages between 1694 and 1792 were the undertakings of noble families, many of them very old families.[26] Whatever the truth of the relation of social structure and social concepts to business methods, institutions, recruitment, and behaviour, it is certainly not simple. The cliché of French/English dichotomy is far too simplistic. That variety of attitudes and destinies evident in so small a group as Dugard and Company is perhaps a reflection of cross-currents in society at large. In this as in so many ways, the period 1730–70 may have been one of basic transition.[27] Did the departure of the France family from commerce in the 1740s constitute a social transformation increasingly less necessary, even less attractive? Was it increasingly easy for a man like D'Haristoy to feel fully at ease while conversing with ministers of the Crown about looms and dye vats? Certainly, he did not blush to tell the Intendant, De la Bourdonnaye, that he was "born for great tasks" and that while only one man he was undertaking the work of a king![28]

At least three of the families united in the Société du Canada were Protestant. It is thus natural to ask whether religion influenced their business behaviour and made it markedly different from that of their Catholic partners. Historians influenced by Max Weber would undoubtedly find Dugard and Laurens examples of Protestant capitalism and explain France's retreat from business in terms of his Catholicism. Such an explanation takes no account of D'Haristoy, the real progenitor of modern times in the story, and ignores the obvious fact that the Catholic Guillaume France was responding to opportunities of social advancement closed to the Protestant Dugards, Laurenses, and Vincents. The shaky foundations of the scholarship that supports the notion of an important relation between the Protestant ethic and the spirit of capitalism has been thoroughly exposed elsewhere.[29] The mentality of all the members of the Société du Canada seems in certain particulars to have been so consistent and to have been so similar to that attributed to Catholic French bourgeois of the period that a more common ground of ethics and attitude formation than the Protestant Reformation must be sought. Is not the common ground trade itself, which encourages attitudes, values, and a singular way of life by which it is in turn reinforced?

In 1675 Jacques Savary published one of the most influential books in French history, *Le parfait négociant*, wherein the mercantile middle class found the very model of its social type:

> If one looks at all the families of traders and those that have left commerce for the robe, it will be found that these great establishments began with ancestors born without wealth but with much virtue that they acquired by doing business under other merchants, who being content with their conduct took them as associates because of the indispensable necessities of their business, first for a sixth or a twelfth, bringing nothing to the partnership but their industry. And thus little by little they advanced in such a way that eventually they remained alone masters of the boutique or warehouse of their masters and thus conserved the habits that rendered them rich and opulent.[30]

Much virtue, a humble and respectful attitude towards superiors, regular habits, including rising at 5 a.m. and retiring at 11 p.m., were part of a constellation of qualities that constituted a kind of class and occupational ethic. The *parfait négociant* was sober, hard-working, and a man of probity, as he hoped his business associates would also be: trade depended upon trust.

It is easy to see from their letters that Robert Dugard and his friends accepted this philosophy. They prized work very highly. When Dugard in all but name became bankrupt in 1761, he instinctively explained the injustice of his fate in terms of his having worked hard and having persevered in working hard even in the face of heavy losses. What was equally important, he believed that he had avoided luxury. When François Havy was ruined by the British conquest of Quebec, he too felt that the times were out of joint. Why? Because he believed that he had worked harder than any other metropolitan factor, but many of his competitors had grown very rich.

Bankruptcy itself was also regarded in the light of Savary's ethic. For Dugard, not being able to meet his obligations was the supreme dishonour that would permanently blemish the family name. Almost everything he owned he sold to pay his creditors (Bonneval excepted) and from a rented office he spent the last nine years of his life making minimal payments here and there, holding his creditors at bay while suing his own debtors with vigour. Neither this conception of work nor this attitude towards bankruptcy were a part of the outlook of the French upper classes. They regarded work as at very best a necessary evil and certainly unconnected with reward, which they expected as their birthright. To them debts and bankruptcy were of small account.

Savary counselled that young merchants should undertake trade "with traders who are already established in trade with whom they can ally themselves by marrying their daughters."[31] Marrying the daughter of a businessman was the key to success or failure "because in marrying the daughter, one marries the good or bad business of the house."[32] Thus it is not surprising that Dugard and Company is an example of a number of young men forming a company with two older men past age of retirement, Gédéon Vincent and David Laurens père, and a man in middle age, Guillaume France père. It is not surprising that Dugard sealed the relation by marrying Laurens's daughter.

Le parfait négociant was the bourgeois heritage of the seventeenth century: probity, hard work, caution, a business organization that might be described as an extension of the institution of the family. In an age of heady expansion, it was perhaps too unaspiring, too self-limiting. The common business venture was no longer founded upon a modest capital and minimal fixed assets, being of short duration with a speedy division of large profits. There was perhaps in the Savary ethic an outmoded fear of bigness that one can see reflected in the elder Guillaume France's complaint, "I would never have believed that our enterprise would have lasted so long without returning our investment." [33] But it was a policy of expansion, even reckless expansion, that carried the day. The most significant aspect of the history of Dugard and Company may then be that it represents a transition from seventeenth-century norms that might be called "static capitalism" towards a more open-ended economic endeavour, "expansionist capitalism." This would reinforce the notion of social change that might be divined in the diverse destinies of the members of the company: the breakup of an old order.

Robert Dugard and his friends lived out their lives beneath the eyes of a sleepless God. They were governed by His Divine Providence. The passages in the Dugard Papers testifying to a submission to Providence are many and striking. Some examples may be recalled from earlier chapters, all of them reactions to economic or other personal disasters: "God above all. . . . Everything must be placed in the hands of Divine Providence," (Havy).[34] "We must be patient and offer this new loss to the Lord," (France fils).[35] "It seems that heaven has arranged things in a very unfortunate manner for me," (Dugard).[36] "We must make a sacrifice of it and submit to the decrees of Providence," (France fils).[37] "We must adore the hand of God that strikes us," (France fils).[38]

Belief in a Divine Plan could sometimes be an inestimable source of strength. Dugard wrote in the midst of financial calamity that he was sustained "by the consideration that all events are directed by the hand of God and that we ought to submit to his will and to the trials he sends us." [39] François Havy's letters are rich in the expectation of divine help. But the more the businessman believed in the reality of Providence, the more his unsettling ambition and social ascension must have weighed upon him. Providence meant Order, the harmony of the world—and that included the social order—established by God.[40] With some difficulty the Church had found a place for the merchant in this social hierarchy. It told him that to pursue his calling was to utter a prayer. The idea of Providence, the idea of the calling and the idea of an immutable social order were all shared by Huguenots and Roman Catholics. But in the pursuit of his calling the merchant all too often upset the social order in which he still believed. The successful merchant must have seen himself committing a sin as old as western civilization, the sin of hubris. Modern psychiatry would call his situation a "double bind." Entrance into the nobility meant the cutting loose of even the memory of a mercantile past, forgetting ever having been a party to the disruption of the social order. To reach the pinnacle of success and remain an active merchant was perhaps to maintain a psychically difficult position. To reach the pinnacle of success and immediately come crashing down was easily explained in terms of hubris. This would seem to be the meaning of Rémy Bansa's pronouncements on the life of Robert Dugard. As Dugard himself lamented, he had followed "too vast ideas."[41]

Far across the Atlantic, in Canada and the West Indies, to which ambitions even more vast than the schemes of Pierre D'Haristoy had carried French trade and empire, were new societies. To what extent did the ideas and the problems of those of Dugard's class influence these frontier groups of Frenchmen? The little community of metropolitan merchants in Quebec's Lower Town, of which Havy and Lefebvre were for so many years a part, constituted an intrusion of French business into the Canadian colony. Did they transmit their own bourgeois attitudes and habits of mind to the native Canadian business community with which they were in continuous interaction? Or was the Lower Town something set apart from the mainstream of Canadian life, too weak to influence a society established on norms other than its own, evolving through the interaction of other, more pertinent aspects of French society with the imperatives of a new and singular environment? What aspects of French society could most adequately flourish in the West Indies, at once so intimate a part of the French economy and so outlandishly different from anything French at all?

The history of Dugard and Company, like an old map, includes a terrain known with some high degree of accuracy, extends to peninsulas, capes and bays drawn in with less assurance of reliability and ends with tentative sketchings in the area of historical terra incognita. For many old questions it provides answers, for others suggestions; inevitably it raises new questions. While it is intended to illuminate history in its broadest outlines, it also has as its object the more modest task of restoring to memory a certain set of men who, although unexceptional in themselves, for a time did the business of the world and helped to shape it in its continual process of becoming. They merit the recognition and the sympathy that the historian reserves for those spent souls in whom he so perversely attempts to conjure up a spark of their old life.

Profiles of the Dugard Fleet

The *Louis Dauphin*, 1729–34, a *brigantin* variously described as of 80 and 90 tons burden, was probably built at Le Havre in 1728–29 at a cost of 21,574 livres 12/5 *tournois*, including initial equipping.[1] She was built and owned by R. Dugard, D. Laurens, G. Vincent père et fils, G. France, P. D'Haristoy of Rouen, and Pedro Beckveldt of Bilbao.[2] By a decision of 22 January 1733 Beckveldt was bought out by the other members of this Société du *Louis Dauphin* since his decision to participate in the value of freight only and not in cargoes resulted in a financial loss for him.[3] A letter of 8 December 1743 announces the ship as lost on its fourteenth voyage, returning to Honfleur from Cul de Sac Marin, Martinique.[4]

The *St. Mathieu*, 1730–44, was a *navire* described in a bill of lading of 1743 as of 120 tons burden with five cannon and a crew of 20.[5] Most sources, however, describe her as of 90 to 100 tons, and an estimate as low as 80 tons has been found.[6] The vessel was purchased in 1730 by R. Dugard, G. Vincent père et fils, and P. D'Haristoy for 11,100 livres.[7] On 14 May 1732 she was offered to the Société du *Louis Dauphin* to charter.[8] However, an accounting statement dated 9 June 1732 shows that one-fifth interest was ceded to David Laurens, and the accounts of Guillaume France show that he too was credited with a fifth.[9] The *St. Mathieu* had thus become the property of the company. She had left Fort Royal, Martinique, on 13 September 1744 and was returning from her thirteenth voyage for the company when she was captured by the English.[10]

The *Ville de Québec* (later the *Union*), 1733–47, was a *navire* usually described as of 300 tons burden.[11] Her draught was of ten feet unladen and 14 feet laden. She was pierced for 18 cannon, had two

decks and according to a *rôle d'équipage* had one *gaillard* although
one would have expected her to have had two, a quarter deck, and a
forecastle.[12] Crews of 33 and of 50 men are recorded,[13] and at different times she was mounted with as few as 12 and as many as 20
guns.[14] Sometime between 28 January and 10 March 1733 she was
purchased at London from the South Sea Company by Robert Dugard
and François Vangellikom Vandelle on behalf of the Société du
Canada.[15] The price was 45,801 livres 14/2 *tournois*.[16] She was
brought to Le Havre, named the *Ville de Québec*, and Vandelle became her captain.[17] In 1741 she was sent to Quebec for a complete
refitting, possibly because of ice damage she may have suffered leaving
the St. Lawrence the previous November. That all-new sculpture was
provided by Noel Levasseur, indicates that this refit may have been
almost a rebuilding.[18] After refitting, the vessel was renamed the
Union.[19] She perished in a storm near Ile de Ré on 27 February 1747
while returning from Martinique on her tenth voyage.[20]

The *Alçion*, 1736–43, said to have been a *bon voilier*,[21] is variously
described as of 200, 230, and 250 tons burden.[22] What is probably the
most accurate source describes it as a *navire* of 200 tons, pierced for
18 cannon and carrying 12, with a draught of nine feet unladen and
15½ feet fully laden. She was manned by a crew of 34.[23] This was the
first ship built at Quebec for the company by Havy and Lefebvre. Her
cost was 55,747 livres 18/4 *tournois*, and she was launched in September or October 1736, carrying her first cargo to Léoganne, St.
Domingue.[24] She was lost in a storm off "La Petite Caique au Débouquement de St. Domingue" on 29 April 1743, while returning to
Bordeaux from her fifth voyage. The Captain, Pierre Gautier, was ac-
cused by the colonial jurisdiction of St. Marc of deliberately abandon-
ing the vessel without due cause in concert with Robert Dugard to
secure both insurance money and profits on cargo sent aboard other
vessels. Charges against Dugard were never seriously considered, and
Gautier was exonerated by the Admiralty Court of Guienne at Bordeaux.[25]

The *Fleury*, 1738–46, was described in a *rôle d'équipage* as a *navire*
of 300 tons burden, draught unladen of ten and one-half feet and
laden of 14 feet, pierced for 26 cannon and carrying 22, with a crew of
39.[26] She was built at Quebec at a cost of 62,865 livres 2/11 *tournois*
and was launched in 1738.[27] She may have been decorated with
sculpture by Noel Levasseur.[28] She made five commercial voyages before being leased to the King on 30 March 1746.[29] The *Fleury* sailed to
Chebucto Bay with the squadron of the Duc d'Anville. On return she
was damaged during a storm, separated from the fleet and was being

conducted to Guadeloupe by a French ship when encountered by the *Greyhound* of New York. The crippled *Fleury* was captured and taken to New York where she was adjudged a prize on 19 February 1746.[30]

The *St. Louis*, 1739–51, was a *brigantin*[31] described variously as of 70 tons burden with a crew of 18, 80 tons with a crew of 14, and 90 tons with a crew of 15.[32] The most reliable source is an official estimate of 82½ tons burden.[33] Her sculpture was by Noel Levasseur.[34] The ship was built for Dugard and Company at Quebec in 1739 at a cost of 15,995 livres 18/9 *tournois*.[35] She undertook four trading voyages before 1744, was laid up during the War of the Austrian Succession, and thereafter used for fishing, being shipwrecked at Côte de Loix, Ile de Ré on 4 March 1751, at the beginning of her third fishing voyage.[36] Letters of 21 September and 27 June 1754 describe the sale of her debris.[37]

The *Centaure*, 1740–56, was a *navire* of 350 tons burden,[38] with a draught of ten feet empty and 15 feet fully laden, pierced for 24 guns and with a keel of 80 feet.[39] At different times she carried 12, 15, and 16 guns and crews of 40 and 50 men.[40] Her sculpture was also by Noel Levasseur.[41] She was built at Quebec for Dugard and Company at a cost of 62,338 livres 18/9 *tournois* and was launched in November 1740, carrying part of cargo 11 in return.[42] The *Centaure* was at Le Havre when war was declared in 1744 and was unable to enter the Channel during the four years of conflict because the local *commissaire de la Marine* had commandeered her 12 cannon.[43] In 1748 she recommenced trading activity. On 27 June 1756 she was captured on the high seas by Capt. James Campbell of the *Nightingale*. She was taken to the port of New York and there adjudged a prize, 2 August 1756.[44] She had undertaken nine voyages and was the last of the Dugard fleet.

The *Imprévû*, 1740–44, was a *brigantin*[45] of between 100 and 120 tons burden which carried from four to ten cannon on different occasions.[46] She was built for Dugard and Company at Quebec for 19,670 livres 3/4 *tournois*, and was launched in 1740.[47] Sculpture was by Noel Levasseur.[48] Caught in the ice at Kamouraska, she did not reach France on her maiden voyage until 1741.[49] While returning from Martinique on her fourth voyage in 1744, she was captured by an English ship and taken to Exeter as a prize.[50]

The *Astrée*, 1745–51, was a *navire* variously described as of 243, 300, 350, and 400 tons burden! At different times she carried 18 and 20 cannon and one statement numbers the crew at 45.[51] Launched in 1745, this was the last ship built in Canada for Dugard and Company and was also the most expensive, costing 80,407 livres 7/11 *tour-*

nois.[52] Noel Levassseur's sculpture alone cost 400 livres.[53] The *Astrée* lay in the stocks for nearly four years before being launched and received a terrible beating on her first voyage, facts that may account for her short life.[54] Her refit and sheathing for southern waters took two years, 1746–47.[55] Thereafter she made two voyages and was subsequently dismantled and sold.[56]

The *Trois Maries*, 1742–44, an old vessel described as a *navire* of 140 tons burden, mounted with ten cannon and with a crew of 23, was purchased and outfitted in 1742 for 18,676 livres 13/3 *tournois* by Robert Dugard, Pierre D'Haristoy, and two persons not members of the Société du Canada, LeMoyne and Collineau.[57] She made three voyages, all of them carrying cargoes to Quebec for Dugard and Company. On 4 December 1744 she collided with the *Brillant*, a 600-ton ship of the Compagnie des Indes, while the two were returning in convoy to France from Canada. She sank to the bottom with a loss of 14 lives.[58]

The Ships and Their Voyages

The following tables are based upon the accounts of members of the Société du Canada, which are to be found in the *Fonds Dugard, Archives Nationales, 62AQ40:*

LIASSE O:

Guillaume France, son compte courant avec Robert Dugard, 1729–38, dated 4 October 1738.

Pierre D'Haristoy, son compte courant avec Robert Dugard, 1728–38, dated 31 December 1739.

Vincent père et fils, leur compte courant avec Robert Dugard, 1729–38, dated 31 December 1739.

David Laurens, son compte courant avec Robert Dugard, 1729–38, dated 21 July 1739.

LIASSE S:

Compte de Monsieur France avec DuGard de Rouen dressés par Epoques de Payements et de Recette, 1729–42, no date.

Pierre D'Haristoy, son compte courant avec Robert Dugard, 1737–59, no date.

LIASSE 9:

Monsieur Vincent et ses heritiers, leur compte courant avec Robert Dugard, 1737–59, dated 29 May 1759.

LIASSE R:

Monsieur Guillaume France et ses heritiers, leur compte courant avec Robert Dugard, 1737–59, dated 14 May 1759.

In addition many other sources have been used and these are referred to in the notes to the tables. To save space these citations are very brief, yet they explain the nature of the document cited and where it may be found.

TABLE 20.

Voyages of the Louis Dauphin

Year	Port (France)	Agent	Dep.	Destination (Col. or For)	Arr.	Dep.
1729[1]	Le Havre via La Rochelle	LeVaillant		Bilbao		
1730[2]				Quebec		
				Martinique		
1731[3]				Quebec		
1732[4]				Quebec		
1733[5]				Ile à Vache, St. Dom. (charter out)		
1734[6]				Cadiz		
1735[7]	Le Havre			Quebec	5/7/35	
				Louisbourg		
				Quebec	27/9/35	
1736[8]	Le Havre		after 26/4/36	Quebec	17/7/36	
1737[9]				Quebec		
1738[10]	Le Havre via Bordeaux			Martinique	4/10/38	
				Quebec (?)		
1739[11]				St. Pierre, Martinique		17/6/39
1740[12]	Le Havre	J. Bernard	early spring	St. Pierre, Martinique	16/5/40	23/7/40
1741[13]	Honfleur	J. B. Prémond		St. Pierre, Martinique	28/3/41	26/5/41
				Louisbourg		
				St. Pierre, Martinique	16/10/41	
1742	—					
1743[14]	Honfleur	J. B. Prémond	Feb. or March	Cul de Sac Marin, Martinique	16/4/43	

†This voyage does not appear in the balance sheets. The *Louis Dauphin* may have wintered at Quebec (or Louisbourg) going to Martinique in the spring, returns being included in Cargo 9. If this voyage was made from a French port, the absence of a debit and credit is difficult to explain.

Sources: Associates' Accounts and the following:

[1] AN. 62AQ39, Délibérations, 16/5/1732; 62AQ40, V c/c 1729–38.

[2] AN. 62AQ40, FH c/c 1730–31.

[3] AN. 62AQ39, Délibérations, 6/2/1734; 62AQ40, FH c/c 1731.

[4] AN. 62AQ40, FH c/c 1732; AC. F2B 11, Etat.

[5] AN. 62AQ39, Délibérations, 20/7/1733, 6/2/1734.

[6] AN. 62AQ40, D'H c/c 1728–38.

[7] AN. 62AQ40, H & L c/c 1735; AC. CIIA 121 f157, Etat.

[8] AC. B 64 f38, Lettre; CIIA 65 f240, Etat; F2B 11, Etat.

[9] AN. 62AQ40, H & L Compte général de balance; AC. B 65 f51, Lettre; F2B 11, Etat.

Return	Date	Agent	Captain	Debit	Credit	Voyage #
	before June 1730		Vandelle	unknown		—
Le Havre		LeVaillant	Vandelle	25,753.4.2	28,979.7.6	Cargo 1
Le Havre		LeVaillant	Vandelle	58,773.18.9	64,857.2.1	Cargo 2
Le Havre		LeVaillant	Vandelle	multiship		Cargo 3
				10,054.12.6	10,054.12.6	—
				(Dugard's Estimate)		
				8,041.2.1	5,248.6.3	—
Le Havre			R. Mollard	multiship		Cargo 6
Le Havre			Mollard (out) DeL'Estre (ret)	multiship		Cargo 7
Le Havre			P. DeL'Estre	multiship		Cargo 8
			P. DeL'Estre	multiship		Cargo 9
Le Havre		LeVaillant	P. DeL'Estre			†
Le Havre			Fortin	36.172.-.5	27,962.4.7	—
Honfleur	c. 3 May	Prémond	Fortin	80,468.3.9	98,351.3.9	—
Lost on return to Honfleur			Fortin	133,517.17.1	150,642.2.6	—

[10] AN. 62AQ39, Délibérations, 30/12/1737; AC. CIIA 70 f167, Etat, F2B 11, Etat.

[11] AC. C8B 20, Etat.

[12] AC. C8A 52 f248, Etat; C8B 20, Etat.

[13] AN. 62AQ40, RD c/c avec J. B. Prémond; 62AQ41, RD c/c avec Fautoux, 1739–45; AC. C8B 20, Etat; CIIA 121 f174, Etat.

[14] AN. 62AQ40, RD c/c avec Prémond; AC. B77 f160, Lettre; C8B 20, Etat.

TABLE 21.
Voyages of the St. Mathieu

Year	Port (France)	Agent	Dep.	Destination (Colonies)	Arr.	Dep.
1731[1]	Bordeaux	P. Roncante	22/9/31	West Indies		
1732[2]	Le Havre			Quebec		
				Martinique		
1733[3]	Le Havre		after 20/1/33	Cap Français, St. Dom. (charter out)		
				St. Pierre, Martinique		8/5/33
1734[4]	Bordeaux			Quebec	7/10/34	
1735[5]	Le Havre		14/6/35	Quebec		
1736[6]	Le Havre		after 26 April	Quebec		
1737[7]	Le Havre		after 3 May	Quebec		before 19 Dec.
1738[8]	Le Havre			Quebec		
1739[9]	Le Havre	LeVaillant		St. Pierre, Martinique	29/4/39	20/7/39
1740[10]	Bordeaux	Luetkens		St. Pierre, Martinique	26/3/40	
				Louisbourg	13/7/40	
				St. Pierre, Martinique		19/12/40
1741[11]	Le Havre	Christinat		Ft. Royal, Martinique	30/8/41	
				St. Pierre, Martinique		26/12/41
1742[12]	Le Havre	Christinat		St. Pierre, Martinique	21/6/42	
1743[13]	Le Havre	Christinat	21/8/43	Cul de Sac Marin, Mart.	29/10/43	18/8/44
				Ft. Royal, Martinique		13/9/44

#Figures for 1739 combined with *Fleury* to Guadeloupe.

†This voyage (1742) is not mentioned in the balance sheets. Either Admiralty officials erred in recording its arrival at St. Pierre or Dugard erred in not assigning debit and credit or they are "hidden" in those of another voyage.

Sources: Associates' Accounts and the following:

1   AD Gironde. 6B 93 f187, Soumission avant départ.
2   AN. 62AQ39, Délibérations, 14/5/1732; AC. F23 11, Etat.
3   AN. 62AQ39, Délibérations, 20/7/1733; AC. C8B 17, Etat.
4   AN. 62AQ40, H & L c/c 1734; F2B 11, Etat.
5   AN. 62AQ39, Délibérations, 6/4/1735; 62AQ40, H & L c/c 1735; AC. F2B 11, Etat.
6   AN. 62AQ40, H & L c/c 1736; AC. B 64 f38, Lettre; F2B 11, Etat.
7   AN. 62AQ40, H & L c/c 1737; AC. B 65 f51, Lettre; F2B 11, Etat.
8   AN. 62AQ40, H & L c/c 1738.
9   AN. F12 26 pp. 605, 618, Registre du Bureau de Commerce; AC. C8B 20, Etat.
10 AN. 62AQ41, RD c/c avec Fautoux; AC. C8A 52 f248, Etat; C8B 20, Etat; F2B 11, Etats.
11 AC. C8B 20, Etats.
12 AC. B 75 15/11/1742, Lettre; C8B 20, Etat.
13 AC. C8B 20, Etat; C8B 21, Etats.

Return	Date	Agent	Captain	Debit	Credit	Voyage #
Le Havre			F. LeProvost	Voyage not for S.D.C.		—
			F. LeProvost		multiship	Cargo 3
Le Havre			F. LeProvost	11,809.10.–	10,054.12.6	—
Le Havre			F. LeProvost		multiship	Cargo 5
Le Havre			F. LeProvost		multiship	Cargo 6
Le Havre			Védérie		multiship	Cargo 7
Le Havre			Hurel		multiship	Cargo 8
					multiship	Cargo 9
Bordeaux			Hurel		multiship	#
Le Havre			Hurel	45,724.2.11	49,269.–.–	—
Le Havre		Christinat	Hurel	62,090.13.9	60,725.18.4	—
Le Havre			Hurel			†
Taken on return voyage			Hurel	49,845.15.11	46,337.7.1	

TABLE 22.

Voyages of the Ville De Québec/Union

Year	Port (France)	Agent	Dep.	Destination (Colonies)	Arr.	Dep.
1733[1]	Le Havre		between 19/5, 1/7	Quebec		
1734[2]	Le Havre		c. 11/3/34	Cap Français, St. Dom.		
1735[3]	Le Havre via		c. 10/12/34			
	Bordeaux	Luetkens	14/4/35	St. Pierre, Martinique	13/6/35	5/7/35
				Léoganne, St. Domingue		29/11/35
1736[4]	Bordeaux	Luetkens	12/7/36	St. Pierre, Martinique	3/9/36	4/12/36
				also at Ft. Royal		after
				Léoganne, St. Domingue		27/5/37
1737	(above)					
1738[5]	Bordeaux	Luetkens	2/4/38	Louisbourg		
				Quebec	14/7/38	
				Louisbourg		
1739[6]	(?) via					
	Le Havre			Quebec	2/9/39	
1740[7]	Le Havre			Quebec	20/7/40	$\frac{13}{14}$/11/40
1741[8]	Le Havre			Quebec (FOR REFITTING RENAMED UNION)		
		First voyage as UNION:		Louisbourg	most conceivably in 1742	
1742	(above)					
1743	—					
1744[9]	Le Havre	Christinat	3/2/44	St. Pierre, Martinique	23/3/44	9/2/45
1745	(Relache at Nantes, 11 months.)					
1746[10]	Nantes via Ile d'Aix	Souhigaray	15/3/46			
	(Convoy)		29/4/46	Martinique	15/6/46	8/1/47

Sources: Associates' Accounts and the following:

1 AN. 62AQ39, Délibérations, 10/3/1733; 62AQ40, FH c/c 1733; GF c/c avec RD 19/8/1733; AC. B 58 f43 & 54, Lettres; F2B 11, Etat.

2 AN. 62AQ39, Délibérations, 11/1/1734, 14/6/1735; 62AQ42, factures.

3 AN. 62AQ39, Délibérations, 18/1/1735, 1/3/1735; 62AQ42, factures; AC. C8B 17, Etat; C9B 10, Etat; AD Gironde. 6B 94 f209, Soumission avant départ.

4 AN. 62AQ42, Facture; AC. C8A 47 f273, Etat; C8B 17, Etat; AD Gironde, 6B 95 f48, Soumission avant départ.

5 AN. 62AQ40, H & L c/c 1738; H & L Compte général de balance; AC. CIIA 70, f167, Etat; AD Gironde. 6B 96 f98, Soumission avant départ; 6B 387, Rôle d'Equipage.

6 AN. 62AQ39, Délibérations, 25/3/1739; 62AQ40, H & L Compte général de balance; AC. F2B 11, Etat.

Return	Date	Agent	Captain	Debit	Credit	Voyage #
Le Havre			Vandelle	multiship		Cargo 4
Le Havre			Vandelle	31,801.15.–	52,480.11.3	
						—
Bordeaux	23/4/36		Vandelle	48,707.17.11	75,405.13.4	—
Bordeaux	9/12/37		Vandelle	65,219.11.3	101,907.15.5	
			Vandelle or Paris	multiship		Cargo 9
			Vandelle	multiship		Cargo 10
				multiship		Cargo 11
				81,266.5.5	89,148.13.9	—
						—
						—
Nantes	27/3/45	Souhigaray	Fremont (out) Dumesnil (ret.)	181,892.3.9	172,323.19.7	—
						—
Lost on return.			Dumesnil	56,707.–.10	52,166.13.4	—

7 AN. 62AQ40, H & L c/c 1740; H & L Compte général de balance; AC. CIIA 73 f411, Etat; CIIA 75 f83, Lettre.
8 AN. 62AQ40, H & L c/c 1741; H & L Compte général de balance; 62AQ41, RD c/c avec Fautoux.
9 AN. 62AQ42, Papiers de cargaison.
10 AN. 62AQ42, Papiers de cargaison.

TABLE 23.
Voyages of the Alçion

Year	Port (France)	Agent	Dep.	Destination	Arr.	Dep.
1736[1]	(MAIDEN VOYAGE FROM PORT OF CONSTRUCTION, QUEBEC)					
				Louisbourg		
				(Martinique?)		
				Léoganne, St. Domingue		c. 27/5/37
1737	(above)					
1738[2]	Bordeaux	Luetkens	19/1/38	Martinique and		
				Léoganne, St. Domingue		5/10/38
1739[3]	Bordeaux		23/3/39	Léoganne, St. Domingue	May, 1739	15/11/39
1740[4]	Bordeaux		12/5/40	St. Domingue		
1741	(above)					
1742[5]	Bordeaux	Luetkens	5/3/42	Léoganne, St. Domingue		15/4/43

Sources: Associates' Accounts and the following:

1 AN. 62AQ39, Délibérations, 15/5/1736; 62AQ42, Lettre, 27/5/1737; 62AQ45, Factures de cargaison.

2 AN. 62AQ42, Lettres, 4/10/1738, 23/4/1739; AD Gironde, 6B 386, Rôle d'Equipage.

3 AN. 62AQ42, Lettres, 29/5/1739, 23/11/1739; 62AQ45, RD c/c avec Luetkens; AC. C9B 12, Etat; AD Gironde. 6B 96 f168, Soumission avant départ.

4 AD Gironde. 6B 96 f249, Soumission avant départ.

5 62AQ44, Papiers de cargaisons; AD Gironde. 6B 97 f107, Soumission avant départ.

Return	Date	Agent	Captain	Debit	Credit	Voyage #
Bordeaux			Mollard	18,132.1.8	(see Ville de Qué. 1736)	1st
						—
Bordeaux	28/12/38	Luetkens	Mollard	62,801.14.2	81, 951.9.2	2nd
Bordeaux		Luetkens	Mollard	57,648.15.10	70,756.18.9	3rd
Bordeaux	7/7/41	Luetkens	Mollard	87,689.7.1	115,350.12.6	4th
						—
Lost on return			P. Gauthier	120,003.10.–	132,896.15.–	5th

TABLE 24.
Voyages of the Fleury

Year	Port (France)	Agent	Dep.	Destination (Colonies)	Arr.	Dep.
1738[1]	(MAIDEN VOYAGE FROM PORT OF CONSTRUCTION, QUEBEC)					
1739[2]	Le Havre			Guadeloupe		
1740[3]	Bordeaux via Rochefort	Luetkens	6/7/40	Ft. Royal, Martinique	23/8/40	
				St. Pierre, Martinique		13/6/41
1741	(above)					
1742[4]	Le Havre	Christinat	late Feb. or March	St. Pierre, Martinique	20/4/42	
1743	(above)					
1744[5]	Le Havre via	Christinat	28/3/44			
	Lorient	Perrault	27/5/44	Senegal (charter party, Comp. des Indes)		
1745	—					
1746[6]	Lorient	Perrault	May, 1746	"affretté au Roy" To Chibuctou Bay		20/10/46

†Figures for 1739 combined with *St. Mathieu* to Martinique.

Sources: Associates' Accounts and the following:

   1 AN. 62AQ40, H & L c/c 1738; AC. B67 f143, Lettre.

   2 AN. F12 86 pp. 605, 618, Registre du Bureau de Commerce.

   3 AN. F12 88 f67, Registre du Bureau de Commerce; 62AQ45, RD c/c avec Luetkens; AC. C8A 51 f250, Lettre; C8A 52 f248, Etat; C8B 20, Etat; AD Gironde. 6B 96 f256, Soumission avant départ; 6B 388, Rôle d'Equipage.

   4 AN. F12 88 f67 & 89 f55, Registres du Bureau de Commerce; AC. C8B 20, Etat.

   5 AN. 62AQ44, Papiers de cargaison.

   6 AN. 62AQ44, Papiers de cargaison, Relation de la Prise.

Return	Date	Agent	Captain	Debit	Credit	Voyage #
Le Havre	c. 8/12				multiship	Cargo 9
Bordeaux			Védérie		multiship	1st †
Le Havre (?)			Tilly LePelly	204,403.3.9	254,942.2.1	2nd
						—
Le Havre		Christinat	Tilly LePelly	376,907.6.3	398,645.1.8	3rd
						—
Lorient	3/12/44	Perrault	E. Escallier	31,492	40,494.15.–	4th
—						—
Captured on return.				40,847.4.2	119,392.–.10	

TABLE 25.
Voyages of the St. Louis

Year	Port (France)	Agent	Dep.	Destination (Colonies)	Arr.	Dep.
1739[1]	(MAIDEN VOYAGE FROM PORT OF CONSTRUCTION, QUEBEC)					28/10/39
				St. Pierre, Martinique	22/12/39	
1740	(above)					
1741[2]	Le Havre via					
	La Rochelle		Jan. 1741	Louisbourg		
1742[3]	Le Havre		Aug. 1742	Louisbourg		
				Martinique		
1743[4]	Le Havre	Christinat	Mar. 1743	Louisbourg	30/5/43	10/8/43
				Cul de Sac Marin,		
				Martinique	2/9/43	22/11/43
1744	—					
1745	—					
1746	—					
1747	—					
1748[5]	Le Havre to					
	Honfleur					
1749[6]	Honfleur via	J. B. Prémond				
	St. Martin					
	de Ré		17/4/49	The Grand Banks		
1750[7]	Honfleur	J. B. Prémond		The Grand Banks		
	(St. Martin?)					
1751[8]	Honfleur via					
	St. Martin					
	de Ré		1/2/51	Lost near Côte de Loix, Ile de Ré.		

† This voyage does not appear in the balance sheets. Debit and credit might be included with Cargo 10 or with voyages of *Louis Dauphin* or *St. Mathieu* to Martinique, 1739. But no debit and credit exists for *Louis Dauphin* for 1739 and figures for *St. Mathieu* are combined with those of *Fleury* to Guadeloupe, leaving the company's activities for 1739 somewhat unclear.

Sources: Associates' Accounts and the following:

1   AC. C8B 20, Etat; CIIA 71 f182, Etat; CIIA 72 f78, Exercise, 1739 (Government Expenses).
2   AN. FI2 89 f331, Registre du Bureau de Commerce; 62AQ41, RD c/c avec Fautoux, AC. B75 f112, Lettre.
3   AN. FI2 89 f331, Registre du Bureau de Commerce; 62AQ41, RD c/c avec Fautoux.
4   AN. 62AQ41, RD c/c avec Fautoux; 62AQ44, Papiers de cargaison; AC. C9A 62, Liste des Navires, 10/3/1743; C8B 20, Etat.
5   AN. 62AQ44, J. B. Prémond, Compte de Débours, janvier, 1749.
6   AN. 62AQ44, Papiers de cargaison.
7   AN. 62AQ40, J. B. Prémond c/c avec RD; 62AQ44, Papiers de cargaison.
8   AN. 62AQ44, Papiers de cargaison, Rôle d'Equipage.

Return	Date	Agent	Captain	Debit	Credit	Voyage #
			B. Paris	multiship		†
La Rochelle	Mar. 1742			9,141.2.6	9,577.3.9	1st L.B.
Le Havre				18,094.1.8	20,874.17.1	2nd L.B.
Le Havre	28/1/44	Christinat	Le Roche Couvert	31,886.19.7	30,998.17.6	3rd L.B.
—						—
—						—
—						—
				Expenses of refitting included below		—
Honfleur	14/10/49	Prémond	P. Robinet	24,743.9.–	14,344.10.5	1st N.F.L.
Honfleur	18/7/50	Prémond	P. Robinet	6,486.7.11	6,862.10.10	2ndN.F.L.
			P. Robinet	4,971.9.7	1,823	3rd N.F.L.

TABLE 26.

Voyages of the Centaure

Year	Port (France)	Agent	Dep.	Destination (Colonies)	Arr.	Dep.
1740[1]	(MAIDEN VOYAGE FROM PORT OF CONSTRUCTION, QUEBEC)					12/11/40
1741[2]	Le Havre			Quebec	Oct. 1741	
1742[3]	Le Havre	Christinat		Quebec	15/8/42	3/11/42
1743[4]	Le Havre	Christinat	20/6/43	Quebec	17/9/43	5/11/43
1744[5]	UNABLE TO LEAVE HAVRE DE GRACE IN TIME OF WAR WITHOUT CANNON.					
1745	—					
1746	—					
1747	—					
1748[6]	Le Havre	Christinat	18/10/48	Cap Français & Léoganne St. Dom. (charter to Com. des Indes)		
1749	(above)					
1750[7]	Nantes via	Souhigaray	27/2/50			
	Bordeaux	Goudal	9/7/50	Léoganne, St. Domingue		
1751[8]	(Refitting at Le Havre)					
1752[9]	Le Havre via	Christinat	24/7/52			
	Bordeaux	Goudal	27/11/52	St. Pierre, Martinique	27/12/52	5/7/53
1753	(above)					
1754[10]	Bordeaux	Goudal	7/6/54	St. Pierre, Martinique	11/7/54	1/3/55
1755[11]	Bordeaux	Goudal	9/8/55	Fort Royal, Martinique St. Pierre, Martinique	27/9/55	21/5/56

Sources: Associates' Accounts and the following:

1   AN. 62AQ40, H & L c/c 1740; AC. B71, Lettre à RD, 30/12/1740; CIIA 75 f83, Lettre.

2   AC. CIIA 76 f3, Lettre.

3   AN. 62AQ40, H & L c/c 1743; 62AQ41, Papiers de cargaison; AC. B77 f36, Lettre; CIIA 78 f87, Lettre; CIIA 78 f95, Etat.

4   AN. 62AQ40, H & L c/c 1743; 62AQ41, Papiers de cargaison; AC. B77 f155, Lettre; CIIA 79 f20, Liste des Lettres . . . ; CIIA 79 ff285, 300, Lettres; CIIA 80 ff250, 262, Lettres.

5   AN. 62AQ35, Lettre, F à RD, 28/10/1745.

6   AN. 62AQ35, Lettre, F à RD, 7/6/1748; 62AQ42, Papiers de cargaison.

7   AN. 62AQ42, Papiers de cargaison; AD Gironde. 6B 101 f151, Soumission avant départ; 6B 398, Rôle d'Equipage.

8   AN. 62AQ42, Compte de Radoub . . .

9   AN. 62AQ42, Papiers de cargaison; AC. CIIB 21, Etat.

10   AN. 62AQ42, Papiers de cargaison; AD Gironde. 6B 99 f45, Soumission avant départ.

11   AN. 62AQ35, Lettre, F à RD, 4/8/1756; 62AQ42, Papiers de cargaison.

Return	Date	Agent	Captain	Debit	Credit	Voyage #
Le Havre	c. 24 Dec.				multiship	Cargo 11
					multiship	Cargo 12
Le Havre	c. 12/1/43		Vandelle		multiship	Cargo 13
Le Havre	9/12/43	Christinat	Vandelle		multiship	Cargo 14
						—
						—
						—
						—
Nantes	9/7/49	Souhigaray	Vandelle	58,308.13.9	82,834.17.6	1st
Le Havre	4/9/51	Christinat	Vandelle	72,799.5.5	67,236.13.4	2nd
						—
Bordeaux	18/8/53	Goudal	Gosselin	63,352.3.4	40,179.2.6	3rd
						—
Bordeaux	25/7/55	Goudal	Gosselin	59,084.10.10	82,986.7.6	4th
Captured on return.			Bellanger	127,416.15.5	151,042.7.6	5th

TABLE 27.
Voyages of the Imprévû

Year	Port (France)	Agent	Dep.	Destination	Arr.	Dep.
1740[1]	(MAIDEN VOYAGE FROM PORT OF CONSTRUCTION, QUEBEC)					
				Ile Royale (Louisbourg?)		
				Quebec	8/10/40	
				Louisbourg	31/10/40	
				Quebec	13/11/40	
				Kamouraska (caught in the ice)		Jun. 1741
1741	(above)					
1742[2]	Bordeaux	Luetkens	Feb. 1742	Cul de Sac Marin, Martinique	17/3/42	
1743[3]	Le Havre	Christinat	28/5/43	Cul de Sac Marin, Martinique	17/7/43	19/8/44

Sources: Associates' Accounts and the following:

1 AC. B73 f133, Lettre; CIIA 73 f411, Etat; CIIA 75 f83, Lettre; CIIA 76 f322, Mémoire; F2B 11, Etat; APQ, Ordonnances des Intendants (NF 2) Cahier 29, 3/4/1741, 16/6/1741.

2 AN. 62AQ43, Papiers de cargaison & *Imprévû* c/c avec Renault; 62AQ45, RD c/c avec Luetkens, 1741–42; AC. B 75, Lettre, 15/11/1742; C8B 20, Etat.

3 AN. 62AQ43, Papiers de cargaison, Conte de la Perte de . . . , Assurance de . . . ; AC. C8B 20, Etat; C8B 21, Etat; C9A 62, Liste des navires en armement au Port du Havre. . . .

TABLE 28.
Voyages of the Astrée

Year	Port (France)	Agent	Dep.	Destination (Colonies)	Arr.	Dep.
1745[1]	(MAIDEN VOYAGE FROM PORT OF CONSTRUCTION, QUEBEC)					10/11/45
1746[2]	(REFITTING AND SHEATHING OF HULL AT MORLAIX)					
1747	(above)					
1748[3]	Morlaix via	Jacquelin	13/8/48			
	Bordeaux	Goudal	31/10/48	Martinique		
1749[4]	Nantes via	Souhigaray	18/7/49			
	Bordeaux	Goudal	9/5/50	Quebec		8 or 9/50
				Ft. Royal, Martinique	1/11/50	
				St. Pierre, Martinique		26/2/51

Sources: Associates' Accounts and the following:

1 AN. 62AQ41, Papiers de cargaison, Extrait du Registre des Declarations et Rapports du Greffe de l'Amirauté de Léon, Etabli au Port Oblique de Roscoft, 29/12/1745.

2 AN. 62AQ43, Compte du Radoub et Doublage.

Return	Date	Agent	Captain	Debit	Credit	Voyage #
			B. Paris		multiship	Cargo 11
						—
Le Havre	c. 6/11/42		B. Paris	71,445.3.4	70,351.9.2	1st
			Renault (out)			
Captured on return.			LaMoisse (ret.)	189,532.11.8	152,752.7.11	2nd

Return	Date	Agent	Captain	Debit	Credit	Voyage #
Roscoff	29/12/45					
Morlaix	Jan. 1746	Jacquelin	A. Olivier	multiship		Cargo 15
				(costs included below)		—
Painboeuf	5/6/49					
Nantes		Souhigaray				
Bordeaux	24/7/49		Gosselin	70,944.14.2	44,038	1st
Bordeaux	8/5/51	Goudal	Gosselin	45,991.1.3	57,473.10.–	2nd

3 AN. 62AQ43, Papiers de cargaison; AD Gironde. 6B 101 f2, Soumission avant départ.
4 AN. 62AQ43, Papiers de cargaison; AD Gironde. 6B 101 f125, Soumission avant départ.

TABLE 29.
Voyages of the Trois Maries

Year	Port (France)	Agent	Dep.	Destination (Colonies)	Arr.	Dep.
1742[1]	Bordeaux via La Rochelle	Goudal	23/3/42			
				Quebec	13/8/42	
				Louisbourg		18/11/42
1743[2]	Bordeaux	Goudal	12/4/43	Quebec		18/8/43
1744[3]	Honfleur	Prémond	20/4/44	Quebec	23/8/44	5/11/44
				Louisbourg (for convoy)	24/11/44	30/11/44

Sources: Associates' Accounts and the following:

1 AN. 62AQ41, Papiers de cargaison; AC. CIIA 78 f98, Etat; AD Gironde. 6B 97 f122, Soumission avant départ.

2 AN. 62AQ41, Papiers de cargaison; AC. CIIA 79 f200, Lettre; AD Gironde. 6B 97 f185, Soumission avant départ.

3 AN. 62AQ41, Papiers de cargaison; AC. CIIA 81 f260, Lettre.

Return	Date	Agent	Captain	Debit	Credit	Voyage #
Bilbao and	Dec. '42 or		Gosselin	18,676.13.4	13,563.18.–	
Bordeaux	Jan. '43			(Includes purchase)		1st
Honfleur	c. 2 Nov.	Prémond	Gosselin	7,666.14.8	11,670.4.8	2nd
Lost on return.			B. Paris	36,778.4.–	37,369	3rd

Voyages: Chronological List

1729   The *Louis Dauphin* from Le Havre to Bilbao via La Rochelle, returning to France.

1730   The *Louis Dauphin* to Quebec and Martinique, returning to France.

1731   The *Louis Dauphin* to Quebec, returning to Le Havre.

1732   The *Louis Dauphin* from Le Havre to Quebec and Martinique, returning to France.
The *St. Mathieu* from Le Havre to Quebec and Martinique, returning to France.

1733   The *Louis Dauphin* to Ile à Vache, St. Domingue, returning to Le Havre.
The *St. Mathieu* from Le Havre to Cap Français, St. Domingue, returning to Le Havre.
The *Ville de Québec* from Le Havre to Quebec, returning to Le Havre.

1734   The *Louis Dauphin* to Cadiz.
The *St. Mathieu* from Bordeaux to Quebec, returning to Le Havre.
The *Ville de Québec* to Cap Français, St. Domingue, returning to Le Havre.
The *Précieuse* to Quebec, returning to France.

1735   The *Louis Dauphin* from Le Havre to Quebec, Louisbourg, Quebec, returning to Le Havre.

The *St. Mathieu* from Le Havre to Quebec, returning to Le Havre.

The *Ville de Québec* from Le Havre and Bordeaux to St. Pierre, Martinique, and Léoganne, St. Domingue, returning to Bordeaux.

1736   The *Louis Dauphin* from Le Havre to Quebec, returning to Le Havre.

The *St. Mathieu* from Le Havre to Quebec, returning to Le Havre.

The *Ville de Québec* from Bordeaux to St. Pierre and Ft. Royal, Martinique, and Léoganne, St. Domingue, returning to France.

The *Alçion*'s maiden voyage from Quebec to Louisbourg, Léoganne, and Bordeaux.

1737   The *Louis Dauphin* to Quebec, returning to Le Havre.

The *St. Mathieu* from Le Havre to Quebec, returning to Le Havre.

1738   The *Louis Dauphin* from Le Havre and Bordeaux to Martinique, possibly wintering at Quebec and returning to Le Havre via Martinique in 1739.

The *St. Mathieu* from Le Havre to Quebec, returning to France.

The *Ville de Québec* from Bordeaux to Louisbourg, Quebec, and Louisbourg, returning to France.

The *Alçion* from Bordeaux to Martinique and Léoganne, St. Domingue, returning to Bordeaux.

The *Fleury*'s maiden voyage from Quebec to Le Havre.

1739   The *St. Mathieu* from Le Havre to St. Pierre, Martinique, returning to Bordeaux.

The *Ville de Québec* via Le Havre to Quebec, returning to France.

The *Alçion* from Bordeaux to Léoganne, St. Domingue, returning to Bordeaux.

The *Fleury* from Le Havre to Guadeloupe, returning to Bordeaux.

The *St. Louis*'s maiden voyage from Quebec to Louisbourg and St. Pierre, Martinique.

1740   The *Louis Dauphin* from Le Havre to St. Pierre, Martinique, returning to Le Havre.

The *St. Mathieu* from Bordeaux to St. Pierre, Martinique,

Louisbourg, and St. Pierre, Martinique, returning to Le Havre.

The *Ville de Québec* from Le Havre to Quebec, returning to France.

The *Alçion* from Bordeaux to St. Domingue, returning to Bordeaux.

The *Fleury* from Bordeaux and Rochefort to Ft. Royal and St. Pierre, Martinique, returning to Le Havre.

The *Centaure*'s maiden voyage from Quebec to Le Havre.

The *Imprévû*'s maiden voyage from Quebec to Ile Royale to Quebec to Louisbourg to Quebec to Kamouraska (winter) to France.

1741   The *Louis Dauphin* from Honfleur to St. Pierre, Martinique, to Louisbourg to St. Pierre, Martinique, returning to Honfleur.

The *St. Mathieu* from Le Havre to Ft. Royal and St. Pierre, Martinique, returning to Le Havre.

The *Ville de Québec* from Le Havre to Quebec for refit to Louisbourg (as *Union*), returning to France.

The *St. Louis* from Le Havre and La Rochelle to Louisbourg, returning to La Rochelle and Le Havre.

The *Centaure* from Le Havre to Quebec, returning to France.

The *Nouvelle Galère* from Bordeaux to Quebec.

1742   The *St. Mathieu* from Le Havre to St. Pierre, Martinique, returning to Le Havre.

The *Alçion* from Bordeaux to Léoganne, St. Domingue; lost on return.

The *Fleury* from Le Havre to St. Pierre, Martinique, returning to France.

The *St. Louis* from Le Havre to Louisbourg and Martinique, returning to France.

The *Centaure* from Le Havre to Quebec, returning to Le Havre.

The *Imprévû* from Bordeaux to Cul de Sac Marin, Martinique, returning to Le Havre.

The *Trois Maries* from Bordeaux to Quebec to Louisbourg to Bilbao, returning to Bordeaux.

1743   The *Louis Dauphin* from Honfleur to Cul de Sac Marin, Martinique; lost on return.

The *St. Mathieu* from Le Havre to Cul de Sac Marin, Martinique; taken on return.

The *St. Louis* from Le Havre to Louisbourg to Cul de Sac
Marin, Martinique, returning to Le Havre.
The *Centaure* from Le Havre to Quebec, returning to Le
Havre.
The *Imprévû* from Le Havre to Cul de Sac Marin, Mar-
tinique; taken on return.
The *Trois Maries* from Bordeaux to Quebec, returning to
Honfleur.

1744   The *Union* from Le Havre to St. Pierre, Martinique, return-
ing to Nantes.
The *Fleury* from Lorient to Senegal, returning to Lorient for
the Compagnie des Indies.
The *Trois Maries* from Honfleur to Quebec, returning via
Louisbourg; sunk in collision.
The *Andromède* from La Rochelle to Canada, returning to
France.

1745   The *Astrée*'s maiden voyage from Quebec to Roscoff and
Morlaix.
The *Thétis* from Le Havre to Martinique; lost on outward
voyage.

1746   The *Union* from Nantes to Martinique; lost on return.
The *Fleury* from Lorient to Chebucto Bay for the King; captured on return.

1747   No voyages.

1748   The *Centaure* from Le Havre to Cap Français, St. Domingue,
returning to Nantes.
The *Astrée* from Morlaix to Bordeaux to Martinique, returning to Nantes and Bordeaux.

1749   The *St. Louis* from Honfleur to St. Martin de Ré to the
Grand Banks, returning to Honfleur.
The *Astrée* from Nantes to Bordeaux to Quebec to Ft. Royal
and St. Pierre, Martinique, returning to Bordeaux. Dismantled.

1750   The *St. Louis* from Honfleur to St. Martin de Ré to the
Grand Banks, returning to Honfleur.
The *Centaure* from Nantes to Bordeaux to Léoganne, St.
Domingue, returning to Le Havre.

1751   The *St. Louis* from Honfleur to St. Martin de Ré; lost.

1752   The *Centaure* from Le Havre to Bordeaux to St. Pierre, Martinique, returning to Bordeaux.

1753   No voyages.

1754   The *Centaure* from Bordeaux to St. Pierre, Martinique, returning to Bordeaux.

1755   The *Centaure* from Bordeaux to Ft. Royal and St. Pierre, Martinique; taken on return.

Investment, Outlay, and Profit

Two sets of current accounts prepared by Robert Dugard in 1738 and 1759 for his partners and another account showing Guillaume France's interest until 1742 with special reference to his drawings against capital, all in Archives nationales, series AQ62, volume 40, provide the only extant information on the total of investments and outlays, profits and losses, of the Société du Canada. They are fragmentary evidence of an extensive double entry bookkeeping system that reposed upon the journal and the ledger. Dugard's knowledge of double entry can be inferred from the impeccable Amsterdam account books of 1722 and from the scattered references to various accounts. This is worthy of note, given that not even in Parisian business circles was double entry accounting universal.[1] However, the long delays in the rendering of accounts suggest that the whole system was used in a slack manner, with, for example, no annual balancing of books.

The unit of business undertaking was not the year but the voyage. All the costs of sending off an expedition to Canada, Martinique, or St. Domingue were added together and regarded as the outlay on the voyage, or debit. (Figure 3 provides graphic presentation of these outlays as well as investment in shipping.) As far as the accounts were concerned, what happened to ship and cargo while far from the coasts of France was unknown. The activities of captains and factors were monitored by means of their own extensive double entry accounts, but these latter were not integrated into the metropolitan accounting system. For example, the accounts took no cognizance of the profit on French merchandise sold in the colonies or on colonial merchandise sold in France. When the return cargo was sold in Europe, the many attendant costs were deducted from the gross profit and a net figure was entered to the credit of the voyage to offset the original debit. It was the comparison of these two figures that was fundamental to the notion of profit. This practice of recognising only the metropolitan figures was behind the needs and means of the time, a fragment of insularity as yet unaffected by an ever-expanding world. Pairing the outfitting debit figure and the net return figure was also a violation of double entry, which would more logically lead to the assigning of all expenses to the debit column and all profits to the credit column. Although the resulting entries always showed the correct amount of profit, they falsified the per cent profit and thus may have given the partners an unduly optimistic view of their business. This will be clear from the following example, which shows an outlay of 10 livres and a gross profit on the return cargo of 20 livres, with expenses of 2 livres alternately added to the outlay or deducted from the return:

Return	Outlay	Profit
20	12	8
18	10	8

In both cases the profit is 8, but what a difference there is between $\frac{8}{10}$s and $\frac{8}{12}$s when a profit is calculated in percentage terms. Deduction of expenses from the return figure increases the per cent level of profit. Thus all profit figures in Dugard's current accounts are too high. There is, however, reason to believe that Dugard assigned the most significant costs of a voyage to the current account debits.[2] In any case, the profits as Dugard and his associates understood them were always calculated using a credit figure from which some deductions had been made in addition to the direct costs of selling return cargo that were an invariable preliminary deduction. In the case of the fourteenth cargo, these additional "fraix" totalled more than 27,000 livres.[3] A table of profits has been prepared by calculating the difference of outlay and return as a percentage of the former (table 30, figures outside parentheses). Although the figures are too high, they nevertheless serve to show the difference between different branches of trade, change over time, and presumably reflect the thinking of the company.

The difficulty is not only with percentage figures, however; even the profit stated as a plain number is not exact. The debits and credits for voyages take no account of investment in shipping. Ships were the company's only fixed assets. Eighteenth-century businessmen had an aversion to fixed assets and kept them to a minimum. Business ventures tended to be of short duration, the average merchant being involved in many businesses at once. At any given moment some were dissolving, others were being founded, and some were in between.

Fixed assets were a bother to such unfixed businesses. They also tied up capital and the merchants' view of capital, in their picturesque phrase, was "to make it roll," not to keep it tied up. Thus if a merchant could not store all his merchandise in his house, he *rented* a warehouse; if it became inconvenient to maintain his counting house in his home, as happened in the case of Robert Dugard after 1762, he *rented* space. Captains and factors abroad *rented* warehouses and living quarters. But there were the ships. How should they be handled in accounting terms?

G. V. Taylor's statement that "The concept of depreciation costs . . . was unknown"[4] to eighteenth-century French businessmen is familiar. True as far as it goes, it should not be taken to mean that ships were not amortized in the accounts, but rather that they were not amortized over an extended period of time. The amortization of the *Louis Dauphin*, the company's first ship, is a good example of the traditional method employed. The debit and credit entries in the account of Vincent père et fils, 1738, read as follows:

Debit:
June 14th, 1729, For a sixth in the construction of the Ship the *Louis Dauphin* and outfitting for Bilbao . . . . .3595„–„6

Credit:
June 14th, 1729, For the return on the voyage of the *Louis Dauphin* to Bilbao . . . . .71„13„–

In this example the cost of the ship has been amalgamated with the outfitting costs of its first voyage, a freighting venture with no cargo costs to obscure the proceedings. Thus the combined investment and outlay are much greater than the profit on returns; the operation has resulted in a deficit. But the ship is fully amortized—or would be if the result were not a deficit. Subsequent voyages were free of this charge.

There is a second good example of this type in the account of Pierre D'Haristoy, partner of the Société au Navire *Les Trois Maries*. This was a typical short-term undertaking. The cost of the ship was debited to the first voyage. Subsequent voyages took no account of it; and as the *Trois Maries* was sunk on its third voyage, the insurance money was credited to that voyage. It all makes a tidy package:

Debit:
For his quarter interest in the ship the *Trois Maries* and outfitting, 1742 . . . . .4669„3„4
For idem in the 2nd outfitting of the said ship . . . . . .1698„14„8
For his part of the insurance on the said ship . . . . 217„11„2

For his quarter in the 3rd outfitting of the said ship and
Cargo 9194,,11,,–

Credit:
For his quarter in the product of the first voyage of the *Trois
Maries,* 1742 3390,,19,,6
For idem of the 2nd voyage, 1743 2919,,11,,2
For idem of the 3rd voyage, 1744 9342,,5,,–

The amortization of company ships acquired between 1732 and
1745 did not follow the traditional pattern as given above and is therefore evidence that there was a change in the company's conception of
itself following the first voyage of the *Louis Dauphin.* The other ships
were debited independently of any voyages. That they were set against
the company's operations as a whole rather than those of a year or a
single voyage is a distinct recognition that traditional forms were inadequate for the long-lived and extensive business that the Société au
Navire *Le Loùis Dauphin* was on its way to becoming in 1732. But
lacking a concept of amortization over time, Dugard carried each ship
as a debit at its original value until either the vessel was lost or the
company wound up. These debits had no corresponding credits.
Dugard was well aware that this was an accounting fiction and that
each partner's resulting credit balance was too low. Therefore each
account ended with the proviso that the small credit figure was accorded "Without Prejudice for [D'Haristoy, France, etc.] for his fifth
in each of our ships."

The total absence of systematic depreciation, or amortization over
time, made sense in the business world of the eighteenth century. Ship-
owners had no access to long-term credit and were in fact required to
pay for their vessels on delivery or shortly thereafter. By the time of its
second voyage a ship really was paid for, and its owners could forget
about its value until the time came to dissolve the partnership and sell
the assets. The sale price would be entered into the ship's own account,
which was then closed, the balance figure being carried to the profit
and loss account. Secondly, as there was no tax calculated on the basis
of annual business profits, there was no need to assign a share of depreciation to each voyage. Yet to the extent that either immediate
amortization or the failure to amortize at all may have led merchants
to overestimate profits on most of their voyages, this convention was
detrimental. The absence of depreciation draws attention to the fact
that any kind of cost accounting lay in the future. The only real purpose of the journal and ledger was to keep track of debtor and creditor

and to provide the raw material for casting the balance sheet when the company dissolved.

Dugard and Company's policy of building ships in Canada requires special comment. The only direct evidence of the manner in which these ships were paid for is the account "Messrs. Havy and Lefebvre of Quebec, their current account for the management of cargoes, 1731–1757" (AN, 62 AQ 40, Xb). This account specifies that the *Astrée* constituted part of the returns of the fifteenth cargo. Of the "costs and cargo in return" of 1745 totalling 212,393 livres, 80,406 livres constitutes the fully-outfitted new ship. In another account covering the same year the entire amount is credited simply as "total of purchases and costs" without further explanation. Unfortunately, no other ship is expressly mentioned in any other accounts, but it must be assumed that the other Canadian-built ships also formed part of the "returns." Havy and Lefebvre had no money with which to build ships except that which came from Dugard in the form of merchandise, and all of this had to be accounted for in the account of sales and returns. The presumption is, therefore, that the financing of all Canadian-built ships corresponds to that of the *Astrée*, which is alone explicitly revealed. For purposes of Dugard's accounts, which were not sufficiently flexible to take direct cognizance of colonial investment, it is as if the investment were made in France. The reader of the accounts must imagine that the entire "return" from Canada that included a ship was really salable cargo and that from the amount realized by sale a ship was immediately purchased in metropolitan France. Thus a current account, which gives one-fifth values, shows the following relation of values in 1738:

Debit: Cargo to Quebec, 84112 / Credit: Sale of "Returns," 90999
Construction of the *Fleury*, 12573 / . . . .

Investment in a fixed asset had to be shown as a debit, even though it came into the owner's hands as a credit, a part of return cargo.

There is one case that does not fit this formula exactly, the building of the *Alçion* in 1736. According to the accounts, the returns of the maiden voyage of this ship were combined with those of the *Ville de Québec*'s voyage to St. Domingue and Martinique, while the original cargo aboard *Alçion* was combined with the outward cargo of the *Ville de Québec* from Bordeaux. The maiden voyage was triangular, and *Alçion* was in effect an auxiliary to the *Ville de Québec* in the island trade. Thus the "returns" of the seventh cargo from Quebec are

TABLE 30.

Profits in Colonial Trade, 1729–1755

Unadorned figure based on differences of outlay and return; figure in parentheses takes account of depreciation.

Year	Total	Canada	St. Domingue	St. Dom. & Martinique
1730	12.5 (5.1)	12.5 (5.1)		
1731	10.4 (7.0)	10.4 (7.0)		
1732	9.5 (8.0)	9.5 (8.0)		
1733	9.4 (7.2)	10.9 (9.4)	−5.0 (−63.0)	
1734	14.2 (11.7)	9.2 (8.9)	65.0 (47.3)	
1735	15.3 (13.5)	8.9 (7.9)		54.8 (43.5)
1736	8.1 (5.2)	4.5 (3.6)		22.1 (10.9)
1737	12.7 (11.6)	12.7 (11.6)		
1738	11.1 (7.5)	8.2 (5.2)		30.5 (21.5)
1739	13.6 (10.4)	13.0 (11.6)	22.7 (13.5)	
1740	19.6 (16.4)	19.5 (16.9)	31.5 (24.9)	
1741	10.8 (9.0)	10.8 (8.5)		
1742	9.7 (5.1)	15.3 (13.7)	10.7 (−11.2)	
1743	6.2 (1.0)	18.0 (16.5)		
1744–5	8.6 (5.7)	13.6 (11.6)		
1746	75.9 (40.1)			
1747	No outlay			
1748	−1.8 (−10)		42.1 (30.4)	
1749	1.5 (−36)			
1750	6.5 (−13.6)		−7.6 (−13.8)	
1751	−63.3 (−71)			
1752	−36.6			
1753	No outlay			
1754	40.5			
1755	18.5			

Note: Very high profits greatly reduced by ship depreciation, eg. 65 per cent in 1734, indicate a small cargo or freight venture (high profit on small outlay). High profit of 1746 results from payments made by the Crown for loss of the *Fleury* at Chebucto. (It was grossly overvalued for the charter party.) Profit and loss after 1745 is relatively insignificant because outlays and investment are modest (see Figure 3).

Sources: AN, 62 AQ 40, partners' current accounts; tables of depreciation.

Martinique	Triangular	Grand Banks Fishery
10.0 (2.4)		
17.6 (14.2)	7.8 (6.0)	
−2.0 (−3.3)	22.2 (22.2)	
4.6 (2.8)	15.4 (7.4)	
−6.2 (−11.0)	−2.5 (−6.6)	
−5.2 (−7.1)		
−8.0 (−13.8)		
−37.9 (−43.2)		
	24.9 (−33.3)	−42.0 (−44.9)
		5.9 (−12)
		−63.3 (−71)
	−36.6 (−36.6)	
	40.5 (40.5)	
	18.5 (13.9)	

TABLE 31.
Value of Ships with Amount of Annual
Depreciation

Louis Dauphin	21574	(1797)
St. Mathieu	9000	(750)
Ville de Québec	45801	(3816)
*Union**	56693	(4724)
Alçion	55747	(4645)
Fleury	62865	(5238)
St. Louis	15995	(1333)
Centaure	62338	(5194)
Imprévû	19670	(1639)
Astrée	80407	(6700)

* Value of the *Ville de Québec* at the end of 1740 plus the value of rebuilding.

Source of ship evaluations: AN. 62AQ40, partners' current accounts.

deficient by the value of the fully-outfitted *Alçion* and the value of her cargo of West Indian produce sold in France. This explains the low profit figure for Canadian trade that year. The maiden voyage of other ships along the triangular route may have been similarly credited to the "returns" of direct Caribbean voyages, but this is suggested by no references in the accounts.

The eighteenth-century practice of immediate amortization is not one that must be accepted. A rate of depreciation can easily be determined. The first step is to determine the average life of a Dugard and Company ship. Those captured in war at an early age are left out of the computation, while the *Centaure*, captured at the ripe age of 17 years must be included, for it was the longest-lived ship in the company's history. If it had not been captured, it would undoubtedly have sunk or been broken up for scrap in the near future.

The average life of a ship based upon the ages of those sunk or broken up and upon the age of the *Centaure* is 12.3, or roughly 12 years. Therefore, the value of each ship can be depreciated by one-twelfth each year. When one final deduction would reduce the book value of a ship to zero, the vessel has been carried for the remainder of its existence at whatever value remains, approximately one-twelfth. If amortization, the assigning of the cost of the vessel to successive years, were the only consideration, then the vessels could simply be written off. But the residual value of ships is also important for the calculation of the company's wealth at different times. Establishing a convention for amortization over time and a residual value, even though a purely arbitrary one, for amortized shipping makes it possible to estimate the profits and ownership interest of the company more accurately. The unit of depreciation and the depreciating value of each ship are given in tables 31 and 32. Repairs to the *Ville de Québec* in 1741 were so extensive that the repaired vessel was regarded as a new Canadian-built ship and christened the *Union*. This procedure has been followed here. When the depreciation factor is taken into account, the profits calculated on the difference of voyage outlays and returns are considerably reduced (table 30, figures in parentheses).

Dugard's voyage debit and credit figures are further falsified by the entering of certain debits in special accounts: "Doubtful debts and outstanding paper," "Outstanding debts by bankruptcies," "Costs, advances of capital by correspondents" (includes interest payments), and "Interest on bottomry, 1742." The totals of these accounts are based on *états* drawn up by Robert Dugard, all but one still extant. The values therein appear to date from 1739, the year in which Dugard first kept separate books for the company. It is not clear how these charges were accounted for before that date.

In table 33 a more exact statement of the company's financial history has been essayed, taking into account the total of paid-in capital, the factor of depreciation, as well as the various costs in the separate *états*. This has been limited to the period 1729–48. The period thereafter can be considered as a dénouement; the outlays were miniscule compared with those of the earlier period. It is also known that some distribution of profits was made in 1748 and this may have been repeated. The format of the table is unconventional, but an orthodox balance sheet follows (table 34), the concluding balance being identical.

Table 33 lists all sources of finance (paid-in capital, retained earnings, and borrowing), the amount of investment and outlay, and the net return that corresponds to the latter. All money and inventory left at the end of the year (current assets) are totalled and joined with the depreciated value of shipping to produce a final figure equivalent to the ownership interest of the five partners. (The table is preceeded by a guide giving a detailed statement of the items in each column.) It can be argued that an inaccurate estimate of the residual value of shipping could greatly falsify the ownership interest. However, carrying ships at a minimum of one-half rather than one-twelfth of their original cost would only increase the averaged annual profit for the period 1735 to 1742 by about one per cent. At the same time, it would render the decline of the war years more precipitate.

TABLE 32.
Depreciated Value of Ships at Each Year's End

	L.D.	S.M.	V.Q./Un.	AL.	FL.
1729	19777				
1730	17980				
1731	16183				
1732	14386	8250			
1733	12589	7500	41985		
1734	10792	6750	38169		
1735	8995	6000	34353		
1736	7198	5250	30537	51102	
1737	5401	4500	26721	46457	
1738	3604	3750	22905	41812	57627
1739	1807	3000	19089	37167	52389
1740	(1807)	2250	15273	32522	47151
1741	(1807)	1500	51969	27877	41913
1742	(1807)	750	47245	23232	36675
1743	—	(750)	42521	—	31437
1744		—	37796		26199
1745			33073		20961
1746			28349		—
1747			—		
1748					
1749					
1750					
1751					
1752					
1753					
1754					
1755					

Figure in parentheses indicates that the ship is fully amortized but is being carried at a nominal minimum value computed as a loss when the ship is captured or sunk although not regarded as an operating expense.

Source of ship evaluations: AN. 62AQ40, partners' current accounts.

StL.	CENT.	IMP.	AST.
14662			
13329	57114	18031	
11996	51950	16392	
10663	46756	14753	
9330	41562	13114	
7997	36368	—	
6664	31174		73707
5331	25980		67007
3998	20786		60307
2665	15592		53607
1332	10398		46907
(1332)	5204		40207
—	(5204)		—
	(5204)		
	(5204)		
	(5204)		
	—		

The profit of each year can be computed from the figures in the table. Assets at the company's disposal at the beginning of any year (paid-in capital, retained earnings, shipping) must be compared with the company's assets at the end of the year (the value of return cargo minus finance costs and any expenses not included in the outlay figure plus the value of shipping depreciated from the value assigned it at the beginning of the year). The per cent profit obtained in this manner has been calculated for each year, 1729 to 1742. As the complication of additions and withdrawals of capital does not affect the remaining years, which form a distinct period of war and destruction, it has been sufficient to take the difference of ownership interest at two points, calculate the per cent increase, and compute an annual average. The profit figures obtained in this way are more realistic than the voyage profits in table 30 based solely on the outlay and return figures.

It will be noted, once again, that Dugard used the voyage or Canadian cargo rather than the year as the basis for his accounts. Per cent profits calculated for voyages or cargoes are profits on turnover, not per annum. In the case of Canadian voyages the two might not be very different. The return cargoes of one year might in part be the return on outlay of the previous year (trade goods having been advanced on credit), but once a "rotation" of capital had been set in motion this

---

GUIDE TO FIGURE 3

GRAPH OF THE INVESTMENTS AND OUTLAYS OF THE SOCIÉTÉ DU CANADA, 1729–55

Outlays have been divided into the categories of Canadian trade, Caribbean trade, triangular trade, and Grand Banks fishing expeditions. The company's only long-term investments were ships. Investment in those built in Europe is added to the year of delivery. In the case of Canadian-built ships, they are attributed to the year following delivery. The value of a ship in a return cargo from Canada is reputed to be cash, which is immediately invested in a ship. The result of this proceeding is to even out the differences between investment and outlay of one year and the next. This practice and the exclusion of non-colonial voyages—the *Louis Dauphin* to Bilbao in 1729 and Cadiz in 1734, the *Fleury* under charter to the Compagnie des Indes in 1744 and the King in 1746—account for the difference between the value of bars for those years and values in column E of table 33.

FIG. 3. *The Investments and Outlays of Dugard and Company, 1729–55*

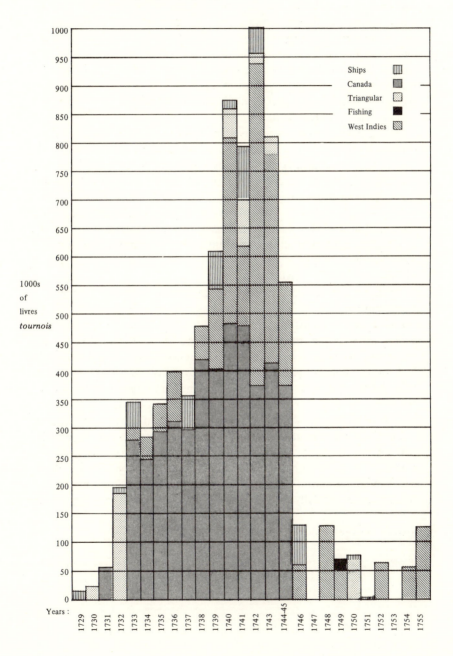

ceased to matter. Each year a substantial sum was returned to offset new outlays. In any case, given the credit terms invariably extended by suppliers, it is probable that little or even none of a cargo was paid for when a ship set sail for Canada. The voyage was accomplished in six to nine months, leaving three to six months for disposal of the cargo before the end of a 12-month period. The problem is more acute in the case of West Indian voyages. These usually took about 14 months, so the period from the payment for most of the outward cargo until the return of a substantial part of the outlay was probably between one and one-half and two years.

As has been pointed out above, the original current account figures on which all calculation must be based presumably overestimate profits. Are these profits then also overestimated? The deficiency cannot, presumably, be entirely overcome. What, then, can be concluded on the subject of profits? It is the nature of numbers to appear to be exact no matter what the circumstances of their collection. While these figures should not be regarded as exact, they are as close to exactitude as the documentation allows. It is, however, most unlikely that the general impression as to the rough magnitude of profits at different places and times is incorrect.

Table 33 also makes it possible to determine roughly how much borrowing must have been necessary and in what years to provide for the company's expansion. The growth of the company's wealth from 22,001 livres at the end of 1729 to 620,182 livres in 1742 and its rapid reduction to 406,926 livres in the six years of business blighted by the War of the Austrian Succession are clearly revealed. It is obvious from this that the rise in costs that can be attributed to insurance premiums, the disappointing market conditions in the West Indies caused by the arrival of all French ships at once in convoy, and the loss of shipping not entirely offset by insurance payments resulted in a very substantial loss for the company. From tables 30 and 33 taken together, it is also clear that in the long run the Canadian trade was more reliable than the West Indian and that the ambitious drive of the company into Martinique, especially at Cul de Sac Marin, was ultimately disastrous.

GUIDE TO TABLE 33

Column A: The year. Figures given are those for undertakings be-
            gun in the given year although they may not have been
            concluded by 31 December.

Column B: Paid-in capital. Contributions by Dugard's associates are given in the accounts. There is no record of Dugard's contributions; therefore, assuming them to have been equal in value to those of his associates, the ownership being divided into five equal shares, a figure equal to one-quarter of the total of the other associates' contributions is added to them.

Column C: Retained earnings. This is the balance left from the previous year after all expenses were met. It is a maximum figure as all current assets might not have been converted into cash.

Column D: Total of B and C.

Column E: Investment and outlay. This includes all investment in ships built or bought in Europe (*Louis Dauphin, St. Mathieu,* and *Ville de Québec*) and all outlays on cargoes and outfitting. Ships built in Canada were paid for from the Canadian profits on cargoes included in these outlay figures.

Column F: Needed finance. If the figure in Column E is larger than that in Column D, then additional finance must have been necessary.

Column G: Surplus. If the figure in Column E is smaller than that in Column D, then there must have been a surplus.

Column H: Profits less Canadian ships. These are the profits on "returns" from which expenses incurred after ships had returned to France were deducted. The value of Canadian-built ships has also been deducted in order to separate current assets (cash, accounts receivable, inventory) from fixed assets (ships). The ultimate effect is the same as if the value of the ships had not been removed and had instead been entered as an investment in the following year, although the depreciated value of shipping would still have to appear in Column K.

Column I: Consolidated costs. Costs totalled by Dugard under the headings of debts owed by bankrupts, advances by correspondents, and interest, bad debts, etc. have been divided on a *pro rata* basis between the period 1739–48 and 1749–55. The share for 1739–48 is divided into ten instalments. For 1742 interest on bottomry is added.

Column J: Total current assets. The total of Columns H and G minus the totals of Columns F and I.

TABLE 33.

*Financial History of Dugard and Company, 1729–1748, Hypothetical
Reconstruction*

A	B	C	D	E	F	G
Year	Paid-in Capital	Retained Earnings	Total, B & C	Investment and Outlay	Needed Finance	Surplus
1729	23306	—	23306	21726	—	1580
1730	26943	2224	29167	25753	—	3414
1731	40919	32393	73312	58774	—	14538
1732	81071	79395	160466	197797	37331	—
1733	78944	169355	248299	348656	100357	—
1734	7664	230858	238522	288247	49725	—
1735	−15667	279375	263708	348167	84459	—
1736	−14529	317074	302545	401619	99074	—
1737	−1900	279559	277659	300028	22369	—
1738	6013	315729	321742	483363	161621	—
1739	—	312464	312464	546609	234145	—
1740	—	338276	338276	860733	522457	—
1741	—	391972	391972	717409	325437	—
1742	—	395276	395276	960395	565119	—
1743	—	438301	438301	821467	383166	—
1744–5	—	456720	456720	586352	129632	—
1746	—	361303	361303	97554	—	263749
1747	No new outlay					
1748	—	370066	370066	129253	—	240813

Source: AN. 62AQ40, partners' current accounts.

Column K: Total fixed assets (ships). The total value of the fleet at
            the end of each year, depreciation taken into account.
Column L: Ownership interest. Total of J and K.
Column M: Profit for the year. Shows increase or decrease in the
            ownership interest, which is the same as the company's
            total worth because it carried no long-term finance.

H	I	J	K	L	M	
Profits Less Cdn. Ships	Con. Costs Deduction	Total Current	Total Fixed (ships)	Ownership Interest	Profit for Year	
644	—	2224	19777	22001	−5.5	
28979	—	32393	17980	50373	2.9	
64857	—	79395	16183	95578	4.6	
206686	—	169355	22636	191991	8.6	
331215	—	230858	62074	292932	8.1	
329100	—	279375	55711	335086	11.5	
401533	—	317074	49348	366422	14.7	Average
378633	—	279559	94087	373646	6.2	1729–43
338098	—	315729	83079	398808	7.2	7.5
474085	—	312464	129698	442162	9.2	
605042	32621	338276	113461	451737	2.1	
947050·	32621	391972	187477	579449	28.2	
753334	32621	395276	205404	600680	3.7	
1053773	50353	438301	181881	620182	3.2	
872507	32621	456720	138714	599434		Average
556177	65242	361303	165579	526882		1743–48
171559	32621	402687	126667	529354		−6.9
	32621	370066	85091	455157		
126873	32624	335062	71864	406926		

TABLE 34.

Reconstructed Balance Sheet of Dugard and Company, 31 Dec. 1748

DEBIT		CREDIT	
Investment in fleet	414817	Depreciated value, fleet	71864
Outlays on cargoes and		Net profits, return	
outfitting	7117527	cargoes	7978587
Bottomry loan, 1742,			
interest	17732		
Misc. costs, incl. bad			
debts, interest, etc.	326213	Paid-in capital less	
		drawings	232764
To Balance	406926		
	8283215	Total	8283215

Source: AN. 62AQ40, partners' current accounts.

Abbreviations Used in the Notes

AC	Archives des Colonies (in the Archives nationales, Paris)
AD	Archives départementales (Seine-Maritime, Gironde, etc.)
AM	Archives de la Marine, Paris
AN	Archives nationales, Paris
ADQ	Archives du Québec
ASQ	Archives du Séminaire de Québec
AJQ	Archives judiciaires de Québec
BMR	Bibliothèque municipale de Rouen
Bib. Prot.	Bibliothèque de la Société de l'Histoire du Protestantisme français, Paris
MG	Manuscript Group (at PAC)
PAC	Public Archives of Canada, Ottawa
SHM	Société historique de Montréal

Notes

Notes to Preface

1. Letter from S. Rumeau, Sous-Directeur des Archives de France (Paris, 3 February 1973).

2. See Bertrand Gille, *Etat sommaire des Archives d'entreprises conservées aux Archives nationales* (Paris, 1957), pp. 149–51, "Le Fonds Dugard."

3. Richard Pares, "The Economic Factors in the History of the Empire," *The Historian's Business and other Essays* (Oxford, 1961), p. 50.

4. Philippe Wolff, "L'étude des économies et sociétés avant l'ère statistique," *L'histoire et ses méthodes*, edited by Charles Samarin (Paris, 1961), p. 852.

Notes to Introduction

1. The most useful studies on the diplomatic history of the period are David B. Horn, *Great Britain and Europe in the Eighteenth Century* (Oxford, 1967); Sir Richard Lodge, "The Anglo-French Alliance, 1716–1731," *Studies in Anglo-French History during the Eighteenth, Nineteenth and Twentieth Centuries*, ed. A Colville and H. Temperley (Cambridge, 1935); Arthur McCandless Wilson, *French Foreign Policy during the Administration of Cardinal Fleury, 1726–1743* (Cambridge, Mass., 1936); and Paul Vaucher, *Robert Walpole et la politique de Fleury, 1731–1742* (Paris, 1924).

2. Wilson, *Fleury*, p. 42, quoting Louis XIV to Amelot, 18 February 1709.

3. "Arlequin actionnaire. Caricature sur la banqueroute de Law, 1720. Gravure au trait, anonyme, Musée Carnavalet, Paris," plate 19, facing p. 272, in E. Labrousse et al., *Histoire économique et sociale de la France*, vol. 2 (Paris, 1970).

4. Eugène LeLong, "Introduction," *Conseil de Commerce et Bureau du Commerce, 1700–1791, Inventaire analytique des procès verbaux*, Louis Jean Pierre Marie Bonnassieux (Paris, 1900); Bernard Wybo, *Le Conseil de Commerce et le commerce intérieur de la France au XVIIIᵉ siècle* (Paris, 1936).

5. Wybo, *Conseil de Commerce*, p. 64; Wilson, *Fleury*, disagrees (p. 66), but Wybo presents sufficient evidence to show that the influential Orry was an inveterate systematizer and maker of rules.

6. For economic and social background, see Pierre Goubert, *Louis XIV et vingt millions de Français* (Paris, 1967); Robert Mandrou, *La France aux XVIIᵉ et XVIIIᵉ siècles*, Nouvelle Clio (Paris, 1967); and Hubert Méthivier, *Le siècle de Louis XV*, Que-sais-je? (Paris, 1966) in addition to Labrousse, *Histoire économique*. The sober and tentative account of the latter should be compared with Mandrou's earlier, more exuberant treatment. The moderation is to be attributed to the influence of Michel Morineau's *Les faux-semblants d'un démarrage économique: agriculture et démographie en France au XVIIIᵉ siècle*, Cahiers des Annales (Paris, 1971), placed at Labrousse's disposal in manuscript.

7. Henri Sée, *La France économique et sociale au XVIIIᵉ siècle*, 7th ed. (Paris, n.d.) has not been superseded with regard to the rise of commerce and industry.

8. Hubert Luthy, *La banque protestante en France*, 2, *De la banque aux finances, 1730–1794* (Paris, 1961), p. 21.

9. Wybo, *Conseil de Commerce*, p. 19.

10. Guy P. Palmade, *French Capitalism in the Nineteenth Century*, trans. and with introduction G. M. Holmes (New York, 1972), p. 49.

11. This treatment of the history of French trade in the Caribbean is based upon C. A. Banbuck, *Histoire politique, économique et sociale de la Martinique sous l'Ancien Régime* (Paris, 1935), L. P. May, *Histoire économique de la Martinique* (Paris, 1930), W. S. Mims, *Colbert's West-India Policy* (New Haven, Conn., 1912), Maurice Filion, *Maurepas, ministre de Louis XV, 1715–1749* (Montreal, 1967). Filion's use of secondary sources is narrow and he sees Maurepas as virtually without allies in the government service. Supplement with Wilson, *Fleury*

12. May, *Martinique*, p. 134.

13. On the naval question see Wilson, *Fleury*, chap. 2.

14. AN, AD vii 2a, "Lettres Patentes du Roy portant Reglement pour le Commerce des Colonies françoises du mois d'avril, 1717," (Paris, 1717); "Lettres Patentes du Roy de France en Forme d'Edit concernant le commerce estranger aux Isles & Colonies de l'Amérique données à Fontainebleau au mois d'octobre, 1727" (Paris, 1727).

15. AN, AC, C8A, 39, fol. 471, Réponse de la Martinique; 40 fol. 31, D'Orgeville au Ministre, 5 février 1729; 42, fol. 118, Champigny au Ministre, 3 septembre 1731; C9A, 32, St. Aubin au Ministre, 9 décembre 1730.

16. AN, AC, C8A, 58, fol. 274, De Caylus au Ministre, 6 octobre 1749.

17. For a sampling of colonial administrators' views see C8A, 39, fols. 471,

115, 155, 173; 41, fol. 112; 42, 15 mars 1731; 51, fol. 384; 58, fol. 266. There is no better example of a ministerial reply than noted in n. 20.

18. AN, AC, C9A, 30, Le Gentil au Ministre, 19 avril 1729.

19. AN, AC, C9A, 37, De Fayet au Ministre, 28 juin 1733. See also 40, De Fayet au Ministre, 11 janvier 1734.

20. AN, AC, B 76, fol. 213, Ministre à Messrs. de Larnage et Maillart (St. Domingue), Versailles, 5 avril 1743. This document is an excellent summary of Maurepas's colonial views. If it was not written by the Minister himself, then he was not the only individual in the department with a sharp tongue.

21. On the economy of New France see W. J. Eccles, *The Canadian Frontier, 1534–1760*, Histories of the American Frontier, ed. R. A. Billington (New York, 1969); A. J. E. Lunn, "Economic Development in New France 1713–1760" (Ph.D. diss., McGill, 1942); Jean Hamelin, *Economie et société en Nouvelle-France* (Quebec, 1960); and Guy Frégault, "La Compagnie de la Colonie," *Le XVIIIᵉ siècle canadien: études* (Montreal, 1968).

22. D. J. Horton, "Gilles Hocquart, Intendant of New France" (Ph.D. diss., McGill, 1975) is the first thorough study of this official.

23. On Ile Royale see Guy Frégault, *François Bigot, administrateur français*, 2 vols. (Montreal, 1948); Charles de La Morandière, *Histoire de la pêche française de la morue dans l'Amérique septentrionale*, vol. 2 (Paris, 1962); and H. A. Innis, "Cape Breton and the French Régime," *Proceedings and Transactions of the Royal Society of Canada*, 3rd series, 29 (1935): 51–87. The latter is nearly incomprehensible, but points out that the Cape Breton fishery was required to compete with the metropolitan fishery, and provides important statistics.

24. La Morandière, *Histoire de la pêche*, 2: 648, quoting AN, AC, F3, 50, fol. 11, Ministre au Sieur Lhermite, 26 janvier 1714.

25. Ibid., p. 652, quoting AN, AC, B 37, fol. 27, Ministre au Contrôleur général Desmaretz, 10 février 1715.

Notes to Chapter Two

1. AM, C⁴ 159, Mémoire sur la Ville de Rouen par Sicard en 1730. Signed, "fait a la hougue le 20 octobre 1730, Sicard." Gives information about the city, its institutions, and its commerce used in this chapter. See in *Précis Académie de Rouen*, H. Wallon, "La Vicomté de l'Eau et le commerce de Rouen au XVIIIᵉ siècle" (1902), p. 185 and J. Lothe, "La douane et la vie économique de Rouen sous l'Ancien Régime" (1930), p. 11.

2. Roger Mols, *Introduction à la démographie historique des villes d'Europe du XIVᵉ au XVIIIᵉ siècles* (Gembloux, 1954–56), 2: 514. Mols limits himself to giving the population of Rouen as more than 50,000. He quotes contemporary estimates for 1726 as 80,690 (Saugrain), for 1745 as 92,480 (Orry), and for 1787 as 68,040 (Calonne).

3. H. Wallon, *La Chambre de Commerce de la Province de Normandie*,

1703–1791 (Rouen, 1903). Chap. 6, "Le Batiment consulaire," discusses Blondel's creation.

4. In addition to Sicard, H. Wallon, *La bourse découverte et les quais de Rouen* (Rouen, 1897).

5. Henri Lafosse, *La Juridiction consulaire de Rouen, 1556–1791* (Rouen, 1922), pp. 21–22.

6. Ibid., pp. 109–11.

7. Wallon, *Chambre de Commerce*, p. 175 and chap. 3.

8. Ibid., chaps. 7, 8, 10.

9. Ibid., p. 99.

10. Ibid., pp. 100–10.

11. Lafosse, *Juridiction*, p. 48.

12. Ibid., pp. 51–54.

13. Ibid. The *juridictions consulaires* and *chambres de commerce* are mercantile "constituted bodies" not discussed in R. R. Palmer's synthesis, *The Age of Democratic Revolution*, vol. 1 (Princeton, 1959).

14. Wallon, *Chambre de Commerce*, p. 79.

15. Pierre Dardel, *Navires et marchandises dans les ports de Rouen et du Havre au XVIIIᵉ siècle* (Paris, 1963), p. 53. This and Dardel's companion volume, *Commerce, industrie et navigation à Rouen et au Havre au XVIIIᵉ siècle* (Rouen, 1966), provide an economic history for which historians of the eighteenth century must be grateful, but social questions are unfortunately not considered. The reader would also gain much by consulting Henri Fouquet, *Histoire civile, politique et commerciale de Rouen depuis les temps les plus réculés jusqu'à nos jours* (Rouen, 1876), a graceful and solid work.

16. Dardel, *Commerce*, pp. 107–19.

17. Ibid., p. 117. See pp. 186–87 for discussion of the various versions of the De la Rue story.

18. Ibid., p. 119.

19. P. Sement, *Les anciennes halles aux toiles et aux cotons de Rouen* (Rouen, 1931), p. 120.

20. Dardel, *Commerce*, p. 116.

21. Dardel, *Navires et marchandises*, p. 164.

22. Ibid., pp. 84–85, 182–83, 186, 196, 206.

23. Ibid., pp. 72, 176–78.

24. Ibid., pp. 102–3, 105, 196.

25. Ibid., p. 105; Sement, *Les anciennes halles*, pp. 117–18.

26. Dardel, *Navires et marchandises*, p. 74.

27. Ibid., p. 198, 201–3.

28. Sicard, Mémoire, 1730.

29. According to Dardel, *Navires et marchandises*, French foreign trade tripled between 1716–20 and 1777–83 (p. 49). The commerce of Rouen and Le Havre shared in this increase, tripling between 1730 and 1753 (p. 49). In 1769, however, their foreign trade (and perhaps that of all France) levelled off, marking a "renversement de la tendance et de la conjoncture" (p. 52). Their trade with the Antilles, increasingly important after 1736, multiplied thirty-

one times in the period 1730–76 and greatly enhanced their positions as major centres of maritime commerce. However, the largest part of their trade remained that with other European countries, and this doubled in the same period (pp. 50–51, 58). Le Havre and Rouen always had an unfavourable balance of foreign trade, importing raw materials from abroad, but selling most of their manufactured goods in the kingdom (p. 53).

30. Bib. Prot., Fonds Lesens, MS 1206–I.

31. Bib. Prot., Fonds Pierre LeGendre, MS 412¹. The *état civil* of the Protestants of Rouen can be traced in the registers of the congregation of Quévilly. In 1791, Pierre LeGendre, first archivist of the Département de la Seine-Inférieure, compiled alphabetical lists of these registers. His manuscript is today in the Bibliothèque de la Société de l'Histoire du Protestantisme français, Paris. There are also copies in the Archives départementales de la Seine-Maritime and the Bibliothèque municipale de Rouen. (See René Rouault de La Vigne, *Les Protestants de Rouen et de Quévilly sous l'Ancien Régime*, Rouen and Paris, 1940, p. 26.) LeGendre's lists are divided into three volumes. The first, MS 412¹, is a "Table Analytique des Baptêmes, 1594–1668, Quévilly près Rouen." Original records were and are missing for the years 1610–March 1619 and 1625–1630 inclusive. The second is MS 412² ("Table Analytique des Mariages et Annonces de Mariage, Quévilly près Rouen, 1609–1669"). Original records for 1620–30 were and are missing.

In April 1667, an ordinance changed the form of registers; thereafter baptisms were kept in a common register with marriages and burials. Thus there is also in MS 412² a "Table Analytique de Baptêmes, Mariages et Inhumations à Quévilly près Rouen, 1668–1685." MS 412³ contains a "Table Analytique de Baptêmes, Mariages et Inhumations à Quévilly près Rouen, 1628–1685," as well as a copy of the register of burials in the Protestant Cimetière de la rue de la Rose, 25 November 1746–11 May 1788. This cemetery was given by Robert Dugard III as a burial place for foreign Protestants. A Déclaration du Roi of 9 April 1736 permitted that *Rouennais* Protestants might also be there interred. (See Pierre La Verdier, "Etablissement d'un cimetière protestant à Rouen, 1786," *Bulletin de la Société de l'Histoire de Normandie* 10 (1909): 213–29.)

Writing near the end of the last century, Emile Lesens maintained that two registers of burials in the cemetery for the period from the end of 1714 to 30 January 1743 recording 313 burials had been discovered since LeGendre had compiled his tables and that they were to be found at the Palais de Justice in Rouen. (See Fonds Emile Lesens, MS 1206–IV.) The archives of the Palais, a building badly damaged in W.W.II, have since been removed to other repositories. A check with the archivists of the Archives départementales, Rouen, the Archives de la Ville de Rouen and the Bibliothèque municipale de Rouen failed to reveal the elusive registers or any knowledge of their fate.

32. Ibid., MS 412².

33. Ibid., MS 412³. If the record is correct, then he was born in April 1613, for which year the registers of Quévilly are lost.

34. Ibid., MSS 412¹, 412³.

35. AD Seine-Maritime, Greffe du notaire Lauvon, 14 novembre 1707. This original marriage contract was made *sous seing privé* on 2 September 1702. At the later date, it was filed with the notary. The latter's signature appears only in a note explaining the deposition.

36. Françoise Porée must have died between 14 November 1707 and 10 April 1712, for on the latter date Robert Dugard III signed another marriage contract with one Marie Mayer. (AD Seine-Maritime, Greffe du notaire Le Coq, 8 juillet 1712, i.e., date of deposition.)

37. AN, 62 AQ, 1, receipts, 1662, 1663.

38. Ibid., bill of exchange, London, 3 January 1658/59.

39. Ibid., bills of exchange, Amsterdam, 6 November 1664; London, 9 September 1664.

40. Bibliothèque municipale de Rouen (BMR), JJ, "Registre alphabétique des noms des marchands qui ont payé le droit de hance en cette ville de Rouen, en execution de l'arrêt du Parlement du seize aoust 16 quatre vingt douze," fol. 14. The register begins in 1650.

41. A. Michel de Boislisle, ed., *Correspondance des contrôleurs généraux des finances* (Paris, 1874–97), 1: 483, no. 1734, "LaBourdonnaye, Intendant de Rouen au contrôleur-général, 7 juillet 1698."

42. Recorded payments of the *droit de hanse* by members of the Société du Canada exhibit the same time lag. In 1698, Robert III's mother, Marie LePlastrier, also paid the fee (Registre alphabétique, fol. 43).

43. AN, 62 AQ 1, "Ensuit la Repartition de la Somme de Sept mille neuf cents quatre vingt dix neuf livres, quinze sols . . ."; there are 51 names on the list taxed as follows: 500–600 livres—four persons; 180–350 livres—13 persons; 91–179 livres—12 persons; and zero–90 livres—24 persons.

44. Ibid., printed form, signed Jean Goujon, Rouen, 15 mars 1720.

45. AN, TT² (Réligionnaires fugitifs), fol. 128, "Placet de R. Dugard de Rouen au Marquis de la Vrillière, secrétaire d'Etat, 19 décembre 1723"; letter of De Gasville, Intendant, 23 décembre 1723.

46. AN, 62 AQ 11, Grand Livre, 1722–26; 62 AQ 12, Journal, 1722–26. Neither volume is signed by Dugard. But the account of German wool in Journal B, fol. 2, shows that wool debited to this account comes under the bale marking –RDG–. Thus RDG of Amsterdam is the owner of the journal and the companion ledger. Since the owner received his capital from his father in 1722 the Robert Dugard in question must be Robert IV.

47. AN, 62 AQ 12, Journal A, Capital Account. Journal A covers 1 February 1722 to 27 August 1722, and comprises the first 108½ pages of the journal register. The profit centre is Amsterdam and the money of account the florin.

48. Ibid. Each item becomes a ledger account.

49. AN, 62 AQ 11, Ledger, accounts of Amsterdamers Cornelis Burius, Cornelis de Boer, Jan van Blanken, Compagnie des Indes Orientales, Louis Docher, Pieter Groenvelt, Daniel Hooywagen, Zacharias Leun, Veuve Rooseboom, Phillip van der Waes, Issac Willing, Creditteurs Divers, and Debitteurs Divers.

50. Ibid., the following foreign accounts: Spiegal, Frederick à Dantzick, m/c [mon compte]; Boeteseur, Joachim, à Hambourg, m/c; Indigo chez J. Boeteseur à Hambourg, m/c; Laines d'Allemagne; Paarling, Jan van, à Hambourg, m/c; Marchandises entre les mains de Paarling, m/c; Indigo entre les mains de Paarling, m/c; Paarling, Jan van, à Hambourg, s/c [son compte], Schelde, Barthelemy van, à Altona, m/c; and Tervoet, Pieter à Bremen, m/c.

51. Ibid., foreign accounts—Soetenou, Michel van, à Londres, m/c; Soutenou, Michel van, s/c; Varin, Claude, à Dunkerque, s/c; Genwith, Simon, à Morlaix, s/c.

52. Ibid., foreign accounts—Jude, Louis, à Rouen, m/c; Jude, Louis, à Rouen, s/c; Marchandises à Rouen m/c chez Louis Jude; Dugard, Robert, à Rouen, m/c; Dugard, Robert, à Rouen, s/c; Marchandises à Rouen en mains du R. Dugard pour compte ⅓ Elie duPuis de la Rochelle, ⅓ Dugard et ⅓ moy; Marchandises à Rouen en Mains de Robert Dugard pour Notre compte à Demie; and Bery, Jean de, à Rouen, s/c.

53. Ibid., foreign accounts—Frémy, Jean et Cie à Nantes, s/c; LeBrun, Laurent, à Nantes, s/c; DuPuis, Elie, à la Rochelle, m/c; DuPuis, Elie, à la Rochelle, s/c; Marchandises pr compte Elie duPuis de la Rochelle; LeClerc, Benjamin à Lisbonne, s/c; LeClerc, Benjamin, à Lisbonne, m/c; Laines de Portugal; Draps; Haro, Henrique de, à Cadix, m/c; Haro, Henrique de, à Cadix, s/c; Marchandises à Cadix entre les mains de Henrique de Haro, m/c; and Marchandises Générales.

54. Ibid., Pieter Rutger's account.

55. Ibid. He sold to Blanken, Groenveldt, Hooywagen, Leun, Rooseboom, Staden, Vitre, and Willing, buying from Burius, Boer, East India Company, Docher, and Waes.

56. Ibid. He bought nothing from Varin, Genwith, Bery, Frémy, and LeBrun, selling nothing to Van Schelde and Tervoet.

57. Henri Lévy-Bruhl, *Histoire de la lettre de change en France aux XVIIe et XVIIIe siècles* (Paris, 1933); R. A. de Roover, *L'Evolution de la lettre de change, XIVe–XVIIIe siècles* (Paris, 1953). These are the two basic works on the bill of exchange; further references are given in chaps. 4 and 8, nn.

58. Ibid. The relevant accounts with Van Paarling are listed in note 50.

59. Ibid., Van Paarling, s/c, Dugard à Rouen, m/c.

60. Ibid., Schelde, m/c.

61. Ibid., Tervoet, m/c.

62. Ibid., Soetenou, m/c; and Genwith, s/c.

63. Ibid., Laines de Compte à Demie avec Samuel LeBlanc.

64. Ibid., Laines pour compte en tiers entre Dirk de Jager de Leyden, S. Leblanc et moy en mains de Jager; 62 AQ 12, Journal B, 20 September.

65. AN, 62 AQ 11, Soetenou, m/c.

66. Ibid., Marchandises à Rouen en mains du R. Dugard pour compte ⅓ Elie du Puis. . . .

67. All relevant accounts are in Ledger, 62 AQ 11, except Marchandises aux Iles which is in Journal B, 62 AQ 12, only.

68. AN, 62 AQ 11, fol. 1.

Original gross capital:	159,116	Original gross capital	159,116
Original debts owed:	16,461	Balance of profit and loss	8,426
Original net capital:	142,655	New gross capital:	167,542
		New debts owed:	17,085
		New net capital:	150,457

The increase in capital is 7,802 or five and one-half per cent. The same result will be found by the alternative method of comparing the trial balance of 27 August, fol. 29, with the entries of 1 February at fol. 1.

69. AN, 62 AQ 12, fol. 9, 16 September 1722.

70. Ibid., 12 October 1722.

71. Ibid. This final journal is as follows: 3 pages for 16 October to 31 December 1723; 7-1/10 pages for 12 February to 29 November 1724; 3½ pages for 18 January to 15 November 1725; and 3½ pages for 12 January to 15 June 1726. There are 17 pages in all. Since none of the entries have the usual d/c sign in the margin, none of them has been posted to a ledger beyond the few scribbles at the back of 62 AQ 11.

72. AN, 62 AQ 38, Mlle. Jeanne Verel, son compte courant avec Robert Dugard, 1 décembre 1738.

73. AN, 62 AQ 32, Baille, 12 novembre, 1733; extracted from *étude* of *notaire* Michel LeCoq.

74. Bib. Prot., Fonds Pierre LeGendre, MS 412[1]. There are three distinct groups of Laurenses. The mercers are all amongst the persons in the register who can be traced back to Abraham Laurens and Marie Dumont (baptism of son Abraham in MS 412[1], January 1631); the *passementiers* can be traced back to Hutius Laurens and Marie Benoist (baptism of son Abraham, 1634 in MS 412[1]); the dinaudier-chaudronnier are in the family lines descended from Nicholas Laurens and Anne Allard (baptism of son Abraham, 15 November 1600 in MS 412[1]).

75. Ibid., parents' marriage, MS 412[2]; baptism of grandparents' eldest son, 19 October 1620 in MS 412[1].

76. BMR, JJ, Registre Alphabétique, fv. 44.

77. Bib. Prot., MS 412[3], Inhumation de David Laurens, 27 avril 1784.

78. Ibid., inhumation de Marie Laurens, 16 juillet 1747.

79. Ibid., Fonds Lesens, MS 1206-V, Baptême Paroisse St. Vincent gives the date of the baptism as 17 November 1731. However, the Contrôle de Rouen, AD Seine-Maritime, dates the marriage contract at 27 January 1735, and its registration at 2 August 1735.

80. Bib. Prot., Fonds LeGendre, MS 412[2], Mariage, 1680.

81. BMR, JJ, Registre alphabétique des noms des marchands . . ., fol. 87.

82. Bib. Prot., Fonds LeGendre, MS 412[2], baptême, 1681.

83. Ibid. Fonds Lesens, MS 1206-V, baptême, 21 janvier 1744.

84. AD Seine-Maritime, G 5.128, Bans de Mariage entre François Guillaume LeMenu de la Noe . . . et Marie Julie Françoise France . . . 11 octobre 1755.

85. G. H. Faucon, *La juridiction consulaire de Rouen, 1556–1905, d'après*

les documents authentiques et avec l'agrément du Tribune de Commerce de Rouen (Evreux, 1905), p. 97.

86. BMR, JJ, Registre alphabétique, fol. 25.

87. AD Seine-Maritime, G 5.128 gives wife's name as Catherine Elizabeth Blard, but her *acte de sépulture* in AD Marne gives her name as Elizabeth-Catherine Besard.

88. AN, 62 AQ 31, Robert Dugard à M. Bourgerel à Nantes, Rouen, 3 juin 1767.

89. Ibid., Richard à Robert Dugard, Paris, 14 juin 1757.

90. BMR, JJ, Registre chronologique, 31 juillet 1743. The chronological register, unlike the alphabetical one, which contains most names, records the fee paid for letters.

91. Dardel, *Commerce*, p. 197; numerous other mentions.

92. AD Seine-Maritime, G 6.506, Comptes de la fabrique de l'église Saint-Etienne des Tonneliers; G 7001 and G 7002, comptes de la fabrique de l'église paroissiale de St. Maclou.

93. AN, 62 AQ 39, Livre de Délibération.

94. Bib. Prot., Fonds LeGendre, MS 412³.

95. AN, 62 AQ 35. Last letter of G. France père is 19 October 1742; the first letter of G. France fils is 20 November 1744.

96. AN, 62 AQ 31, Richard à Robert Dugard, Paris, 9 juin 1757.

97. AN, 62 AQ 37, Dugard fils à Rémy Bansa, Rouen, 5 août 1770.

98. Bib. Prot., Fonds LeGendre, MS 412³.

Notes to Chapter Three

1. AN, 62 AQ 40, liasse O, partners' accounts, 1729–38 (for D'Haristoy, 1728–38).

2. Ibid.

3. Ibid.

4. Pastor Denis Vatinel, *conservateur* of the library of the Société de l'Histoire du Protestantisme français, Paris, has informed the author that François Havy was born at Beuzevillette near Bolbec, the son of François Havy and Suzanne Levesque, and baptised a Roman Catholic on 5 March 1703. His father's name appears in a list of Beuzevillette's "nouveaux convertis" in 1698, and he is described as 25 years old, a merchant and a bachelor, occupying ten acres of ground and living with his mother, aged 66. But the date invalidates the age attributed to Havy in the Quebec Census of 1744— *Rapport de l'archiviste de la Province de Québec pour 1939–40*, ed. P. G. Roy (Quebec, 1940), pp. 1–154—which would place his birth in 1709. Professor John Bosher of York University has communicated to the author the substance of Havy's *acte de sépulture* from the registers in the Archives départementales de la Gironde, Bordeaux; the age given in that document would place Havy's birth in 1699. A baptismal record is undoubtedly the best source for determining age, and it is beyond any reasonable doubt that the document

cited by Pastor Vatinel does indeed refer to the François Havy in question because Havy is known to have been of Norman Protestant descent, the date is within the decade in which all evidence suggests Havy must have been born, the name is itself very rare, and finally and most persuasively, the given parentage is mercantile and explains the relationship of Havy to François Levesque, a cousin who came to work for him in his later years in Canada. Havy's only reference to his family background, in which he claims poverty prevented his receiving a good education, is in AN, 62 AQ 32, Havy à Dugard, 7 juillet 1759.

Beginning in 1732, Havy had a partner at Quebec, his cousin Jean Lefebvre (see chap. 4, p. 70). Lefebvre refers to himself in his last will and testament as "de la province de Caux en Normandie" (APQ, AJQ, Greffe de J. C. Panet, 22 novembre 1758). Pastor Vatinel states that while he is aware of there having been several Protestant Lefebvre families in the Pays de Caux, the only Jean Lefebvre in his records was born on 7 August 1704 at Manneville la Goupil near Bolbec. Nothing proves that this is the Jean Lefebvre in question. If it is, the 1744 census has his age wrong by a full decade. As to religion, both Havy and Lefebvre appear in a "Liste des Personnes de la Religion prétendue réformée qui sont à Québec commis des négociants de la France" (AC, C 11 A, 75, fol. 15).

5. AN, 62 AQ 38, J. Verel, compte courant avec Robert Dugard, 20 mars 1729–8 janvier 1732.

6. AN, 62 AQ 12, 16 août and 3 octobre 1724.

7. E. Lesens, "Liste des Protestants de Rouen qui ont été persécutés à la Révocation de l'Edit de Nantes . . ." in J. Bianquis, *La Révocation de l'Edit de Nantes à Rouen* (Paris, 1885).

8. Bib. Prot., Fonds Lesens, MS 1206-V.

9. AN, 62 AQ 40, liasse X, François Havy s/c de gestion 1730–31; son compte de gages et dépenses, 1731–32; son compte de gestion, cargaison *Louis Dauphin* Québec à Martinique, 1731, dated 1732; son compte de gestion à Québec, 1730–31. Although it is almost certain ships stopped at La Rochelle until 1734, no specific record has been found and so it is not entered on charts in appendix B.

10. Ibid., François Havy, son compte de gestion, Deuxième Cargaison, 1732; son compte de gestion, cargaison *Louis Dauphin* pour Québec, 1734, dated 29 mai 1732.

11. AN, 62 AQ 39, Livre de Délibération de la Compagnie du Canada. A vellum-covered volume of 49 fols., 18 to 48 inclusive having been cut out. There is no trace of ink on the remaining edges, and the pages were probably blanks removed for economy's sake. The volume contains the *acte de société* on fols. 7v–9r, and the minutes of 32 meetings.

12. Ibid., 14 mai 1732.

13. AN, 62 AQ 40, liasse O, accounts, Vincent père et fils, 1729–1738; Pierre D'Haristoy, 1728–1738.

14. All voyages are outlined in as much detail as possible in appendix B,

which includes all documentary references. A condensed chronological list appears in appendix C.

15. Appendix D discusses problems involved in determining the profits of Dugard and Company.

16. AN, 62 AQ 39, délibération 3, 22 janvier 1733; 62 AQ 40, liasse O, accounts, 1729–1738. The reimbursement is entered in the books on 8 February 1732, but is a result of a meeting of 22 January 1733. Probably, because of the slowness of communication, word from Beckveldt was not received by the other partners until the later date. The severance was then carried at the earlier date so that he would have no part in operations after the return of the second cargo.

17. AN, 62 AQ 39, délibération 2, 16 mai 1732.

18. Ibid., délibération 4, 28 janvier 1733.

19. Ibid., délibération 5, 19 mars 1733.

20. Ibid., délibération 3, 22 janvier 1733.

21. Ibid., délibérations 4 et 5, 28 janvier et 10 mars 1733.

22. Ibid., délibération 6, 20 juillet 1733.

23. Ibid.

24. Ibid., délibération 10, 16 mars 1734.

25. Ibid., délibération 9, 11 février 1734.

26. Ibid., délibérations 5 et 9, 10 mars 1733 et 11 février 1734.

27. Ibid., délibération 5, 10 mars 1733.

28. Ibid., délibération 7, 11 janvier 1734.

29. Ibid., délibération 5, 10 mars 1733.

30. Appendix D.

31. AN, 62 AQ 39, délibération 6, 20 juillet 1733.

32. Appendix D.

33. AN, 62 AQ 39, délibération 7, 11 janvier 1734.

34. Appendix D.

35. A. P. Usher, *The Early History of Deposit Banking in Mediterranean Europe* (Cambridge, Mass., 1943), pp. 77–78.

36. Ibid., pp. 33–78 on gradual acceptance of the legal status of the signature; H. Lévy-Bruhl, *Histoire juridique des sociétés de commerce* (Paris, 1938), pp. 76–79 on oral and written agreements.

37. Lévy-Bruhl, ibid., p. 79.

38. Ibid., p. 65.

39. Ibid., pp. 30, 94–100.

40. AN, 62 AQ 39, fols. 7v–9r, "Acte de Société que Dieu veuille benir," Clause Quarto.

41. AN, 62 AQ 40, liasse O, Acte sous seing privé, 26 mai 1742.

42. Lévy-Bruhl, *Histoire juridique*, p. 31.

43. Ibid., p. 32.

44. AN, 62 AQ 39, Acte, Clause Sexto.

45. Lévy-Bruhl, *Histoire juridique*, p. 93.

46. AN, 62 AQ 39, Acte, Preamble.

47. Lévy-Bruhl, *Histoire juridique*, p. 127.
48. AN, 62 AQ 39, Acte, Clause Sexto.
49. Lévy-Bruhl, *Histoire juridique*, pp. 251, 254.
50. AN, 62 AQ 39, Acte, Clause Primo.
51. Ibid., Clause Tertio.
52. Ibid., Clause Septimo.
53. Ibid., Clause Octavo.
54. Ibid., Clause Secundo (quotation) and Clause Quarto.
55. Ibid., Clause Secundo.
56. Ibid., délibération 17, 15 mars 1735.
57. Lévy-Bruhl, *Histoire juridique*, p. 124.
58. AN, 62 AQ 39, Acte, Clause Quinto.
59. Ibid., Clause Nono.
60. Ibid., Clause Decimo.
61. Ibid., Clause Nono. See A. Blanchet and A. Dieudonné, *Manuel de numismatique française* (Paris, 1916), 3: 208. Lévy-Bruhl mentions *jetons* but only with regard to *sociétés de captitaux* (*Histoire juridique*, p. 201).
62. Ibid., délibération 31, 27 juin 1742.
63. AN, 62 AQ 39, délibération 31, 27 juin 1742.
64. Ibid.
65. The information in this and the following paragraph is based upon the graphs and tables in appendices B, C, and D.

Notes to Chapter Four

1. The current accounts of all associates with Robert Dugard in AN, 62 AQ 40, liasse O.
2. The difference of contributions and withdrawals can be read from the current accounts.
3. AN, 62 AQ 40, liasse S, "Compte de Monsieur france avec DuGard, de Rouen dressé par Epoques de Payements & de Recette, 1729–1742," and account prepared by Dugard for France fils in 1766 and referred to by Dugard as the "Tableau." (See n. 5 below.)
4. AN, 62 AQ 40, "Retours de la 14e Cargaison Envoyée à Québec en 1743."
5. AN, 62 AQ 40, liasse R, Lettre de Robert Dugard, 5 avril 1766. This defence of his actions was written by Dugard for Guillaume France fils or his representative during a protracted dispute that followed the termination of the Société du Canada.
6. AN, 62 AQ 35, Guillaume France à Robert Dugard, 15 janvier 1738.
7. Ibid.
8. Ibid., France fils à Robert Dugard, 16 juin 1747, enclosure.
9. Ibid., Guillaume France à Dugard, 15 janvier 1738.
10. AN, 62 AQ 40, liasse R, Lettre de Dugard, 5 avril 1766.
11. Ibid.

12. AN, 62 AQ 39, Livre de Délibération, 13 décembre 1742.

13. In addition to France's accounts and France à Dugard, 15 janvier 1738 (62 AQ 40 and 62 AQ 35 respectively), see 62 AQ 35: "Billets que jay fournis à l'ordre de Monsieur G. France ce jour dhuy 4 Xbre 1738 en deduction de son interest en Diverses Navires et Cargaisons ou il est interessé avec moy dont il se charge cependant de faire les fonds à l'echeance," and "Des billet ou Promesses de Monsieur Dugard . . . 28 sept. 1742." There is yet a third list of promissory notes provided dated 31 October 1743. The intention was for France to negotiate the notes for ready money and repay Dugard when the latter was required to redeem the notes. Most of them were never negotiated.

14. R. de Roover, *Money, Banking and Credit in Medieval Bruges* (Cambridge, Mass., 1948); "Early Accounting Problems of Foreign Exchange," *The Accounting Review*, 19 (1944): 381–407; *Gresham on Foreign Exchange; an Essay on Early English Mercantilism with the text of Gresham's Memorandum for the Understanding of the Exchange* (Cambridge, Mass., 1949); *L'évolution de la lettre de change, XIVe–XVIIIe siècles* (Paris, 1953).

15. Except as otherwise indicated, these comments are based upon Jacques Savary, *Le parfait négociant*, 1 (Paris, 1749), 2 (Paris, 1724), which is the basis for articles in Jacques Savary des Bruslons, *Dictionnaire universel de commerce* and the *Encyclopédie* of Diderot and Dalambert. Savary's treatment is not as clear as the modern reader will wish, particularly on the relative merits of bills and notes. Dugard's partner in another venture (See chap. 8) remarks, "Les lettres à domicile ne sont pas bien accueillies dans le commerce; il faut un Accepteur, mais aussi un bon Endosseur . . ." (Paynel à Dugard, 16 septembre 1752, quoted in 62 AQ 6 Item 2, Réponse, p. 51). De Roover may underestimate the importance of notes in the eighteenth century because he stresses the role of laws against usury in causing European banking to be based upon the bill of exchange and remittance from place to place. In addition to n. 14 above, see his *Business, Banking, and Economic Thought in Late Medieval and Early Modern Europe; Selected Studies of Raymond de Roover*, ed. Julius Kirshner (Chicago and London, 1974), section 4, and Kirshner's introductory essay. At times Savary writes in accord with de Roover's view, e.g., in explaining the popularity of *billets de change* (notes given for or payable in bills) by their sharing the freedom from usury attributable to bills themselves (1: 208). However, he more often seems to consider any loan among merchants as *lucrum cessans* (see chapt. 6, n. 55) and therefore permitted. See "L'art des lettres de change," annex to 1: 89, and especially, parère 21 in 2: 173–74, in which Savary goes well beyond *lucrum cessans* by considering the state of the borrower rather than the lender. The impression of the Dugard Papers for the years 1749–51 is that straight borrowing by discounted notes as well as bills was common although the terms were short, especially for bills. This theme is taken up again in chap. 8; on scruples, see that chap. at n. 109; on discount, see n. 120.

16. AN, 62 AQ 39, délibération 32, 27 juin 1742.

17. AD Gironde, 7B, 2102, Fonds Silva, Dugard à Da Silva, Rouen, 30 mars 1742.

18. Ibid.

19. AN, 62 AQ 45. Numerous papers bound in a bundle and labelled "Procès Luetkens" are a major source of information on this affair. Included is a copy of the 14 bills of exchange and certification of the bankrupt Luetkens's partial payment thereof. The first of these may stand as an example:

Pre [mière]   Londres le 25 janvier 41/42   Pour 1000 # tournois
                               5 février
    A deux usances payer par cette première de change à lordre de Mr abraham Peixotte mille livres tournois en Especes au cours à nous connue ce jour valeur de Mr. Joseph Marquer junior que passerer à compte de M-R-D suivant l'avis de Anth° Clerembault & fils

                                                 [signature]

A Messieurs
Messieurs Luetkens Frères & Drewzen
A Bordeaux
Accepté
Luetkens frères & Drewzen
[signature]

The *parère* bundled with Havy letters in 62 AQ 36, "Parère sur la Pretention de Srs Luetkens de Bordeaux," should also be read.

20. Ibid., "Procès Luetkens." Traittes des Sieurs Luetkens frères de Bordeaux.

21. De Roover, *Medieval Bruges*, p. 66. For an example of credit circulation by French royal financiers, see J. Sperling, "The International Payments Mechanism in the Seventeenth and Eighteenth Centuries," *Economic History Review*, 2nd series 14, no. 3 (1962): 464.

22. AN, 62 AQ 45, "Procès Luetkens." Réponse aux Observations de M. Dugard.

23. AD Gironde, 7B 2102, Fonds Silva, Dugard à Da Silva, Rouen, 16 avril 1742.

24. Ibid., 2 avril 1742.

25. Ibid., 16 avril 1742.

26. Ibid.

27. Ibid., Dugard à Da Silva, Rouen, 16 avril 1742.

28. There are documents relating to the bottomry loan in 62 AQ 40, liasse O and in 62 AQ 45, "Prêt à la Grosse Aventure." A recapitulation in the latter is the most complete list.

29. Ibid., prêt de Valmaletie, 26 mai 1742.

30. Appendix B.

31. Ibid.

32. AN, 62 AQ 40, liasse R, Lettre de R. Dugard, 5 avril 1766.

33. AN, 62 AQ 39, livre de délibération, 27 juin 1742.

34. Ibid.

35. Ibid.

36. Ibid.

37. Ibid.

38. J. N. Myer, *Understanding Financial Statements* (New York, 1964), p. 84.

Notes to Chapter Five

1. Appendix B.

2. AN, 62 AQ 41–44.

3. Ibid., 41, examples, 14ᵉ Cargaison, factures 36, 71.

4. Ibid., 43, *Astrée*, 1749.

5. Ibid., *Centaure*, 1743.

6. Ibid., 42.

7. Ibid., 41, "Etat de la Facture des Marchandises chargez sur le navire landromède, capt Bionneau, 1744."

8. Ibid., 42.

9. Ibid., 44.

10. Ibid., 41, 13ᵉ Cargaison.

11. Ibid., 42, example, connaissement, *Centaure*, 1750.

12. Ibid., 44, *St. Mathieu*, 1743; 42, *Union*, 1744.

13. Ibid., 42, *Centaure*, 1848, Convention.

14. Ibid., *Trois Maries*, connaissement de cargaison; 41, *La Déesse de la Rochelle* à Québec, 1742, connaissement.

15. Ibid., 42.

16. Ibid., 44, example, *Astrée*, Rolle d'Equipage, 5 juin 1751.

17. Ibid., 44 (*Fleury*), 43 (*Thétis*).

18. Ibid., 42.

19. Ibid., 41, *Astrée*, de Québec en France, 10 novembre 1745.

20. Ibid., 41.

21. Ibid., 42, Capt. Belinger à Dugard, New York, 15 septembre 1756; 41, "Extrait du Registre des Declarations et Raports du Greffe de l'Amirauté de Roscoft," 29 décembre 1745; 42, "Declaration de la Perte du Nᵛʳᵉ L'Union du Havre . . . du 4 mars 1747"; 41, Liasse, "la Perte du navire Les Trois Maries," pièce 9; 44, "Observations sur la perte du Navire L'Alçion sur la Petite Caique au Debouquement de St. Domingue le 29 avril 1743" (source of quote, re. Gautier); 44, "Relation de la Prise du Fleury par le maître cannonier."

22. Consideration of Caribbean cargoes is based on the following documents, each of which has been condensed into a table: AN, 62 AQ 44, "Compte de Vente Generalle et Achapts provenant de la Cargaison du Navire Alçion, 1742–43"; ibid., 43, "Compte de Ventes des Marchandises Composant la Cgn du Navire l'Imprévû, Capt. J. B. Renault, vendu au Cul de Sac Marin" (Martinique, 1743); ibid., 42, "Facture des Marchandises chargées au Havre à Bord du Navire le St. Mathieu, Rouen, 12 aoust 1743"; and ibid., 42, "Facture des Marchandises chargées au Havre à bord d'Union, Rouen, le 25 janvier, 1744."

23. L. Vignols, "L'importation en France au XVIIIᵉ siècle du boeuf salé

d'Irelande," *Revue historique*, 159 (1928): 79; G. Debien, "La nourriture des esclaves sur les plantations des Antilles françaises aux XVIIe et XVIIIe siècles," *Caribbean Studies* 4, no. 2: 3–27.

24. Consideration of Canadian cargo is based on the invoices for the fourteenth cargo numbered 1–179 with no pieces bearing numbers 69 and 170 and two invoices missing (AN, 62 AQ 41). Figures given in the discussion of Figure 1 total 168,762, 0.45 per cent more than the total of table 5. The discrepancy results from the inclusion of invoiced costs that could not be assigned to specific merchandise.

25. Ibid., facture 63.

26. Jacques Savary des Bruslons, *Dictionnaire universel de Commerce* (Paris, 1741), 3, supplément.

27. Debien, "La nourriture"; Vignols, "L'importation du boeuf salé." Beef constituted a very small part of the slave's diet, far less than the two pounds per week specified in the *Code Noir*. Debien remarks that the diet contained "fort peu de salaison" (p. 23). Vignols (p. 86) draws attention to the use of salt beef by *engagés*, the poor, and those of "aisance médiocre." These classes ate more beef per person than slaves, but the latter because of their greater numbers consumed most of the imported beef. There is no work of greater precision on this point.

28. Appendix B for departure dates.

29. AN, 62 AQ 41, 14e Cargaison, connaissements, *Le Comte de Matignon*, 10 juin, 15 juin 1743.

30. Ibid., "Etat des debours faits par christinat à la Reception et Expedition des Marchandises cy après chargees d'ordre et pour compte de Monsieur R DuGard de Rouen, sur le Navire le Centaure Capitaine françois Vangellickom Vandelle à l'adresse de Mrs havy et le febvre de Québec, 8 janvier 1745."

Notes to Chapter Six

1. Arrival and departure dates, appendix B.

2. Joseph Conrad, *The Mirror of the Sea* (Garden City, 1925), p. 83. See also *American Practical Navigator* (Washington, 1943), pp. 298–305; A. G. Findlay, *Memoir descriptive and explanatory of the Northern Atlantic Ocean*, 14th ed. (London, 1879).

3. Pehr Kalm, *The America of 1750: Peter Kalm's Travels in North America*, ed. A. B. Benson (New York, 1966), 2: 427.

4. In 1733 and 1734 they lived on Rue St. Pierre (AQ, AJQ, Etude Barolet, 30 septembre 1734). The earliest document to give their address as Place du Marché is from 1736 (*ibid.*, 9 octobre 1736). Their house is specifically identified as that of Fornel in *ibid.*, 3 mars 1737, reprinted in P. G. Roy, *Inventaire des pièces sur la Côte de Labrador*, 2 vols. (Quebec, 1940 and 1942), 1: 302. The most probable year for their move into the house is 1735 rather than 1736, as in that year enlargements of the premises of a commercial nature were undertaken (see n. 5). The correspondence of Havy and Lefebvre with

Pierre Guy makes it clear that they remained in the house until they left Canada (PAC, Collection Baby, fols. 1144–45, 1139–40, examples from 1748).

5. Marcel Gaumond, *La Maison Fornel* (Quebec, 1965), p. 25; photos, p. 26; plan, p. 32.

6. P. G. Roy, *Rapport de l'archiviste de la Province de Québec pour 1939–40* (Quebec, 1940) pp. 1–154.

7. AN, AC, C 11 A, 93, fol. 25 Bigot au ministre, 3 octobre 1749.

8. On Pascaud see *Dictionary of Canadian Biography*, 2 (Toronto, 1969): 508.

9. "Approbation d'une Assemblee des marchands . . . ," 6 October 1740, *Edits et ordonnances: revus et corrigés d'après les pièces originales deposées aux Archives provinciales*, 2 (Québec, 1855): 554–555. Published over a century ago, this document was singled out by Adam Shortt, *Currency, Exchange and Finance during the French Period* (Ottawa, 1925), 2: 705 and by Jean Lunn, "Economic Development in New France, 1713–1760," (Montreal, 1943) in which she noted its dissonance with De la Potherie's analysis of the merchant class: "It is interesting to note that although there were said to have been over a hundred shops in Quebec, the 'principal merchants' who chose the syndic numbered only sixteen" (p. 354). The volume of trade handled by Havy and Lefebvre confirms the social and economic implications of the document. That the import-export trade of Canada was monopolised by a small number of Quebec City merchants, most but not all of them metropolitans, and that most but not all of the large profits made thereby accrued to metropolitan business houses is, of course, precisely the situation described by Gilles Hocquart in his correspondence with Maurepas through a long administration. Examples, AN, AC, C 11 A, 59, fol. 116 (27 octobre 1732); 60, fol. 263 (25 octobre 1733); 77, fol. 143 (1 novembre 1742). The unqualified acceptance of De la Potherie's ill-informed comment in L. R. MacDonald, "France and New France: the Internal Contradictions," *Canadian Historical Review*, 52, no. 2 (June, 1971): 130–31 ("The small merchant ruled") is unacceptable, and the analysis of the import-export trade with regard to capital formation consequently invalid.

10. AN, 62 AQ 40, receipt, 18 juillet 1734; 36, Dugard à Havy, 14 juillet 1760.

11. Ibid., 31, Havy à Dugard, La Rochelle, 10 février, 19 mai, 11 juin 1759.

12. Ibid., 36, Havy à Dugard, La Rochelle, 5 juillet 1760.

13. Ibid., Havy à Dugard, La Rochelle, 16 juin 1761. On *pacotilles*, see chap. 5 above; on private trade by factors in another setting, see Ralph Davis, *Aleppo and Devonshire Square* (London, 1967), chap. 5; on Havy's denial, see below, chap. 8, n. 147.

14. PAC, Collection Baby, fols. 643–44 (letter of Lamaletie), 5 juillet 1745.

15. Ibid., fols. 551–54, 9 février 1745. On Pierre Guy, see *Dictionary of Canadian Biography* 4 (Toronto, 1974): 271.

16. PAC, Collection Baby, 6 mars 1745.

17. Ibid., fols. 153–55, 20 août 1747.

18. Ibid., fols. 707–09, 29 septembre 1745.

19. Kalm, *America*, 2: 431.

20. AN, AC, C 11 A, 75, fol. 15, "Liste des Personnes dela Religion prétendu reformée qui sont à Québec commis des négociants de France," 1741. See also Bigot's comments on Protestants, *ibid.*, 93, fol. 257.

21. PAC, Collection Baby, fols. 769–72, 29 décembre 1745.

22. Ibid., fols. 631–33, 20 juin 1745; fols. 730–36, 20 octobre 1745.

23. Ibid., fols. 704–06, 22 septembre 1745.

24. AN, 62 AQ 31, Havy à Dugard, La Rochelle, 10 février 1759.

25. AQ, Pièces judiciaires et notariales, no. 1296.

26. PAC, Collection Baby, fol. 600, 24 mai 1745; fol. 1060, 1 septembre 1747 (Havy and Lefebvre to Pierre Guy):

> Nous voyons que vous [Guy] contés faire servir votre couteau de chasse et que le ceinturon ne peut vous servir. Sans reproche pourquoy avés vous le ventre sy gros, Il faut tascher de faire alonger ledit ceinturon. Car pour le ventre il ne faut pas penser a le faire diminuer.

> Nous vous avons envoyé le plus long ceinturon de couteau de chasse que nous eussions Mr. Lefebvre la mesure sur son ventre, mais pour vous mon cher monsieur avouez le vous lavez dune grosseur a ni pouvoir ateindre.

True men of the eighteenth century!

27. Ibid., fols. 820–23, 7 mai 1746.

28. Ibid., fol. 618, 11 juin 1748.

29. Ibid., fols. 592–95, 4 mai 1745.

30. See below, n. 105.

31. PAC, Collection Baby, Havy and Lefebvre to Guy, fols. 548–1102 *passim*.

32. Ibid., fols. 1044–47, 20 juillet 1747.

33. Ibid., fols. 853–54, 17 juin 1746.

34. AN, AC, C 11 A, 78, fol. 2, Hocquart au Ministre, 8 octobre 1742.

35. The reader may check this by averaging increases on dry goods, hardware and provisions as given in table 7 and applying to them the per cent divisions of a cargo as given in table 5.

36. AN, AC, C 11 A, 91, fol. 103, "Reflection particulière de Cugnet . . ."

37. PAC, Collection Baby, fol. 569–71, 23 mars 1745. It is evident from scattered references that Havy and Lefebvre almost always favoured Guy with lower prices but they were very insistent that this be kept secret. Others must have done the same. The lowest profit figure for 1740 in table 8 may reflect such a favour. Only in 1741 did the peacetime *bénéfice* rise to 30 per cent. Hocquart noted that the *bénéfice* was higher (AN, AC, C 11 A, 75, fol. 61) but his estimate of a 10–12 per cent increase over the previous year seems rather high. Havy and Lefebvre still sold some goods at 25 per cent in 1741, that being the rate of the previous year.

38. For example, ASQ, Polygraphie 24, 10–10E, "Messieurs du séminaire doivent aux Havy et Lefebvre"; SHM, Collection Pierre Guy, 84 and *passim*; AQ, AJQ, Etude Dulaurant, 23 octobre 1743, facture de Monfort.

39. SHM, Collection Pierre Guy, factures; compare with AN, 62 AQ 41, 14ᵉ cargaison, factures.

40. AN, AC, C 11 A, 66, fols. 171–202.

41. While goods were often imported to fit the needs of particular customers whose bale marks appear in the invoices, Dugard always supplied these goods and recipients paid the invoice inflation plus the *bénéfice*.

42. PAC, Collection Baby, fols. 752–58, 12 novembre 1745; 918–20, 4 octobre 1746.

43. Ibid., fols. 524–27, 7 octobre 1744.

44. Ibid., fols. 981–83, 6 mars 1747; fols. 987–88, 11 mars 1747, and *passim*.

45. AN, AC, C 11 A, 77, fol. 143, Beauharnois au ministre, 1 novembre 1742.

46. Ibid., 67, fols. 109–44, "Réponse au mémoire du roi," 1737.

47. AQ, AJQ, Etude Barolet, nos. 729, 1066; Etude Dulaurant, 3 octobre 1736, 23 octobre 1742, 26 octobre, 15 septembre 1743, 13 août 1747; Etude J. Pinguet, 5 septembre 1743; Etude Saillant, 8 septembre, 25 octobre, 6 novembre, 1753; 5 avril, 18 septembre 1754.

48. ASQ, Polygraphie 24 et Séminaire de Québec, Grande Livre, 1737–40.

49. AN, 62 AQ 40, Comptes de gestion à Québec, 1730–38. The accounts of these years list the notes accepted for each year as well as previous debt returned. Unfortunately, the same information is not available for the years 1739–42 for which condensations made by Dugard are alone extant. All computations concerning debt and debtors are based upon these accounts.

50. See n. 47 above.

51. PAC, Collection Baby, fols. 656–63, 28 juillet 1745.

52. Ibid., fols. 667–80, 28 octobre 1745; 685–90, 13 septembre 1745.

53. Ibid., fols. 977–80, 1 mars 1747.

54. Ibid., fols. 685–90, 13 septembre 1745.

55. Ibid., fols. 970–74, 8 février 1747. The analogy is easily mistaken as modernism, but this is because we are ignorant of scholastic economics; *mea culpa:* "Havy and Lefebvre of Quebec: A Case Study of Metropolitan Participation in Canadian Trade, 1730–60," *The Canadian Historical Review*, 56, no. 1 (March 1975): 22. The Spanish schoolman, Luis Molina, S. J. (1535–1600), may have put this analogy into print for the first time, but he had it from a merchant. See B. W. Dempsey, *Interest and Usury* (Washington, D.C., 1943), pp. 158–59; Joseph Schumpeter, *History of Economic Analysis* (New York, 1954), p. 105, where the author may not be justified in saying Molina and his circle "coined the significant phrase" if it was common coin among merchants. Nearly 150 years after Molina, the Hugenots, Havy and Lefebvre, cling to this scholastic defence of *lucrum cessans* instead of turning to Calvin. There is great need for self justification implicit in the passing on of

this talisman from generation to generation. General orientation: Raymond de Roover, *Business, Banking, and Economic Thought in Late Medieval and Early Modern Europe*, ed. Julius Kirshner (Chicago, 1974).

56. Invoice attached to "Obligation par la Ve Monfort aux Srs. Havy et Lefebvre, 23 octobre 1742," Etude Dulaurant. On the rate in Europe, see AN, AC F 2 B, I, 268, "Messieurs les Directeurs et sindics dela chambre de Commerce dela Rochelle au Bureau de Commerce, 22 janvier 1734." (They state that they charge their Canadian customers eight per cent.)

57. PAC, Collection Baby, fols. 551–54, 9 février 1745.

58. AN, AC, 59, fol. 12, 30 octobre 1732.

59. AN, 62 AQ 40, "Dettes Douteuses et Effets en Souffrance [Robert Dugard, 1749]."

60. Ibid., "Dépouillement des achapts fait à Québec en 1743."

61. PAC, Collection Baby, fols. 893–96, Québec, 11 septembre 1746.

62. Ibid., fols. 543–44, Lamaletie à Guy, 1 janvier 1745.

63. Ibid.

64. Private bills of all sorts are mentioned in AN, 62 AQ 40, "Comptes de gestion de Havy et Lefebvre," "Compte de Balance de Havy et Lefebvre"; "François Havy, son compte courant, 1733–51."

65. Ibid., "Compte de gestion de Havy et Lefebvre, 6e cargaison, 1735," ref. to "Retrait pour lettres protestés remises par M. D'Haristoy."

66. PAC, Collection Baby, fols. 951–54, 24 novembre 1746.

67. AN, 62 AQ 40, comptes de gestion à Québec, 1733–39 and 1744 show dates.

68. PAC Collection Baby, fols. 1107–8, 28 octobre 1747.

69. AN, AC, F 2 B, 11, etats de sortie des marchandises, 1732, 33, 35, 36, 37, 39. Etats do not exist for the 1740s.

70. Ibid., B. 72, f. 352, Ministre à Hocquart, Versailles, 16 avril 1741.

71. Ibid., C 11 A, 76, 318–45, "Mémoire sur le Commerce du Canada, 1741."

72. ASQ, Polygraphie 24, no. 10 B, 10 C, 36 K.

73. The *Ville de Québec* plus two ships launched that year, the *Centaure* and the *Imprévû*, totalled 750 tons.

74. AN, AC, C 11 A, 73, fol. 377, Hocquart au ministre, 2 novembre 1740.

75. Appendix A.

76. See Lunn, "Economic Development," (Montreal, 1942), chap. 10 for a good survey of bounties and shipbuilding; AN, AC, C 11 A, 51, fol. 53, Beauharnois et Hocquart au Ministre, 25 octobre 1729.

77. Ibid., 67, fols. 109–44, "Réponse au mémoire du Roy, 1737."

78. Ibid., 63, 73, "Réponse au mémoire du Roy, 13 octobre 1735."

79. Lunn, "Economic Development," p. 250 n.

80. AN, AC, C 11 A, 67, fols. 109–44, "Réponse au mémoire du Roy, 1737."

81. AQ, AJQ, Etude Barolet, no. 582, "Marché entre Pierre Lupien dit Baron, François Havy et Jean Lefebvre, 9 oct. 1736"; APQ, Pièces judiciaires et

notariales, no. 1242, "Marché entre René de Couagne et les sieurs Havy et Lefebvre, 2 nov. 1741."

82. AQ, AJQ, Etude Barolet, no. 580, "Engagement de Jean Trepany et Pierre Lions aux sieurs Havy et Lefebvre, 8 oct. 1736."

83. AN, AC, C 8 A, 55, fol. 340, "Copie de la lettre ecrite à Mr dela Croix par Messers Havy et Lefebvre, De Québec, 30 May 1743."

84. AQ, Pièces judiciaires et notariales, no. 1290, for information on the shipyard.

85. AN, 62 AQ 40, comptes de gestion à Québec, 1730–41; "Compte général de Balance, 15 juillet 1746." Tables 9 to 11 are constructed on the basis of figures extracted from the *compte de balance*.

86. Correspondence between Hocquart (AC, C 11 A) and Maurepas (AC, B), also summarized in Lunn, "Economic Development," p. 477.

87. Jean Hamelin, *Economie et Société en Nouvelle-France* (Quebec, 1960).

88. This may be traced in the correspondence of Beauharnois and Hocquart with Maurepas printed in Shortt, *Currency, Exchange, etc.*

89. AN, 62 AQ 40, Comptes de gestion à Québec, 1733, 1734.

90. Shortt, *Currency, Exchange, etc.*, 2: 655, Hocquart à Maurepas, 10 oct. 1734.

91. Lunn, "Economic Development," pp. 456, 464–65. Similar tabulation for pounds beaver received by the Compagnie des Indes was made by H. A. Innis in *The Fur Trade of Canada* (Toronto, 1927) and the values of furs entering La Rochelle were tabulated by E. Salone, *La Colonisation de la Nouvelle-France* (Paris, n.d.) and used by Innis. Both of these differ from Lunn's; however, where I have been able to check, Lunn's figures appear to be correct.

92. Hamelin, *Economie et société*, p. 61; AN, AC, C 11 A, letters of Hocquart *passim*; Lunn, "Economic Development," statistics pp. 444–49 and *passim*.

93. Chap. 3, n. 4.

94. Combined value of cargoes bought and sold.

95. AN, AC, C 11 A, 75, fol. 61, Hocquart au ministre, 25 octobre 1741.

96. Ibid., B, 67, fv. 145, Ministre à Dugard, 28 décembre 1738.

97. Ibid., 65, fols. 118v–119r, Ministre à Dugard, 30 décembre 1737; 77, fol. 36, Ministre à Derchigny, 16 janvier 1743; C 11 A, 78, fol. 274, Hocquart au ministre, 4 novembre 1740; 73, fol. 414, Hocquart au ministre, 8 novembre 1740.

98. Alluded to in replies of Maurepas to Dugard, AN, AC, B, 58, fv. 43, 19 mai 1743, fol. 54, 1 juillet 1733; 64, fol. 38, 26 avril 1736; 65, fol. 51, 3 mai 1737, fv. 118, 30 décembre 1737; 67, fv. 145, 28 décembre 1738; 75, fol. 89, 7 mai 1742; 77, fols. 25, 10 janvier 1743, 55, 13 février 1743; 79, fol. 66, 6 avril 1744.

99. Ibid., 65, fol. 51, 3 mai 1737, fols. 118v–119r, 30 décembre 1737; 67, fv. 145, 28 décembre 1738.

100. Ibid., 67, fv. 145, 28 décembre 1738.

101. Ibid., 75, fols. 112–13, 144; 94, fol. 290.

102. Ibid., 77, fol. 55, Ministre à Dugard, 13 février 1743.

103. AN, AC, C 11 A, 80, Hocquart au ministre, 25 octobre 1743.

104. Ibid., fol. 9, Hocquart au ministre, 15 oct. 1743. On clientage, see D. J. Horton, "Gilles Hocquart, Intendant of New France," (Montreal, 1975).

105. PAC, Collection Baby, fols. 500–1, 4 novembre 1743; fol. 1153, 5 novembre 1748. Ref., return of Jean Jacquelin who had been sent to help Havy and Lefebvre, fols. 759–64, 26 novembre 1745. Havy had been in Rouen in 1736 (AN, 62 AQ 40, "François Havy son compte courant avec Dugard, 1733–57"). Bigot's comments, AN, AC, C 11 A, 93, fol. 257.

Notes to Chapter Seven

1. AN, AC, C 8 B, 17–21, "Etats des Batiments arrivés à la Martinique de France," 1733–52; "Etats des Batiments sortis de la Martinique pour la France," 1733–52.

2. AN, AC, C 9 B, 13, "Mémoire sur les Colonies de St. Domingue et de la Martinique par M. Liger cy devant auditeur en la chambre de Bretagne, 24 septembre 1750." The author compares French merchant ships unfavourably with English ones.

3. See appendix B.

4. Written correspondence often gives the impression that ships did not arrive in the islands until February at the earliest. (See C 8 A, 42, fol. 245, D'Orgeville au ministre, Fort-Royal, 27 septembre 1731; 62 AQ 42, Lallement à Dugard, Léoganne, 28 juin 1738, as examples.) But the records of the arrival of ships at St. Pierre extant for the years 1733, 1735, 1737, 1739, 1741, 1742, 1743, 1744, 1745, 1749, and 1752 (see n. 1) suggest a more regular supply as shown in the table below, which lists the total arrivals each month for all years combined. Possibly problems of irregular supply were greater in earlier years.

Ship arrivals at St. Pierre:

Nov.	Dec.	Jan.	Feb.	Mar.	Apr.	May	Jun.	Jul.	Aug.	Sept.	Oct.
129	112	117	104	111	159	131	124	90	7	9	65

5. AN, AC, C 8 A, 42, fol. 245, D'Orgeville au ministre, Fort-Royal, 27 septembre 1731.

6. AN, AC, C 9 A, 82, Maillart au ministre, Léoganne, 6 février 1749.

7. L. P. May, *Histoire économique de la Martinique* (Paris, 1930), p. 1.

8. AN, AC, C 11 B, 23, "Mémoire sur la Martinique," n.d., anon.

9. May, *Histoire économique*, p. 229.

10. See ibid., chap. 6, "La transformation des échanges," for a good description of the *commissionnaires'* rise to prominence.

11. AN, AC, C 8 A, 46, fol. 185.

12. Ibid., 58, Mémoire de M. Caylus, 1749.

13. AN, AC, C 9 A, 35, De Vienne au ministre, 8 janvier 1732; 50, "Compte général de M. de Larnage et Maillart, 28 septembre 1739."

14. Ibid., 48, De Larnage au ministre, Léoganne, 15 novembre 1738.

15. Ibid., 46, De Fayet au ministre, 26 avril 1737; 56, 6 septembre 1741.

16. Ibid., 37, "Observations sur Léoganne, Petit Goave, 27 avril 1733."

17. See chap. 3.

18. See appendices B and C for ship movements in this chapter.

19. AN, 62 AQ 42. The letters of Lallement of Léoganne are filed here with accounting papers of voyages to Léoganne rather than in the correspondence series. There are two of them for 1738 dated 28 June, and 4 October, and five for 1739, dated 23 April, 29 May, 26 September, 14 November, and 23 November.

20. Ibid., 23 avril 1739.

21. For a definitive discussion of this question based primarily on English and Anglo-American sources see Richard Pares, *Yankees and Creoles* (Cambridge, Mass., 1956), p. 66; *Merchants and Planters* (Cambridge, 1960).

22. AN, AC, C 8 A, 55, fol. 340, "Copie de la lettre ecritte à Mr de la Croix par Messers Havy et Lefebvre, De Québec, 30 mai 1743; fol. 344, "Copie de la Lettre à M Dela Croix par M. Dugard, Rouen, 20 août 1743."

23. AN, AC, C 11 A, 79, fol. 319, Hocquart au ministre, 8 octobre 1743.

24. See appendix C. A voyage extending along at least two sides of the Europe, America, Caribbean route is regarded as triangular.

25. AN, 62 AQ 41, "Léon Fautoux, son compte courant avec Robert Dugard, 1738–45, Rouen, 13 nov. 1745." See also "Léon Fautoux," *Dictionary of Canadian Biography* 3 (Toronto, 1974): 216.

26. See n. 22 above.

27. AN, AC, B, 65, fols. 118v–119r, Ministre à Robert Dugard, 30 décembre 1737; C 11 A, 65, fol. 28, Réponse au mémoire du Roy, 1736.

28. Ibid., Réponse.

29. See n. 22 above; A. J. E. Lunn, "Economic Development in New France, 1713–1760" (Montreal, 1942), 361 ff. discusses most of the problems raised by triangular trade.

30. See n. 22 above.

31. Calculated from tables in appendix C.

32. AN, 62 AQ 39, Livre de Délibération, 11 février 1734.

33. AN, F¹², 54–89, Registres du Conseil de Commerce, 1708–13, 1736–42; 86, fols. 402, 605, 618, 703, 704; 88, fol. 67. A ship could return to a port other than that of outfitting only with special permission. The minutes clearly reveal that these particular changes were permitted only because of Maurepas's influence. They were therefore a direct result of the sedulous courting of high officials, so much a part of the company's operations. But, unfortunately, they do not reveal why the changes were made. Reasons given by Dugard were dismissed as spurious, but the permissions granted all the same.

34. F. G. Pariset, ed., *Bordeaux au XVIIIᵉ Siècle* (Bordeaux, 1968), 2:

208–19. (The chapter is by F. Crouzet.) In the pre-war period only five voyages to Canada originated at Bordeaux. The first was that of the *Saint-Mathieu* in 1734, the ship stopping at Bordeaux for provisions. Later, it was more common to have the provisions carried north by coasting vessels (e.g. the loading of the *Centaure*, 1743, in chap. 5 above). The only other instances of loading at Bordeaux occurred when the *Ville de Québec* was transferred to the Canada trade from the sugar trade and when vessels based in Bordeaux were chartered (*La Nouvelle Galère*) or purchased (*Les Trois Maries*). See appendix B and AN, F¹², 89, fol. 212.

35. Pariset, *Bordeaux*, pp. 306–12; Pierre Dardel, *Navires et marchandises dans les ports de Rouen et du Havre au XVIIIe siècle* (Paris, 1963), p. 51.

36. Dugard and Company was by no means the only one to seek out-of-the-way markets. See AN, AC, C 8 A, 50, fol. 370, De la Croix au ministre, 2 novembre 1739.

37. AN, 62 AQ 43, "Instructions pour Capitaine Renault, Rouen, 27 mai 1743."

38. Ibid., "Instructions pour M. F. Hurel Capitaine du Navire Le St. Mathieu, Au Havre 20 août 1743."

39. Ibid., "Instructions pour Capitaine Renault, Rouen, 27 mai 1743."

40. Ibid., 44, "Instructions pour Monsieur La Roche Couvert, Capitaine du Navire Le St. Louis allant du Havre à Louisbourg, 1743."

41. Ibid., 43, "Instructions pour Capitaine Renault, Rouen, 27 mai 1743."

42. Ibid., 42, "Introductions pour Monsieur François Martin Fremont, Capitaine du navire l'Union . . . au Havre et Rouen, 29 janvier 1744."

43. This paragraph and the following one constitute a summary of important clauses in the many extant instructions written by Dugard. In addition to those addressed to Renault, Hurel, La Roche Couvert, and Fremont there are in 62 AQ 44 those to Capt. Escallier, 25 March, 1744, voyage to Senegal, Capt. P. Robinet, 28 January 1751, voyage to Grand Banks, and Pierre Gauthier, 1742, voyage to Léoganne.

44. Pares, *Yankees*, p. 66.

45. AN, 62 AQ 42, "Instructions . . . Fremont"; Ibid., 43, "Mémoire de la Dépense Particulière faite au Cul de Sac Marin pour le Compte du Navire L'Imprévû tant pendant quil à resté au Dt Cul de Sac Marin qu'après son Depart. Depuis le 18 juillet 1743 à 5 septembre 1748" (Renault).

46. Ibid., mémoire.

47. Ibid., 42, "Compte de Gestion de la Cgn du navire l'Union à la Martinique par le Capitaine Martin Fremont parti du Havre en 1744."

48. AN, AC, C 8 A, 58, fol. 97, Caylus au ministre, 9 septembre 1748.

49. AN, AC, C 9 A, 30, Le Gentil, subdélégué au ministre, Le Cap, 5 juin 1729.

50. AN, AC, C 8 A, 46, fol. 185, D'Orgeville au ministre, Fort-Royal, 10 juin 1735.

51. AN, AC, C 8 B, 9, "Observations sur le Projet d'ordonnance pour regler l'estimation du prix des sucres . . . d'Orgeville, 10 décembre 1735."

52. AN, AC, C 9 A, 50, "Compte général de Mrs. de Larnage et Maillart, 28 sept. 1739."

53. Ibid., 57, De Larnage et Maillart au ministre, Léoganne, 10 mai 1742. In 1742 the one-price system was still current, the then rising price of sugar in Europe extinguishing all complaint. Regulations that De Fayet and Du Clos had made for the determination of sugar prices by arbitors were said in this memo never to have been closely obeyed (ibid., 35, Ordonnance, 10 décembre 1732).

54. AN, AC, C 8 A, 54, fol. 278, De la Croix au ministre, 25 septembre 1742.

55. Ibid., 39, fols. 337–72, "Mémoire sur le service des Isles du Vent de l'Amérique, 6 décembre 1728"; C 9 A, 34, Le Gentil au ministre, Au Cap, 7 janvier 1731.

56. AN, AC, C 9 A, 57, De Larnage et Maillart au ministre, Léoganne, 10 mai 1742.

57. AN, AC, C 8 A, 59, fol. 410, "Joint à la Lettre de M. Thomassin Dufarres, 9 février 1742."

58. AN, AC, C 9 A, 35, "Projet d'Ordonnances qui regle le poid des sucres & indigo et le jauge des futailles, 1732"; 57, De Larnage et Maillart au ministre, Léoganne, 10 mai 1742; n. 57.

59. Ibid., 61, De Larnage et Maillart au ministre, Petit Goave, 16 avril 1743; C 9 B, 20, "Extrait des Registres du Greffe du Conseil Superieur de Léoganne, 20 décembre 1729"; C 9 A, 54, De Larnage et Maillart au ministre, 15 juin 1741.

60. See also May, *Histoire économique*, chap. 4.

61. Esp. AN, 62 AQ 42, "Instructions pour . . . Fremont"; 62 AQ 43, "Instruction pour . . . Renault."

62. Cf. the works of Richard Pares, esp. *A West India Fortune* (London, 1950).

63. AN, 62 AQ 43, "Instructions pour . . . Fremont."

64. AN, C 9 A, 40, De Fayet au ministre, 26 janvier 1734.

65. AN, AC, B, 81, fol. 50, Ministre aux Mrs. de Caylus et Ranché, Paris, 11 juin 1745; AN, AD, VII a, Déclaration du Roy, 12 juin 1745; C 9 A, 66, De Larnage et Maillart au ministre, Petit Goave, 21 avril 1745; Assembly of the Province of Canada, *Edits et Ordonnances: revus et corrigés d'après les pièces originales déposées aux Archives provinciales*, 1 (Quebec, 1854): 258–64 (règlement, 12 janvier 1717).

66. AN, F 2 B, 1, fol. 417, "Mémoire des négociants & armateurs de la Rochelle pour la Chambre de Commerce sur une affaire des plus importantes, concernant le commerce de Saint-Domingue, 19 mai 1743."

67. AN, AC, C 8 A, 46, fol. 185, D'Orgeville au ministre, Fort-Royal, 10 juin 1745.

68. AN, 62 AQ 43, Mémoire de la Depense (Renault).

69. Ibid., J. B. Renault à Dugard, Le Havre, 22 août 1751.

70. Ibid., 38, J. H. Donis à Dugard, Bourg Marin, 16 décembre 1763. Many

debts left at Léoganne had the same result (ibid., 44, Bonniot à Dugard, Léoganne, 6 décembre 1749).

71. AN, AC, C 8 A, Observations.

72. Pares, *Fortune*, pp. 243–46.

73. In chap. 6 an estimate was made of the percentage of total imports to Canada from France for which Dugard and Company was responsible. Although the total figures for imports taken from Hocquart's reports are only rough estimates, it was deemed meaningful to report that the company's imports equalled a tenth or a quarter of these estimates. To attempt to apportion such an estimate into small units of one per cent and less would be to use rough figures to produce a result of apparent but spurious accuracy. In addition, unless the figure produced is very large, there is no occasion for comment. In a nutshell, in Canada the company was a big fish in a small pond; in the Caribbean it was a very ordinary fish in an ocean. This is another way of underscoring the disparity in size between the West Indian sugar economy and the Canadian economy, from which the Ministry of Marine so unreasonably expected such large results. It would appear that the greater opportunity of the West Indian trade did not produce larger business units. Rather, trading operations had an optimum size independent of the scale of colonial markets. It took comparatively few of these to service Canada and a great many to service the West Indies. The size of these units was governed by the personal nature of business, the short life of businesses, and the limited means of finance.

74. AN, 62 AQ 42, "Instructions pour . . . Fremont."

75. R. Richard, "A propos de Saint-Domingue; la monnaie dans l'économie coloniale, 1674–1803," *Revue d'histoire des colonies* (1954), p. 28; S. Ricard, *Traité général du Commerce* (Amsterdam, 1781), 2: 147.

76. The official rate was livres *tournois* $\times \frac{4}{3}$ = livres *argent des îles*; *argent des îles* $\times \frac{3}{4}$ = livres *tournois*. This occurs in Renault's "Etat de différents effets dont je dois faire raison à la Cargaison du navire l'Imprévû . . ." along with the rate livres *tournois* $\times \frac{5}{4}$ = livres *argent des îles*; livres *argent des îles* $\times \frac{4}{5}$ = livres *tournois*. The depreciation of 15.5 per cent occurs in *pièce* 61, "Billet de Jean Varin," 3 octobre 1744 (livres *tournois* $\times \frac{6}{5}$ = livres *argent des îles*; livres *argent des îles* $\times \frac{5}{6}$ = livres *tournois*—approx.), all in AN, 62 AQ 43, *Imprévû* en Retour. In the papers of the *St. Mathieu* en Retour, 1743, also in 62 AQ 43, is a certificate signed by the commander of Cul de Sac Marin at Rouen, 1750, stating that in 1744 he paid money owed to Dugard to Captain Hurel at Cul de Sac Marin at the $\frac{4}{5}$ (20 per cent depreciation) rate. The depreciation of 30 per cent appears in "Les interessés au navire l'Imprévû, Captne Renault, leur compte court. avec Renault" (62 AQ 43, *Imprévû* en Retour, 1743) and "Les interessés au navire l'Astrée Captne Gosselin leur compte court. avec Renault" (62 AQ 44, *Astrée* en Retour, 1749–51). The letter is Renault à Dugard, Le Havre, 12 août 1754.

77. AN, 62 AQ 43, *Imprévû* en Retour, 1743, pièce 59 "Billet de Dufour, 25e aoust 1744."

78. AN, 62 AQ 43, *Imprévû* au Cul de Sac Marin, 1743; ibid., 44, *Alçion* à

Léoganne, 1742. In both cases original invoices from manufacturers or commission agents to Robert Dugard have been compared with the sales figures in the captains' accounts. The base figure is the price of the commodity plus some small packaging costs that frequently occur in invoices. Considerable costs which from time to time also occur in invoices have been excluded for the sake of uniformity. To admit those that occur in the invoices, it would be necessary to add those that do not so occur, arriving at F.O.B. prices; this the data will not permit.

79. The prices in table 14 do not include any additional costs.

80. Chap. 8, n. 4.

81. AN, 62 AQ 43, *Centaure*, 1754, 1756; Ibid., 44, *Astrée*, 1749.

82. Ibid., *St. Louis*, 1743, *Astrée*, 1749.

83. In the British Empire, where cargoes were ordered by planters and sent by London or Bristol factors, the factors are said to have gained little on them, their aim being to get the commission on returning sugar. They even paid the transport on outward cargoes to ingratiate the planters. See Pares, *Fortune*, pp. 187, 224.

84. Jean Cavignac, *Jean Pellet, commerçant de gros, 1694–1772* (Paris, 1967), p. 209. The data presented by Cavignac do not support his statement, for they very clearly show that in many instances outward cargo profits were higher than those on return cargoes. The latter were bought with the proceeds of the outward cargoes; and while it is true that they were larger and so netted more even when at a lower percentage rate, they could only be larger if the sale of the outward cargo were successful.

Notes to Chapter Eight

1. AN, 62 AQ 35, France fils à Dugard, Paris, 28 octobre 1745; Enclosure, being a copy of a *mémoire* to Maurepas outlining the problem of the cannon.

2. Ibid., 7 mai 1745.

3. There is considerable information concerning the flour contract, showing how all levels of government, from Maurepas to Hocquart at Quebec and La Bourdonnaye at Rouen were involved: AC, B, 78, fol. 358; 79, fols. 41, 53, 58, 62, 63, 65, 66, 85, 92, 93, 102; 81, fol. 267; 82, fol. 97; 83, fols. 98, 285; C 11 A, 79, fol. 62; 80, fol. 6; 81, fol. 300; Archives départmentales de la Seine Maritime, C 831, 4 janvier 1744, 11 janvier 1744.

4. AN, AC, C 8 A, 56, fol. 73, Champigny au ministre, 16 novembre 1744.

5. AN, AC, C 9 A, 65, Maillart au ministre, Petit Goave, 10 août 1744.

6. PAC, Collection Baby, fols. 543–44, Lamaletie à Guy, Québec, 1 janvier 1745; fols. 545–47, ibid., 22 janvier 1745.

7. AN, AC, C 11 A, 81, fol. 300, Hocquart au ministre, 9 octobre 1744; 83, fol. 270, Hocquart au ministre, 16 octobre 1745.

8. Ibid., 85, fol. 380, Hocquart [au Duc D'Anville], 22 octobre 1746. Re.

Indians: "Ils sont nus, Ils n'ont n'y chassé ni cultivé leurs Terres parce quils ont Toujours Esté occupés à guerre."

9. PAC, Collection Baby, fols. 524–27, Havy et Lefebvre à Guy, Québec, 7 octobre 1744.

10. AN, 62 AQ 40, "Inventaire chez Havy et Lefebvre, Québec, 8 novembre 1745."

11. PAC, Collection Baby, fols. 536–42, Havy et Lefebvre à Guy, Québec, 16 décembre 1744.

12. AN, AD vii, 2a, arrêts, 20 avril 1744; 4 mai 1745.

13. "Novembre, 1746: Mémoire sur l'estat actuel de la marine et sur les arrangements à prendre pour le service de 1747 [de Maurepas]", printed in R. Lamontagne, Aperçu structural du Canada au XVIIIᵉ Siècle (Montreal, 1964), p. 86 ff.

14. AN, 62 AQ 35, France fils à Dugard, Paris, 5 décembre 1744. See also appendices B and C for reference to ship voyages.

15. Ibid., 26 décembre 1744.

16. Ibid., Paris, 2 janvier 1745. Ibid., 41, Liasse, perte des Trois Maries, pièce 9.

17. Ibid., 35, France fils à Dugard, Paris, 5 janvier 1745.

18. Ibid., Paris, 29 mars 1745.

19. Ibid., Paris, 7 mai 1745.

20. Ibid., 43, Charte-partie, La Thétis, 17 février 1745.

21. Ibid., 35, France fils à Dugard, Paris, 11 juin 1735.

22. Ibid., Paris, 4 juillet 1745.

23. "Mémoire de Maurepas," Lamontagne, Aperçu, p. 90.

24. AN, 62 AQ 35, France fils à Dugard, Paris, 7 mai, 29 juin, 13 juillet, 1745.

25. PAC, Collection Baby, fols. 586–89, Havy et Lefebvre à Guy, 28 avril 1745.

26. Ibid., fols. 548–50, 23 jan. 1745.

27. Ibid., fols. 602–4, 25 mai 1745.

28. Ibid., fols. 608–10, 3 juin 1745.

29. Ibid., fols. 629–30, 19 juin 1745; 6 juillet 1745,.645–48.

30. Ibid., fols. 656–63, 28 juillet 1745. Olivier had sent letters ahead for the authorities and on his arrival was questioned by them. It was he who made the first report of the surrender of Louisbourg and not as G. F. G. Stanley claims in New France: The Last Phase, 1744–60 (Toronto, 1968), p. 14, the officer Paul Marin, who did not arrive back at Quebec until August.

31. Ibid., fols. 685–90, Havy et Lefebvre à Guy, 30 juin 1745.

32. Ibid., fols. 724–26, 18 octobre 1745.

33. Ibid., fols. 711–15, 5 octobre 1745.

34. Ibid., fols. 694–97, 23 septembre 1745.

35. Ibid., fols. 707–9, 29 septembre 1745. (The second letter of this date.)

36. Ibid., fols. 677–80, 28 août 1745.

37. Ibid., fols. 759–64, 26 novembre 1745.

38. Ibid., fols. 741–44, 29 octobre 1745.

39. AN, 62 AQ 41, 15ᵉ cargaison en retour, pièce 66, "Robert Dugard, son compte courant avec Léon Fautoux de Louisbourg, 13 novembre 1745, Rouen."

40. Ibid., 35, France fils à Dugard, Paris, 3 décembre 1745.

41. Ibid., 41, "Extrait du Registre des Declarations et Raports du Greffe de l'Amirauté de Léon, Etably au Port Oblique de Roscoff, 29 décembre 1745."

42. Ibid., 35, France fils à Dugard, Paris, 29 janvier 1746; 62 AQ 43, Liasse Radoub de L'Astrée.

43. Ibid., France fils à Dugard, Paris, 2 janvier 1745.

44. Pierre Dardel, *Commerce, industrie et navigation à Rouen et au Havre aux XVIIIᵉ Siècle* (Rouen, 1966), pp. 145–50.

45. AN, 62 AQ 45, four *actes de société* for chambers of three to six years duration renewable, dated 1736, 1742, 1748, and 1754. Also reference to Guillaume France, ibid., 35, France à Dugard, Paris, 29 mai 1748.

46. Information is drawn from extant insurance policies in voyage accounts, AN, 62 AQ 41–44. Each policy is found in the folder of the ship and voyage in question. With regard to English insurance rates, T. S. Ashton, *An Economic History of England: The 18th Century* (London, 1961), confines himself to saying "But generally rates were lower in London [p. 134]." L. Sutherland, *A London Merchant* (London, 1962), an important work on English insurance, is no more helpful. A. H. John, "The London Assurance Company and the Marine Insurance Market of the Eighteenth Century," *Economica* (May 1958), pp. 127 and 138, confirms the view that English advantage in insurance was related to the solidity of insurers, not low rates.

47. AN, 62 AQ 35, France fils à Dugard, Paris, 7 avril 1745.

48. Ibid., France fils à Dugard, Paris, 16 octobre 1745.

49. Ibid., Letters of 22 novembre 1744, 1 octobre 1745, 28 octobre 1745, 7 mai 1745.

50. Ibid., Paris, 13 juillet 1746.

51. AN, AC, C 9 A, Samson au ministre, 29 mars 1746.

52. AN, 62 AQ 35, France fils à Dugard, Paris, 6 mai 1746. See also appendix C; Richard Pares, *War and Trade in the West Indies 1739–1763* (London, 1963).

53. AN, 62 AQ 42, Facture de cargaison, *Union* to Martinique, 1746.

54. For confirmation, see Pares, *War and Trade*, p. 341.

55. AN, C 9 A, 65, Maillart au ministre, Petit Goave, 10 août 1744.

56. AN, 62 AQ 35, France fils à Dugard, Paris, 6 mai 1746.

57. Ibid.

58. PAC, Collection Baby, fols. 798–801, Havy et Lefebvre à Guy, 20 mars 1746.

59. Ibid., fols. 816–19, 2 mai 1746.

60. Ibid., fols. 820–23, 7 mai 1746.

61. Ibid., *passim*, 1746.

62. Ibid., fols. 859–62, 28 juin 1746.

63. Ibid., fols. 829–33, 19 mai 1746. They were less impressed by the glittering profits of war than was Guy Frégault, "Essai sur les finances canadiennes," in *Le XVIIIe siècle canadien: études* (Montreal, 1968), pp. 332–33.

64. Ibid., fols. 865–68, 6 juillet 1746.

65. Ibid., fols. 918–20, 4 octobre 1746.

66. Ibid., fols. 933–36, 24 octobre 1746.

67. AN, C 11 A, 86, fol. 4, Hocquart au ministre, 3 novembre 1746.

68. AN, 62 AQ 44, "Relation de la Prise du Fleury par le maître cannonier"; "Province of New York, Extract, Court of Admiralty, City Hall, New York, 19 February 1746."

69. Ibid., 42, "Du 4 mars 1747, Declaration de la Perte du Nvre L'Union du Havre nauffragé à la pointe de la baleine en l'Isle de Ré."

70. Ibid., 35, France fils à Dugard, Paris, 12 mars 1747.

71. Ibid.

72. Ibid., 20 juillet 1747, 6 Septembre 1747.

73. Pares, *War and Trade*, pp. 324–25.

74. PAC, Collection Baby, fols. 1020–22, 17 juin 1747; fols. 1100–2, 17 octobre 1747.

75. Ibid., fols. 1040–41, 9 juillet 1747; fols. 1082–84, 7 septembre 1747.

76. AN, 62 AQ 40, "Extrait de le Lettre des Sr. Havy et Lefebvre, Ecrit à Quebec Le 3 novembre 1747." There is no mention of the crucial letter of Dugard (to which this is an extract of the reply) in the letters of Havy and Lefebvre to Guy. Thus it was probably received in the period between 22 July and 8 August, when Guy was in Quebec on militia duty. Similarly, there is no mention of the company decision in the letters of France to Dugard, although the general idea that it was time to close the business is mentioned in several letters, two quoted above. The only specific mention is therefore this extract.

77. AN, 62 AQ 35, France fils à Dugard, Paris. Several letters, 8 January 1748, 28 April 1748. The quote is from the last letter.

78. Ibid., 5 mai 1748.

79. AN, 62 AQ 35, France fils à Dugard, Paris, 24 mai 1748.

80. Ibid., 7 juin 1748; appendix B.

81. AN, 62 AQ 35, France fils à Dugard, Paris, 29 mai 1748.

82. Ibid., 6 octobre 1749; Dugard à France fils, 11 août 1755.

83. Ibid., France fils à Dugard, Paris, 7 avril 1750.

84. Ibid., *passim*. France referred to the post-war proceedings in a letter to his cousin as "le commencement dune nouvelle société" (Paris, 2 août 1750).

85. Ibid., France fils à Dugard, Paris, 16 juin 1747, with enclosure, "Etat Estimatif de la situation de la société de commerce etablie entre Mrs. Robert Dugard, etc., le 11 février 1744."

86. Ibid., 5, Dugard à Madame D'Haristoy, 11 janvier 1760; 62 AQ 40, "D'Haristoy, compte courant avec Dugard, mai 1759."

87. BN, Nouvelles acquisitions françaises, no. 339, pp. 30–32, "Notte sur les Manufactures de Rouen," Papiers de Taillet de Couronne et de Noël de la Morinière sur l'histoire de Normandie.

88. AN, AM, B 3, 473, fol. 145, Machault à Maurepas, 29 mars 1748.

89. AN, 62 AQ 2, Acte de société.

90. Ibid., 5, D'Haristoy à Dugard, Paris, 24 décembre 1746; Expense account dated 24 May 1748.

91. Ibid., 3 février 1747.

92. Ibid., 2, Mémoire ("Société pour le Rouge d'Adrinople") probably written by Jean Hellot; Acte de Société, Aubenas, 12 août 1747, Rouen, 20 août 1747.

93. Ibid., Extrait des Registres du Conseil d'Etat, 26 août 1747.

94. Ibid., 6, Item 2, "Réponse," 10.

95. Ibid., Extrait, Livre de Délibération, 28 janvier 1748.

96. Ibid., Item 2, Réponse, 6–11.

97. Ibid., Extrait, Livre de Délibération, 24 novembre 1748; ibid., 5, D'Haristoy à Dugard, Paris, 25 juin 1740; 62 AQ 2, "Mémoire pour repondre au dépir de M. Trudaine qui souhaite que nous teignons pour le public (1754)."

98. Ibid., D'Haristoy à Dugard, Paris, 19 juin 1749.

99. Ibid., D'Haristoy à Dugard, Paris, 3 février 1747; Paynel à Dugard, Rouen, 21 décembre 1754.

100. Ibid., D'Haristoy à Dugard, Paris, 20 juin 1749.

101. Ibid., Paynel à Dugard, Rouen, 29 juin 1749.

102. Ibid., 6, Item 2, Réponse, 23, 36.

103. Ibid., 5, D'Haristoy à Dugard, Paris, 28 novembre 1749.

104. Ibid., 3 janvier 1750.

105. Ibid.

106. Ibid., 23 janvier 1750.

107. Ibid., 28 novembre 1749.

108. Ibid., 23 janvier 1750.

109. Ibid., 14 décembre 1749. Louvet states (ibid., à Dugard, 5 décembre 1749) that D'Haristoy's relatives were scrupulous about lending at interest without contract, that is, they would consider *constitutions de rente* or bills of exchange but not notes.

110. Ibid., 26 décembre 1749; à Paynel, 5 décembre 1749. That D'Haristoy conceived of *actions* as a species of bond or debenture seems clear from his statement, "Je nay encore rien décider pour les actions parce qu'on n'a pas rendu réponse si on en prendra ou *si on me pretera d'une autre façon* (italics added). Ibid., à Dugard, 19 décembre 1749. On the ambiguity of the action, see J. Savary des Bruslons, *Dictionnaire universel de commerce* (Amsterdam, 1726), 1: 1547, and H. Lévy-Bruhl, *Histoire juridique des sociétés de commerce* (Paris, 1938), p. 225.

111. AN, 62 AQ 5, à Dugard, 26 décembre 1749.

112. Ibid., Louvet le jeune à Dugard, Paris, 16 janvier 1750. As Louvet was not the type that Dugard and other company members would have called a man of probity, the "appears" is a necessary qualification to even the least suspect information from his pen.

113. For general background see the works of R. de Roover. G. Rambert, ed., *Grande histoire du commerce de Marseille*, vol. 4 (Paris, 1954) is also useful.

114. AN, 62 AQ 5, Dugard à D'Haristoy, Rouen, 26 novembre 1749.

115. Ibid., D'Haristoy à Dugard, Paris, 6 décembre 1749.

116. Ibid., 23 janvier 1750.

117. Ibid., Louvet à Dugard, Paris, 16 janvier 1750.

118. Ibid., Dugard à D'Haristoy, Rouen, 26 novembre 1749.

119. Ibid.

120. Letters of Louvet le jeune and Le Leu le jeune in 62 AQ 5 are helpful in understanding these financial machinations. The various operations, conducted principally via the banker Le Leu, raise the question of the nature of discount or "escompte" at Paris, circa 1750. De Roover states categorically, "Sous l'Ancien Régime, les lettres de change se negociaient au cours de la bourse et sans escompte," *L'Evolution de la lettre de change, XIVe–XVIIIe siècles* (Paris, 1953), p. 133. The word *escompte* originally implied that when an acceptor paid before maturity, the bearer accepted less as the debt did not last as long, whereas today the word implies that the bill is originally sold for face value minus interest to maturity. But when Dugard writes to Le Leu that he sends him three "Traittes de M Louvet le Je notre amy à mon ordre sur M Ripondelly Lesquelles je vous ai endossées sur l'esperence que ledit amy ma donnée que vous voudrier bien vous charger de les Escompter dont je prendrai le montant sur vous après l'avis" and adds that he will need the bulk of the proceeds in only five days; and when Le Leu replies that "La difficulté quil y a de placer ce papier provient de ce que Paris est farcy de l'accept(ati)on du Sr. Ripandelly et qu'un chacun veut voir comment cette sorte de Banque tournera," it seems clear that *escompte* in the modern sense is intended. But it is also apparent that it is regarded as something new. (62 AQ 5, Dugard à Le Leu, Rouen, 18 août 1750; Le Leu à Dugard, Paris, 25 août 1750). Thus we have an example of the evolution of usage in this transitional period. De Roover's own quotation from P. Giraudeau's contemporary manual (p. 121) suggests this practice. See below, "Conclusion," n. 21.

121. AN, 62 AQ 6, Item 2, Réponse, pp. 18, 29, 39, 44–6 with quote at p. 39.

122. Ibid., pp. 44–6; ibid., p. 5, D'Haristoy à Dugard, Darnétal, 3 mars 1750.

123. The affair is extremely difficult to unscramble from the records available and the above is a very sketchy account. Most of the sources are letters: 62 AQ 5, Louvet le jeune à Dugard; D'Haristoy à Dugard; 62 AQ 3: Le Leu à Dugard; 62 AQ 5: Dugard à Louvet; 62 AQ 31: Vasse à Dugard; Dugard à Morisse et fils; Dugard à Vasse; Dugard à Premond; Dugard à Bourgerel; as well as "Mémoire pour les sieurs Bosquillon, Aubrelique, Rousseau, et Lefebvre, 23 juin 1763" and 62 AQ 6, Item 2, Réponse. This series of incidents, could it be faithfully reconstructed with the aid of other archives which in all probability do exist, may provide valuable insight into business and

government finance as well as the hopeless state of the French judicial system at the time.

124. AN, 62 AQ 6, Item 2 Réponse, pp. 34, 51, 54; ibid., p. 5, Paynel à Dugard, Rouen, 16 septembre 1752.

125. Ibid., 6, Item 2, Réponse, p. 58.

126. Ibid., p. 5, D'Haristoy à Dugard, 25 juin 1749.

127. Ibid., 2, "Pour repondre au depir de M. Trudaine qui souhaite que nous teignons pour le Publique"; "Observations sur les difficultes qui se sont presentes aux entrepreneurs. . . ."

128. Ibid., 5, D'Haristoy à Dugard, 9 janvier 1754. The English also sought the secret of "Turkey Red." In 1756 the Royal Society of Arts offered a reward for it. C. H. Wilson, *England's Apprenticeship* (New York, 1966), p. 297.

129. Ibid.

130. Ibid., D'Haristoy à Dugard, Rouen, 2 janvier 1755.

131. Ibid., p. 2, "Sur la requeste presentée au Roy par les Srs Dugard, D'Haristoy et Paynel. . . ."

132. Ibid., D'Haristoy à Dugard, Paris, 21 juin 1752; 6 décembre 1749, respectively.

133. Ibid.

134. Ibid., 29 janvier 1752.

135. AN, F 12, 1411 a, Copie s.d. anonyme [John Holker]. Account of his expenditure of 7,000 livres received to bring to France English Catholic workmen and machines; ibid., De Montigny à Crones, 4 janvier 1752; André Rémond, *John Holker, manufacturier et grande fonctionnaire en France au XVIIIe siècle, 1719–1786* (Paris, 1946).

136. AN, F 12, 1411 a, "Mémoire concernant l'etablissement projeté d'une manufacture d'etoffes de coton façon d'Angleterre [D'Haristoy] 1752."

137. Ibid., Machault à M. de la Bourdonnaye, 6 mars 1752. See also "Etat de dénombrement des noms et talents des ouvriers anglois venu par ordre du Gouvernement et qui sont actuellement à Darnétal depuis le 3 du present mois de mars sous la direction de M. D'Haristoy (1752)"; Morel à Trudaine, 23 mars 1752; Morel à Monseigneur, 13 mars 1752.

138. Ibid., "Instruction [de Machault] à M. de Montigny, 2 juillet 1752."

139. Ibid., Arrêt du Conseil d'Etat, 19 septembre 1752, Versailles.

140. Ibid., "Observations de de Montigny," 26 août to 16 octobre 1753.

141. Ibid., Garde des Sceaux [Trudaine] à M. de la Bourdonnaye, 15 août 1752; De la Bourdonnaye à Trudaine, 9 septembre 1752.

142. AN, 62 AQ 5, letters of D'Haristoy dated 6 juillet 1752, 17 janvier 1754, 25 juillet 1754, all to Dugard; to Trudaine, 17 novembre 1754; ibid., 6 letters of Torrent to Dugard, 24 juillet 1752 to 19 novembre 1752; ibid., 2, "Mémoire de l'Emprunte de 1757."

143. Pierre Dardel, *Commerce, industrie et navigation à Rouen et au Havre aux XVIIIe siècle* (Rouen: 1966), p. 159.

144. AN, 62 AQ 5, D'Haristoy à Dugard, Paris, 9 juin 1752.

145. Lunn, "Economic Development," appendix, pp. 466–67.

146. AN, 62 AQ 40, Comptes de gestion à Québec, 1737, 1738.

147. It is difficult to credit Havy's assertion in Havy à Dugard, La Rochelle, 16 juin 1761 (62 AQ 31) that "tout Letems que Jay Esté avotre service qui a esté depuis 1732 Jusquen et compris lannée 1748 Jene Travaillois Pas non plus que Le defuns lefebvre Pour Mon Compte." None of the vessels built and employed in the sealing enterprises are debited as Société du Canada assets. Oil sent to France as return cargo (see cargo account items in 62 AQ 41) always appears as having been sold to the company by some partner of Havy and Lefebvre, e.g. Sr. Volant, Fornel et Cie, etc. The present interpretation is therefore that the sealing stations were undertakings by which Havy and Lefebvre stood to gain or lose for their own account.

148. P. G. Roy, *Inventaire des pièces sur la Côte de Labrador* (Québec, 1940 and 1942), 2: 50, 51, 56, 151; 1: 293 (Acte de Société. Original in AQ, AJQ Etude Barolet, 3 mai 1737).

149. AN, AC, C 11 A, 81, fol. 77, Beauharnois et Hocquart au ministre, 25 octobre 1744.

150. AN, AC, B, 81, fol. 271, Ministre aux Beauharnois et Hocquart, 26 avril 1745.

151. Roy, *Côte de Labrador*, 2: 229; AN, AC, C 11 A, 92, fol. 259, "Representations Respectueuses, s.d."

152. Roy, *Côte de Labrador*, 2: 90; AQ, NF 17, "Registres de l'Amirauté de Québec," vol. 2, 1749–56, "Laudiance des Criées tenant par Extrord^{re} le mercredy vingt quatre avril 1754 deux heures de relevé."

153. AQ, AJQ, Etude LaTour, Acte de Société, 17 mai 1740, published in Roy, *Côte de Labrador*, 2: 177.

154. AQ, Pièces judiciaires et notariales, no. 4129, published in Roy, *Côte de Labrador*, 2: 352.

Notes to Chapter Nine

1. AN, 62 AQ 40, "Messieurs Havy et Lefebvre de Québec, Leur Compte Courant pour la Gestion des Cargaisons, 1731–57"; 62 AQ 31, Havy à Dugard, La Rochelle, 19 avril 1757.

2. Ibid., Havy à Dugard, La Rochelle, 16 juillet 1757.

3. PAC, Collection Baby, fols. 691–92, 789–91, 1020–22, 1057–58, 1059–61, 1142–43, 1148–50 (Letters to Pierre Guy, 1745–48); AQ AJQ, Etude Dulaurant, 4 juin 1748; Etude Panet, 19 août 1751.

4. Ibid., Etude Saillant, 17 septembre 1754, 7 octobre 1752; AQ, NF 11, Jug. et Del. du Con. Sup., arrêt, 11 septembre 1752.

5. AQ, AJQ, Etude Dulaurant, 10 novembre 1746; AN, 62 AQ 31, Havy à Dugard, La Rochelle, 20 mai 1760.

6. See the brief biographical sketch of Jean-Louis Fornel in *Dictionary of Canadian Biography*, 3 (Toronto, 1974): 224.

7. P. G. Roy, *Inventaire des pièces sur la Côte de Labrador* (Quebec, 1940 and 1942), 2: 234, 235–38, 244–45, 249–55, 255; 1: 91–2, 99–101.

8. Ibid., 2: 88, 259–61; PAC, AC, C 11 A, 100, fol. 337, "Mémoire sur l'exploitation des Traittes. . . ."

9. Ibid., "Mémoire sur l'exploitation. . . ."

10. AN, 62 AQ 31, Havy à Dugard, La Rochelle, 21 janvier 1756.

11. Ibid., 19 avril 1757.

12. Ibid., 5 août 1758.

13. Ibid., 35, France fils à Dugard, Metz, 4 août 1756.

14. Ibid., 42, liasse *Centaure*, 1755–56, extract of court record, Province of New York (signed) Lewis Morris, 30 December 1756.

15. Ibid., 35, France fils à Dugard, 21 août 1756.

16. Ibid.

17. Ibid., 31, Havy à Dugard, La Rochelle, 19 avril 1757.

18. Ibid., Richard Pares, *War and Trade in the West Indies, 1739–1763* (London, 1963), pp. 359–75.

19. AN, 62 AQ 31, Havy à Dugard, La Rochelle, 5 août 1758.

20. Ibid.

21. Ibid., 16 septembre 1758.

22. Ibid.

23. Ibid., 5 août 1758.

24. Ibid., 22 décembre 1758.

25. Ibid.

26. Ibid., 16 septembre 1758.

27. PAC, Collection Baby, fols. 2010–13, S. Jauge à F. Baby, Bordeaux, 15 mai 1763.

28. AN, 62 AQ 31, Havy à Dugard, La Rochelle, 10 février 1759.

29. Ibid., 40, liasse o, current accounts.

30. Ibid., 5, Dugard à France fils, Rouen, 6 décembre 1759.

31. Ibid., 35, Enclosure, "Etat Estimatif de la situation de la société de commerce etablie entre M$^{rs.}$ Robert Dugard . . . 11 février 1744" in France fils à Dugard, Paris, 16 juin 1747.

32. Ibid., 5, Dugard à France fils, Rouen, 11 juillet 1759.

33. Ibid.

34. Ibid., 35, France fils à Dugard, Vaugency, 19 juillet 1759.

35. Ibid., 5, Dugard à France fils, Rouen, 6 décembre 1759.

36. Ibid., 37, Dugard à France fils, Rouen, 7 juillet 1760.

37. Ibid., 5, Dugard à France fils, Rouen, 6 décembre 1759.

38. Ibid., 35, France fils à Dugard, Vaugency, 1 juin 1759, 29 juillet 1760; France fils à Duperreux, Vaugency, 15 avril 1766. See also correspondence of Dugard and Baraguay in 62 AQ 36.

39. Ibid., 5, Dugard à France fils, Rouen, 6 juillet 1759.

40. Ibid., 36, Havy à Dugard, La Rochelle, 5 juillet 1760.

41. Ibid., 31, Havy à Dugard, La Rochelle, 19 mai 1759.

42. Ibid., 11 juin 1759.

43. Ibid., 7 juin 1760.

44. Ibid., 36, Havy à Dugard, La Rochelle, 5 juillet 1760; Dugard à Havy, Rouen, 14 juillet 1760.

45. Ibid., Havy à Dugard, 17 janvier 1761; 62 AQ 40, "Monsieur Havy son compte courant avec Robert Dugard."

46. Ibid., 31, Havy à Dugard, La Rochelle, 26 décembre 1761.

47. Ibid., 11 juin 1759.

48. PAC, Collection Baby, fols. 1697–1701, Havy à Baby frères, 12 février 1759.

49. Ibid.

50. AN, 62 AQ 31, Havy à Dugard, 20 mai 1760.

51. Ibid., 27 décembre 1759.

52. PAC, Collection Baby, vol. 3, J. Lefebvre à M. le Chevalier Dargenteuil, Québec, 13 octobre 1760.

53. AN, 62 AQ 36, Havy à Dugard, La Rochelle, 17 janvier 1761.

54. PAC, Collection Baby, fols. 1989–91, Havy à Baby, Bordeaux, 16 avril 1763.

55. Ibid., fols. 1931–36, S. Jauge à F. Baby, Bordeaux, 4 février 1763.

56. Ibid., and fols. 2010–13, 15 mai 1763.

57. Ibid., fols. 2445–47, Thouron frères aux Baby frères, La Rochelle, 6 mars 1767; chap. 3, n. 4.

58. AN, 62 AQ 31, Havy à Dugard, La Rochelle, 27 décembre 1759.

59. See Dugard's comments in 62 AQ 31, Dugard à Grand et Labbard, 4 avril 1760; à Bansa frères, 4 avril 1760.

60. Ibid., Ridel et Cie. à Dugard, Paris, 13 juin 1760.

61. Ibid., 6, Dugard à Paynel fils ainé, 5 juillet 1760.

62. Ibid., 31, Dugard à J. B. Prémond, Rouen, 5 octobre 1761.

63. Ibid.

64. Ibid., 31, Dugard à L. Chef d'Hôtel, 12 novembre 1761.

65. AN, Minutier central du département de la Seine, Etude CXXII (Jacques Felize), liasse 674, Mariage de Robert Dugard et Marguerite Esther Lecourt, 23 août 1749; 62 AQ 31, Dugard à J. B. Prémond, 21 octobre 1761.

66. AN, 62 AQ 31, Dugard à J. de Cuisy, Rouen, 18 octobre 1761.

67. Ibid., 3, Dugard à Christinat et Turpin, 1 mars 1762.

68. Ibid., 31, J. de Cuisy à Dugard, Caen, 10 novembre 1761.

69. Ibid., a legal paper of 15 May 1767 marked "copy," which gives details of purchase of the property from Haren de Bonneval on 5 October 1743. The estate was paid for by a *rente viagère*.

70. Ibid., Dugard à J. de Cuisy, Rouen, 27 juin 1762, Dugard à Christinat et Turpin, Rouen, s.d., states that de Cuisy and Laurens were given the power of attorney to sell Bonneval for 65,000 livres. Perhaps this was closer to the market value, as there are many indications of market slump.

71. Ibid., Dugard à De La Fosse Châtry, s.d.; "Accord des créanciers Dugard, 23 mars 1762, Rouen."

72. Ibid., Correspondence of Dugard and Cuisy beginning 10 November 1761: Dugard à Christinat et Turpin, s.d.; reference to endorsements, De Cuisy à Dugard, Caen, 8 septembre 1762.

73. Ibid., Dugard à Christinat et Turpin, Rouen, 26 novembre 1761; same to same, n.d.

74. Ibid., Dugard à Christinat et Turpin, Rouen, 30 novembre 1761.

75. Ibid., 5, Dugard à Veuve D'Haristoy, s.d.

76. Ibid., Dugard à Veuve P. de Labat et fils, Rouen, 6 juillet 1766.

77. Some idea of the progress of this audit may be gained from 62 AQ 31, Dugard à Bourgerel, Rouen, 3 juin 1767; same to same, 31 juillet 1766. Many of the *mémoires* and judgements are preserved in 62 AQ 6.

78. Ibid., 31, Dugard à De Cuisy, Rouen, 17 juillet 1762.

79. Ibid., 32, leases of 12 November 1731 and Christmas, 1763.

80. Ibid., 31, Dugard à Bourgerel, 31 juillet 1766; Dugard in reply to Doutreleau, written on the back of Doutreleau à Dugard, Paris, 19 juillet 1766, in 62 AQ 35.

81. Ibid., 31, Dugard à Bansa frères, Rouen, 20 mars 1762; à Bourgerel, Rouen, 30 novembre 1768.

82. Ibid., 38, Journal de Dugard, 30 octobre 1761 to 3 juin 1770 (with gaps). One of Dugard's few book purchases in this period was a volume on agriculture. His land had suddenly become of greater relative economic importance than ever before, and he found his own knowledge of farming woefully inadequate. In this period he also consulted an expert, an "ancien cultivateur," who advised that barley would be best for his poor soil. (62 AQ 33, De la Cours à Dugard, Tournay, 9 septembre 1763.)

83. Ibid., 31, Dugard à De Cuisy, Rouen, 20 juin 1762.

84. Ibid., 21 juin 1762.

85. Ibid., 35, Dugard à Bourgerel, Rouen, 5 août 1769.

86. Ibid., 31, Dugard à Bourgerel, 3 février 1768; same to same, 22 juillet 1769.

87. Ibid., 10 mars 1770.

88. See esp. in 62 AQ 31, "Billets que Mrs. de Cuisy & Laurens ont endossé le 1 octobre 1762," as well as many receipts and financial statements here.

89. Ibid., 5, Dugard à France fils, Rouen, 6 décembre 1759.

90. Ibid., 31, Dugard à Christinat & Turpin, Rouen, 26 novembre 1761.

91. Ibid.

92. Ibid., 5, Dugard à France fils, Rouen, 6 décembre 1759.

93. Ibid.

94. Ibid., 10 juillet 1759.

95. Ibid., 6, Dugard à Paynel fils ainé, Rouen, 5 juillet 1760.

96. Ibid., 31, Dugard à France fils, Rouen, 6 octobre 1761.

97. Ibid., Dugard à Bourgerel, 30 novembre 1768.

98. Ibid., 5, Dugard à Paynel, Rouen, 28 juillet 1761.

99. Ibid., 36, Dugard à Baraguay, Rouen, 22 mars 1762.

100. Ibid., 5, Dugard à France fils, Rouen, 10 février 1764.

101. Ibid., Charlet à Dugard, 19 avril 1768.

102. Ibid., 31, Dugard à Bourgerel, 30 novembre 1768; for 1768 and 1769 see also 62 AQ 35, Christinat et Turpin à Dugard, Le Havre, 2 décembre 1768, same to same, 22 mai 1769.

103. Ibid., 31, Dugard à Bourgerel, 20 janvier 1770.

104. Ibid.

105. Ibid., Dugard à Bourgerel, 20 janvier 1770.

106. Ibid., 37, Dugard fils à Rémy Bansa, Rouen, 5 août 1770. Monsieur I. Cloulas, directeur des Services d'Archives de l'Eure, has reported to me that there is no mention of the death of Dugard in the *état civil* of La Haye Aubrée. The most reasonable interpretation of this fact is that as a Protestant he was buried privately, thus not being mentioned in the parish registers.

107. Ibid., 34, Rémy Bansa à Dugard fils, Frankfurt, 6 novembre 1767.

108. Ibid., *passim*.

109. Ibid., 33, De Cuisy à Dugard fils, Caen, 4 septembre 1763.

110. Ibid., 34, Bansa à Dugard fils, Frankfurt, 13 août 1770.

111. Ibid., 37, Dugard fils à Bansa, Rouen, 3 septembre 1770.

Notes to Conclusion

1. AN, 62 AQ 5, Torrent à Dugard, Paris, 7 septembre 1752.

2. See chap. 8, n. 120.

3. Jean Meyer, *L'armement nantais dans la deuxième moitié du XVIIIe siècle* (Paris, 1969); Jean Cavignac, *Jean Pellet, commerçant de gros, 1694–1772* (Paris, 1967); Ralph Davis, *Aleppo and Devonshire Square* (London, 1967); Richard Pares, *A West India Fortune* (London, 1950); Lucy Sutherland, *A London Merchant* (London, 1962).

4. Ellis T. Powell, *The Evolution of the Money Market, 1385–1915* (London, 1966), chap. 6.

5. Davis, *Aleppo*, p. 68.

6. Powell, *Money Market*, p. 131.

7. D. M. Joslin, "London Private Bankers, 1720–1785," *Economic History Review*, 2nd S., 7, no. 2 (1954–55): 185–86.

8. Adam Smith, *An Inquiry into the Nature and Causes of the Wealth of Nations* (New York, 1965), Bk. I, chap. 9.

9. Ibid., p. 97.

10. G. V. Taylor, "Noncapitalist Wealth and the Origins of the French Revolution," *American Historical Review*, 72, no. 2 (January 1967): 474–78; Smith, *Wealth of Nations*, p. 90.

11. Smith, *Wealth of Nations*, p. 87.

12. Ibid., p. 97.

13. Sutherland, *A London Merchant*, pp. 30–1.

14. Smith, *Wealth of Nations*, p. 89.

15. Davis, *Aleppo*, pp. 223–24.

16. Meyer, *L'armement*, p. 231.

17. Ibid., p. 239.

18. Louis Dermigny, *Cargaisons indiennes; Soliers & Cie. (1781–1793)* (Paris, 1960), 1: 81.

19. Cavignac, *Jean Pellet*, p. 208.

20. Meyer, *L'armement*, p. 220 ff.

21. Smith, *Wealth of Nations*, p. 93. One work in which bills and discount are not ignored is T. J. A. LeGoff, "An eighteenth-century grain merchant: Ignace Advisse Desruisseaux," in *French Government and Society, 1500–1850*, ed. by J. F. Bosher (London, 1973) pp. 92–122.

22. See p. 000.

23. AN, 62 AQ 37, Dugard fils à Bansa, 26 octobre 1765.

24. Davis, *Aleppo*, p. 72. See also Sutherland, *A London Merchant*, p. 5; Pares, *Fortune*, p. 332.

25. Taylor, "Noncapitalist Wealth," p. 473.

26. Meyer, *L'armament*, pp. 92–3.

27. Renversement de la conjoncture? See Robert Mandrou, *La France aux XVIIᵉ et XVIIIᵉ siècles* (Paris, 1967), p. 95.

28. AN, 62 AQ 5, D'Haristoy à Dugard, Paris, 3 janvier 1750.

29. Kurt Samuelsson, *Religion and Economic Action: A Critique of Max Weber* (New York, 1961).

30. Jacques Savary, *Le parfait négociant*, (Paris, 1721), 1: 136.

31. Ibid., 1: 282.

32. Ibid., 1: 288–89.

33. See p. 41.

34. See p. 72.

35. See p. 121.

36. See p. 151.

37. See p. 141.

38. See p. 127.

39. See p. 151.

40. Bernard Groethuysen, *The Bourgeois; Catholicism vs. Capitalism in Eighteenth-Century France* (Paris, 1927; English ed., New York, 1968), a brilliant but almost ignored work.

41. See p. 151.

Notes to Appendix A

1. AC C8A 52, fol. 248, Etat. Mentioned in four états in C8B, vol. 20.

2. AN, 62AQ 40, D. Laurens c/c avec R. Dugard, 1729–38; P. D'Haristoy c/c avec R. Dugard, 1728–38; Vincent père et fils c/c avec R. Dugard, 1729–38.

3. AN 62AQ39, Livre de Délibération, 22 janvier 1733.

4. AN 62AQ42, "Instructions pour le Capt. Fremont, 29 janvier 1744"; AC B77 fol. 160, Maurepas à J. B. Prémond, 25 décembre 1743.

5. AN 62AQ43, Facture de Cargaison, Le Havre, 18 août 1743.

6. AC C8A 52, Etat 1740 describes it as eighty tons. Other descriptions: C8B 20 Etats 1739, 1741; C8B 21 Etats 1744; F2B 11 Etat 1740.

7. AN 62AQ40 Vincent père et fils c/c avec Robert Dugard, 1729–38; P. D'Haristoy c/c avec R. Dugard, 1728–38.

8. AN 62AQ39, Livre de Délibération, 14 mai 1732.

9. AN 62AQ40, D. Laurens c/c avec Robert Dugard, 1729–38; G. France c/c avec R. Dugard, 1729–42.

10. AN 62AQ43, Various "Comptes de Recouvrement d'Assurances" at Bordeaux, Nantes, La Rochelle, and London.

11. AC C8B 17, Three états; C8B 21, état, 1744; F2B 11, état 1739; AN 62AQ43, Facture de cargaison, 8 novembre 1746.

12. AD Gironde, 6B 387, Rôle d'Equipage, 1 avril 1738.

13. AN 62AQ43, Facture de cargaison, 8 novembre 1746; AD Gironde. 6b 387, Rôle d'Equipage, 1 avril 1738.

14. In addition to n. 3, AC F2B 11, état 1739.

15. AN 62AQ39, Livre de Délibération, 28 janvier 1733 et 10 mars 1733.

16. AN 62AQ40, One-fifth of the cost listed in each associate's account, 1730–38.

17. AN 62AQ39, Livre de Délibération, 19 mars 1733.

18. ADQ NF 11 or PAC. FM8 A2, 7 mars 1747, "Arrêt dans le cause entre les Sieurs Havy et Lefebvre, négociants de Québec . . . et Noel Levasseur, sculpteur. . . ."

19. AN 62AQ40, The reference to the refit is in all associate's accounts. Only "Compte de Monsieur France avec DuGard de Rouen dressés par Epoques de Payements & de Recettes" states specifically that the *Ville de Québec* and the *Union* are the same vessel: "Radoub de la V. de Québec nommée lunion."

20. AN 62AQ40. Mentioned in all associates' closing accounts.

21. AN 62AQ44. Luetkens frères et Cie à Robert Dugard, Bordeaux, 27 juin 1743.

22. AD Gironde. 6B 96 fols. 80, 249, Soumissions avant départ; 6B 97 fol. 107, Soumission avant départ; 6B 242, Rapport de Mer.

23. AD Gironde. 6B 386, Rôle d'Equipage, 4 janvier 1738.

24. AN 62AQ39, Livre de Délibération, 15 mai 1736; 62AQ40, One-fifth of cost listed in each associate's closing account; 62AQ45, Facture de cargaison de l'Alçion de Québec à Louisbourg (1737).

25. AN 62AQ44, "Observations sur la Perte du Navire l'Alçion sur la Petitte Caique au Débouquement de St. Domingue le 29 avril 1743. . . ." (Probably written by Dugard); AD Gironde. 6B 1311, Numerous documents related to the trial of Pierre Gautier at Bordeaux; 6B 1330, Placet de Pierre Gautier; 6B 790, "Appointemens de l'Amirauté."

26. AD Gironde. 6B 388, Rôle d'Equipage, 6 juillet 1740.

27. AN 62AQ 40, One-fifth of cost listed in each associate's closing account.

28. ADQ NF 11 or PAC FM8 A2, 7 mars 1747, Arrêt. . . .

29. AN 62AQ 44, Mémoire, septembre 1749.

30. Ibid. "Relation de la Prise de Fleury par le maître canonnier"; "Province of New York, Extract Court of Admiralty, City Hall, New York, n.d."

31. AC F2B 11, Etat 1739.

32. AN 62AQ44, Factures de cargaison, 22 novembre 1743 et 20 mars 1743; "Rôle d'Equipage du Navire le St. Louis d'Honfleur. . . ."

33. AC C11A 71 fol. 182.

34. APQ NF 11 or PAC FM8 A2, 7 mars 1747, Arrêt. . . .

35. AN 62AQ40, One-fifth of the cost listed in each associate's closing account.

36. AN 62AQ44, "Rôle d'Equipage du Navire le St. Louis d'Honfleur. . . ."

37. Ibid., Baussen à Robert Dugard, 27 juin et 21 septembre 1754.

38. AN 62AQ41, Police d'Assurance, Rouen, 18 juin 1743; 62AQ42, Facture de cargaison, 10 octobre 1748; Police d'Assurance, Rouen, 7 juillet 1749.

39. AN 62AQ35, D'Haristoy à Robert Dugard, Paris, 24 janvier 1747; AD Gironde. 6B 101 fol. 151, "Soumission avant départ, 3 juillet 1750."

40. N. 1 and 2.

41. APQ NF11 or PAC FM8, 7 mars 1747, Arrêt. . . .

42. AN 62AQ40, One-fifth of cost listed in each associate's closing account.

43. AN 62AQ35, G. France fils à R. Dugard, 28 octobre 1745.

44. AN 62AQ42, Capt. Belinger à Robert Dugard, New York, 15 septembre 1756; Declaration, Province of New York, Court of Vice Admiralty, 30 December 1756 (signed Lewis Morris).

45. AC C11A 73 fol. 411, "Etat des Liquers et Vins de Liquers, 16 octobre 1740."

46. AC C8B 20, etats 1742 et 1743; C8B 21, etat, 1744; F2B 11, etat 1740.

47. AN 62AQ40, One-fifth of cost listed in each associate's closing account.

48. APQ NF 11 or PAC. FM8 A2, 7 mars 1747, Arrêt. . . .

49. AC C11A 75 fol. 83, Beauharnois au Ministre, 3 février 1741; ibid., 76 fols. 318–45, "Mémoire sur le Commerce du Canada," 1741; APQ NF 2, Cahier 29, 3 avril, 16 juin.

50. AN 62AQ43, "Conte de la Perte de #1735 Assurance faite l'Imprévû pris et mené à Exeter condamé."

51. AN 62AQ43, Facture de cargaison, Québec, 10 novembre 1745; "Acte de Propriété du navire l'Astrée, Amirauté de Morlaix, 1 août 1748"; Police d'Assurance, Rouen, 8 octobre 1748.

52. AN 62AQ40, One-fifth of cost listed in each associate's closing account.

53. APQ NF 11 or PAC FM8 A2, 7 mars 1747, Arrêt. . . .

54. Note 3 and AN 62AQ41, "Extrait du Registre des Déclarations et Raports du Greffe de l'Amirauté de Léon, Etably au Port Oblique de Roscroft, 29 décembre 1745."

55. AN 62AQ43, "La Présente liasse concernant le Radoub et Armement du Navire l'Astrée à Morlaix contient 56 pièces d'Ecriture."

56. Ibid., "Compte de Vente de la Cosse du navire l'Astrée du Havre avec parti de ses agrés & apareaux le reste desdits agrés & apareaux avant servy au navire le Centaure commandé par M. Gosselin."

57. AN 62AQ40, One-quarter of cost appears in Pierre D'Haristoy's closing account.

58. AN 62AQ43, Liasse, Perte du Trois Maries, esp. Extrait des Registres de

L'Amirauté (pièce 9); Decision des Arbitres (pièce 31). These are the source of all above information except cost of vessel.

Notes to Appendix D

1. Jean Meyer, *L'armement nantais dans la deuxième moitié du XVIIIe siècle* (Paris, 1969), pp. 129, 125.

2. I have made several attempts to total debits and credits from voyage papers and arrive at the same totals as given in the current accounts. None of these attempts has been successful. The closest I have come, calculation of debits and credits for the *Union*, voyage of 1744, resulted from including all return cargo costs except wartime insurance premiums and Dugard's commission in the debit column. The error is only 2,891 out of 181,892 on the debit and 1,336 out of 172,323 on the credit.

3. AN, 62 AQ 41, "Compte provisionel du Produit de Retour en attendant supplement de linvendu et dettes à rentrer, 6 février, 1745," 14e Cargaison en Retours.

4. G. V. Taylor, "Types of Capitalism in Eighteenth-Century France," *English Historical Review* 79 (1964): 483.

Primary Sources

The present work is based primarily on collections of private papers. The most important of these, as noted in the Preface, is the Fonds Dugard in the Archives d'entreprises (série AQ), Archives nationales, Paris. A list of the contents of these 45 cartons of business letters and accounts is to be found in Bertrand Gille, *Etat sommaire des Archives d'entreprises conservées aux Archives nationales* (Paris, 1957), 149–51. A useful guide to the documents is available to researchers in the Salle des Inventaires, Archives nationales. The letters of François Havy and Jean Lefebvre in the Collection Baby at the Université de Montréal, with transcripts at the Public Archives of Canada, Ottawa, together with the Collection Pierre Guy in the possession of the Société historique de Montréal, also available at the Public Archives of Canada, extend this private documentation, revealing in considerable detail many aspects of the Canadian side of Dugard and Company's business. Private collections are always prized for their rarity; the existence of three so closely interrelated series is a good fortune beyond expectation. The value of these archives, so rich in information on business, society, attitudes, and even public affairs, is by no means exhausted by the present study.

The archives of notaries in France and more particularly in Canada have been used to supplement this central documentation. Having become more easy of access in recent years, these archives are quickly proving their worth in the domain of social and economic history. Their nature is such that they provide many different uniform series of information—on marriages, dowries, and debts, for example—which makes them an ideal source for the statistical studies upon which social history is more and more coming to repose.

Private papers are here used in conjunction with public documentation, each making up for the deficiencies of the other to provide a more holistic view of the past than could otherwise be had. The Archives de la Marine and the Fonds des Colonies at the Archives nationales are the most important of the many public series used. The great value of these archives has been commented on and proven by performance so often that no testimonial in their favour is required.

Primary Sources in French Archives

Archives nationales, Paris

AD   Textes administratifs du pouvoir central ou d'institutions locales, xiie–xviiie siècles. VII (Marines et colonies) 2ª, 2ᵇ, 6.

TT²   Réligionnaires fugitifs.

F¹²   Administration générale de la France, Commerce et Industrie. Registres du Bureau du Commerce (54, 55, 58, 83, 87, 88, 89); Avis des députés au bureau (698–708); Teintures (1330, 1334A, 1334B–1335); Manufacture de St. Sever (1411A).

62 AQ   Archives d'entreprises. Fonds Dugard, 1–45.

Fonds des Colonies.

B   Correspondance envoyée. Ordres du Roi (53–102).

C 8 A   Correspondance générale. Lettres reçues. Martinique (39–61).

C 8 B   Martinique (9, 10, 17, 20–23).

C 9 A   Correspondance générale. Lettres reçues. St. Domingue (29–85).

C 9 B   St. Domingue (9–14).

C 11 A Correspondance générale. Lettres reçues. Canada (51–109, 121, 125).

F 1 A   Mélanges. Commerce aux colonies (35).

F 2 B   Mélanges. Commerce aux colonies (1,2,11).

Archives de la Marine, Paris

B 3   Correspondance. Lettres reçues (328–79, 508).

C 4   Classes, amirautés et police de la navigation (159, Mémoires sur les ports de France).

Archives départementales de la Marne et de la Province de Champagne, Chalons-sur-Marne

G 1501 & E 706. Actes paroissiaux, Vaugency (Saint-Quentin-sur-Coole).

Archives départementales de la Gironde, Bordeaux

7 B 2102 Fonds Silva.

6 B Soumissions avant départ; rôles d'équipage.

Archives départementales de la Seine-Maritime, Rouen

C Administration provinciales (225, 831).

G Clergé séculier. Comptes de fabrique (G 6.506, 7.001, 7.002); bans de mariage (G.5.1285).

Archives notariales. Etudes LeCoq, Lauvon.

Bibliothèque de l'Arsenal, Paris
Affaire du Canada (1761–71), 12,142–12,148.

Bibliothèque de la Société de l'histoire du Protestantisme français, Paris
Fonds Emile Lesens. 1206 I–V; 1208, I–VII.
Fonds Pierre LeGendre. 412¹, 412², 412³, 413¹. (See above, p. 48, n. 31.)

Bibliothèque municipale de Rouen
JJ Registres de droit de hanse.

Bibliothèque nationale, Paris
Nouvelles acquisitions françaises, 339. Papiers de Haillet de Couronne et de
     Noel de la Morinière sur l'histoire de Normandie.

Minutier central, Paris
Etude Jacques Felize (CXXII), liasse 674.

Primary Sources in Canadian Archives

Public Archives of Canada, Ottawa
Collection Baby (transcripts of originals at the Université de Montréal), I–IV
     (primarily letters of Havy and Lefebvre).
Collection Pierre Guy (microfilm of originals in possession of Société his-
     torique de Montréal).

Archives du Québec, Quebec
NF 2 Ordonnances des Intendants.
NF 5 Cahiers d'Intendance.
NF 11 Registres du Conseil supérieur.
NF 17 Registres de l'Amirauté de Québec.
NF 25 Collection de pièces judiciaires et notariales.
Archives judiciaires de Québec aux Archives du Québec.
Etudes: Barolet, Claude (1728–60); Louet, Jean-Claude (1718–37); Dulaur-
     ant, C-Hilarion (1734–59); Pinquet, Nicholas (1749–51); Panet,
     Jean-Claude (1744–75); Saillant, Simon, père (1748–71); Lanouillier
     des Granges, P. A. (1748–60).

Archives du Séminaire de Québec, Quebec
Polygraphies 24: 10–10E, 36K (Comptes avec Havy et Lefebvre).
Polygraphie 27: 2L.
Grand Livre, 1737–40.

Bibliography

Ashton, T. S. *An Economic History of England: The 18th Century*. London: Methuen & Co., 1961.

Banbuck, C. A. *Histoire politique, économique et sociale de la Martinique sous l'Ancien Régime*. Paris: M. Rivière, 1935.

Beaurepaire, Charles de Robillard de. *Collection des inventaires sommaires des Archives départementales de la Seine-Inférieure, Première Partie, C&D*. Paris, 1864.

Bi-centenaire de la fondation de la Chambre de Commerce de Rouen, 1703–1903; Aperçu historique. Rouen: Imprimerie Lecerf fils, 1908.

Blanchet, A. and Dieudonné, A. *Manuel de numismatique française*, 3. Paris: A. Picard et fils, 1916.

Boislisle, A. M. de, ed. *Correspondance des contrôleurs généraux des finances*. 3 vols. Paris, 1874–97.

Bonnassieux, Louis Jean Pierre Marie. *Conseil de Commerce et Bureau du Commerce, 1700–1791, Inventaire analytique des procès verbaux*. Introduction et table par Eugène LeLong. Paris: Imprimerie nationale, 1900.

Canada, Assembly of the Province of. *Edits et ordonnances: revus et corrigés d'après les pièces originales déposées aux Archives provinciales*, vols. 1 and 2. Quebec, 1854–55.

Cavignac, Jean. *Jean Pellet, commerçant de gros, 1694–1772*. Paris: S.E.V.P.E.N., 1967.

Conrad, Joseph. *The Mirror of the Sea*. Garden City: Doubleday, Page & Co., 1925.

Dardel, Pierre. *Navires et marchandises dans les ports de Rouen et du Havre au XVIIIe siècle*. Paris: S.E.V.P.E.N., 1963.

———. *Commerce, industrie et navigation à Rouen et au Havre au XVIIIe siècle*. Rouen: Société libre d'émulation de la Seine-Maritime, 1966.

Davis, Ralph. *Aleppo and Devonshire Square*. London: Macmillan, 1967.

Debien, Gabriel. "La nourriture des esclaves sur les plantations des Antilles françaises aux XVIIᵉ et XVIIIᵉ siècles." *Caribbean Studies*, 4, no. 2 (July, 1964): 3–27.

Dempsey, B. W. *Interest and Usury*. Washington, D.C.: American Council on Public Affairs [1943].

Dermigny, Louis. *Cargaisons indiennes; Soliers & Cie. (1781–1793)*. 2 vols. Paris: S.E.V.P.E.N., 1960.

Dictionary of Canadian Biography, vol. 3 (1741–1770). Edited by Francess G. Halpenny. Toronto: University of Toronto Press, 1974.

Dorn, Walter L. *Competition for Empire, 1740–1763*. The Rise of Modern Europe, edited by W. L. Langer. New York: Harper and Row, 1940.

Eccles, W. J. *The Canadian Frontier, 1534–1760*. Histories of the American Frontier, edited by R. A. Billington. New York: Holt, Rinehart and Winston, 1969.

Edey, Harold C. *Introduction to Accounting*. London: Hutchinson University Library, 1963.

Faucon, G. H. *La juridiction consulaire de Rouen, 1556–1905, d'après les documents authentiques et avec l'agrément du Tribune de Commerce de Rouen*. Evreux: C. Hérissey, 1905.

Filion, Maurice. *Maurepas, ministre de Louis XV, 1715–1749*. Montreal: Les Editions Leméac, 1967.

Findlay, A. G. *Memoir descriptive and explanatory of the Northern Atlantic Ocean*. 14th ed. London, 1879.

Ford, F. L. *Robe and Sword; The Regrouping of the French Aristocracy after Louis XIV*. New York: Harper and Row, 1965.

Fouquet, Henri. *Histoire civile, politique et commerciale de Rouen depuis les temps les plus reculés jusqu'à nos jours*. Rouen, 1876.

Frégault, Guy. *François Bigot, administrateur français*. 2 vols. Montreal: Les Etudes de l'Institut de l'histoire de l'Amérique française, 1948.

———. *Le XVIIIᵉ siècle canadien: études*. Montreal: Editions H.M.H., 1968.

Gaumond, Marcel. *La maison Fornel*. Quebec: Ministère des Affaires culturelles, 1965.

Gille, Bertrand. *Etat sommaire des Archives d'entreprises conservées aux Archives nationales*. Paris: Imprimerie nationale, 1957.

Goubert, Pierre. *Louis XIV et vingt millions de Français*. Paris: Bibliothèque de culture historique, 1967.

Groethuysen, Bernard. *The Bourgeois; Catholicism vs. Capitalism in Eighteenth-Century France*. Translated and condensed by Mary Ilford. New York: Holt, Rinehart & Winston, 1968.

Gruder, Vivian. *The Royal Provincial Intendants: A Governing Elite in Eighteenth-Century France*. Ithaca, N.Y.: Cornell University Press, 1968.

Hamelin, Jean. *Economie et société en Nouvelle-France*. Quebec: Les Presses de l'université Laval, 1960.

Harris, R. W. *Absolutism and Enlightenment, 1660–1789*. New York: Harper and Row, 1964.

Henderson, W. O. *England and Industrial Europe*. Liverpool: Liverpool University Press, 1954.

Horn, David B. *Great Britain and Europe in the Eighteenth Century*. Oxford: At the Clarendon Press, 1967.

Horton, D. J. "Gilles Hocquart, Intendant of New France." Ph.D. dissertation, McGill University, 1975.

Innis, H. A. *The Fur Trade of Canada*. Toronto: University of Toronto Press, 1927.

———. "Cape Breton and the French Régime." *Proceedings and Transactions of the Royal Society of Canada*, 3rd series, 29 (1935): 51–87.

Jackson, W. *Book-keeping in the True Italian Form of Debtor and Creditor by Way of Double Entry; or, Practical Book-keeping Exemplified from the Precepts of the late Ingenious D. Dowling, author of Mercantile Arithmetic*. Dublin, 1815.

John, A. H. "The London Assurance Company and the Marine Insurance Market of the Eighteenth Century." *Economica*, 25, no. 98 (May, 1958): 126–41.

Joslin, D. M. "London Private Bankers, 1720–1785." *Economic History Review*, 2nd s., 7, no. 2 (1954–55): 167–86.

Kalm, Pehr. *The America of 1750: Peter Kalm's Travels in North America*. Edited by A. B. Benson. 2 vols. New York: Dover Publications Inc., 1966.

Labrousse, Ernest et al. *Histoire économique et sociale de la France, II, Des derniers temps de l'âge seigneurial aux préludes de l'âge industriel (1660–1789)*. Paris: Presses universitaires de France, 1970.

Lafosse, Henri. *La juridiction consulaire de Rouen, 1556–1791*. Rouen: H. Defontaine, 1922.

Lamontagne, Roland. *Aperçu structural du Canada au XVIIIe siècle*. Montreal: Les Editions Leméac, 1964.

La Morandière, Charles de. *Histoire de la pêche française de la morue dans l'Amérique septentrionale*. Vol. 2. Paris: Gustave-Paul Maisonneuve, 1962.

La Verdier, Pierre. "Etablissement d'un cimetière protestant à Rouen, 1786." *Bulletin de la Société de l'Histoire de Normandie*, 10 (1909): 213–29.

Le Goff, T. J. A. "An eighteenth-century grain merchant: Ignace Advisse Desruisseaux." *French Government and Society, 1500–1850; Essays in memory of Alfred Cobban*, edited by J. F. Bosher. London: The Athlone Press of the University of London, 1973, pp. 92–122.

Lesens, Emile. "Liste des Protestants de Rouen qui ont été persécutés à la Revocation de l'Edit de Nantes. . . ." In J. Bianquis, *La révocation de l'Edit de Nantes à Rouen*. Paris, 1885.

Lévy-Bruhl, Henri. *Histoire de la lettre de change en France aux XVIIe et XVIIIe siècles*. Paris: Recueil Sirey, 1933.

———. *Histoire juridique des sociétés de commerce*. Paris: Domat-Monchrestien, 1938.

Lodge, Sir Richard. "The Anglo-French Alliance, 1716–1731." In *Studies in*

Anglo-French History during the Eighteenth, Nineteenth and Twentieth Centuries, edited by A. Colville and H. Temperley. Cambridge: The University Press, 1935.

Lothe, J. "La douane et la vie économique de Rouen sous l'Ancien Régime." *Précis Académie de Rouen*, 1930.

Lunn, A. J. E. "Economic Development in New France, 1713–1760." Ph.D. dissertation, McGill University, Montreal, 1942.

Luthy, Hubert. *La banque protestante en France*, vol. 2, *De la banque aux finances, 1730–1794*. Paris: S.E.V.P.E.N., 1961.

MacDonald, L. R. "France and New France: the Internal Contradictions." *Canadian Historical Review*, 52, no. 2 (June, 1971): 121–143.

Mandrou, Robert. *La France aux XVIIe et XVIIIe siècles* ("La Nouvelle Clio; L'Histoire et ses Problèmes"). Paris: Presses universitaires de France, 1967.

Marion, M. *Dictionnaire des institutions de la France aux XVIIe et XVIIIe siècles*. 1923. Reprint. Paris: A. Picard et fils, 1968.

May, L. P. *Histoire économique de la Martinique*. Paris: Les Presses modernes, 1930.

Méthivier, Hubert. *Le siècle de Louis XV*. Que-sais-je? Paris: Presses universitaires de France, 1966.

Meyer, Jean. *L'armement nantais dans la deuxième moitié du XVIIIe siècle*. Paris: S.E.V.P.E.N., 1969.

Mims, W. S. *Colbert's West-India Policy*. New Haven: Yale University Press, 1912.

Miquelon, Dale. "Havy and Lefebvre of Quebec: A Case Study of Metropolitan Participation in Canadian Trade, 1730–60." *The Canadian Historical Review*, 56, no. 1 (March, 1975): 1–24.

Mols, Roger. *Introduction à la démographie historique des villes d'Europe du XIVe au XVIIIe siècles*. Gembloux: J. Duculot, 1954–56.

Morineau, Michel. *Les faux-semblants d'un démarrage économique: agriculture et démographie en France au XVIIIe siècle*. Cahiers des Annales, no. 30. Paris: Armand Colin, 1971.

Myer, J. N. *Understanding Financial Statements*. Mentor series. New York: New American Library, 1964.

Palmade, Guy P. *French Capitalism in the Nineteenth Century*. Translated and with introduction by G. N. Holmes. New York: Barnes and Noble, 1972.

Palmer, R. R. *The Age of Democratic Revolution*, vol. 1. Princeton, N.J.: Princeton University Press, 1959.

Pares, Richard. *A West India Fortune*. London: Longmans, Green, 1950.

———. *Yankees and Creoles*. Cambridge, Mass.: Harvard University Press, 1956.

———. *Merchants and Planters*. Cambridge: At the University Press, 1960.

———. *The Historian's Business and other Essays*. Oxford: At the Clarendon Press, 1961.

———. *War and Trade in the West Indies, 1739–1763*. London: F. Cass, 1963.

Pariset, F. G., ed. *Bordeaux au XVIIIe siècle*. Histoire de Bordeaux, sous la direction de Charles Higounet. Bordeaux: Fédération historique du Sud-Ouest, 1968.

Pirenne, Jacques. *Les grands courants de l'histoire universelle*, vol. 3, *Des traités de Westphalie à la Révolution française*. Neuchatel: Editions de la Baconnière, 1948.

Powell, Ellis T. *The Evolution of the Money Market, 1385–1915*. 1915. Reprint. London: Cass, 1966.

Quebec, Province of. *Rapport de l'archiviste de la Province de Québec pour 1939–40*. Edited by P. G. Roy. Quebec: Redempti Paradis, Imprimeur de Sa Majesté le Roi, 1940.

Rambert, G., ed. *Grande histoire du commerce de Marseille*, vol. 4. Paris: Plon, 1954.

Rémond, André. *John Holker, manufacturier et grand fonctionnaire en France au XVIIIe siècle, 1719–1786*. Paris: M. Rivière, 1946.

Ricard, Samuel. *Traité général du Commerce*. Amsterdam, 1781.

Richard, R. "A Propos de Saint-Dominque; la monnaie dans l'économie coloniale, 1674–1803." *Revue d'histoire des colonies* (1954), pp. 22–46.

Roberts, Penfield. *The Quest for Security, 1715–1740*. The Rise of Modern Europe, edited W. L. Langer. New York: Harper and Row, 1947.

Roover, Raymond de. "Early Accounting Problems of Foreign Exchange." *The Accounting Review*, 19 (1944): 381–407.

———. *Money, Banking and Credit in Medieval Bruges: Italian Merchant Bankers, Lombards, and Money-changers*. Cambridge, Mass.: The Mediaeval Academy of America, 1948.

———. *Gresham on Foreign Exchange; an Essay on Early English Mercantilism with the text of Gresham's Memorandum for the Understanding of the Exchange*. Cambridge, Mass.: Harvard University Press, 1949.

———. *L'évolution de la lettre de change, XIVe–XVIIIe siècles*. Paris: Armand Colin, 1953.

———. *Business, Banking, and Economic Thought in Late Medieval and Early Modern Europe; Selected Studies of Raymond de Roover*. Edited by Julius Kirshner. Chicago and London: The University of Chicago Press, 1974.

Rouault de La Vigne, René. *Les Protestants de Rouen et de Quévilly sous l'Ancien Régime, registres de l'état civil, cimetières*. Rouen and Paris: Société libre d'émulation, du commerce et de l'industrie de la Seine-Inférieure, 1940.

Roy, P. G. *Inventaire des pièces sur la côte de Labrador*. 2 vols. Quebec: No imprint, 1940 and 1942.

Salone, E. *La colonisation de la Nouvelle-France*. Paris: E. Guilmoto, n.d.

Samarin, Charles, ed. *L'histoire et ses méthodes*. Paris: Gallimard, 1961.

Samuelsson, Kurt. *Religion and Economic Action: A Critique of Max Weber*. New York: Harper and Row, 1961.

Savary, Jacques. *Le parfait négociant*. 2 vols. Various editions cited: vol. 1, Paris, 1721 and 1749; vol. 2, Paris, 1721 and 1724.

Savary des Bruslons, Jacques. *Dictionnaire universel de commerce*. Various
    editions cited: Paris, 1723–30 and 1741; Amsterdam, 1726–32;
    Geneva, 1744; Copenhagen, 1759–65.
Schumpeter, Joseph A. *History of Economic Analysis*. Edited by Elizabeth
    Boody Schumpeter. New York: Oxford University Press, 1954.
Scoville, Warren C. *The Persecution of the Huguenots and French Economic
    Development, 1680–1720*. Berkeley and Los Angeles: University of
    California Press, 1960.
Sée, Henri. *La France économique et sociale au XVIIIᵉ siècle*. 7th ed. Paris:
    Armand Colin, n.d.
Sement, P. *Les anciennes halles aux toiles et aux cotons de Rouen*. Rouen:
    Imprimerie de la Vicomté, 1931.
Shortt, A. *Documents relating to Canadian Currency, Exchange and Finance
    during the French Period*, 2 vols. Ottawa: The King's Printer, 1925.
Smith, Adam. *An Inquiry into the Nature and Causes of the Wealth of
    Nations*. New York: The Modern Library, 1965.
Sperling, J. "The International Payments Mechanism in the Seventeenth and
    Eighteenth Centuries." *Economic History Review*, 2nd series, 14, no. 3
    (1962): 446–68.
Stanley, G. F. G. *New France: The Last Phase, 1744–60*. The Canadian
    Centenary Series. Toronto: McClelland and Stewart, 1968.
Sutherland, Lucy. *A London Merchant*. 1933. Reprint. London: F. Cass,
    1962.
Taylor, G. V. "Types of Capitalism in Eighteenth-Century France." *English
    Historical Review*, 79 (1964): 478–97.
———. "Noncapitalist Wealth and the Origins of the French Revolution."
    American Historical Review, 72, no. 2 (January 1967): 469–96.
Temple, Nora. "The Control and Exploitation of French Towns during the
    Ancien Régime." *History*, 51 (February 1966): 16–34.
U.S. Hydrographic Office. *American Practical Navigator*. Washington, 1943.
Usher, A. P. *The Early History of Deposit Banking in Mediterranean Europe*.
    Cambridge, Mass.: Harvard University Press, 1943.
Vaissière, P. de. *St. Domingue, 1629–1789; la société et la vie créole sous
    l'Ancien Régime*. Paris: Perrin, 1909.
Vaucher, Paul. *Robert Walpole et la politique de Fleury, 1731–1742*. Paris:
    Plon-Nourrit, 1924.
Vignols, Léon. "L'importation en France au XVIIIᵉ siècle du boeuf salé
    d'Irelande." *Revue historique*, 159 (1928): 79ff.
———. "L'asiento français (1701–1713) et anglais (1713–1750) et le com-
    merce franco-espagnol vers 1700 à 1730." *Revue d'histoire
    économique et sociale*, 17 (1929): 403–436.
Wallon, H. *Une page d'histoire locale: La bourse découverte et les quais de
    Rouen*. Rouen, 1897.
———. "La Vicomté de l'Eau et le commerce de Rouen au XVIIIᵉ siècle."
    Précis Académie de Rouen, 1902.

————. *La Chambre de Commerce de la Province de Normandie, 1703–1791.* Rouen: Cagniard, 1903.

Wilson, Arthur McCandless. *French Foreign Policy during the Administration of Cardinal Fleury, 1726–1743.* Cambridge, Mass.: Harvard University Press, 1936.

Wilson, C. H. *England's Apprenticeship.* New York: St. Martin's Press, 1966.

Wolf, John B. *The Emergence of the Great Powers, 1685–1715.* The Rise of Modern Europe, edited W. L. Langer. New York: Harper and Row, 1951.

Wybo, Bernard. *Le Conseil de Commerce et le commerce intérieur de la France au XVIIIe siècle.* Paris: Domat-Montchrestien, 1936.

Index

Académie des Sciences, 130, 135
Accounts
  general: in company, trial balance
    of, 22; and bill of exchange, 44;
    and mentality, 47; current, and
    credit, 77
  of Dugard and Company: setting
    up of, 39–41; limited use of,
    46–47; and windup, 142–45;
    criticized; 143–44; cognizance
    of colonial transactions in,
    197–98; calculation of profit in,
    198; amortization in, 200; cog-
    nizance of Canadian-built ship-
    ping in, 201–4; a rate of de-
    preciation applied to, 204–5;
    cognizance of debt in, 205;
    hypothetical reconstruction of,
    205–10; with Havy and
    Lefebvre, 145
  of company voyages: outfitting in,
    49–50; invoices in, 50–51; bill
    of lading in, 51–52; freight in,
    52–53; crew rolls in, 53; in-
    flated invoices in, 51, 73; of
    Martinique trade, 101–2; ex-
    change rate in, 108
Acte de société, 32–35
Actions (debentures, stock), 132,
  156–57, 247 n.110
Admiralty, 14, 50, 54; jurisdiction of,
  over cargo debts, 104–5
Adrianople red, 129–34
Agricultural sector, 6
Ailleboust, (François?) D', 78
Albany, 64
Altona, 19
Amsterdam: Dugard's first business
  at, 19; insurance at, 123–25; men-
  tioned, 31, 42, 43
Anglo-French alliance, 3
Anville, Duc d', 126–27
Argent des iles, 107–8, 242 n.76
Asiento, 2
Assortment (cargo), 76
Aubenas, 130
Auger (Canadian trader), 78
Austria, 3
Austrian Succession, War of: and
  Canadian trade, 85, 120–21; and
  Louisbourg, 97; and company
  trade, 119–29; and shipping prob-
  lems, 125, 139; and company
  profits, 210; and Indians, 243–
  44 n.8

Baie des Châteaux, 137
Baie des Esquimaux, 139

Bale marks, 51, 73

Bank of Amsterdam, 19

Bankruptcy, 47, 160; of Clerembault and Luetkens, 43–44; of Dugard, 147–50; and Coûtume de Normandie, 148; attitudes towards, 150–52; and Savary, 164

Bansa, Rémy, 153, 166

Barraguay (auditor), 143

Bayonne, 25, 96; insurance at, 123

Bazil, Louis, 137

Beauvais, 58

Beckveldt, Pedro, 25, 29, 227 n.16

Beef, Irish salt, 8, 59, 232 n.27

Bénéfice (Quebec), 74–76, 127

Béner (Canadian trader), 78

Besard, Elizabeth Catherine, 25, 225 n.87

Beuzevillette, 28, 225 n.4

Bigault (weaver at Rouen), 15

Bigot, François, 70, 140

Bilbao, 16, 17, 23, 25, 28, 65

Bill of exchange: defined, 20; at Amsterdam, 21; in Canadian exports, 28, 80, 86–87; as credit instrument, 42–44, 130–34, 156; and multilateral adjustments, 97; and Jacques Savary, 229 n.15; example of, 230 n.19; and discount, 248 n.120

Bolbec, 28

Bond (posting), 54, 104

Bonneval, 148–51, 252 n.70

Bonny and Hody (Bilbao), 68

Bordeaux, 29; first company ship sails from, 31; in bill circulation, 43–44; in company operations, 66, 98, 239–40 n.34

Bottomry, 45

Bouffe, Marguerite, 24

Bourse de Rouen, 14

Bouteiller, Maison (Nantes), 159

Braund, William, 159

Bremen, 16, 19

Brittany, 55–57

Brokerage, 50

Buffon, Georges-Louis Leclerc, comte de, 89

Bureau of Commerce, 4, 7–8, 14

Business units: optimum size, 424 n.73

Cadiz, 15–16, 21–22; insurance at, 123–24

Caen, 28, 68

Cambrai, 131

Canada: economic limitations of, 9–10; smugglers in, 10; and Louisbourg, 11, 82; and military expenditures, 16, 126; renewed French interest in, 11, 17; and shipping timetables, 49, 69; as market, 64, 82; a poor country, 76; diversification of exports of, 82; agricultural economy of, 82, 87–88, 97, 120; shipbuilding in, 82–84; trade balance of, 82, 84–85; money supply of, 86–87; fur trade of, 82, 87, 141; economic downturn in, 90; profits on exports from, 112; and bourgeois values, 166; trade of, reliable, 210; mentions, 29, 30, 32, 48

Cap Français, 28, 92

Capital, 39, 41

Capitalism, 155, 165

Captain: as businessman, 55, 95, 100–102

Card money, 87

Cargaison: defined, 76, 235 n.41

Caylus, Marquis de, 9, 92

Chambers of commerce, 4, 14

Chambly, 83

Champigny (Intendant at Martinique): on high prices, 109

Chapeau (perquisite), 50, 52

Charter-party, 32, 53

Chaurand, Maison (Nantes), 159

Chebucto Bay, 126

Chinoiserie, 1

Christinat, Veuve (Le Havre), 50, 53, 68

Clerembault, Antoine and Son (London), 43–44

Clos, Du (Intendant of St. Domingue), 241 n.53

Colbert, Jean Baptiste, 7

Commission agent, 50, 71

Commissions, 34, 50, 54, 71

Commissionnaires (St. Pierre), 92, 99

Commodities of trade: at Rouen-LeHavre, 15–17; at Amsterdam, 19–20; re-export of colonial, 36; sent to West Indies, 55–60; sent to Canada, 61–68; in sale of cargoes, Imprévû, 1743, Union, 1744, 108–9

Compagnie des calandres à l'anglais, 135

Compagnie des Indes, 4, 32, 52, 53, 80, 87, 119, 120, 128

Compagnie du plomb laminé, 134

Compte à demi, 22–23

Compte en tiers, 22

Congé et passeport, 53, 54

Congnard (Cougnard?), David, 18

Congnard (Cougnard?), Peter, 18

Consignment (of cargo), 50–51

Consular Jurisdiction, 14, 25

Contrôle-général, 4

Convoy system, 109, 125, 127

Cork (Ireland), 66, 68

Corroyer (bookkeeper), 144

Corruption: false invoices, 51, 73; false weights and measures, 103; bribing of officials, 131; Hocquart on, 141

Corvée des grands chemins, 5

Cotton industry, 6, 15

Cougnard, Judith, 24

Coûtume de Normandie, 143

Credit: in ship purchase, 23; suppliers', 40, 49; Dugard's free advance of, 41; and promissory notes, 42, 130–34; and bills of exchange, 42–44, 130–34; and bottomry, 45; and charter-parties, 53; in Canada, 76–77; and current ac-

counts, 77; in West Indies, 101, 104–6, 160; and règlement of 12 January 1717, 104; and déclaration of 12 June 1745, 105, 119; in France and England compared, 157–58

Cugnet, François Etienne, 74, 140

Cuisy, Jean de, 148–53 passim

Cul de Sac Marin, 55, 58, 99, 210

Curve of returns: defined, 85; illustrated, 86

Customs (revenue), 50, 73, 82

Dangicourt, Madeleine, 24

Danré de Blanzy (Canadian notary), 78

Danzig, 19

Darnétal: production of woollens and blankets at, 15, 62

Darnétal enterprises, 129–34, 139, 144, 147, 156

Debt. See Credit

Demographic rise, 6

Departure dates (ships), 49, 69

Depreciation (shipping), 40, 198–205

Desmond, Capt. David, 68

Déville-les-Rouen, 25

D'Haristoy. See Haristoy

Dictionnaire universel de Commerce, 64

Dieppe, 68

Dourgne, 66

Droit de hanse (Rouen), 18

Dugard and Company: first voyage of, 17; recorded meetings of, 20–30; establishes principles of operation, 31; emancipation of, from La Rochelle, 31; articles of association of, 32–35, 155; and problem of excess capacity, 32; names Dugard manager, 34; decline of meetings of, 35; ratification of Dugard's administration by, 36, 45; builds ships, 36; growth of, to 1742, 36–37; weaknesses of, 37, 45; use of credit by, 40–47, 156; ploughback of profits by, 41; rationalization of accounts by, 41; geographic impact of purchases by, 66; establishes trading factory at Quebec, 30, 69; diversification of activities of, in Canada, 82–84; and accounts of Quebec factory, 84–88; share of Canadian trade of, 84–85; volume of Canadian trade of, 88; does not get supply contract, 90; selects Louisbourg agent, 96; gets flour supply contract, 119; reduces shipments to Canada, 126; ceases Canadian trade, 128; manifests early interest in West Indies trade, 92–93; share of West Indies trade of, 242 n.73; keeps Canadian and West Indies trade separate, 93; uses various navigation patterns, 93–95; prefers Martinique, 95; favours West Indian over Canadian trade, 99, 106; mature trading system of, 95, 99; uses triangular trade, 95–97; uses port of Bordeaux, 98, 99; ships cod to Bilbao, 97; trades at Cul de Sac Marin, 99–102; loses goods in fire at St. Pierre, 121; becomes caretaker operation, 128; suffers from diversion of capital, 135; definitive end of, 141; windup of, 142–45; and shipowning, 160; credit policy of, 76–79, 104, 160; rate of profit of, 115, 158–60; accounts of, analysed, 197–210; and Savary's dicta, 164; self-conception of, 200

Dugard, Marguerite Esther née Lecourt: and Dugard's bankruptcy, 148

Dugard, Robert I, 17

Dugard, Robert II, 17, 18

Dugard, Robert III, birth of, 18; as nominal Catholic, 17; first marriage of, 18; business of, 18, 19; as

Robert IV's correspondent, 19, 21; extant records of, 23; second marriage of, 222 n.36; provides cemetery, 222 n.31

Dugard, Robert IV ("Dugard of Rouen"); birth of, 18; ancestry of, 17–19; Amsterdam years of, 19–23; ledgers of, identified, 222 n.46; assists father, 23, 24; as part owner of *St. Mathieu*, 29; first marriage of, 24; signs first minutes, 25; authority of, in company affirmed, 29–31; named manager, 34; earns commissions, 34; actions of, ratified, 36; character of management of, 48; makes interest-free advances, 41; business reputation of, 43, 44; obtains ratification of operations, 46; as lobbyist, 5, 89, 131, 239 n.33; views of, on Cul de Sac, 100; belongs to insurance companies, 123; promises to limit trade, 127; signs Darnétal paper, 130–31; takes over negotiation of Darnétal paper, 133; demands LeLeu discount notes, 248 n.120; partnership of, with Havy and Lefebvre, 139; overvalues company, 129, 142; is creditor to partners, 143; self-justification of, 144, 151; possible dishonesty of, 144–45; undeclared bankruptcy of, 147–51; second marriage of, 148; dispute of, with Paynel heirs, 150; stoicism of, vs. despair, 151–52; death of, 11, 26, 152; is typical of Rouen bourgeosie, 6, 135–36; middle class values of, 162; as Protestant, 163; as landowner, 253 n.82; comments on Canada-West Indies Trade, 98, on credit, 104, on Louvet, 133, on negotiation of paper, 133

Dugard, Robert V: birth of, 24; modest aims of, 152–53

Dunkirk, 19

Duperreaux (auditor), 143
Dupuis, Elie, 20–22
Duroy et Fils (Montauban), 66
Dutch East India Company, 19

England, 3, 16, 20, 119
Elbeuf, 15, 17, 23
Epinay, 58
Escalier, Capt., 120
Excess capacity, 32
Exchange rates, 107–8, 242 n.74

Factors: in Canada, 70–71
Fautoux, Léon, 96, 100, 122
Fauxsauniers, 83–84
Fayet, De (Governor of St. Domin-
    gue), 9, 241 n.53
Fécamp, 24
Ferrant, Anne, 24
Fesquet, André, 129, 134
Flanders, 2, 58
Fleury, André-Hercule, Cardinal de,
    3, 8
Forges de St. Maurice, 10, 89
Fornel, Louis, 36–37, 70, 139
Fornel, Marie-Anne, 70, 140
Fort-Royal, 92, 121
Foucher, François, 78
France (family): traditional values of,
    161–62
France: Guillaume, fils: birth of, 25;
    belongs to insurance companies,
    123; usefulness of, to company,
    125; background and capacities of,
    124; as a Catholic, 163; desires to
    liquidate company, 127; differs
    with partners, 128, 246 n.84; re-
    ceives no dividend, 129; withholds
    money, 142; does not accept
    Dugard's accounts, 143; on calam-
    ity, on fate, 121; on life, 122; on
    Fautoux, 122; on obedience, 126;
    on royal treasury, on Frenchmen,
    128; on Providence, 141
France, Guillaume, père: background
    of, 24–25; death of, 26; fears ex-

pansion, 41; receives notes from
    Dugard, 42, 229 n.13; mentioned,
    33, 39, 46, 47
France: trade of, 6, 8, 220–21 n.29
François (family), 142
Fraud: in West Indies, 103
Freight rates: and war, 125
Fremont, Capt. François-Martin, 52;
    remains at St. Pierre, 101–2, 106,
    121, 125; leaves St. Pierre, 127
Fur trade (Canada), 10, 82, 87, 141
Fusil boucannier, 58
Fusil de chasse, 64

Gabelle, 50
Gardère, Jean, 139
Garisson (trader of Bordeaux), 139
Garonne River, 66
Gaudar, François, 130
Gaudet, (Dominique?), 78
Gazette d'Hollande, 141
Genwith (trader of Morlaix), 21
Gibraltar, 2
Godefroy, Pierre, 147, 152
Goguet, Denis, 70
Gosselin, Capt., 53
Goudal, Henri, 51, 66
Grande St. Modet, 137
Guadeloupe, 19
Guy, Pierre, 71; favoured customer
    of Havy and Lefebvre, 75, 77–78,
    234 n.37; buys from Lamaletie,
    76; sells furs, 80; girth of,
    234 n.26; on militia duty,
    246 n.76

Halles de Rouen, 16, 65
Hamburg, 19, 22, 31, 42, 43
Hamelin, Jean, 87
Hamilton Inlet, 139
Haristoy, Mme. Pierre D': dispute of,
    with Dugard, 150
Haristoy, Pierre D': background of,
    25; death of, 26; sells St. Mathieu,
    29, 33, 39; proposes end to expan-
    sion, 46–47; belongs to insurance

company, 123; discovers Adrianople red, 129; borrows for Darnétal, 131–33; plans velour factory, 135; estate of, owes Dugard, 143; bravado of, 132, 163; conscience of, 133; typicality of, 135–36; modernity of, 161–62; on the Darnétal enterprises, 131; on courtiers, 132; on Louvet, 133; on Trudaine, 134–35; on liberalism, 134
Haro, Henrique de, 22–23
Havy and Lefebvre: rent quarters, 70; contemporary description of, 71; as *raison sociale*, 71; private trade of, 71, 250 n.47; as Protestants, 72; as salaried clerks, 145; and travel, 73; composition of *mémoires* by, 76; extend credit, 77–78; and bills of exchange, 80; accounts of, 81–82, 84–88; export flour, 82; build ships, 82–84; as entrepreneurs, 84; good performance of, 85; returns of, 86–87; volume of trade of, 88; private ships of, 96; extend credit to selves, 136; sealing activity of, 136–37; as commission agents, 139; hold real estate and mortgages, 139, 146; last ties of, with Dugard, 139; and King's Posts, 140; plan return to France, 140; final accounts of, for Dugard, 145; war losses of, 146; attitude of, to debtors, 78–79; attitude of, to money, 79, 235–36, n.55; aspirations of, 88; are impatient of paternalism, 121; on shipbuilding, 84; on Canada-West Indies trade, 98; on war, 120; on the King, 121; on the general good, 122, on wartime prosperity, 126; addresses of, 232–33 n.4
Havy, François: background of, 28, 225–26 n.4; founds Quebec factory, 30, 69; years of, in Canada, 70; as a principal trader of Quebec, 71; character of, 72; age of, 88; visits France, 90; final return of, to France, 140; visits Dugard, 140; marries, 142; settles at La Rochelle, 142; quarrels with Dugard, 145; dies, 146–47; on autumn, 82; on Louisbourg, the Navy and war policy, 141; on Canada, 142, 146; on Canadian business, 145; on Providence, 146
Hellot, Jean, 130–31
Hocquart, Gilles, 10, 73; reports favourable balance of trade, 82; and Dugard and Company, 89; talks to merchants, 88–89; and Pascaud Frères, 90; refuses permission, 121; favours Bazil, 137; refuses concession, 139; on debtors, 79; on Havy's shipbuilding, 83; on money supply, 86–87; on Ile Royale and triangular trade, 96; on corruption, 141
Holker, John, 135
Holland, 3, 20; insurance in, 30, 58
Honfleur, 68, 99
Hôpital Général (Rouen), 34
Horses: difficult to ship, 97
Hubris, 165
Hudson Bay, 2
Huguenot, 42
Hurel, Capt. F(rançois?), 52

Ile Royale, 10–11
Indians (Canada): as consumers, 64–65
Industry (France), 6, 60
Insurance, 30; wartime premiums for and business profits, 114–15, 210; rates of, in war and peace, 123–25
Interest rates, 41, 158
Invoices: false, 51, 73–74
Ireland, 59
Iroquois, Wars of the, 10

Jacquelin, Jean, 139
Jager, Dirk de, 22
Jenkins' Ear, War of, 3
Joint-stock companies, 32, 156

Kalm, Peter, 72
Kessessakiou River, 139
King's Posts, 139

La Bourdonnaye, De (Intendant of Rouen), 132, 163
Labrador, 84, 136–37
Labrousse, Ernest, 5
La Flotte, 63
Lagroix, Capt., 121
La Haye-Aubrée, 148
La Hougue, Battle of, 7
Lallement, Raymond, 94–95
Lamaletie, Jean-André, 76, 80
La Muette, 132
Land: and prestige, 162
La Roche Couvert, Capt., 100
La Rochelle: in early company voyages, 17, 28–29, 93; becomes secondary in company trade, 31, 66, 68; receives beaver, 87; geographical advantages of, 90; insurance at, 123–24
La Rue, Etienne de, 15, 151
Laurens, David, fils: birth of, 24; death of, 26; borrows for company, 32–33, 47; belongs to insurance company, 123; and Dugard's bankruptcy, 148–51; posts bond for nephew, 152; middle class values of, 161; as Protestant, 163
Laurens, David, père: birth of, 24; death of, 25, 39
Laurens, Marie, 24
Laurens, Thomas, 24
Law, John, 4, 132
Law of Nations, The, 126
Lay days: defined, 53
League of Augsburg, War of, 7
LeBlanc, Marie, 23

LeBlanc, Samuel, 22
Leclerc, Benjamin, 23
Lefebvre, Jean: years of, in Canada, 70; character of, 72–73; age of, 88; death of, 146; identification of, difficult, 226 n.4; girth of, 234 n.26
Le Havre, 29, 66; distance of, from Rouen, 13; import function of, 15–16; rise of colonial trade of, 16–17, 220–21 n.29; primacy of, in company operations, 31, 98; company agent at, 34; export of 14th cargo from, 68; late entry of, in colonial trade, 99; takes over maritime trade of Rouen, 136
LeLeu, Alexandre, le jeune, 133–34
Lemercier, Michel, 147
Léoganne, 92
Le parfait négociant, 163–65
Le Plastrier, Marie, 17, 222 n.42
Le Provost, Capt. François, 29
LeTellier, Madeleine, 24
Letters Patent of April 1717, 8, 31
Letters Patent of October 1727, 8
Lettres de hanse, 18, 24, 25
Le Vaillant, Louis, 34
Levesque, François, 146, 226 n.4
Lévy-Bruhl, Henri, 33
Leyden, 22
Liability, 33, 155
Liberalism, 134–35
Lille, 58
Lisbon, 23
Livre: stabilized, 5
Loire River, 66
London, 18, 19, 42–43; insurance at, 123–24
Lorient, 120
Louisbourg, 11; as market for Canada, 82; and triangular trade, 95–97; company's first trade at, 96; fall of, in 1745, 121; fall of, in 1758, 141
Louis XIV, 2, 4

Louis XV, 3
Louvet, Jean-Joseph, le jeune, 129;
    negotiates Darnétal paper, 131,
    133; defrauds partners, 133–34;
    escapes to England, 134
Louviers, 15, 23
Lubeck, 16
Lucas (Vincent guardian), 143
Lucrum cessans, 229 n.15
Luetkens Frères et Drewzen (Bor-
    deaux), 43–44, 230 n.19
Lunn, Jean, 87
Luthy, Hubert, 6
Luxembourg, Duc de, 131
Lyons, 58, 63–64

Maastricht, 128
Machault d'Arnouville, Jean-
    Baptiste, 141
Mail, 73
Maine, 57–58
Manuel du Fabricant, 15
Manufacture de velours de coton
    façon d'Angleterre, 135
Manufacture du plomb laminé, 25
Manufacture royale de teinture de
    coton et de fil en rouge d'An-
    drinople, 130
Marchand domicilié, 70–71
Marchand forain, 70–71
Marine, Department of, 7, 8; mer-
    cantilist aims of, 10; war
    preparations of, 120; financial
    strain on, 121; policy of, on neu-
    tral shipping, 141; stops payment,
    146
Martinique: increase of plantations
    in, of exports to, 7; in company's
    first colonial voyage, 28, 29, 30,
    48; staple of, 60; as market 59–60
Martin's Bank, 157
Maurepas, Jean-Frédéric Phélypeaux,
    Comte de: as able minister, 7–8;
    views of, on smuggling, 9; views
    of, on Dugard and Company and
    on horse trade, 89, 97; disgrace of,
131; instructions of, on Baie des
    Châteaux, 137; colonial views of,
    219 n.20; favours Dugard,
    239 n.33
Mayer, Marie, 222 n.36
Mazamet, 66
Mentalité: fate and Providence, 2, 72,
    121, 127, 146; conservatism, 4;
    elitist values, 7, 14–15; piety, 19;
    association of young and old mer-
    chants, 22; business and marriage,
    24; duration of business unit, 41;
    accounts, partnership, capitalism,
    47; West Indian food preferences,
    60; Canadian preference for Euro-
    pean goods, 64–65; drinking hab-
    its, 71–72; debt, 78–79; attitude
    towards money, 79, 235–36 n.55;
    hubris, luxury, 153; values and be-
    haviour, 161–66
Metropolitanism, 64–65, 70, 77,
    161
Marseilles: insurance at, 123–24
Mingan, 136
Minorca, 2
Minute-book, 35–36
Mississippi Bubble, 4
Molina, Luis, 235 n.55
Mollard, Capt., 93
Monetary policy, 2
Monetary stock, 6
Monfort (Canadian trader), 78
Montaran, de (Intendant of com-
    merce), 130–31
Montauban, 31, 62, 66
Montigny, de (Académie des Sci-
    ences), 135
Montreal, 72–73, 161
Morel (Inspector of Manufactures),
    135
Morlaix, 19
Mortagne, 31

Nadeau, Commandant (Cul de Sac
    Marin), 100, 105
Nantes, 20, 28; insurance at, 123–24

Naval policy, 8
Nérac, 59
New England, 9
Newfoundland, 2
New York Province, 10
New York City, 127
Niort, 62, 66, 68
Normandy, 55–57, 59
North Shore, 136–37

Obligation: defined, of Canadian traders, 77
Octroi des marchands, 14
Olivier, Capt. Abel: brings news of fall of Louisbourg, 121, 244 n.30; brings Astrée to France, 123
Orléans, 66
Orléans, Philippe III, Duc d', 3
Orry, Philibert, 5

Paarling, Jan van, 21–22
Pacotilles, 32; defined, 34, 51; captains', carried free, 52, 71; wine and spirits not part of, 76; belonging to partners, 96; company shipments reduced to, 128
Palais des Consuls, 14
Pannié d'Orgeville (Intendant of Martinique), 92, 105
Pantaleo: insurance at, 123
Pares, Richard, 101, 105
Paris: distance of, from Rouen, 13; in credit circulation, 43–44; commodities from, 58, 63, 66
Partnership, 47, 155–57
Pascaud, Antoine, 70
Pascaud Frères (La Rochelle), 73–74, 90
Paternalism, 10, 121
Paynel Frères (Rouen): declare bankruptcy, 151
Paynel, Louis: and Darnétal, 129; as self-styled commanditaire, 147, 156; death of, 150
Pays de Caux, 28

Peirenc de Moras (Minister of Marine), 141
Pellet, Jean, 159
Philip V, 3
Pictet (Paris banker), 134
Poirier (notary?), 78
Pompadour, Antoinette Poisson, Marquise de, 131
Porée, Franqise, 17, 222 n.36
Porée, Jonas, 18
Pothier, Robert-Joseph, 35
Prêt à la grosse aventure, 45
Price rise, 5–6
Prices: determination of, in Canada, 73–74, 79–80; determination of, in Martinique, 102; determination of, in St. Domingue, 102–3, 241 n.53; in Canada and West Indies compared, 102, 106; in Canada and War of Spanish Succession, 121–22; and convoys, 109; in colonies and War of Austrian Succession, 120, 121, 126, 127
Printed textiles, 15
Privateers, 8
Profits: at Amsterdam, 22, 222 n.68; on first voyages, 29; remain steady to 1742, 31, 39; of Canadian and West Indian trades compared, 32; do not cover costs of succeeding year, 40; and bottomry, 45; at Quebec, 74–76; at Quebec and credit, 78; in West Indies, 99, 106–12; and Seven Years War, 110; in Canada and Martinique compared, 110; on Canadian cargoes in West Indies, 110–11; on return cargoes, 112–17; and insurance premiums, 114–17; in Canada and war, 126; overestimated by Dugard, 142; overall, of company, 158–60; company's overall, and methods of calculation, 197–214
Promissory note: early use of, by

Dugard, 42; use of, by Havy and Lefebvre in Canada, 77–78; use of, by Darnétal enterprises, 130–34; inadequacy of, 156; Jacques Savary on, 229 n.15

Protestants: in Canada, 72; and society, 163

Provision (bill of exchange): defined, 42, 43

Pufendorf, Samuel, 126

Quebec City: first cargo to, 27–28; second cargo to, 28; third cargo to, 29–30; trading factory established at, 30; fourteenth cargo to, 66, 68; principal traders of, 71, 233 n.9; described by contemporary, 72; sale of cargoes at, 73–79; credit at, 76–79; trade in furs at, 79–80; trade by factors at, 69–70, 160; and freight seekers, 160; hinterland of, 161

Quesnay, François, 7

Quévilly-près-Rouen (Protestant congregation), 17, 24, 161, 221 n.31

Rauly Père et Fils (Montauban), 51

Renault, Capt. J. B.: remains at Cul de Sac Marin, 101–2, and debtors, 105, 127; writes to Dugard, 121, 125

Rennes, 58, 68

Revocation of Edict of Nantes, 17–18

Ricard, Samuel, 107–8

Richard, R., 107–8

Richelieu River, 83

Ricouart, De (Intendant at Rochefort), 90

Ridel Frères (Paris), 42, 44, 147

Ripandelly (Parisian banker), 248 n.120

Roads, 1

Roanne, 65–66

Rochefort, 90

Roover, Raymond de, 42, 44

Roscoff, 123

Rouen: institutions, topography, population of, 13–14, 219 n.2; import function of, 15, 220–21 n.29; revived interest of, in colonial trade, 16–18; connection of, with Bilbao, 17; company's only voyage from, 17, 19, 21, 23; insurance companies in, 30; faience of, 58; siamoise of, 62; as entrepôt, 65

Rouillé, Antoine-Louis, Comte de Jouy, 5, 130

Ruette d'Auteuil, François, 78

St. Charles River, 84

St. Domingue: late development of, 7; little need for New England goods at, 9; as market, 59–60

St. Etienne, 62, 66

St. Eustache, 19

St. Georges-du-Vièvre, 16

St. Lawrence River, 69, 84

St. Malo: insurance at, 123

St. Pierre, Martinique: described, 91–92; company trade at, 102; fire at, 114, 121; compared with Montreal, 161; ship arrivals at, 228 n.4

St. Sever enterprises: founding of, 135–36; require Dugard's money and time, 144; credit of, and war, 147; conclusions on, 156

Savary, Jacques: on merchant behaviour, 163–65; on notes and bills, 229 n.15

Savary des Bruslons, Jacques, 64

Schelde, Barthélemy van, 121

Seal fishery, 84, 136

Seine River, 68

Séminaire de Québec, 77

Senegal, 53

Seven Years War: British declaration of, 141; Havy and Lefebvre and, 140–47; and inflation, 141–42

Sèvre Niortaise River, 66

Ships: characteristics of, 91

Ships of Dugard and Company
  Alçion, 44, 45; mention of, in
    examples, 49–68; cargo of,
    1742–43, 55–60; building of,
    83; maiden voyage of, 93; as
    company's first ship to Louis-
    bourg, 96; carries horses, 97;
    sale of cargo of, 1742, analysed,
    108–9; loss of, 119; profile of,
    168; evaluation of, as return
    cargo, 201, 204
  Astrée: mention of, in examples,
    49–68; high cost of, 84; launch-
    ing of, 122; profile of, 169–70;
    as item of return cargo, 201
  Centaure, 68, 82; building of, 84,
    89; 90; trapping of, at LeHavre,
    119; profile of, 169; longevity
    of, 204
  Eleanor, 96
  Fleury, 45; building of, 83; as last
    company ship to visit Louis-
    bourg, 97; mention of, in exam-
    ples, 49–68; commandeering of,
    by Crown, 127; 143; profile of,
    168–69
  Imprévû, 45; mentioned in exam-
    ples, 49–68; cargo of, 1743,
    55–60; building of, 84; trapping
    of, in ice, 96; initiates company
    trade at Cul de Sac Marin, 99;
    capture of, 120; mention of, 169
  Louis Dauphin; building of, 27;
    early voyages of, 28–32 passim;
    initiates company trade to
    Louisbourg, 96; loss of, 119;
    profile of, 167; amortization of,
    199
  St. Louis: building of, 84; trapping
    of, at Le Havre, 119; consigning
    of, to fishery, 128; profile of,
    169
  St. Mathieu: purchase of, by com-
    pany, 29; early voyages of,
    30–34; mention of, in examples,
    49–68; cargo of, 1743, 55–60;
    capture of, 120, profile of, 167
  Ville de Québec/Union: purchase
    of, 30; lease of, to Compagnie
    des Indes, 32; mention of, in
    examples, 49–68; cargo of,
    1744, 55–60; initiates com-
    pany's West Indies trade, 93;
    visits Louisbourg, 96; costs and
    profits of voyage of, 1744,
    113–15; voyage of, 1744 and
    war, 125; loss of, 127; profile of,
    167–68
Ships strangers to Dugard and Company: Aimable Raechal, 102; Andromède, 119, 123; Brillant, 120;
  Cézar, 68; Comte de Matignon,
  68; Fortune, 23; Greyhound, 127;
  Grande St. François, 22; Heureux,
  68; Marianne, 96; Marie, 68; Parfaite Union, 139; Reine Marie, 19,
  23; St. Charles, 96; St. Charles de
  l'Ile Dieu, 68; St. Louis, 68; Sul-
  tanne, 119; Thétis, 53, 121; Trois
  Maries (mentioned in examples,
  49–68; sinking of, 120; profile of,
  170; accounts of, reproduced,
  199–200); Triomphant, 68
Silva, Gabriel Da, 43–45
Slaves: food of, 232 n.27
Smith, Adam, 158–60
Smugglers, 8–9, 11, 89
Société au navire le Louis Dauphin,
  29
Société du Canada: as raison sociale,
  32. See also Dugard and Company
Société en commandite, 147, 156
Société générale, 33, 156
Society: different models, French vs.
  English, 161–65
Soetenou, Van (trader of London),
  19, 22
Solier et Cie. (Marseilles), 159
South Sea Company, 30
Spain, 3, 8, 16
Spanish Succession, War of, 4, 7
Spiegal, Frederick, 19

Tarn River, 66
Taylor, G. V., 199
Taxes, 50, 121, 222 n.43
Tervoet, Peter, 21
Tessard, Marie Anne, 28
Texier (Canadian trader), 78
Thierry (weaver at Rouen), 15
Tokens (*jetons de présence*), 35
Tonneaux de port permis (perquisite), 52
Torrent, Claude, 134
Toulouse, Louis Alexandre, Comte de, 8
Tours, 58
Traité général du Commerce, 108
Triangular voyages, 28–30; problems of, 93, 95–97
Trudaine, Daniel-Charles, 5, 131, 134–35
Trudaine de Montigny (Director of Commerce), 5
Turnover, 159

Usance, 42–43
Usury, 156, 229 n.15
Utrecht, Treaty of, 2

Valmaletie (creditor of Dugard and Company), 45
Vandelle, François Vangellikom: background, birth of, 28, 30; salary and perquisites of, 52; initiates

company's West Indies trade, 93; 96, 126
Vasse, Jacques, 144, 248–49 n. 123
Verel, Jeanne, 23
Viart, Catherine, 17
Vincent estate, 143
Vincent, Gédéon, 24–25
Vincent, Gédéon Samuel I, 24–25
Vincent, Gédéon Samuel II, 24–25
Vincent, Jean, 24
Vincent Père et Fils (Rouen), 29, 33, 39, 47
Volant d'Hautebourg, Jean-Louis, 78, 136

Wealth of Nations, The, 158
West India Company, 7
West Indies, French: unsatisfied market demand of, 9, 29, 32, 42, 48; ships leave for, 49; as market, contrasted to Canada, 64; trade at, by captains, 160; and bourgeois values, 166; trade of, bad choice for company, 210; provisions in, 232 n.27. *See also individual islands and towns*
"Westphalia system," 3
Wines and spirits: in West Indian cargoes, 58–59; in Canadian cargoes, 63, 75–76
Woollen industry, 15